2006

FIREARMS
AND
VIOLENCE

A CRITICAL REVIEW

Committee to Improve Research Information and Data on Firearms
Charles F. Wellford, John V. Pepper, and Carol V. Petrie, editors
Committee on Law and Justice
Division of Behavioral and Social Sciences and Education

NATIONAL RESEARCH COUNCIL
OF THE NATIONAL ACADEMIES

THE NATIONAL ACADEMIES PRESS
Washington, D.C.
www.nap.edu

THE NATIONAL ACADEMIES PRESS 500 Fifth STREET, N.W. Washington, DC 20001

NOTICE: The project that is the subject of this report was approved by the Governing Board of the National Research Council, whose members are drawn from the councils of the National Academy of Sciences, the National Academy of Engineering, and the Institute of Medicine. The members of the committee responsible for the report were chosen for their special competences and with regard for appropriate balance.

This study was supported by the National Academy of Sciences and Grant No. 2000-IJ-CX-0034 from the National Institute of Justice, Grant No. 200-2000-00629 from the Department of Health and Human Services, the Joyce Foundation (grant not numbered), Grant No. 200-8064 from the Annie E. Casey Foundation, and Grant No. 2001-16212 from the Packard Foundation. Any opinions, findings, conclusions, or recommendations expressed in this publication are those of the author(s) and do not necessarily reflect the views of the organizations or agencies that provided support for the project.

Library of Congress Cataloging-in-Publication Data

National Research Council (U.S.). Committee to Improve Research Information and Data on Firearms.
 Firearms and violence : a critical review / Committee to Improve Research Information and Data on Firearms ; Charles F. Wellford, John V. Pepper, and Carol V. Petrie, editors ; Committee on Law and Justice, Division of Behavioral and Social Sciences and Education.
   p. cm.
 Includes bibliographical references and index.
 ISBN 0-309-09124-1 (hardcover) — ISBN 0-309-54640-0 (pdf)
 1. Firearms and crime—United States. 2. Firearms and crime—Research—United States. 3. Firearms ownership—United States. 4. Violence—United States. 5. Violence—United States—Prevention. I. Wellford, Charles F. II. Pepper, John, 1964- III. Petrie, Carol. IV. National Research Council (U.S.). Committee on Law and Justice. V. Title.
 HV6789.N37 2004
 364.2—dc22
                                    2004024047

Additional copies of this report are available from National Academies Press, 500 Fifth Street, N.W., Lockbox 285, Washington, DC 20055; (800) 624-6242 or (202) 334-3313 (in the Washington metropolitan area); Internet, http://www.nap.edu.

Printed in the United States of America.

Suggested citation: National Research Council. (2005). *Firearms and Violence: A Critical Review*. Committee to Improve Research Information and Data on Firearms. Charles F. Wellford, John V. Pepper, and Carol V. Petrie, editors. Committee on Law and Justice, Division of Behavioral and Social Sciences and Education. Washington, DC: The National Academies Press.

THE NATIONAL ACADEMIES
Advisers to the Nation on Science, Engineering, and Medicine

The **National Academy of Sciences** is a private, nonprofit, self-perpetuating society of distinguished scholars engaged in scientific and engineering research, dedicated to the furtherance of science and technology and to their use for the general welfare. Upon the authority of the charter granted to it by the Congress in 1863, the Academy has a mandate that requires it to advise the federal government on scientific and technical matters. Dr. Bruce M. Alberts is president of the National Academy of Sciences.

The **National Academy of Engineering** was established in 1964, under the charter of the National Academy of Sciences, as a parallel organization of outstanding engineers. It is autonomous in its administration and in the selection of its members, sharing with the National Academy of Sciences the responsibility for advising the federal government. The National Academy of Engineering also sponsors engineering programs aimed at meeting national needs, encourages education and research, and recognizes the superior achievements of engineers. Dr. Wm. A. Wulf is president of the National Academy of Engineering.

The **Institute of Medicine** was established in 1970 by the National Academy of Sciences to secure the services of eminent members of appropriate professions in the examination of policy matters pertaining to the health of the public. The Institute acts under the responsibility given to the National Academy of Sciences by its congressional charter to be an adviser to the federal government and, upon its own initiative, to identify issues of medical care, research, and education. Dr. Harvey V. Fineberg is president of the Institute of Medicine.

The **National Research Council** was organized by the National Academy of Sciences in 1916 to associate the broad community of science and technology with the Academy's purposes of furthering knowledge and advising the federal government. Functioning in accordance with general policies determined by the Academy, the Council has become the principal operating agency of both the National Academy of Sciences and the National Academy of Engineering in providing services to the government, the public, and the scientific and engineering communities. The Council is administered jointly by both Academies and the Institute of Medicine. Dr. Bruce M. Alberts and Dr. Wm. A. Wulf are chair and vice chair, respectively, of the National Research Council.

www.national-academies.org

COMMITTEE ON LAW AND JUSTICE
2003-2004

CHARLES F. WELLFORD (*Chair*), Department of Criminology and Criminal Justice, University of Maryland, College Park

MARK H. MOORE (*Vice Chair*), Hauser Center for Non-Profit Institutions and John F. Kennedy School of Government, Harvard University

DAVID H. BAYLEY, School of Criminal Justice, University of Albany, SUNY

ALFRED BLUMSTEIN, H. John Heinz III School of Public Policy and Management, Carnegie Mellon University

RICHARD BONNIE, Institute of Law, Psychiatry, and Public Policy, University of Virginia Law School

JEANETTE COVINGTON, Department of Sociology, Rutgers University

MARTHA CRENSHAW, Department of Political Science, Wesleyan University

STEVEN DURLAUF, Department of Economics, University of Wisconsin, Madison

JEFFREY FAGAN, School of Law and School of Public Health, Columbia University

JOHN FEREJOHN, Hoover Institution, Stanford University

DARNELL HAWKINS, Department of Sociology, University of Illinois, Chicago

PHILLIP HEYMANN, Harvard Law School, Harvard University

ROBERT L. JOHNSON, Adolescent and Young Adult Medicine, New Jersey Medical School

CANDACE KRUTTSCHNITT, Department of Sociology, University of Minnesota

JOHN H. LAUB, Department of Criminology and Criminal Justice, University of Maryland, College Park

MARK LIPSEY, Center for Crime and Justice Policy Studies, Vanderbilt University

DANIEL D. NAGIN, H. John Heinz III School of Public Policy and Management, Carnegie Mellon University

RICHARD ROSENFELD, Department of Criminology and Criminal Justice, University of Missouri-St. Louis

CHRISTY VISHER, Justice Policy Center, Urban Institute, Washington, DC

CATHY SPATZ WIDOM, Department of Psychiatry, New Jersey Medical School

CAROL V. PETRIE, *Director*
RALPH PATTERSON, *Senior Project Assistant*

Contents

Appendixes

Preface

Few topics engender more controversy than "gun control." Large segments of the population express contradictory opinions and assert contradictory facts when they discuss the role of firearms in violence and especially how to reduce violent injuries and deaths that involve firearms. The report of the Committee on Improving Research Information and Data on Firearms was not intended to, nor does it reach any conclusions about the issue of gun control. Rather, we have addressed what empirical research tells about the role of firearms in violence. Our recommendations address how to improve the empirical foundation for discussions about firearms policy. Until that foundation is better established, little progress is likely in the ongoing public debate over firearms.

One theme that runs throughout our report is the relative absence of credible data central to addressing even the most basic questions about firearms and violence. As we often state in the report, without much better data, important questions will continue to be unanswerable. This is unacceptable when we see the impact that firearm-related violent injury and death have on American society and especially some of the most vulnerable segments of that population. The fact that little can be said about the prevention and control of these levels of death and injury—when for some segments of the population they are the leading causes of death and injury—is of concern to us as citizens and scientists.

Reaching consensus on a controversial topic for which research is limited and in conflict requires an exceptional committee and staff. The committee has spent the past two years learning about research and data on firearms and seeking to learn from each other how our disciplines evaluate and use this knowledge. It is only because committee members had diverse backgrounds, uncommon respect for each other, and a willingness to apply common scientific standards to our deliberations that we were able to complete our work in what I think is an exceptional manner. Some may disagree with our analysis, but none can question our effort to raise the science of firearms research so that it can begin to inform public policy. I thank committee members for their work and patience.

Needless to say, the staff for the committee carried a very heavy load. Without them we would have not been able to complete our work. John Pepper in particular deserves special recognition as the study director. John not only provided outstanding staff support but he also helped form the structure of our report, edited and contributed to many of the chapters, was the primary drafter of one chapter, and always managed to see a way forward when we seemed stymied. Carol Petrie, staff director of the Committee on Law and Justice, provided invaluable insight into the way we could deal with controversial topics, helped keep us on track, and edited every chapter. Brenda McLaughlin, research associate, provided valuable assistance, and Michelle McGuire, program assistant, and Ralph Patterson, senior project assistant, performed superbly.

The committee is grateful to Anthony Braga, Harvard University, whose work as a consultant to the committee throughout its period of operation was invaluable. And the committee wants to thank Christine McShane, of the Division on Social and Behavioral Sciences and Education, for her invaluable assistance in preparing the manuscript for review and publication. She provided clear and sensible guidance on chapter and appendix organization, and she did an outstanding job of editing the entire report, several times.

The committee could not have completed its work without the assistance of many scholars and policy officials who gave unstintingly of their time and shared their resources, their work, and their thinking. To gather information on a variety of subjects from a diversity of perspectives, we held four public workshops: the Workshop on Firearms Research and Data, August 30-31, 2001; the Workshop on Intentional Injuries and Firearms, November 15-16, 2001; the Workshop on Self-Defense, Deterrence and Firearm Markets, January 16-17, 2002; and the Workshop on Firearm Injury Prevention and Intervention, May 28-29, 2002. We thank all of the individuals who served as presenters and discussants at these meetings. They are listed here alphabetically, and with their affiliations at the time of each workshop: Roseanna Ander, Joyce Foundation; J. Lee Annest, Centers for Disease Control and Prevention; Arthur Berg, Harvard University; Paul Blackman, National Rifle Association; Alfred Blumstein, Carnegie Mellon University; David Bordua, University of Illinois-Urbana/Champaign; Anthony Braga, Harvard University; David Brent, University of Pittsburgh;

Stephen Bronars, University of Texas, Austin; Philip Cook, Duke University; Patti Culross, David and Lucile Packard Foundation; Peter Cummings, University of Washington; Mike Dowden, Bureau of Alcohol, Tobacco, and Firearms; Jeffrey Fagan, Columbia University; Scott Gast, University of Virginia; Susan Ginsburg, Independent Consultant; Robert Hahn, Centers for Disease Control and Prevention; Marjorie Hardy, Eckerd College; Stephen Hargarten, Medical College of Wisconsin; David Hemenway, Harvard University; Sally Hillsman, Office of Research and Evaluation, National Institutes of Justice; David Kennedy, Harvard University; Gary Kleck, Florida State University; Christopher Koper, University of Pennsylvania; Colin Loftin, State University of New York-Albany; John Lott Jr., American Enterprise Institute; Jens Ludwig, Georgetown University; John Malone, Bureau of Alcohol, Tobacco, and Firearms; Michael Maltz, University of Illinois, Chicago; David McDowall, State University of New York-Albany; James Mercy, Centers for Disease Control and Prevention; Victoria Ozonoff, Massachusetts Department of Public Health; Glenn Pierce, Northeastern University; Jeffrey Roth, University of Pennsylvania; Eric Sevigny, Carnegie Mellon University; Lawrence Sherman, University of Pennsylvania; Kevin Strom, Research Triangle Institute; Stephen Teret, Johns Hopkins University; Robyn Thiemann, U.S. Department of Justice; Douglas Weil, The Brady Center to Prevent Gun Violence; Timothy Wheeler, Claremont Institute; Brian Wiersema, University of Maryland; Deanna Wilkinson, Temple University; James Wright, University of Central Florida; and Franklin Zimring, University of California.

This report has been reviewed in draft form by individuals chosen for their diverse perspectives and technical expertise, in accordance with procedures approved by the Report Review Committee of the National Research Council (NRC). The purpose of this independent review is to provide candid and critical comments that will assist the institution in making the published report as sound as possible and to ensure that the report meets institutional standards for objectivity, evidence, and responsiveness to the study charge. The review comments and draft manuscript remain confidential to protect the integrity of the deliberative process.

We thank the following individuals for their participation in the review of this report: Esther Duflo, Department of Economics, Massachusetts Institute of Technology; John A. Ferejohn, Hoover Institution, Stanford University; Arthur S. Goldberger, Department of Economics, University of Wisconsin; Lawrence Gostin, Georgetown University Law Center; Ken Land, Department of Sociology, Duke University; Steven Messner, Department of Sociology, University of Albany, State University of New York; Jeffrey Miron, Department of Economics, Boston University; Lee N. Robins, Department of Psychiatry, Washington University School of Medicine; Paul Rosenbaum, Department of Statistics, Wharton

School, University of Pennsylvania; Arlene Rubin Stiffman, School of Social Work, Washington University; and Michael Tonry, Institute of Criminology, University of Cambridge.

Although the reviewers listed above have provided many constructive comments and suggestions, they were not asked to endorse the conclusions or recommendations nor did they see the final draft of the report before its release. The review of this report was overseen by Elaine Larson, School of Nursing, Columbia University, and Christopher Sims, Department of Economics, Princeton University. Appointed by the National Research Council, they were responsible for making certain that an independent examination of this report was carried out in accordance with institutional procedures and that all review comments were carefully considered. Responsibility for the final content of this report rests entirely with the authoring committee and the institution.

Charles F. Wellford, *Chair*
Committee on Improving Research
Information and Data on Firearms

Executive Summary

There is hardly a more contentious issue in American politics than the ownership of guns and various proposals for gun control. Each year tens of thousands of people are injured and killed by firearms; each year firearms are used to defend against and deter an unknown number of acts of violence; and each year firearms are widely used for recreational purposes. For public authorities to make reasonable policies on these matters, they must take into account conflicting constitutional claims and divided public opinion as well as facts about the relationship between guns and violence. And in doing so they must try to strike what they regard as a reasonable balance between the costs and the benefits of private gun ownership.

Adequate data and research are essential to judge both the effects of firearms on violence and the effects of different violence control policies. Those judgments are key to many important policy questions, among them: Should regulations restrict who may possess and carry a firearm? Should regulations differ for different types of firearms? Should purchases be delayed and, if so, for how long and under what circumstances? Should restrictions be placed on the number or types of firearms that can be purchased? Should safety locks be required? While there is a large body of empirical research on firearms and violence, there is little consensus on even the basic facts about these important policy issues.

Given the importance of these issues and the continued controversy surrounding the debate on firearms, the Committee to Improve Research Information and Data on Firearms was charged with providing an assessment of the strengths and limitations of the existing research and data on gun violence and identifying important gaps in knowledge; describing new methods to put research findings and data together to support the design and implementation of improved prevention, intervention, and control strategies for reducing gun-related crime, suicide, and accidental fatalities; and utilizing existing data and research on firearms and firearm violence to develop models of illegal firearms markets. The charge also called for examining the complex ways in which firearm violence may become embedded in community life and considering whether firearm-related homicide and suicide have become accepted as ways of resolving problems, especially among youth. However, there is a lack of empirical research to address these two issues.

MAJOR CONCLUSIONS

Empirical research on firearms and violence has resulted in important findings that can inform policy decisions. In particular, a wealth of descriptive information exists about the prevalence of firearm-related injuries and deaths, about firearms markets, and about the relationships between rates of gun ownership and violence. Research has found, for example, that higher rates of household firearms ownership are associated with higher rates of gun suicide, that illegal diversions from legitimate commerce are important sources of crime guns and guns used in suicide, that firearms are used defensively many times per day, and that some types of targeted police interventions may effectively lower gun crime and violence. This information is a vital starting point for any constructive dialogue about how to address the problem of firearms and violence.

While much has been learned, much remains to be done, and this report necessarily focuses on the important unknowns in this field of study. The committee found that answers to some of the most pressing questions cannot be addressed with existing data and research methods, however well designed. For example, despite a large body of research, the committee found no credible evidence that the passage of right-to-carry laws decreases or increases violent crime, and there is almost no empirical evidence that the more than 80 prevention programs focused on gun-related violence have had any effect on children's behavior, knowledge, attitudes, or beliefs about firearms. The committee found that the data available on these questions are too weak to support unambiguous conclusions or strong policy statements.

Drawing causal inferences is always complicated and, in the behavioral and social sciences, fraught with uncertainty. Some of the problems that the committee identifies are common to all social science research. In the case of firearms research, however, the committee found that even in areas in which the data are potentially useful, the complex methodological problems inherent in unraveling causal relationships between firearms policy and violence have not been fully considered or adequately addressed.

Nevertheless, many of the shortcomings described in this report stem from the lack of reliable data itself rather than the weakness of methods. In some instances—firearms violence prevention, for example—there are no data at all. Even the best methods cannot overcome inadequate data and, because the lack of relevant data colors much of the literature in this field, it also colors the committee's assessment of that literature.

DATA RECOMMENDATIONS

If policy makers are to have a solid empirical and research base for decisions about firearms and violence, the federal government needs to support a systematic program of data collection and research that specifically addresses that issue. Adverse outcomes associated with firearms, although large in absolute numbers, are statistically rare events and therefore are not observed with great frequency, if at all, in many ongoing national probability samples (i.e., on crime victimization or health outcomes). The existing data on gun ownership, so necessary in the committee's view to answering policy questions about firearms and violence, are limited primarily to a few questions in the General Social Survey. There are virtually no ongoing, systematic data series on firearms markets. Aggregate data on injury and ownership can only demonstrate associations of varying strength between firearms and adverse outcomes of interest. Without improvements in this situation, the substantive questions in the field about the role of guns in suicide, homicide and other crimes, and accidental injury are likely to continue to be debated on the basis of conflicting empirical findings.

Emerging Data Systems on Violent Events

The committee reinforces recommendations made by past National Research Council committees and others to support the development and maintenance of the National Violent Death Reporting System and the National Incident-Based Reporting System. These data systems are designed to provide information that characterizes violent events. No single system will provide data that can answer all policy questions, but the necessary first step is to collect accurate and reliable information to describe the basic facts about violent injuries and deaths. The committee is encouraged by the efforts of the Harvard School of Public Health's Injury Control Research Center pilot data collection program and the recent seed money provided to implement a Violent Death Reporting System at the Centers for Disease Control and Prevention.

Ownership Data

The inadequacy of data on gun ownership and use is among the most critical barriers to better understanding of gun violence. Such data will not by themselves solve all methodological problems. However, its almost complete absence from the literature makes it extremely difficult to understand the complex personality, social, and circumstantial factors that intervene between a firearm and its use. Also difficult to understand is the effect, if any, of programs designed to reduce the likelihood that a firearm will cause unjustified harm, or to investigate the effectiveness of firearm use in self-defense. We realize that many people have deeply held concerns about expanding the government's knowledge of who owns guns and what type of guns they own. We also recognize the argument that some people may refuse to supply such information in any system, especially those who are most likely to use guns illegally. **The committee recommends a research effort to determine whether or not these kinds of data can be accurately collected with minimal risk to legitimate privacy concerns.**

A starting point is to assess the potential of ongoing surveys. For example, efforts should be undertaken to assess whether tracing a larger fraction of guns used in crimes, regularly including questions on gun access and use in surveys and longitudinal studies (as is done in data from the ongoing, yearly Monitoring the Future survey), or enhancing existing items pertaining to gun ownership in ongoing national surveys may provide useful research data. To do this, researchers need access to the data. **The committee recommends that appropriate access be given to data maintained by regulatory and law enforcement agencies, including the trace data maintained by the Bureau of Alcohol, Tobacco, and Firearms; registration data maintained by the Federal Bureau of Investigation and state agencies; and manufacturing and sales data for research purposes.**

In addition, researchers need appropriate access to the panel data from the Monitoring the Future survey. These data may or may not be useful for understanding firearms markets and the role of firearms in crime and violence. However, without access to these systems, researchers are unable to assess their potential for providing insight into some of the most important firearms policy and research questions. Concerns about security and privacy must be addressed in the granting of greater access to these data, and the systems will need to be continually improved to make them more useful for research. Nevertheless, there is a long-established tradition of making sensitive data available with appropriate safeguards to researchers.

Methodological Approaches

Difficult methodological issues exist regarding how different data sets might be used to credibly answer the complex causal questions of interest.

The committee recommends that a methodological research program be established to address these problems. The design for data collection and analysis should be selected in light of particular research questions. For example, how, if at all, could improvements in current data, such as firearms trace data, be used in studies of the effects of policy interventions on firearms markets or any other policy issue? What would the desired improvements contribute to research on policy interventions for reducing firearms violence? Linking the research and data questions will help define the data that are needed. We recommend that the results of such research be regularly reported in the scientific literature and in forums accessible to investigators.

RESEARCH RECOMMENDATIONS

Firearms, Criminal Violence, and Suicide

Despite the richness of descriptive information on the associations between firearms and violence at the aggregate level, explaining a violent death is a difficult business. Personal temperament, the availability of weapons, human motivation, law enforcement policies, and accidental circumstances all play a role in leading one person but not another to inflict serious violence or commit suicide.

Because of current data limitations, researchers have relied primarily on two different methodologies. First, some studies have used case-control methods, which match a sample of cases, namely victims of homicide or suicide, to a sample of controls with similar characteristics but who were not affected by violence. Second, some "ecological" studies compare homicide or suicide rates in large geographic areas, such as counties, states, or countries, using existing measures of ownership.

Case-control studies show that violence is positively associated with firearms ownership, but they have not determined whether these associations reflect causal mechanisms. Two main problems hinder inference on these questions. First and foremost, these studies fail to address the primary inferential problems that arise because ownership is not a random decision. For example, suicidal persons may, in the absence of a firearm, use other means of committing suicide. Homicide victims may possess firearms precisely because they are likely to be victimized. Second, reporting errors regarding firearms ownership may systemically bias the results of estimated associations between ownership and violence.

Ecological studies currently provide contradictory evidence on violence and firearms ownership. For example, in the United States, suicide appears to be positively associated with rates of firearms ownership, but homicide is not. In contrast, in comparisons among countries, the association between rates of suicide and gun ownership is nonexistent or very weak but there is a substantial association between gun ownership and homicide. These cross-country comparisons reflect the fact that the suicide rate in the United States ranks toward the middle of industrialized countries, whereas the U.S. homicide rate is much higher than in all other developed countries.

The committee cannot determine whether these associations demonstrate causal relationships. There are three key problems. First, as noted above, these studies do not adequately address the problem of self-selection. Second, these studies must rely on proxy measures of ownership that are certain to create biases of unknown magnitude and direction. Third, because the ecological correlations are at a higher geographic level of aggregation, there is no way of knowing whether the homicides or suicides occurred in the same areas in which the firearms are owned.

In summary, the committee concludes that existing research studies and data include a wealth of descriptive information on homicide, suicide, and firearms, but, because of the limitations of existing data and methods, do not credibly demonstrate a causal relationship between the ownership of firearms and the causes or prevention of criminal violence or suicide. The issue of substitution (of the means of committing homicide or suicide) has been almost entirely ignored in the literature. What sort of data and what sort of studies and improved models would be needed in order to advance understanding of the association between firearms and suicide? Although some knowledge may be gained from further ecological studies, the most important priority appears to the committee to be individual-level studies of the association between gun ownership and violence. Currently, no national surveys on ownership designed to examine the relationship exist. **The committee recommends support of further individual-level studies of the link between firearms and both lethal and nonlethal suicidal behavior.**

Deterrence and Defense

Although a large body of research has focused on the effects of firearms on injury, crime, and suicide, far less attention has been devoted to understanding the defensive and deterrent effects of firearms. Firearms are used by the public to defend against crime. Ultimately, it is an empirical question whether defensive gun use and concealed weapons laws generate net social benefits or net social costs.

Defensive Gun Use

Over the past decade, a number of researchers have conducted studies to measure the prevalence of defensive gun use in the population. However, disagreement over the definition of defensive gun use and uncertainty over the accuracy of survey responses to sensitive questions and the methods of data collection have resulted in estimated prevalence rates that differ by a factor of 20 or more. These differences in the estimated prevalence rates indicate either that each survey is measuring something different or that some or most of them are in error. Accurate measurement on the extent of defensive gun use is the first step for beginning serious dialogue on the efficacy of defensive gun use at preventing injury and crime.

For such measurement, the committee recommends that a research program be established to (1) clearly define and understand what is being measured, (2) understand inaccurate response in the national gun use surveys, and (3) apply known methods or develop new methods to reduce reporting errors to the extent possible. A substantial research literature on reporting errors in other contexts, as well as well-established survey sampling methods, can and should be brought to bear to evaluate these response problems.

Right-to-Carry Laws

A total of 34 states have laws that allow qualified adults to carry concealed handguns. Right-to-carry laws are not without controversy: some people believe that they deter crimes against individuals; others argue that they have no such effect or that they may even increase the level of firearms violence. This public debate has stimulated the production of a large body of statistical evidence on whether right-to-carry laws reduce or increase crimes against individuals.

However, although all of the studies use the same basic conceptual model and data, the empirical findings are contradictory and in the committee's view highly fragile. Some studies find that right-to-carry laws reduce violent crime, others find that the effects are negligible, and still others find that such laws increase violent crime. The committee concludes that it is not possible to reach any scientifically supported conclusion because of (a) the sensitivity of the empirical results to seemingly minor changes in model specification, (b) a lack of robustness of the results to the inclusion of more recent years of data (during which there were many more law changes than in the earlier period), and (c) the statistical imprecision of the results. The evidence to date does not adequately indicate either the sign or the magnitude of a causal link between the passage of right-to-carry laws and crime rates. Furthermore, this uncertainty is not likely to be resolved with the existing data and methods. If further headway is to be made, in the committee's judgment, new analytical approaches and data are needed. (One committee member has dissented from this view with respect to the effects of these laws on homicide rates; see Appendix A.)

Interventions to Reduce Violence and Suicide

Even if it were to be shown that firearms are *a* cause of lethal violence, the development of successful programs to reduce such violence would remain a complex undertaking, because such interventions would have to address factors other than the use of a gun. Three chapters in this report focus specifically on what is known about various interventions aimed at reducing firearms violence by restricting access, or implementing prevention programs, or implementing criminal justice interventions. These chapters focus largely on what is known about the effects of different interventions on criminal violence. Although suicide prevention rarely has been the basis for public support of the passage of specific gun laws, such laws could have unintended effects on suicide rates or unintended by-products. **Thus, in addition to the recommendations related to firearms and crime below, the committee also recommends further studies of the link between firearms policy and suicide.**

Restricting Access

Firearms are bought and sold in markets, both formal and informal. To some observers this suggests that one method for reducing the burden of firearm injuries is to intervene in these markets so as to make it more expensive, inconvenient, or legally risky to obtain firearms for criminal use or suicide. Market-based interventions intended to reduce access to guns by criminals and other unqualified persons include taxes on weapons and ammunition, tough regulation of federal firearm licensees, limits on the number of firearms that can be purchased in a given time period, gun bans, gun buy-backs, and enforcement of laws against illegal gun buyers or sellers.

Because of the pervasiveness of guns and the variety of legal and illegal means of acquiring them, it is difficult to keep firearms from people barred by law from possessing them. The key question is substitution. In the absence of the pathways currently used for gun acquisition, could individuals have obtained alternative weapons with which they could have wrought equivalent harm? Substitution can occur in many dimensions: offenders can obtain different guns, they can get them from different places, and they can get them at different times.

Arguments for and against a market-based approach are now largely based on speculation, not on evidence from research. It is simply not known whether it is actually possible to shut down illegal pipelines of guns to criminals nor the costs of doing so. Answering these questions is essential to knowing whether access restrictions are a possible public policy. The committee has not attempted to identify specific interventions, research strategies, or data that might be suited to studying market interventions, substitution, and firearms violence. **Rather, the committee recommends that work be started to think carefully about possible research and data designs to address these issues.**

Prevention Programs and Technology

Firearm violence prevention programs are disseminated widely in U.S. public school systems to children ages 5 to 18, and safety technologies have been suggested as an alternative means to prevent firearm injuries. The actual effects of a particular prevention program on violence and injury, however, have been little studied and are difficult to predict. For children, firearm violence education programs may result in *increases* in the very behaviors they are designed to prevent, by enhancing the allure of guns for young children and by establishing a false norm of gun-carrying for adolescents. Likewise, even if perfectly reliable, technology that serves to reduce injury among some groups may lead to increased deviance or risk among others.

The committee found little scientific basis for understanding the effects of different prevention programs on the rates of firearm injuries. Generally, there has been scant funding for evaluation of these programs. For the few that have been evaluated, there is little empirical evidence of positive effects on children's knowledge, attitudes, beliefs, or behaviors. Likewise, the extent to which different technologies affect injuries remains unknown. Often, the literature is entirely speculative. In other cases, for example the empirical evaluations of child access prevention (CAP) laws, the empirical literature reveals conflicting estimates that are difficult to reconcile.

In light of the lack of evidence, the committee recommends that firearm violence prevention programs should be based on general prevention theory, that government programs should incorporate evaluation into implementation efforts, and that a sustained body of empirical research be developed to study the effects of different safety technologies on violence and crime.

Criminal Justice Interventions

Policing and sentencing interventions have had recent broad bipartisan support and are a major focus of current efforts to reduce firearms violence. These policies generally do not affect the ability of law-abiding citizens to keep guns for recreation or self-defense, and they have the potential to reduce gun violence by deterring or incapacitating violent offenders. Descriptive accounts suggest that some of these policies may have had dramatic crime-reducing effects: homicide rates fell dramatically after the implementation of Boston's targeted policing program, Operation Ceasefire, and Richmond's sentencing enhancement program, Project Exile.

Despite these apparent associations between crime and policing policy, however, the available research evidence on the effects of policing and sentencing enhancements on firearm crime is limited and mixed. Some sentencing enhancement policies appear to have modest crime-reducing effects, while the effects of others appear to be negligible. The limited evidence on Project Exile suggests that it has had almost no effect on homicide. Several city-based quasi-random interventions provide favorable evidence on the effectiveness of targeted place-based gun and crime suppression patrols, but this evidence is both application-specific and difficult to disentangle. Evidence on Operation Ceasefire, perhaps the most frequently cited of all targeted policing efforts to reduce firearms violence, is limited by the fact that it is a single case at a specific time and location. Scientific support for the effectiveness of the Boston Gun Project and most other similar types of targeted policing programs is still evolving.

The lack of research on these potentially important kinds of policies is an important shortcoming in the body of knowledge on firearms injury interventions. These programs are widely viewed as effective, but in fact knowledge of whether and how they reduce crime is limited. Without a stronger research base, policy makers considering adoption of similar programs in other settings must make decisions without knowing the true benefits and costs of these policing and sentencing interventions.

The committee recommends that a sustained, systematic research program be conducted to assess the effect of targeted policing and sentencing aimed at firearms offenders. Additional insights may be gained from using observational data from different applications, especially if combined with more thoughtful behavioral models of policing and crime. City-level studies on the effect of sentencing enhancement policies need to engage more rigorous methods, such as pooled time-series cross-sectional studies that allow the detection of short-term impacts while controlling for variation in violence levels across different areas as well as different times. Another important means of assessing the impact of these types of targeted policing and sentencing interventions would be to conduct randomized experiments to disentangle the effects of the various levers, as well as to more generally assess the effectiveness of these targeted policing programs.

1

Introduction

There is hardly a more contentious issue in American society than the ownership of firearms and various proposals for their control. To make reasonable decisions about these matters, public authorities must take account of conflicting constitutional claims and divided public opinion as well as the facts about the relationship between firearms and violence. In performing these tasks, policy makers must try to strike a reasonable balance between the costs and the benefits of private firearm ownership.

The costs seem obvious. In 2000, over 48,000 victims suffered nonfatal gunshot wounds (Centers for Disease Control and Prevention, 2001) and over 10,000 were murdered with a firearm (Federal Bureau of Investigation, 2001). Many more people, though not shot, are confronted by assailants armed with a gun. Young people are especially affected by this, so much so that firearm fatalities consistently rank among the leading causes of death per capita for youth. In 2000, people ages 20 to 24 accounted for almost one-fourth of all victims of homicides with a firearm (Federal Bureau of Investigation, 2001). Moreover, there are more suicides than homicides that are committed with firearms. And firearm-related accidents result in many serious injuries.

These grim facts must be interpreted with caution. Firearms are involved in homicides and suicides, but determining how many would have occurred had no firearm been available is at best a difficult task. Between 1980 and 1984 there were more than three times as many nongun homicides per capita in America than in England (Zimring and Hawkins, 1998). There were over 41,000 nongun homicides and over 63,000 gun homicides in the United States during this period. New York City has had a homicide rate that is 8 to

15 times higher than London's for at least the last 200 years, long before either city could have had its rates affected by English gun control laws, the advent of dangerous drugs, or the supposedly harmful effects of the mass media (Monkkonen, 2001). Thus, the United States arguably has a high level of violence and homicide independent of firearm availability. Nonetheless, today homicides by a firearm occur in the United States at a rate that is more than 63 times that of England, so firearms, though not the sole source of violence, play a large role in it (Zimring and Hawkins, 1998).

The problem is the same with suicide. People often kill themselves with firearms. There is some evidence that states with the highest rates of private firearm ownership tend to be those with the highest proportion of suicides committed with firearms (Azrael et al., 2004), and there are studies suggesting that homes with firearms in them have more suicides than homes without firearms (Hardy, 2002). However, it is difficult to determine how many people would kill themselves by other means if no firearms were available.

Explaining a violent death is a difficult business. Personal temperament, mental health, the availability of weapons, human motivation, law enforcement policies, and accidental circumstances all play a role in leading one person but not another to inflict serious violence. Furthermore, the impact that a gun has on a situation depends critically on the nature of the interaction taking place. A gun in the hand of a robber may have different consequences than a gun in the hands of a potential robbery victim, a drug dealer, or someone who is suicidal. The relationship between the individuals may also be important in determining the impact of a gun. In a domestic dispute, for instance, both parties might be well informed as to whether the other person has a firearm. In a burglary or street robbery, the offender is less likely to know whether the victim is armed.

In addition, the presence or threat of a gun may influence an interaction along multiple dimensions. A firearm may increase or decrease the likelihood that a potentially violent situation will arise. For instance, an offender with a firearm may be more likely to attempt a robbery, but knowing the victim has a firearm may lead the offender to forgo the crime. The presence of a firearm may also affect the likelihood that an interaction ends in violence or death. For example, it might be that the presence of a gun in a robbery is associated with higher death rates, but lower injury rates.

The intent of the persons, the nature of their interaction and relationships, the availability of firearms to them, and the level of law enforcement are critical in explaining when and why firearm violence occurs. Without attention to this complexity it becomes very difficult to understand the role that firearms play in violence. Even if firearms are shown to be *a* cause of lethal violence, the development of successful prevention programs remains a complex undertaking, as such interventions would undoubtedly have to address the many factors other than the firearm that are involved in any violent situation.

Many people derive benefits from firearm ownership. Some people hunt or shoot at target ranges without ever inflicting harm on any human. It is estimated that there are 13 million hunters in the United States (U.S. Department of the Interior, Fish and Wildlife Service, 2002) and more than 11,000 shooting tournaments sanctioned by the National Rifle Association each year (National Rifle Association, 2002). Others have firearms because they believe the weapons will help them defend themselves. Many people carry their weapons on their person or in their cars. We do not know accurately how often armed self-defense occurs or even how to precisely define self-defense. The available data are believed to be unreliable, but even the smallest of the estimates indicates that there may be hundreds of defensive uses every day (Cook, 1991; Kleck and Gertz, 1995).

OUR TASK

Given the importance of this issue and the continued controversy surrounding the debate on firearms, the need was clear for an unbiased assessment of the existing portfolio of data and research. Accordingly, the National Academies were asked by a consortium of both federal agencies—the National Institute of Justice and the Centers for Disease Control and Prevention—and private foundations—the David and Lucile Packard Foundation, the Annie E. Casey Foundation, and the Joyce Foundation—to assess the data and research on firearms.

The Committee to Improve Research and Data on Firearms was charged with providing an assessment of the strengths and limitations of the existing research and data on gun violence and identifying important gaps in knowledge; describing new methods to put research findings and data together to support the design and implementation of improved prevention, intervention, and control strategies for reducing gun-related crime, suicide, and accidental fatalities; and utilizing existing data and research on firearms and firearm violence to develop models of illegal firearms markets. The charge also called for examining the complex ways in which firearm violence may become embedded in community life and whether firearm-related homicide and suicide become accepted as ways of resolving problems, especially among youth; however, there is a lack of empirical research to address these two issues.

The task of the committee was not to settle all arguments about the causes and cures of violence but rather to evaluate the data and research on firearms injury and violence. Over the past few decades, there have been many studies of the relationship between access to firearms and firearm violence, family and community factors that influence lethal behavior, the extent and value of defensive firearm use, the operation of legal and illegal firearms markets, and the effectiveness of efforts to reduce the harms or increase the benefits of firearm use. We have evaluated these data and studies. In doing so, we have:

- Assessed current data bases so as to make clear their strengths and limitations.
- Assessed research studies on firearm use and the effect of efforts to reduce unjustified firearm use.
- Assessed knowledge of illegal firearms markets.

This report presents the committee's findings.

GUN CONTROL AND THE SECOND AMENDMENT

Many people reading this report will ask whether the committee favors or opposes gun control, accepts or rejects the right of people to own guns, and endorses or questions the conflicting interpretations of the Second Amendment to the U.S. Constitution ("the right of the people to keep and bear arms shall not be infringed").

Resolving these issues, though important, is not the task the committee was given. We were asked to evaluate the data and research on firearm violence to see what is known about the causal connection, if any, between firearms on one hand and violence, suicide, and personal defense on the other. In carrying out this task, we have tried to do what scholars are supposed to do—namely, assess the reliability of evidence about the ownership of firearms and discern what, if anything, is known about the connection between firearms and violence. This involves looking at not only how many firearms are owned and who owns them but also the complex personality, social, and circumstantial factors that intervene between a firearm and its use and the effect, if any, of programs designed to reduce the likelihood that a firearm will cause unjustified harm.[1] It also includes investigating the effectiveness of firearm use in self-defense. It does not include making judgments about whether individuals should be allowed to possess firearms or whether specific firearm control proposals should be enacted.

Questions of cause-and-effect and more-or-less are not how many Americans think about firearms. Some individuals believe that firearm ownership is a right that flows directly from the Second Amendment or indirectly from every citizen's right to self-defense. Others believe that there is no right to bear arms, and that firearms play little or no role in self-defense.

---

[1] A harm is unjustified if it involves a homicide, an accident, or a suicide. It is justified if it involves the reasonable use of force by law enforcement personnel or by people defending themselves against crimes. It is difficult, of course, to count justified and unjustified harms accurately and even harder to discover whether a program intended to reduce unjustified harm has actually done so and, if it has, whether it did so in ways that have not inappropriately reduced justified harms. For a more detailed discussion of the definition of these terms, see *Black's Law Dictionary* (Gardner, 1999).

These competing beliefs are important and will inform the decisions political leaders have to make. America did not, after all, suddenly become a gun-owning nation. The private possession of weapons has been an important feature of American life throughout its history. But important as these beliefs are, they are not questions that can be easily resolved through scientific inquiry. Committee members have no special qualifications for deciding who has what rights or what the Second Amendment may mean. If the Supreme Court had spoken out clearly on this part of the Bill of Rights, the committee could assume something about what rights, if any, it confers. But the Court has not spoken so clearly. It has allowed Congress, for example, to ban the sale of sawed-off shotguns, but only on the narrow grounds that no one had shown that having a weapon with a barrel less than 18 inches long would contribute to the maintenance of a "well-regulated militia." And the Court has accepted restrictions on the sale of firearms to felons. But so far, the Court has held that the Second Amendment affects only federal action, presumably leaving states free to act as they wish. (For a review of holdings on the Second Amendment, see Appendix C.)

Our report is not for or against "gun control." (We put *gun control* in quotation marks because it is so vague: "gun control" can range from preventing four-year-old children from owning guns to banning their ownership by competent adults.) Knowing how strongly so many Americans feel about firearms and various proposals to control or prevent controls on their ownership, we here state emphatically that our task is to determine what can be learned from existing data and studies that rely on them and to make recommendations about how the knowledge base could be effectively improved. Readers of this report should not be surprised that the committee often concludes that very little can be learned. The committee was not called into being to make policy about firearms. Political officials, responding not only to data and studies but also to widely held (and often passionately opposed) public beliefs, will have to make policy. They should do so, however, with an understanding of what is known and not known about firearms and violence.

SOURCES OF DATA FOR RESEARCH ON FIREARMS VIOLENCE

We may have some advantage, however, in understanding what consequences flow from current levels of firearm availability and from efforts by policy makers to alter those consequences. Or to state our task even more humbly, we may be better than many other people in understanding what the *studies* of these consequences may mean. A consequence of some action is the concrete, practical reality that is caused by that action. But in the field we address here, many if not most studies of consequences must make do, not with direct knowledge of the altered reality, but with data that attempt to measure that alteration.

The quality of these data is highly variable. We explain in this report how limited is the knowledge of some of the basic facts. For example, we do not know exactly who owns what kinds of firearms or how the owners use them. Moreover, it may not be easy to improve this knowledge. Asking people whether they own a firearm, what kind it is, and how it is used is difficult because ownership is a controversial matter for one or more of several reasons: some people may own a firearm illegally, some may own it legally but worry that they may use it illegally, and some may react to the intense public controversy about firearm ownership by becoming less (or even more) likely to admit to ownership.

Of course these same problems accompany attempts to measure other behaviors (e.g., illicit use of drugs) and yet ways have been developed to address these problems in those instances (for a review see National Research Council, 2001). While not perfect, many substantial resources have been devoted to addressing the measurement issues that the collection of sensitive data raises. As we discuss in this report, this has not happened in the firearms area, in part, because of the substantial opposition to data collection by interest groups resulting in legal restrictions on collecting information about firearms ownership.[2]

STANDARDS AND METHODS FOR FIREARMS RESEARCH

All research must follow some basic standards to be accepted by the community of scholars in a field—firearms research is no different. These standards are well known to scientists, although all of them are not achieved in every research effort and meeting these minimal standards does not guarantee that the completed research will be judged to be a contribution to knowledge. These are necessarily minimal standards. Meeting them does not guarantee a piece of research is sufficiently sound to warrant acceptance of its findings. Another National Research Council committee (2002) recently described the scientific process in terms of "six interrelated but not necessarily ordered, principles of inquiry" (pp. 3-5):

- Pose significant questions that can be investigated empirically.
- Link research to relevant theory.
- Use methods that permit direct investigation of the question.

---

[2]For example, the 1986 Firearms Owners Protection Act, also known as the McClure-Volkmer Act, forbids the federal government from establishing any "system of registration of firearms, firearm owners, or firearms transactions or distribution."

- Provide a coherent and explicit chain of reasoning.
- Replicate and generalize across studies.
- Disclose research to encourage professional scrutiny and critique.

While any group of scholars might modify this list, it poses some commonly accepted standards that our committee used to begin its evaluation of the literature on firearm violence. In so doing we have sought to ensure that often controversial research issues are subjected to these minimum standards for research and to encourage future research in this area to strive for greater rigor.

The committee also noted that certain research strategies are very prevalent in firearms research. These include various interrupted time-series approaches (before-after studies) and the use of case-control techniques. Because these are so frequently utilized in this area of research, we provide an analysis of their use. In Appendix D there is a discussion of the difficulties of before-after type studies, and in Chapter 7 there is one on case-control designs. For advances to be made in firearm violence research, researchers must be careful to use these techniques and approaches with due recognition of their limitations and carefully consider the effect of research design on findings.

In our analysis of the use of these methods in firearms research, we found too often that the conclusions reached require the acceptance of assumptions that are at best implausible. For example, many studies (e.g., Duggan, 2001; Kaplan and Geling, 1998; Kleck and Patterson, 1993; Miller et al., 2002) of the relationship between the access to firearms and firearm violence are conducted with the state as the unit of analysis (a measure of the rate of firearm ownership is correlated with the rate of firearm violence). These results are used to advance the argument that an individual's probability of access to firearms explains that individual's probability of committing a violent crime with a weapon. While the problems associated with such cross-level interpretations are well known (the "ecological fallacy"; that is, inferences about individual behavior cannot be drawn from aggregate data about a group; Robinson, 1950), these authors and many who use their work to advance various firearms policies all too frequently draw inferences that cannot be supported by their analysis. Similarly in interrupted-time-series designs, the length of the series and the well-known problems associated with nonexperimental and quasi-experimental designs (see Campbell and Stanley, 1966) are frequently not given the attention required for the work to be judged acceptable. Throughout this report we hold all the research we reviewed to these reasonable standards. Especially in areas of research in which there is much public controversy, it is vital that such standards be maintained.

Using the conventional standards of science, we have reviewed the data and research on firearms and have suggested ways by which these data and studies can be improved. Our readers will judge how well we have done this. We hope they will bring to that assessment the same standards of evidence that we applied in our work.

GUIDE TO THE REPORT

The chapters that follow review and analyze what is known about firearms and violence. Chapter 2 describes the major data sources for research on firearms and violence. This summary assesses the strengths and weaknesses of each system and suggests improvements necessary to make significant advances in understanding the role of firearms in violence. Chapter 3 is a summary of the data describing the extent of firearm violence, firearm ownership, the perpetrators and victims of firearm violence, and the context in which firearm violence occurs. Descriptive in form, it also identifies gaps in understanding of some of the basic facts about the role firearms play in intentional violence. Chapter 4 addresses how criminals and those who use firearms to commit suicide gain access to them. It includes an assessment of various attempts to limit access by everyone and by selected subsets of the population. Chapter 5 assesses the research on the use of firearms to defend against crime, and Chapter 6 examines the impact of laws that facilitate the carrying of weapons.

The committee paid close attention to these issues because they have been central to the recent scholarship on firearms and because they demonstrate many of the difficulties of doing research on firearms and violence. Committee member Joel Horowitz further discusses these issues in Appendix D. Committee member James Q. Wilson has written a dissent that applies to Chapter 6 only (Appendix A), and the committee has written a response (Appendix B).

Chapter 7 considers the role of firearms in suicide. While some of the issues are similar to those encountered in the study of violence, the differences are such that separate attention is required, especially for issues of motivation, firearm acquisition, and lethality. In Chapter 8 we analyze the research on the prevention of firearm violence, reviewing research on the effectiveness of primary, secondary, and tertiary prevention programs. Special attention is given to efforts to prevent gun use by youth. Chapter 9 examines the role criminal justice interventions can play in reducing firearm violence. While many of these efforts are new and have not been adequately evaluated, they are frequently thought to hold promise for immediate impact.

2

Data for Measuring Firearms Violence and Ownership

Scientists in the social and behavioral sciences deal with many data-related obstacles in conducting empirical research. These include lack of relevant data, data that are error-ridden, and data that are not based on properly designed statistical samples (i.e., are unrepresentative) of the targeted population. These obstacles are particularly difficult in firearms research. In firearms and violence research, the outcomes of interest, although large in absolute numbers, are statistically rare events that are not observed with great frequency, if at all, in many ongoing national probability samples. Moreover, response problems are thought to be particularly severe in surveys of firearms ownership and violence. In the committee's view, the major scientific obstacle for advancing the body of research and further developing credible empirical research to inform policy on firearms is the lack of reliable and valid data.

This chapter summarizes some of the key data collection systems used to assess firearms policies, describes some of the key properties of useful research data, and offers some suggestions for how to begin to develop data that can answer the basic policy questions. There are no easy solutions to resolving the existing data-related problems. Often, we find that the existing data are insufficient, but how and whether to develop alternative data sources remain open questions. For these reasons the committee urges a significant increase in methodological work on measurement in the area of firearms ownership and violence.

The committee does not wish to paint an overly pessimistic picture of this research area. The existing body of research, as described in the other chapters of the report, has shed light on some of the most fundamental questions related to firearms and violence. However, in key data areas—the availability of firearms, the use of firearms, and the role of firearms in injuries and death—critical information is absent.

A PATCHWORK OF DATA SETS

To study firearms and violence, researchers and policy makers rely on a patchwork of data sources collected for more general purposes of monitoring the nation's health and crime problems. No authoritative source of information exists to provide representative, accurate, complete, timely, and detailed data on the incidence and characteristics of firearm-related violence in the United States. Rather, there are many different sources of data that researchers use to draw inferences about the empirical questions of interest. Some information on firearms and violence is found in probability samples of well-defined populations, such as the National Crime Victimization Survey (NCVS) and the Generalized Social Survey (GSS). Other information comes from administrative data, such as the Uniform Crime Reports (UCR) and the trace data of the Bureau of Alcohol Tobacco and Firearms (BATF). Still other information comes from case studies, social experiments, and other one-time surveys conducted on special populations. Table 2-1 lists characteristics of some of the commonly used data sources.

Perhaps because these data sets serve many purposes, the strengths and limitations of each source have been generally well documented in the literature.[1] This section provides a brief description of the some of the key data sources used in the research literature on firearms injury and violence and discussed in the report. This summary is not an exhaustive treatment of the data sources listed in Table 2-1, nor is it complete in its assessment of the specific data sources considered. Rather, it is intended to provide relevant background material on the key data.

Data on Violence and Crime

It is axiomatic that reliable and valid surveys on violence, offending, and victimization are critical to an understanding of violence and crime in the

---

[1]See, for example, Annest and Mercey (1998); Biderman and Lynch (1991); Maltz (1999); MacKenzie et al. (1990); Jarvis (1992); Wiersema et al. (2000); and Riedel (1999). The National Opinion Research Center (NORC) produces an ongoing series of methodological reports on the GSS, covering topics ranging from item order and wording, to nonresponse errors, and hundreds of other methodological topics. The reports are available directly from the NORC and are listed on http://www.icpsr.umich.edu:8080/GSS under "GSS Methodological Reports."

United States and for any assessment of the quality of activities and programs aimed at reducing violence (National Research Council, 2003). Detailed data on firearm-related death, injury, and risk behaviors are limited.

Most measurement of *crime* in this country emanates from two major data sources. The FBI's Uniform Crime Reports has collected information on crimes known to the police and arrests from local and state jurisdictions throughout the country for almost seven decades. The National Crime Victimization Survey, a general population survey designed to discover the extent, nature, and consequences of criminal victimization, has existed since the early 1970s. Other national surveys that focus on specific problems, such as delinquency, violence against women, and child abuse, also provide important data on crime, victims, and offenders. A variety of data sources have been used to assemble information on suicide and accidents, and the National Violent Death Reporting System (NVDRS) has been funded via the Centers for Disease Control and Prevention (CDC) to collect information on all violent deaths.

In this section, we describe four datasets used to monitor and assess firearms-related violence: the National Crime Victimization Survey, the Uniform Crime Reports, and two emerging systems, the National Incident-Based Reporting System and the National Violent Death Reporting System. The latter two are thought to hold some promise for improving the research information on firearms and violence. Many of the other data collection sources (listed in Table 2-1) have very limited information on firearms and have been assessed elsewhere (see, for example, Annest and Mercy, 1998; Institute of Medicine, 1999).

National Crime Victimization Survey

The National Crime Victimization Survey, which relies on self-reports of victimization, is an ongoing annual survey conducted by the federal government (i.e., the Census Bureau on behalf of the Department of Justice) that collects information from a representative sample of nearly 100,000 noninstitutionalized adults (age 12 and over) from approximately 50,000 households. It is widely viewed as a "gold standard" for measuring crime victimization. The largest and oldest of the crime victimization studies, it uses a rotating panel design in which respondents are interviewed several times before they are "retired" from the sample. It uses a relatively short, six-month reporting period. Respondents are instructed to report only incidents that have occurred since the previous interview and are reminded of the incidents they reported then. The initial interview is done face-to-face to ensure maximum coverage of the population; if necessary, subsequent interviews are also conducted in person. The

TABLE 2-1 Selected Sources of Firearm Data

Title of Data Set	Sponsoring Agency	Information Available
Firearm-Related Injury/Death		
National Vital Statistics System—Final Mortality Data (NVSSF)	National Center for Health Statistics/ Centers for Disease Control and Prevention	Includes total numbers of firearm related deaths; death rates from homicide, suicide, unintentional, and undetermined shootings broken out by age, race, and sex
National Vital Statistics System—Current Mortality Sample (NVSS)	National Center for Health Statistics/ Centers for Disease Control and Prevention	Provides data on selected major causes of death, as well as sex, race, age, date of death, state in which death occurred
National Violent Death Reporting System (NVDRS)	Centers for Disease Control and Prevention	Data on violent deaths linked from medical examiners and coroners, police departments, death certificates, and crime labs; would include circumstances of firearm-related incidents
National Census of Fatal Occupational Injuries (CFOI)	Bureau of Labor Statistics	Complete count of all work-related injury fatalities; includes job-related homicides broken out by weapon
Survey of Occupational Injuries and Illnesses (SOH)	Bureau of Labor Statistics	Includes information on circumstances surrounding firearm-related injuries in the workplace
National Traumatic Occupational Fatality Surveillance System (NTOF)	National Institute for Occupational Safety and Health	Includes narrative text on industry, occupation, cause of death, and injury data on age, race, and sex; includes numbers and rates of firearm-related homicides, suicides, and other deaths occurring at work
National Electronic Injury Surveillance System All Injury Program (NEISS-AIP)	U.S. Consumer Products Safety Commission	Includes intentional and nonintentional nonfatal firearm-related injuries by gender, age, type of injury, type of gun, and nature of incident
National Hospital Ambulatory Medical Care Survey (NHAMCS)	National Center for Health Statistics	Injury visits to hospital emergency departments, including those caused by firearms

Population	Geographic Areas	Frequency/ Year Started
Deceased individuals (data from death certificates)	National	Annual/death registration for all states started 1933, detailed demographic data ftom 1989
Deceased individuals (data from death certificates)	National	Annual death registration for all states started 1933
Homicide, suicide, and unintentional firearm-related deaths, and deaths of undetermined causes	National	Under development
Employed civilians 16 years of age and older, plus resident armed forces	National	Annual/ started 1992
Injuries reported by employers in private industry	National	Annual/ started 1992
Workers age 16 and older certified on death certificate as injured at work	National	Data available from 1980
Admissions to hospital emergency departments	National	Updated daily/ redesigned 1978; all injuries included starting in 2000
Admissions to hospitals with emergency departments	National	Annual/ started 1992

continued

TABLE 2-1 Continued

Title of Data Set	Sponsoring Agency	Information Available
National Ambulatory Medical Care Survey (NAMCS)	National Center for Health Statistics	Includes age, sex, race, ethnicity, source of payment, and circumstances of injury-related visits, including firearm involvement
National Health Interview Survey (NHIS)	National Center for Health Statistics	Demographic information, physician and hospital visits, and other health-related information; includes gunshot wounds and type of gun; 1994 supplement on firearm storage and safety
National Mortality Followback Survey (NMFS)	National Center for Health Statistics	1993 survey included information on firearm access, and circumstances of homicide, suicide, and unintentional injury deaths
Data Elements for Emergency Department Systems (DEEDS)	National Center for Injury Prevention and Control (CDC)	Standardized data definitions, coding, and other specifications
International Classification of External Causes of Injury (CECI)	World Health Organization	External causes of injury in mortality and morbidity systems, including mechanism of injury

Firearms Industry and Retail

Annual Firearms Manufacturing and Exportation Report (AFMER)	Bureau of Alcohol, Tobacco, and Firearms	Number of firearms produced, by type
Census of Manufacturers	Bureau of the Census	Number of manufacturers, shipments, value, employment, payroll, and shipments by type of product for small arms manufacturing and small arms ammunition industries
Producer Price Index (PPI)	Bureau of Labor Statistics	Prices and price change at wholesale level for various categories of firearms, including "small arms" in general, "pistols and revolvers," "shotguns," and "rifles, centerfire"

Population	Geographic Areas	Frequency/ Year Started
Patient visits to office-based, nonfederally employed physicians	National	Annual/ 1995—detailed injury questions added,1997- intent of injury added
Civilian, noninstitutionalized U.S. households	National	Annual/ 1996—detailed injury section added
Persons age 15 and older who died in the year of the survey	National	Irregular frequency/ started in 1960s
24-hour, hospital-based emergency departments	National	Under development
Hospital emergency department records	International	Under development

Population	Geographic Areas	Frequency/ Year Started
Firearms manufacturers	National	Annual
Manufacturers	National	
Producers in the mining and manufacturing industries	National	Monthly/ started 1902

continued

TABLE 2-1 Continued

Title of Data Set	Sponsoring Agency	Information Available
Federal Firearms Licensee (FFL) List	Bureau of Alcohol, Tobacco, and Firearms	Licensee name, trade name, address, phone, and license number

Criminal Use of Firearms

National Crime Victimization Survey (NCVS)	Bureau of Justice Statistics	Victimizations, involving a firearm, by type of crime
Uniform Crime Reporting Program (UCR): Monthly Return of Offenses Known to Police	Federal Bureau of Investigation	Total numbers of specific violent and property crimes, includes counts of weapon type used for robberies and aggravated assaults
Uniform Crime Reporting Program: National Incident-Based Reporting System (NIBRS)	Federal Bureau of Investigation	Incident, victim, property, offender, and arrestee data on each incident and arrest in 22 crime categories
Uniform Crime Reporting Program: Supplemental Homicide Reports (SHR)	Federal Bureau of Investigation	Detailed descriptions of homicides, including weapon used
Youth Crime Gun Interdiction Initiative (YCGII)	Bureau of Alcohol, Tobacco, and Firearms	Proportion of crime guns that are recovered from juveniles, youth, and adults; top source states; type of gun used; "time to crime"
BATF Firearms Trace Data	Bureau of Alcohol, Tobacco, and Firearms	Firearms transaction records kept by federal firearms licensees, including date of sale and name of purchaser
Law Enforcement Officers Killed and Assaulted (LEOKA)	Federal Bureau of Investigation	Duty-related deaths and assaults of law enforcement officers, by weapon used in incident
Federal Justice Statistics Program (FJSP)	Bureau of Justice Statistics	Data on federal criminal case processing from the receipt of a criminal matter or arrest of suspect to release from prison into supervision

Population	Geographic Areas	Frequency/ Year Started
Federal firearms licensees, except collectors of curios and relics	National	
Persons 12 years of age and older	National	Annual/ started 1973
Crimes reported by city, county, and state law enforcement agencies	National	Monthly/ started 1930
Criminal incidents reported by local, state, and federal law enforcement agencies	National	Started 1989, under development
Criminal incidents reported by police departments	National	Started 1976
Guns recovered from juveniles and adult criminals	55 cities in 2001	Annual/ started 1997
Firearms submitted by law enforcement for tracing	National	Record-keeping started 1968
Local, state, and federal law enforcement officers	National	Annual
Defendants in criminal cases, suspects in investigative matters, and offenders under supervision	National	Annual

continued

TABLE 2-1 Continued

Title of Data Set	Sponsoring Agency	Information Available
Census of State and Federal Correctional Facilities	Bureau of Justice Statistics/ Bureau of the Census	Demographic, socioeconomic, and criminal history characteristics, including gun possession and use
National Violence Against Women Survey (NVAWS)	National Institute of Justice/ Centers for Disease Control and Prevention	Prevalence, incidence, characteristics, risk factors, circumstances, responses, and consequences of rape, intimate-partner assault and stalking; includes data on firearm use in these events
Arrestee Drug Abuse Monitoring (ADAM~-gun addendum	National Institute of Justice	Gun acquisition and use among arrestees, including gun carrying, reasons for owning a gun, being threatened with a gun, and drug use

Firearms and Youth

Monitoring The Future (MTF)	National Institute on Drug Abuse	Range of behaviors and attitudes with focus on drug use; includes frequency of gun carrying at school
Youth Risk Behavior Surveillance System (YRBSS)	Centers for Disease Control and Prevention	Prevalence of health risk behaviors including gun-carrying, weapon carrying on school property, and weapon-related threats or injuries on school property

Law and Enforcement

Firearm Inquiry Statistics (FIST)	Bureau of Justice Statistics	Handgun applications made to FFLs, applications rejected, and reasons for rejection

Population	Geographic Areas	Frequency/ Year Started
State correctional facility inmates	National	Every 5 to 7 years/started 1974
U.S. households	National	Unrepeated/ conducted 1996
Arrestees charged with felonies and misdemeanors	National (gun addendum includes 11 of the 35 sites)	1996—gun addendum
6th, 8th, 10th, and 12th graders and young adults up to age 19	National	Annual/ started 1972, gun question added in 1996
School-age youth grades 9 through 12; also 12- to 21-year-olds in 1992 and college students in 1995	National	Every two years/started 1990
Chief law enforcement officers	States operating under the Brady Act and states with statutes comparable to the Brady Act	Started 1995

continued

TABLE 2-1 Continued

Title of Data Set	Sponsoring Agency	Information Available
Survey of State Procedures Related to Firearm Sales	Bureau of Justice Statistics	State laws, regulations, procedures, and information systems related to sales and other transactions of firearms
Firearms Ownership		
General Social Survey (GSS)	National Opinion Research Center	Prevalence of ownership, type of gun owned, opinion on permit and control issues, and gun threat incidents
National Study of Private Ownership of Firearms in the U.S.	National Institute of Justice	Firearm ownership, acquisition, storage, and defensive use; size, number, and type of firearms owned
Survey of Gun Owners in the U.S.	National Institute of Justice	Characteristics of gun ownership, gun carrying, and circumstances of weapon-related incidents

NCVS and its predecessor, the National Crime Survey, underwent lengthy development periods featuring record check studies and split-ballot experiments to determine the best way to measure crime victimization (Tourangeau and McNeeley, 2003).

Although the NCVS data do many things right, they are, like any such system, beset with methodological problems of surveys in general as well as particular problems associated with measuring illicit, deviant, and deleterious activities (see National Research Council, 2003). Such problems include nonreporting and false reporting, nonstandard definitions of events, sampling problems such as coverage and nonreponse, and an array of other factors involved in conducting surveys of individuals and implementing official data reporting systems. Measurement problems have been particularly controversial in using the NCVS to assess defensive gun uses (see Chapter 5 and National Research Council, 2003, for further details).

In contrast to the NCVS, many other data sources used to measure or monitor violence and crime are assembled as part of administrative records.

Population	Geographic Areas	Frequency/ Year Started
Federal, state, and local agencies, including law enforcement, statistical analysis centers, and legislative research bureaus	National	Annual/ 1996
Noninstitutionalized adults	National	Biannual/ started 1972
U.S. households	National	Unrepeated/ conducted in 1994
Adults age 18 and older	National	Unrepeated/ conducted in 1996

Uniform Crime Reports

Every month, local law enforcement agencies are asked to record for their jurisdictions the total number of murders, rapes, robberies, aggravated assaults, burglaries, larcenies, motor vehicle thefts, and arsons on a form known as UCR Return A.[2] For robberies and aggravated assaults, counts broken down by type of weapon (firearms; knives or cutting instruments; other weapons; and personal weapons, such as hands, feet, fists, etc.) are requested. Participation in the UCR program is voluntary.

The UCR Return A data offer a relatively long monthly time series of robberies and assaults by firearms and other weapons occurring in local police jurisdictions across the country. However, administrative data such as UCR have a different set of problems than the NCVS. Foremost among them is that these data alone cannot be used to draw inferences about firearms use or victimization in the general population.[3] The UCR is a sample of crimes reported to and recorded by local law enforcement agen-

---

[2]The UCR program excludes jurisdictions covered by federal law enforcement agencies.

[3]In fact, the NCVS was created to address this problem by capturing data on both reported and unreported crimes, to develop a clearer picture of national crime trends.

cies in the United States. Ideally, they reveal the number of crimes per month for each of the reporting jurisdictions. Of course, many crimes are not reported to the police, so increases or decreases in reports for certain offenses, such as burglary and auto theft, can result in large differences in outcomes and misleading conclusions about crime trends.

Other reporting problems may further limit the usefulness of these data. First, the accuracy of UCR data can be compromised by differences in definitions of crimes and reporting protocols. Local authorities, for example, might choose criminal charges to achieve certain objectives (e.g., increasing plea bargains by downgrading what might otherwise be a charge of aggravated assault, armed robbery, or rape to a lesser charge that then gets reported in the UCR).

Second, participation in the UCR program is voluntary, with smaller, more rural police agencies less likely to submit reports than larger, urban departments. A review of the preliminary 2000 UCR data posted on the FBI's web site indicates that in one large midwestern state, only six cities with 10,000 and over population reported arrest data between January and June. In all, there were six states that could provide only limited data. For example, rape data were unavailable for two states because the state reporting agencies did not follow the national UCR guidelines (http://www.FBI.gov/ucr/ 99cius.htm). The committee is not aware of research that details how this nonresponse problem affects inferences in firearm-related research. Maltz and Targonski (2002) argue that underreporting in the UCR data may bias the results of research on right-to-carry laws, but they do not document the magnitude of these biases (see Chapter 6 for further details).

Finally, because these data are based on monthly counts and not on individual incidents, only limited detail is available regarding crime circumstances. There is no information, for example, on the nature or severity of the injuries inflicted. The Supplemental Homicide Report (which is part of the UCR program) provides limited information on the relationship between victim and offender and event circumstances (e.g., whether the homicide is related to an argument or the commission of another felony).

National Incident-Based Reporting System

The National Incident-Based Reporting System (NIBRS) is designed to provide detailed incident-level information on crimes, including firearm-related crimes. It is administered through the FBI's UCR program and augments the crime reports of local law enforcement agencies in several key respects: offense categories are greatly expanded; attributes of individual crime incidents (offenses, offenders, victims, property, and arrests) can be collected and analyzed; arrests and clearances can be linked to specific incidents or offenses; and all offenses in an incident can be recorded and counted.[4] NIBRS is intended to replace the UCR as the nation's comprehensive, standardized crime data source based on crimes known to the police.

However, since its blueprint was published in 1985 (Poggio et al., 1985), only 16 percent of the U.S. population is covered by NIBRS data (Bureau of Justice Statistics, 2001), with few large cities or urban areas participating. Thus, at this time, NIBRS is not an effective data set for studying firearms violence.

National Violent Death Reporting System

In 2002, Congress appropriated funds to the CDC to begin creating the NVDRS. This system builds on earlier pilot work sponsored by private foundations coordinated through the Harvard School of Public Health's Injury Control Research Center. The NVDRS aims to create a comprehensive individual-level data set in each state that links data from medical examiners and coroners, police departments, death certificates, and crime labs on each death resulting from violence (homicide, suicide, unintentional firearm-related deaths, and undetermined causes). A set of uniform data elements has been proposed that would allow a set of minimum plus desirable variables to be collected using standardized definitions and codes. The NVDRS is designed to provide detailed characteristics of the circumstances surrounding firearm-related deaths, including detailed descriptions of the firearms used. Because similar characteristics would be collected on nonfirearm-related violent incidents, a more complete picture of all violent incidents would be available for analysis than from any existing ongoing data collection effort. The prototype that CDC is implementing in the first six states (Maryland, Massachusetts, New Jersey, Oregon, South Carolina, and Virginia) is being carried out with an initial investment of $2.25 million. Expansion to the remaining states is estimated to cost approximately $20 million (http://www.aast.org/nvdrs).

The NIBRS and the NVDRS are emerging data sources designed to provide more information on the circumstances involved in violent events. The NIBRS would provide details on violent crimes. The NVDRS would provide details on violent deaths. Whether and to what extent these data, if fully implemented, could be effectively used to answer some of the complex firearms policy questions is an open question. Consistency of definitions and data protocols over many different administrative data sources is a highly

---

[4]This description is adapted from that provided by the Justice Research and Statistics Association (http://www.jrsa.org). Other useful information sources on NIBRS, including downloadable data sets and codebooks, are the FBI's Uniform Crime Reporting program (http://www.fbi/ucr/nibrs) and the National Consortium for Justice Information and Statistics (http://www.search.org/nibrs).

complex undertaking that is nearly certain to result in reporting errors. Even if the data are reliable and accurate, the NIBRS and the NVDRS, as with the UCR, are administrative data that by their nature provide information on events rather than people. Neither survey alone will provide information on the use of firearms in the general population, how firearms are acquired, or how they are used in noncriminal and nonfatal instances.

Data on Firearms Ownership, Use, and Markets

Almost every empirical question about firearms and violence requires periodic, scientifically acceptable measures of firearms acquisition, availability, and use. The difficulty of measuring the extent of firearms possession, the ways in which firearms are acquired, and the myriad uses of firearms comes up in every chapter of the report.

Several types of ownership data are used in the literature: (1) surveys to measure acquisition, availability and use; (2) administrative data or other convenience samples providing information on possession and use among particular populations (e.g., arrestees) or associated with particular events (e.g., crime); or (3) proxies that indicate firearms possession and use.

Surveys

Surveys would seem to be the most direct approach to measuring firearms possession, availability, and perhaps use. The *General Social Survey* is the primary source of information for tracking U.S. household firearms ownership over time since the early 1970s. The GSS is an ongoing, nationally representative set of sample surveys on a broad range of social issues conducted by the National Opinion Research Center (NORC). A total of 23 national surveys have been conducted since the inception of the GSS in 1972 (annually until 1993, biennially since 1994, with samples of approximately 1,500 subjects). As an omnibus survey, many topics are covered, but no topic area is treated with a great deal of depth. Because the GSS is designed to provide information on trends in attitudes and opinions, many questions are repeated from year to year. Pertinent to firearms research, the GSS includes questions on whether guns (handguns, rifles, shotguns) are owned by the respondent or other household members. Surveys prior to 1995 included an item on prevalence of being threatened by or shot at with a gun, but these questions have been omitted in recent years.[5]

---

[5]NORC incorporates methodological experiments into each year of the GSS data collection, involving item wording, context effects, use of different types of response scales, and other assessments of validity and reliability (see http://www.norc.uchicago.edu/projects/gensoc1.asp).

The GSS surveys provide basic information on household ownership in the United States and the nine census regions, but not much else specific to firearms policy. They cannot be used to infer ownership at finer geographic levels.[6] They do not inquire into the number of guns owned, the reasons for owning them, or how they are used in practice. As a household survey, the GSS sampling frame omits transients and others without a stable residence who may be at high risk for firearm violence. The data offer no direct indication of illicit firearms transfers.

Many other surveys of varying quality have been used to reveal possession or use of firearms. The NCVS, for example, has been used to study what victims of crime report about the weapons used in the crimes against them and to provide rough estimates of the characteristics of offenders using those weapons (Bureau of Justice Statistics, 1994). In 1994, the National Institute of Justice funded the Police Foundation to conduct a nationally representative telephone survey on private ownership and the use of firearms by adults in the United States. The study covered topics such as the size, composition, and ownership of the nation's private gun inventory; methods of and reasons for firearms acquisition, storage, and carrying of guns; and defensive use of firearms against criminal attackers. The study oversampled racial minorities and gun-owning households. The data provide greater detail about patterns of firearms ownership than the GSS, and they provide an estimate of the use of firearms for defense against perceived threats. Chapter 5 reviews other surveys used to elicit information on defensive gun use, such as the National Self-Defense Survey.

While surveys of firearms acquisition, possession, and use are of varying quality and scope, they all share common methodological and survey sampling-related problems. The most fundamental of these is the potential for response errors to survey questionnaires. Critics argue that asking people whether they own a firearm, what kind it is, and how it is used may lead to invalid responses because ownership is a controversial matter for one or more reasons: some people may own a firearm illegally, some may own it legally but worry that they may use it illegally, and some may react to the intense public controversy about firearm ownership by becoming less (or even more) likely to admit to ownership (Blackman, 2003).[7] Because only one member of the household is selected to respond, even well-intentioned

---

[6]Area identifiers permit use of the GSS survey data to assess household ownership prevalence across a representative sample of U.S. metropolitan areas and nonmetropolitan counties, although access to the area-identified data requires special permission from NORC.

[7]While in most surveys respondents are provided confidentiality, the concern is still expressed that violations of that confidentiality directly or through data mining could lead to the identification of specific respondents in a way that might allow the identification of firearms owners.

respondents may not know about household possession or use. In addition, critics of survey approaches have raised concerns about how survey data might be used to establish what would be close to a national registry of firearm possessors.

The committee is not aware of any research assessing the magnitude or impact of response errors in surveys of firearms ownership and use. Similar concerns have been expressed about other sensitive behaviors for which research evidence on misreporting may be relevant. Surveys on victimization, such as the NCVS, and on the prevalence of drug use, such as Monitoring the Future and the National Household Survey of Drug Abuse, have undergone continuing and careful research efforts to identify the sources of response error and to correct for them (see National Research Council, 2001, 2003; Harrison and Hughes, 1997). The large literature assessing the magnitude of misreporting self-reported drug use surveys, for example, reveals consistent evidence that some respondents misreport their drug use behavior and that misreporting depends on the social desirability of the drug (see National Research Council, 2001, and Harrison and Hughes, 1997, for reviews of this literature).[8] Moreover, the validity rates can be affected by the data collection methodology. Surveys that can effectively ensure confidentiality and anonymity and that are conducted in noncoercive settings are thought to have relatively low misreporting rates. Despite this large body of research, very little information exists on the magnitude or trends in invalid reporting in illicit drug use surveys (National Research Council, 2001).

While there is some information on reporting errors in surveys on other sensitive topics, the relevance of this literature for understanding invalid reporting of firearms ownership and use is uncertain. In many ways, the controversy over firearms appears exceptional. There is, as noted in the introduction, hardly a more contentious issue, with the public highly polarized over the legal and research foundations for competing policy options. Furthermore, the durable nature of firearms may arguably lead some respondents to provide invalid reports because of fears about future events (e.g., a ban on certain types of guns) even if they have no concerns about the legality of past events.

Nonresponse creates a similar problem. Response rates in the GSS are between 75 and 80 percent (Smith, 1995), less than 65 percent in the Police Foundation Survey, and even lower in some of the defensive gun use

---

[8]These studies have been conducted largely on samples of persons who have much higher rates of drug use than the general population (e.g., arrestees). A few studies have attempted to evaluate misreporting in broad-based representative samples, but these lack direct evidence and instead make strong, unverifiable assumptions to infer validity rates (National Research Council, 2001).

surveys described in Chapter 5. Nonresponse rates make it difficult to draw precise inferences about ownership rates and use as the data are uninformative about nonrespondents. With nonreponse rates of 25 percent or more, the existing surveys alone cannot reveal the rates of ownership or use. Prevalence rates can be identified only if one makes sufficiently strong assumptions about the behavior of nonrespondents. Generally, nonresponse is assumed to be random, thus implying that prevalence among nonrespondents is the same as prevalence among respondents. The committee is not aware of empirical evidence that supports the view that nonresponse is random. Indeed, studies of nonresponse in surveys of drug consumption provide limited empirical evidence to the contrary (see National Research Council, 2001). These studies find differences between respondents and nonrespondents in terms of both drug use and other observed covariates (Caspar, 1992; Gfroerer et al., 1997).

Concerns about response errors in self-reported surveys of firearms possession and use require much more systematic research before surveys can be judged to provide accurate data to address critical issues in the study of firearms and violence. The many substantial resources that have been devoted to addressing the measurement issues in the collection of other sensitive data will almost certainly be useful, yet the issues surrounding firearms may be unique. The committee thinks that new research will extend and strengthen what is currently known about response errors on sensitive topics generally. Without systematic research on these specific matters, scientists can only speculate.

Administrative and Convenience Samples

A number of administrative data sets have been used or suggested as a way to study the market for firearms possession and use. In this section, we describe the administrative data collected as part of the Bureau of Alcohol, Tobacco, and Firearms' tracing system, the trace data, and a proposed addendum on firearms to the National Institute of Justice survey of arrestees, the Arrestee Drug Abuse Monitoring (ADAM) survey.

BATF Firearms Trace Data: One federal source of information on firearms related to violence is the firearms trace data compiled by the Bureau of Alcohol, Tobacco, and Firearms of the U.S. Department of Justice. Because trace data are quite distinct from the other federal data sources, and because they have been subject to more criticism than most of the other systems, we provide a more extensive description of the regulatory background related to firearm tracing, the nature of the tracing process, and the uses and limitations of the resulting data.

The Gun Control Act of 1968 established the legal framework for regulating firearms transactions and the associated record-keeping. The act was intended to limit interstate commerce in guns, so that states with strict regulations were insulated from states with looser regulations (Zimring, 1975). To that end, the act established a system of federal licensing for gun dealers, requiring that all individuals engaged in the business of selling guns must be a federal firearms licensee (FFL). The FFLs were established as the gatekeepers for interstate shipments: only they may legally receive mail-order shipments of guns, and they may not sell handguns to residents of another state. FFLs are required to obey state and local regulations in transacting their business.

The Gun Control Act established conditions on the transfer of firearms. FFLs may not sell handguns to anyone under the age of 21, or long guns to anyone under the age of 18, nor may they sell a gun of any kind to someone who is proscribed from possessing one. The list of those proscribed by federal law includes individuals with a felony conviction or under indictment, fugitives from justice, illegal aliens, and those who have been committed to a mental institution. FFLs must require customers to show identification and fill out a form swearing that they do not have any of the disqualifying conditions specified in the Gun Control Act. Beginning in 1994, the Brady Violence Prevention Act required that FFLs initiate a background check on all handgun purchasers through law enforcement records; in 1998 that requirement was expanded to include the sale of long guns as well.

The 1968 Gun Control Act also established requirements that allowed for the chain of commerce for any given firearm to be traced from its manufacture or import through its first sale by a retail dealer. Each new firearm, whether manufactured in the United States or imported, must be stamped with a unique serial number. Manufacturers, importers, distributors, and FFLs are required to maintain records of all firearms transactions, including sales and shipments received. FFLs must report multiple handgun sales and stolen firearms to BATF and provide transaction records in response to its trace requests. When FFLs go out of business, they are to transfer their transaction records to BATF, which then stores them for tracing (Bureau of Alcohol, Tobacco, and Firearms, 2000a). In essence, the 1968 act created a paper trail for gun transactions that can be followed by BATF agents.

The tracing process begins with a law enforcement agency's submission of a trace request to BATF's National Tracing Center (NTC). The form requires information regarding the firearm type (i.e., pistol, revolver, shotgun, rifle), the manufacturer, caliber, serial number, and importer (if the gun is of foreign manufacture), the location of the recovery, the criminal offense associated with the recovery, and the name and date of birth of the firearm possessor (Bureau of Alcohol, Tobacco, and Firearms, 2000a). This information is entered into BATF's Firearms Tracing Center at the NTC and checked against the records of out-of-business FFLs that are stored by BATF, as well as records of multiple handgun purchases reported on an ongoing basis by FFLs. If the gun does not appear in these databases, NTC contacts the firearm manufacturer (for domestic guns) or the importer (for foreign guns) and requests information on the distributor that first handled the gun. BATF then follows the chain of subsequent transfers until it identifies the first retail seller. That FFL is then contacted with a request to search his or her records and provide information on when the gun was sold and to whom.

In 1999, trace requests for 164,137 firearms were submitted by law enforcement agencies to NTC. Of these, 52 percent (85,511) were successfully traced to the first retail purchaser. The 48 percent of trace requests that failed did so for a variety of reasons. Nearly 10 percent of the guns (15,750) were not successfully traced because they were too old (pre-1968 manufacture) and another 11 percent (17,776) failed because of problems with the serial number (Pierce et al., 2002). The majority of the remaining unsuccessful trace requests failed because of errors on the submission forms or problems obtaining the information from the FFL who first sold the gun at retail. It is important to note that, even when a trace is "successful," it provides limited information about the history of the gun (Cook and Braga, 2001). Most successful gun traces access only the data on the dealer's record for the first retail sale of the gun. Generally, subsequent transactions cannot be traced from the sorts of records required by federal firearms laws.

Beginning in 1993, the Clinton administration was concerned about the apparent ease with which criminals and juveniles obtained guns. BATF was charged with initiating a concerted effort to increase the amount of crime gun tracing, improve the quality of firearms trace data, increase the regulation of gun dealers, educate law enforcement on the benefits of tracing, and increase investigative resources devoted to gun traffickers. Comprehensive tracing of all firearms recovered by police is a key component of BATF's supply-side strategy to reduce the availability of illegal firearms. In 1996, BATF initiated the Youth Crime Gun Interdiction Initiative with commitments from 17 cities to trace all recovered crime guns (Bureau of Alcohol, Tobacco, and Firearms, 1997). This program expanded to 38 cities in 1999 (Bureau of Alcohol, Tobacco, and Firearms, 2000a) and to 55 cities in 2001 (Bureau of Alcohol, Tobacco, and Firearms, 2002b). Other jurisdictions have also expanded their use of gun tracing; six states, for example, have recently adopted comprehensive tracing as a matter of state policy, either by law (California, Connecticut, North Carolina, and Illinois), by executive order (Maryland), or by law enforcement initiative (New Jersey) (Bureau of Alcohol, Tobacco, and Firearms, 2000a).

Understandably, research studies based on analyses of firearms trace data have been greeted with a healthy dose of skepticism. Although the quality of firearms trace data has improved over the past decade (Cook and Braga, 2001), trace data analyses are subject to a number of widely recognized problems (see Kleck, 1999; Blackman, 1999; Congressional Research Service, 1992).[9] All are based on firearms recovered by police and other law enforcement agencies, which may not be representative of firearms possessed and used by criminals. Trace data are also influenced by which guns are submitted for tracing, a decision made by law enforcement agencies. Beyond that, not all firearms can be traced. The trace-based information that results is biased to an unknown degree by these factors.

Furthermore, trace data cannot show whether a firearm has been illegally diverted from legitimate firearms commerce. Trace studies typically contain information about the first retail sale of a firearm and about the circumstances associated with its recovery by law enforcement. These studies cannot show what happened in between: whether a firearm was legitimately purchased and subsequently stolen, sold improperly by a licensed dealer, or any other of a myriad of possibilities. As such, trace analysis alone cannot reveal the extent and nature of illegal firearms trafficking.

Ultimately, the validity of the conclusions drawn from these data depends on the application. In general, trace data are not informative about populations of interest, such as offenders, potential offenders, victims, and the general population.

Administered until recently by the National Institute of Justice, Arrestee Drug Abuse Monitoring (ADAM, formerly known as the Drug Use Forecasting program, or DUF) contains survey data and urine samples from samples of arrestees charged with felonies and misdemeanors at 35 sites across the county. Data collection occurred four times a year. Response rates were relatively high: about 85 percent of arrestees agreed to interview (http://www.adam-nij.net). ADAM focused on drug use patterns among criminal suspects and did not regularly collect data on firearms use. However, in 1996 researchers appended a "gun addendum" to the surveys in 11 sites to study patterns of gun acquisition and use among arrestees (Decker et al., 1997).

Decker and colleagues (1997) suggested how the addendum might be used to provide estimates of the frequency and characteristics of arrests in which the arrested persons owned and used firearms (National Research

---

[9]Comprehensive tracing of all firearm recoveries reduces some of the problems in trace data introduced by police decision making. Jurisdictions that submit all confiscated guns for tracing can be confident that the resulting data base of trace requests represents the firearms recovered by police during a particular period of time.

Council, 2003).[10] Tracking firearms possession through arrest might also serve to detect emerging problems in high-risk populations. Quarterly data collection, such as that conducted by ADAM, permits monitoring of local trends over short time intervals.

Such data, however, may not be useful for answering many of the policy-related questions considered in this report. Although the ADAM samples are representative of the local arrestee populations for which the surveys were administered, the 35 data collection sites are not a representative sample of urban areas nationwide. Moreover, a survey of arrestees cannot be used to infer acquisition and use among criminals or the general population. The data are not representative of the relevant populations and can be influenced heavily by police priorities and procedures. Thus, these data alone cannot be used to infer the effects of guns on crime or the effects of interventions on gun use or the market for weaponry in general.

Suppose, for example, one found that the fraction of arrestees reported to possess firearms does not vary by the strength of local regulations. It may be, as suggested by the data, that regulation has no effect on the market. It may also be that regulation affects the crime and the ownership rates, but among the arrested populations the ownership and use rates are unchanged. And it may be that regulations influence policing and the accuracy of self-reporting in unknown ways. ADAM data do not reveal the association between regulation and the behavior of offenders, potential offenders, the crime rate, or policing. Thus, observing that the prevalence of gun ownership and use among arrestees changes after some interventions does not reveal how gun use or crime more generally changed in the population of interest.

Proxy Measures of Ownership

Using proxy measures of ownership raises different issues and questions. In the proxy approach to measuring ownership (proxy approaches have not been developed as measures of firearms use) researchers have sought to find measures that would indicate whether firearms were available. A variety of these have been proposed, but it appears that the one the research community has settled on is the proportion of suicides committed with a firearm (Kleck, 1991; Cook, 1991). This measure has been found to

---

[10]This study, for example, reveals that 14 percent of arrestees carried firearms almost all of the time, that arrestees who tested positive for drugs were no more likely than others to own or use firearms, that the most frequently cited reason given for owning a gun was the need for protection or self-defense (two-thirds), that more than half of the arrestees (55 percent) said that guns are easy to obtain illegally, that 23 percent of arrestees who owned a gun reported using a gun to commit a crime, and that 59 percent of arrestees reported that they had been threatened with a gun.

correlate better than other possible proxies with measures of gun violence (homicide and gun assaults).

As we discuss in Chapter 7, proxies raise two somewhat related but distinct methodological issues. First, proxies have been used at aggregated levels, most often the state level, to infer something about the impact of availability at the individual level on violent outcomes. For example, if the proxy is correlated with gun homicides at the state level, then it is often assumed that availability at the individual level of analysis is associated with individual manifestations of violence. More generally, these studies are used to infer whether an individual's probability of access to firearms explains his or her probability of committing a violent crime or suicide. Aggregate measures of ownership, however, may or may not be related to actual availability in the households in which these rare events (homicides and suicides) occur.

A second issue with proxies is to what extent they are inaccurate indicators of firearms availability at the geographic level of interest. Proxies create biases, yet there is almost no research on these statistical problems in the firearms literature. Without more rigorous evaluations on the impact of proxies, it is difficult to assess the research on ownership and violence. Once these biases have been assessed, proxies may be useful because they are cheaper to collect, their collection is less intrusive, and for other reasons of economy or design. The research community in this area needs to focus more attention on assessing the biases created by proxies and on the development of better direct measures of availability and use.

GENERAL OBJECTIVES FOR DEVELOPING USEFUL RESEARCH DATA

In this section, we discuss several basic features that data on firearm ownership and violence ought to exhibit, individually or in combination, in order for researchers, practitioners, and policy makers to better understand the role of firearms in violent injury and death, both self- and other-inflicted. In particular, the following qualities of data sets are minimally necessary for credible research and evaluation on firearm violence: representativeness, accuracy, comprehensiveness, standardization, and timeliness.

Representativeness

A fundamental component of any scientific data set is that it represents some population of interest in a known way. The textbook scheme is to randomly sample from a known population, but other well-defined sampling schemes are also used to draw inferences about known populations. The NCVS uses a complex random sampling scheme. In Chapter 7, there is a detailed discussion of case-control schemes that can be especially useful for studying rare events like violence and crime.

Many of the data sets used to study firearms and violence are not random samples from well-defined populations of interest, nor are they exhaustive enumerations of any population. These types of data may provide some information, as described above, but using them to assess the effects of policy can be more complicated.

Accuracy

Accuracy of measurement is an essential criterion for a data source to be useful for understanding firearms and violence. Two key features of accuracy are the *validity* and *reliability* of measurement. In general terms, a measure is valid to the degree that it represents the underlying phenomenon of interest, and it is reliable to the degree that it yields the same data over repeated applications. Many of the debates over the relationship between firearms and violence center on questions of validity and reliability. For example, some analysts question the validity of the NCVS for measuring the prevalence of defensive firearms use because, as a survey of crime victims, the NCVS may not fully capture crimes that are averted by the use of firearms. Other researchers question the reliability of one-time sample surveys for measuring rare events, such as defensive use of guns. The chief function of data standardization is to ensure reliability of measurement. The more comprehensive a system, the more likely it will yield valid measurements of the connection between firearms and violence.

Response errors are a vital component of the validity of any data. The validity of data that measure firearms ownership, use, and violence on the basis of respondent self-reports depends on the ability and willingness of persons to disclose highly personal and sometimes incriminating or traumatic information to interviewers. As discussed above, there are reasons to expect response errors in regard to questions about ownership and use, as elicited in the GSS and other gun use surveys. Although there is much speculation on the extent and nature of response errors (see Chapter 5), there is almost no relevant research. Likewise, validity is compromised by nonresponse rates ranging from 20 percent (in the GSS) to over 50 percent in some of the phone surveys used to measure ownership. Without making unsubstantiated assumptions about gun ownership among nonrespondents, the GSS data cannot reveal whether ownership is increasing or decreasing over time.

Comprehensiveness

The criterion of comprehensiveness refers to both a data set's scope and richness of detail with respect to firearm-related violence.

Scope

Scope can be subdivided into the types of events that are captured and the populations covered. The scope of the NCVS, for example, is restricted to nonfatal incidents and to the characteristics of crime victims rather than offenders. Vital statistics and hospital-based information on firearm violence is also limited to the victims. The UCR, by contrast, captures information on both crime victims and offenders, but they are limited to offenses that are known to and recorded by law enforcement agencies. The NCVS includes data on both crimes reported to the police and those that victims do not report. Household-based surveys such as the NCVS and the GSS are limited to the population of persons with stable residences, thereby omitting transients and other persons at high risk for firearm violence. Such persons are included in the ADAM program, which collects information on persons who come into contact with the criminal justice system.

Geographic coverage is another dimension of scope. The GSS, for example, is representative of the United States and the nine census regions, but it is too sparse geographically to support conclusions at finer levels of geographical aggregation. This lack of individual-level data from small geographical areas is a significant shortcoming in the firearms data. Presumably, we would like to be able to make statements about, for example, the probability that an individual commits suicide conditional on owning a gun (or having one available) and other covariates. This cannot be done if the smallest geographical unit that the data resolve is a multistate region. Similar statements can be made about other forms of gun violence.

Perhaps no better illustration of the patchwork character of information on firearms violence in the United States exists than the multiple and nonoverlapping or partially overlapping coverage of the data sets. That should come as little surprise, inasmuch as many of the data sets were expressly intended to provide information about crime, violence, or injury that was not available from other sources. The major impetus for the development of the NCVS, for example, was to gather information on crime incidents that do not come to the attention of law enforcement agencies. The collection of information on violence from hospitals and emergency departments is intended to reveal types of violence, such as partner abuse, thought to be underreported in crime data sources.

The patchwork of existing data sources, in other words, has been created with the best of intentions and has shed light on aspects of violence, including the role of firearms, that otherwise would have remained hidden from view, such as the burden on hospital emergency departments of firearm injuries (Zawitz and Strom, 2000). However, insufficient attention has been devoted to linkages across data in population coverage and the types of firearm violence covered. Can data from the UCR, the NCVS, and emergency departments be effectively linked to draw inferences about the firearms violence in the population? As with data standardization, continuing assessments of remaining gaps in the scope of firearms data should be part of an ongoing program of methodological research on firearm violence.

Context

An often-highlighted limitation of existing data on firearms is the lack of detail regarding the context and circumstances of firearm violence. The Supplemental Homicide Report provides limited information on the relationship between victim and offender and event circumstances (e.g., whether the homicide is related to an argument or the commission of another felony). The National Incident-Based Reporting System extends such information to other crime types, but it covers less than 20 percent of the population more than 20 years after nationwide implementation began. Youth surveys, such as Monitoring the Future (MTF) and the Youth Risk Behavior Surveillance System, collect data on multiple attributes of respondents in addition to firearm behaviors, but little information on the situations in which youth carry and use firearms. The MTF survey also includes a longitudinal component that tracks respondents over time. These panel data might be especially useful for assessing firearms acquisition and use over time. However, citing agreements with respondents regarding confidentiality, the University of Michigan's Institute for Social Research has not made these data available to external researchers (see National Research Council, 2001). The most promising emerging data source with respect to information on the context and circumstances of firearm violence is the National Violent Death Reporting System, which will compile individual-level data from both criminal justice and public health sources on event circumstances, as well as detailed descriptions of the weapons used in violence. The NVDRS offers a model of a comprehensive data set that bridges existing data sources on individuals, events, and weapons.

Standardization

An essential quality of any measurement system is the collection of standard data elements from reporting units for purposes of reliable classification and comparison. Good examples of standardized data sets for measuring firearm violence are the FBI's UCR program, the National Crime Victimization Survey, and the mortality files available from the National

Vital Statistics System. Each of these data sets provides detailed formats and instructions for data collection, coding, and entry to ensure standard measurement of underlying data elements. For example, the UCR program regularly compiles information on eight serious "index offenses" (murder and nonnegligent manslaughter, rape, robbery, aggravated assault, burglary, larceny, vehicle theft, and arson) and requires local law enforcement agencies to use the same crime classification when compiling data on these offenses for reporting to the UCR. The National Vital Statistics System classifies deaths according to the International Classification of Diseases codes for cause of death.

Such standard classification and coding schemes, however, are necessary but not sufficient for ensuring valid and reliable measurement. Ultimately, all data must rely on the faithfulness of their reporting units in adhering to the standard protocols, which requires continuous monitoring of data collection and adequate training of data entry personnel. All of the federally sponsored data sets that collect information on firearm violence have procedures in place to maintain standard data collection, although they vary in the degree of compliance exhibited by reporting units. Generally speaking, systems with direct control over reporting units are able to maintain higher levels of standardization. The NCVS, administered by the Census Bureau in cooperation with the Bureau of Justice Statistics, is a good example of a data source with direct control over data collection. The UCR, in contrast, has no direct control over local data collection and must rely on data checks conducted by state UCR programs, as well as its own quality controls, to ensure adherence to standard coding and classification criteria. The National Vital Statistics System mortality series lie somewhere between the NCVS and the UCR with respect to direct control over local data collection.

We have limited our discussion thus far to standardization within data sets. However, because data on firearms violence comes from multiple sources and will continue to for the foreseeable future, we also must be concerned with standardization of data elements between data sources. Ongoing investigations of comparable data elements from different sources should constitute an essential part of a program of methodological research on firearm-related violence. Moreover, new and emerging data sets should be designed to ensure transparent linkages of data elements with existing data sources.

Two of the most important needs identified in public health and criminological research on violence and other injuries are for the standardization of data elements and the availability of detailed characteristics surrounding each event. Several efforts under way to address these concerns, if successful, may improve the usefulness and quality of data on firearm-related deaths and injuries: the National Incident-Based Reporting System, the

National Violent Death Reporting System, the Data Elements for Emergency Department Systems, and the International Classification of External Cause of Injury coding system. The NIBRS and the NVDRS have been discussed; the latter two systems are described below.

Data Elements for Emergency Department Systems: CDC's National Center for Injury Prevention and Control is coordinating an effort to develop uniform specifications for data entered into emergency department records. These specifications, known as DEEDS, are intended for use in 24-hour, hospital-based emergency departments throughout the United States. If the data definitions, coding conventions, and other recommended specifications were widely adopted, incompatibilities between emergency departments records would be substantially reduced. DEEDS does not specify an essential or minimum data set, but is designed to foster greater uniformity among individual data elements chosen for use. DEEDS also specifies standards for electronic data interchange so that data can be accessed for research purposes while maintaining confidentiality of patient records. DEEDS was first released in 1997 for testing and review. Systematic field studies, however, are still needed to assess the utility and practicality of the system.

International Classification of External Causes of Injury: An international effort, under the auspices of the World Health Organization, is currently under way to develop a new classification system for coding external causes of injury in mortality and morbidity systems. This system, known as the International Classification of External Causes of Injury (ICECI) is designed to capture details about the place of occurrence, activity at time of injury, alcohol and drug involvement, objects or substances involved, intent of injury, and mechanism of injury (e.g., firearms). Specific modules that focus on injuries related to violence, transportation, sports, and work are also under development. The first draft was released in 1998; the present version, ICECI 1.0, was released in 2001. A number of shortened versions have been tested for use as injury surveillance tools in places with limited resources for surveillance. CDC has tested its own short version as a means for capturing external cause of injury information from hospital emergency departments records in the United States with promising results. The European Union is also testing portions of ICECI as part of its efforts to create a minimum data set on injuries. ICECI is designed to replace the International Classification of Diseases coding system, which is thought to lack the scope and specificity needed to inform injury research. The present version of ICECI is undergoing formal review at the World Health Organization.[11]

---

[11]Details about ICECI 1.0, including the data dictionary, are available at http://www.iceci.org.

Timeliness

One remarkable feature of all existing data sources on firearms violence is their lack of timeliness. Other social indicators, particularly those measuring economic activity and performance, are available on a quarterly or monthly basis. By contrast, researchers, practitioners, and policy makers concerned with violent injury and death must contend with data that are infrequently collected and made available at least a year or more after they have been collected. The result is that nearly all studies of firearms violence are, in a real sense, historical in nature. Lack of timeliness in the availability of data is not a problem for investigating behavioral phenomena that change slowly over time, but the risk of firearms violence in the United States is not necessarily such a phenomenon. For example, rates of firearms violence, especially among youth, rose very rapidly to unprecedented levels during the early 1990s, only to peak and turn downward just as rapidly over the next few years. The popular characterization of those changes as an epidemic was not a misnomer, at least with respect to the speed with which they took place. Needless-to-say, monitoring such rapid and abrupt changes requires timely information.

Technical barriers no longer stand in the way of the timely collection, coding, and dissemination of key indicators of firearms violence. Local law enforcement agencies report data on a monthly basis to the FBI on serious assaults, robberies, and homicides by weapon type. Emergency departments and hospitals collect information on violent injuries and death just as frequently. Electronic data entry, coding, and checking have greatly reduced the time required to compile data on firearms violence, and the Internet permits nearly instantaneous dissemination both to special access users and broader audiences.

To better monitor trends in firearms and violence, the committee thinks that an important implementation objective of emerging data sets, such as the NIBRS and the NVDRS, should be dissemination of data on firearms violence on a quarterly basis. In addition, monitoring capabilities might be greatly improved if firearm-related behaviors could be added to any proposed revision of the ADAM survey, perhaps on a rotating schedule with the more detailed questions on drug use, and disseminated regularly.

CONCLUSION

None of the existing data sources, by itself or in combination with others, provides comprehensive, timely, and accurate data needed to answer many important questions pertaining to the role of firearms in violent events. Even some of the most basic descriptive questions cannot be answered with existing data. For example, the existing data do not reveal information pertinent to answering the following questions: [12]

1. Where do youth who shoot themselves or others obtain their guns?

2. In what proportion of intimate-partner homicides committed with a gun does the offender also take his or her own life or the lives of the victim's children or protectors?

3. Did the number of people shot with assault weapons change after the passage of the 1994 ban on assault weapons?

4. What are the most common circumstances leading to unintentional firearm-related deaths? Are particular types or makes and models of firearms overrepresented in unintentional firearm-related deaths?

5. What proportion of suicide or homicide victims were under the care of a mental health professional? What proportion were intoxicated with alcohol or illicit drugs at the time of death? How do these proportions compare with those for suicides committed by other means?

There are many other such "unanswerable questions" about firearm-related violence, and even more that can be answered only with great ambiguity. Data for estimating firearm-related mortality lack timeliness and contain only limited information on key circumstantial and weapon-related variables. For firearm-related morbidity data, key circumstantial and weapon-related information is also limited, and no nationally representative data sources monitor firearm-related hospitalizations and disabilities. Data on firearm storage practices, weapon carrying, and gun safety training are not routinely collected. Data for studying noncriminal violence are lacking.

Significant gaps exist in the nation's ability to monitor firearm-related injury and assess firearm-related policies. In the committee's view, the most important step to improve understanding of firearms and violence is to assemble better data. In the absence of improved data, the substantive questions addressed in this report are not likely to be resolved.

Emerging data have the potential to make important advances in understanding firearms and violence. In particular, the National Incident-Based Reporting System and the National Violent Death Reporting System can provide a wealth of information for characterizing violent events. Whether these data will also be effective for evaluating the effects of firearms, injury reduction policies, or other firearm-related policy ques-

---

[12]We thank Catherine Barber and David Hemenway of the Harvard School of Public Health for providing these examples by personal communication.

tions is unknown and will almost certainly depend on the particular application. No one system will be effective at answering all questions, but it is important to begin by collecting accurate and reliable data to describe the basic facts about violent injury and death. Thus, we are encouraged by the efforts of the Harvard School of Public Health's Injury Control Research Center pilot data collection program, as well as the recent seed money devoted to implement such a system at the CDC. **We reiterate recommendations made by past National Academies committees (e.g., Institute of Medicine, 1999) and others to support the development and maintenance of the National Violent Death Reporting System and the National Incident-Based Reporting System.** We also recognize that these types of data systems have been the subject of great controversy and, in light of well-founded concerns, strongly urge that special care be taken to ensure the credibility of these data.

The design and implementation plans for these and other proposed data sets need to explicitly consider whether and how some of the more complex and important policy questions regarding firearms and violence might be resolved. There are many obstacles for developing better data:

• Methodological issues regarding how different data sets and prior information might be used to credibly answer the complex causal questions of interest.
• Survey sampling issues, including how to design surveys to effectively obtain information on rare outcomes, geographical aggregation, sample nonrepresentativeness, uncertain accuracy of self- and informant reports, lack of standardization in data elements, and uncertain reliability of cause-of-injury and fatality codes.
• Legal and political barriers that may make collecting important data difficult if not impossible. For example, the 1986 Firearms Owners Protection Act (the McClure-Volkmer Act) forbids the federal government from establishing any "system of registration of firearms, firearm owners, or firearms transactions or distribution."

All of these issues should be carefully considered before new data collection efforts are proposed or undertaken. The proliferation of firearm data sources, without basic efforts to evaluate their validity and reliability, to determine the possibility for linkages across data sets, and most importantly to assess exactly which questions can be addressed with a particular data set, will not lead to better policy research and violence prevention.

Thus, the committee urges that work be started to think carefully about the prospects for developing data to answer specific policy questions of interest. The design for collecting data and the analysis of that data should be selected in light of the particular research question. For example, what data are needed to support research on a causal model of the relation between gun ownership or availability and suicide? Building such a model would presumably involve estimating the probability that an individual commits suicide conditional on gun ownership (or availability in some sense). What data are needed to do this? What data are needed to estimate the effects of policy interventions on the probability of suicide or on the substitution of other means of suicide for guns? What other prior information is relevant? What covariates should be included? Are data on them currently available? Do data on covariates exist in a form that could be combined with gun ownership or availability data? Is it necessary to construct a new data set that includes both ownership or availability data and the covariates?

If one is interested in answering the question of whether adolescents with a gun in the home are more likely to successfully commit suicide than adolescents who do not have a gun in their home, then home-level data on gun possession and adolescent suicide are needed rather than aggregate data concerning the numbers of guns in circulation. This type of information could be used to address the basic question of what proportion of the adolescents with a gun in their home eventually commit suicide with a gun. Answering causal questions about firearms and suicide may require additional information.

The same questions can be asked about the probability of committing a violent crime with a gun conditional on ownership or availability. Similarly, what data are needed to support improved research on firearms markets and how criminals or suicide victims obtain firearms? How, if at all, would improvements in trace data be used in studies of the effects of policy interventions on firearms markets or any other policy issue? What would the desired improvements contribute to research on policy interventions for reducing firearms violence? How can trace data be used, considering the deficiencies of these data?

Ultimately, linking the research and data questions will help define the data that are needed. For example, attempting to answer the seemingly basic research question, "How many times each year do civilians use firearms defensively?" by using samples of data collected from crimes reported to the police is a mismatch between the data source and the research question. These surveys cannot reveal successful forms of resistance that are not reported to the police.

This effort to think carefully about the data needed to answer some of the basic research questions should take place in collaboration with survey statisticians, social scientists, public health researchers, and representatives from the Bureau of Justice Statistics, the National Institute of Justice, the Centers for Disease Control and Prevention, the Bureau of Alcohol, Tobacco, and Firearms, and others. The research program should assess data limitations of the existing and proposed data sets, regularly report the results of that research both in the scientific literature and in forums accessible to data users, and propose modifications to the data sources when needed.

Careful attention should be paid to ownership, and use data. As we demonstrate repeatedly in this report, the lack of credible data on gun ownership and limited understanding of the relationship between ownership and violence are among the most critical data barriers to better understanding firearm-related violence. **Thus, the committee recommends a research effort to identify ways in which firearms acquisition, ownership, and use data can be accurately collected with minimal risk to legitimate privacy concerns.**

A starting point is to assess the potential of ongoing surveys. For example, efforts should be undertaken to assess whether tracing a larger fraction of guns used in crimes, longitudinal data from the Monitoring The Future survey, or enhancement of items pertaining to gun ownership in ongoing national surveys may provide useful research data.

To do this, researchers need access to the data. **Thus, the committee recommends that appropriate access for research purposes be given to the Monitoring The Future survey, as well as to the data maintained by regulatory and law enforcement agencies, including the trace data maintained by BATF, registration data maintained by the FBI and state agencies, and manufacturing and sales data.**[13] These data may or may not be useful for understanding firearms markets and the role of firearms in crime and violence. However, without access to these systems, researchers are unable to assess their potential for providing insight into some of the most important firearms policy and other research questions. We realize that many have deeply held concerns about expanding the government's knowledge of who owns what type of guns and how they are used. We also recognize the argument that some may refuse to supply such information, especially those who are most at risk to use guns illegally. More generally, we recognize that data on firearms ownership and violence have been the subject of great controversy. Nevertheless, there is a long established tradition of making sensitive data available to researchers. **In light of these well-founded concerns, the committee strongly recommends that special care be taken to ensure the integrity of the data collection and dissemination process.** Concerns over security and privacy must be addressed in the granting of greater access to the existing data and in creating new data on acquisition, ownership, and use.

---

[13]Current law prohibits the FBI from retaining data from background checks. If these data were retained and provided in an individually identifiable form for research purposes, they might provide useful information on firearms markets and measures of known gun owners nationally. To determine the properties of these data, the FBI would need to retain the records and researchers would need access to test their utility for informing policy.

3

Patterns of Firearm-Related Violence

In any given year, firearms accounted for over half of all known suicides, two-thirds of all reported homicides,[1] and less than 1 percent of known accidental fatalities. But firearms do not always cause injury and death. In fact, the vast majority of firearms uses do not result in personal injury and are highly valued by many citizens. Any effort to assess the overall costs and benefits of firearms needs to address the prevalence of the different circumstances in which firearms are used and not just focus on those uses that result in death or injury.

This chapter begins by placing firearm deaths in the United States in the context of how they compare with other countries and how firearm-related deaths in the United States compare to other causes of death. We then turn to data on the availability and ownership of firearms in the United States. Subsequent sections present some basic facts about firearms involvement in violent crime, self-harm and suicide, and unintentional injury in the United States.[2] Because homicides and suicides are not randomly distributed in the population, we describe the variations in these behaviors by gender and race. These variations further demonstrate the need for refined studies and explanations of the role of firearms in violence.

---

[1]We use the term *homicide* for the phrase *criminal homicide*. Criminal homicide is defined as the willful killing of one human being by another and the killing of another person through gross negligence (excluding traffic fatalities).

[2]In Chapter 2 we discussed the strength and weaknesses of some of the data systems we use to describe the patterns of firearm violence. For now we attempt to carefully use the data and to not overinterpret them, without reconsidering the strengths and weaknesses of the data.

HOMICIDE RATES BY COUNTRY

Using international crime data the committee has attempted to compare per capita homicide rates and rates of firearm homicides in the United States with those in other countries. While we recognize that the measurement of these events is not entirely consistent, these data do provide rough but useful comparisons.

International Comparisons

Table 3-1 displays the data on homicides, firearm-related homicides, and firearm availability for 36 countries. Krug et al. (1998) collected these data by surveying ministries of health or national statistical centers in each of these countries. Review of these data indicate that while the United States does not have the highest rate of homicide or firearm-related homicide, it does have the highest rates for these among industrialized democracies. Homicide rates in the United States are two to four times higher than they are in countries that are economically and politically similar to it. Higher rates are found in developing countries and those with political instability. The same is true for firearm-related homicides, but the differences are even greater. The firearm-related homicide rate in the United States is more like that of Argentina, Mexico, and Northern Ireland than England or Canada. While certainly not the highest homicide or firearm-related homicide rate in the world, these rates in the United States are in the upper quartile in each case.

Some researchers have used data like those summarized above to assess the relationship between firearm-related homicides and firearms availability. For the most part this research focuses on industrialized nations and uses various proxies for the measure of firearms availability. While the vast majority of these studies conclude that homicides and availability are closely associated (Lester, 1990; Killias, 1993a, 1993b; Hemenway and Miller, 2000), the methodological problems in this research (measurement of key variables is of questionable validity, the use of nation-states as the unit of analysis may mask subnational variability, and models tested are poorly specified) do not encourage us to place much weight on this research. However, as noted earlier, the level of nongun homicide is much higher in the United States than it is in other countries. A high level of violence may be a cause of a high level of firearms availability instead of the other way around. Further work with better measures and more complete samples might be useful; for now this literature can be considered suggestive but not conclusive.

TABLE 3-1 International Firearms Homicide and Suicide Rates

Country	Year	Total Homicides (per 100,000)	Firearm Homicides (per 100,000)	Total Suicides (per 100,000)	Firearm Suicides (per 100,000)	Percentage Households with Firearms
Estonia	1994	28.21	8.07	40.95	3.13	9 (UN)
Brazil	1993	19.04	10.58	3.46	.73	4.35 (UN)
Mexico	1994	17.58	9.88	2.89	.91	N/A
United States	1993	9.93	7.07	12.06	6.3	39
Northern Ireland	1994	6.09	5.24	8.41	1.34	8.4 (1989)
Argentina	1994	4.51	2.11	6.71	2.89	3
Hungary	1994	3.53	.23	35.38	.88	N/A
Finland	1994	3.24	.86	27.26	5.78	25.2 (1992)
Portugal	1994	2.98	1.28	14.83	1.28	N/A
Mauritius	1993	2.35	.00	12.98	.09	N/A
Israel	1993	2.32	.72	7.05	1.84	N/A
Italy	1992	2.25	1.66	12.65	1.11	16
Scotland	1994	2.24	.19	12.16	.33	4.7 (1989)
Canada	1992	2.16	.76	13.19	3.72	24.2 (1992)
Slovenia	1994	2.01	.35	31.16	2.51	N/A
Australia	1994	1.79	.44	12.65	2.35	15.1 (1992)
Taiwan	1994	1.78	.15	6.88	.12	N/A
South Korea	1994	1.62	.04	9.48	.02	N/A
New Zealand	1993	1.47	.17	12.81	2.14	22.3 (1992)
Belgium	1990	1.41	.60	19.04	2.56	16.5 (1992)
Switzerland	1994	1.32	.58	21.28	5.61	27.2 (1989)
Sweden	1993	1.30	.18	15.75	2.09	15.1 (1992)
Hong Kong	1993	1.23	.12	10.29	.07	N/A
Denmark	1993	1.21	.23	22.33	2.25	N/A
Austria	1994	1.17	.42	12.12	4.06	18-20 (1996)
Germany	1994	1.17	.22	15.64	1.17	8.9 (1989)
Singapore	1994	1.17	.07	14.06	.17	N/A
Greece	1994	1.14	.59	3.4	.84	.03 (UN)
France	1994	1.12	v.44	20.79	5.14	22.6 (1989)
Netherlands	1994	1.11	.36	10.03	.31	1.9 (1992)
Kuwait	1995	1.01	.36	1.66	.06	N/A
Norway	1993	.97	.30	13.64	3.95	32. (1989)
Spain	1993	.95	.21	7.77	.43	13.1 (1989)
Ireland	1991	.62	.03	9.81	.94	N/A
Japan	1994	.62	.02	16.72	.04	.57 (UN)
England and Wales	1992	.55	.07	7.68	.33	4.4

SOURCES: Krug et al. (1998); United Nations (2000).

U.S. Rates

Across the population as a whole, neither homicide nor suicide is one of the 10 leading causes of death in the United States. However, for 15- to 24-year-olds, homicide is the second leading cause of death, and suicide is the third. The rankings are reversed for 25- to 34-year-olds. Considering these data by race, homicide is the leading cause of death for blacks ages 15 to 24 and 25 to 34. And it is the sixth leading cause of death for blacks at all ages.

FIREARM AVAILABILITY AND OWNERSHIP

To understand the relationship between gun violence and gun availability, it is important to have accurate information about gun ownership. How many firearms are there in the United States? How many households own firearms? How many handguns are there in the United States?

Because most states do not require registration or licensing of firearms and therefore have incomplete record-keeping, inaccessible data, and unobserved levels of illegal firearm ownership (Azrael et al., 2004), most firearm research must make use of alternative measures. The two principal methods for directly measuring the U.S. civilian stock of guns are (1) production-based estimates calculated from domestic manufacturing, export, and import data and (2) nationally representative surveys that ask respondents about gun ownership (Kleck, 1997).

Scholars have also used a varied list of indirect measures or proxies to measure firearms availability and ownership patterns, including the percentage of suicides or homicides committed with a firearm, the fatal firearm accident rate, gun magazine subscription rates, the National Rifle Association membership rate, the hunting license rate, and the number of federal firearm licenses (Miller et al., 2002; Azrael et al., 2004; Duggan, 2001; Corzine et al., 2000; Kleck, 1997). While all of these measures shed light on the relationship between gun ownership and violence, they also all suffer from measurement errors that are difficult to estimate.[3] In Chapter 2, the committee recommends a program of research to improve the ability to measure gun ownership. For this section we use production and sales data to give the reader a rough idea of gun ownership in the United States.

Production-Based Estimates

Firearm production statistics are derived from reports of firearms manufacture, import, and export made to the Bureau of Alcohol, Tobacco, and Firearms. Estimates of firearm availability are derived by adding the net growth in the number of firearms (manufactures plus imports minus ex-

---

[3]For a thorough discussion of the limitations of these measures, see Chapter 7.

TABLE 3-2 Estimated Number and Per Capita Ownership (rate per 1,000) of Firearms in the United States, 1950 to 1999

Year	Total Firearms	Handguns	Firearms per 1,000 Persons	Handguns per 1,000 Persons
1950	57,902,081	14,083,195	381.3	93.5
1960	77,501,065	18,951,219	430.6	105.4
1970	111,917,733	31,244,813	548.7	153.2
1980	167,681,587	51,707,269	737.9	227.5
1990	212,823,547	72,499,181	853.3	290.7
1999	258,322,465	93,742,357	925.8	336.0

SOURCES: Data for 1950 to 1990 are from Kleck (1997: Table 3.1). The 1999 estimate was derived by adding the annual net increase in the stock of total firearms and handguns (manufactures + imports − exports) to the 1990 estimate using data from U.S. Bureau of Alcohol, Tobacco, and Firearms (2002: Exhibits 1, 2, and 3).

ports) to a base measure of the firearms stock.[4] Table 3-2 presents production-based estimates of the size of the civilian firearms stock based on a cumulated total since 1999. As the table shows, in 1999 there were more than 258 million firearms in the United States, 36 percent of them handguns. For every 1,000 people in the United States in 1999 there were nearly 926 firearms, 336 of which were handguns.

From 1950 to 1999, the per capita rate of overall firearms availability increased 143 percent, while handguns alone increased 259 percent. These data suggest that in recent years the rate of increase has slowed: the annual number of new handguns introduced to market has declined since 1994, while annual introduction of other firearms has remained relatively stable.

Survey-Based Estimates

Although production-based estimates indicate a 25 percent increase in firearms availability since 1980, survey-based estimates indicate an 11 to 33 percent decrease in households reporting ownership. Three often-used surveys are the General Social Survey (GSS), the Gallup Poll, and the Harris Poll.[5] According to these surveys, the percentage of respondents reporting

---

[4]Production-based data have limitations in that they account for neither additions to the stock from illegal or other uncounted means nor losses from seized, lost, or nonworking firearms. These data also exclude firearms manufactured or exported for the military but include firearms purchased by domestic law enforcement agencies.

[5]Each survey asks a similar question about gun ownership. Gallup asks "Do you have a gun in your home?" Harris asks "Do you happen to have in your home or garage any guns or revolvers?" and the GSS asks "Do you happen to have in your home (or garage) any guns or revolvers?"

that they have a firearm in the home has been declining since the late 1950s. While the estimates vary from year to year, all three surveys indicate a decline in the percentage of households possessing firearms. From 1980, when the percentage of households owning a firearm was between 45 and 48 percent, ownership has decreased by 5 to 16 percentage points to a prevalence of 30 to 43 percent. In discussion with the committee, Cook has suggested that the decline in ownership per household while individual ownership remains constant may be due to the increase in female-headed households during this period. Despite these overall reductions in household ownership, the relative distribution of firearm ownership across attributes of gender, race, age, education, income, and region has been remarkably consistent over time (Maguire and Pastore, 2002: Table 2.70).

Of households owning a firearm, between 59 and 62 percent reported owning a handgun (Maguire and Pastore, 2002: Tables 2.69, 2.71, and 2.72). All three surveys indicate that gun owners are more likely to be male, white, and middle-aged or older. Furthermore, gun ownership was higher among those who live in the South, had less education than a college degree, and had a higher than average income. Among respondents reporting household gun ownership, the percentage of blacks reporting handgun ownership was 6 to 9 percent higher than for whites, and the percentage of blacks reporting long gun ownership was 11 to 29 percent lower than for whites (Maguire and Pastore, 2002: Tables 2.71 and 2.72).

Aggregation of Individual Survey Responses

Recent research has aggregated the individual survey responses about firearms ownership across U.S. communities (Baumer et al., 2002; Rosenfeld et al., 2001). The GSS is based on a national area probability sample composed of 100 primary sampling units (PSUs) (in the 1990 sampling frame) designed to represent the population of people age 18 and older in the United States. Each PSU is a "self-representing" geographic unit, in the sense that the respondents are representative of the PSU adult population.

Aggregating the individual survey responses to the PSU level permits comparisons of the aggregated items, including firearms ownership, across a representative sample of U.S. geographic areas. Figure 3-1 shows the geographic distribution of household firearm ownership for the 100 PSUs in the 1990 GSS sampling frame, covering the period 1993 to 1998.

The figure shows substantial variability in firearm ownership in the United States. The prevalence of household ownership varies from roughly 10 to 80 percent. Most of the PSUs cluster around the mean ownership level of 43 percent, with fewer PSUs located near the extremes of the distribution.

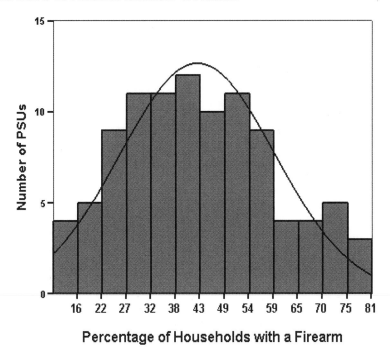

FIGURE 3-1 Distribution of firearms ownership across geographic regions, 1993-1998 (N = 100).
SOURCES: Baumer et al. (2002); Rosenfeld et al. (2001).

FIREARM-RELATED HARM

The majority of firearm-related deaths are the result of murder and suicide, while the majority of nonfatal firearm-related injuries are the result of assaults and accidents. Firearm-related deaths constitute the majority of all homicides and suicides, but firearm-related injuries represent only a minority of nonfatal injuries.[6]

Table 3-3 shows overall and firearm-related deaths by intent based on National Vital Statistics System (NVSS) data. In 1999, there were 28,874 firearm-related reported deaths in the United States. Suicide and homicide accounted for the majority of these fatalities, representing 57 and 37 percent of total firearm-related deaths, respectively. Furthermore, firearm-

---

[6]In this section we use data from the National Vital Statistics System, the National Crime Victimization Survey, the Uniform Crime Reports, and the National Electronic Injury Surveillance System.

TABLE 3-3 Overall Firearm-Related Deaths, 1999

Category	Firearm-Related		Total		% Firearm-Related
	Number	Rate ^{a}	Number	Rate ^{a}	Percent
Suicide	16,599	6.09	29,199	10.71	56.85
Homicide	10,828	3.97	16,899	6.19	64.07
Accident	824	0.30	97,860	35.89	0.84
Legal intervention	299	0.11	398	0.15	75.13
Total	28,874	10.59	148,286	54.30	19.47

^{a}Rate per 100,000 population
SOURCE: National Vital Statistics System data compiled using Web-based Injury Statistics Query and Reporting System (WISQARS). National Center for Health Statistics (2002).

TABLE 3-4 Number and Rate (per 100,000) of Overall and Firearm-Related Nonfatal Injuries by Intent, 2000

	Firearm-Related		Total	
	Number	Rate	Number	Rate
Assault	48,570	17.64	1,672,117	607.37
Legal intervention	862	0.31	63,304	22.99
Suicide attempt	3016	1.10	264,108	95.93
Accident	23,237	8.44	27,550,181	10,007.10
Total	75,685	27.49	29,549,710	10,733.39

SOURCE: NEISS data compiled using WISQARS (National Center for Health Statistics, 2002).

related deaths accounted for the majority of the total number of deaths in each category except accidents. In that case, firearm-related deaths accounted for a tiny fraction of all deaths by accidental means.

Table 3-4 shows overall and firearm-related nonfatal injuries by intent based on National Electronic Injury Surveillance System (NEISS) data. In 2000, there were 75,685 nonfatal firearm-related injuries in the United States. Injuries from violent assault and accidents accounted for the majority of all firearm injuries—64 and 31 percent, respectively. In contrast to completed suicides, firearms account for a small proportion of self-inflicted nonfatal injuries.

How much violent crime involves the use of a firearm?[7] This question can be answered with varying degrees of certainty, depending on the crime and the data source consulted. In general, data on homicide are the

---

[7]By definition, firearm involvement in violent crime includes not only the discharge of a firearm but also the presence of a firearm during the commission of a violent crime.

most reliably reported and provide greater detail about the circumstances of the offense. Of crimes known to police in 2000, the most recent year for which Uniform Crime Reports (UCR) data are available, firearms were involved in 66 percent of the 15,517 murders, 41 percent of the 406,842 robberies, and 18 percent of the 910,744 aggravated assaults. Data from the National Crime Victimization Survey (NCVS) for 2000 indicate about 3 percent of the 260,950 rapes or sexual assaults involved the use of a firearm, although this estimate is based on 10 or fewer sample cases (Rennison, 2001).

Firearms and Homicide

Weaponry in Homicide

According to the UCR, 10,179 murders were committed with firearms in the United States in 2000, corresponding to a rate of 3.6 per 100,000.[8] This count is down from a historic high in 1993 of 17,046 firearm-related murders (6.6 per 100,000). Handguns were used to commit 52 percent of all homicides, and firearms of any kind were used to commit 66 percent of all homicides in that year; 14 percent were committed with knives or other cutting implements, and 7 percent were achieved with hands, feet, or other "personal weapons."

Trends in weapon-specific homicide rates from 1976 to 2000 are shown in Figure 3-2. Handgun homicides rose until 1993 and then fell, tracking closely the overall homicide rate, while the rates for other firearms, knives, and other weapons fell steadily and closely track each other. Thus, handgun homicides accounted for virtually all of the increase in the overall homicide rate between 1985 and 1993, the year the handgun homicide rate reached its 25-year peak of 5.4 per 100,000 (an estimated 14,005 handgun homicides).

The likely use of firearms varies dramatically from one type of homicide to another. For example, in the year 2000, about 17 percent of homicides were known to have occurred during the commission of other crimes; among these, 73 percent of robbery-related homicides were committed with a firearm, but only 9 percent of rape-related homicides were committed with a firearm.

---

[8]These UCR statistics differ slightly from those presented in Table 3-3. Since the UCR collects data from police sources and the NVSS from medical examiner records, the disparity between the two systems arises because of data collection differences. Despite these differences, the systems are highly concordant in their estimates of firearm-related murder. Here we present UCR-Supplemental Homicide Report data because they provide information about offenders, weaponry, and circumstances surrounding the offense—information not found in the NVSS.

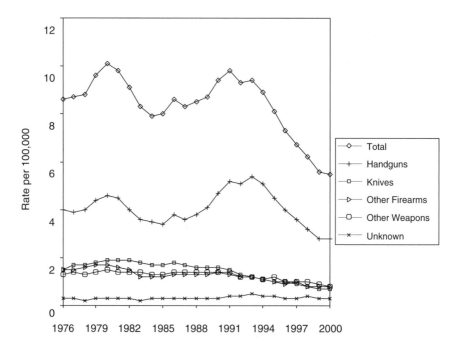

FIGURE 3-2 Murder rates by weapon type.
SOURCES: Fox (2001); U.S. Department of Justice (2001); U.S. Census Bureau (2001a, 2001b, 2002).

Victims

Males are more likely to be victims of homicide than females, and they are even more likely to be killed by firearms. In 1999, male victims accounted for 83 percent of firearm-related homicides and 64 percent of other homicides.[9] The male firearm-related homicide victimization rate was 6.71 deaths per 100,000, compared with a female rate of 1.35 (Bureau of Justice Statistics, 2002a, 2002b). From 1981 to 1999, trends in firearm-related homicides of males seem to explain much of the trends in the total homicide rate.

Young adults and adolescents are disproportionately victimized by firearm-related homicide. The rise and decline of the firearm-related homicide rate beginning in the mid-1980s was largely confined to the young adult and adolescent males (Wintemute, 2000). From 1981 to 1999, 20- to 24-year-olds were most likely to be victims of homicide, especially by firearms, but victimization rates among 15- to 19-year-olds rose and fell more dra-

---

[9]SHR data for 1999 are nearly identical for male involvement in firearm- and nonfirearm-related murder at 83 and 62 percent, respectively (calculated from Fox, 2001).

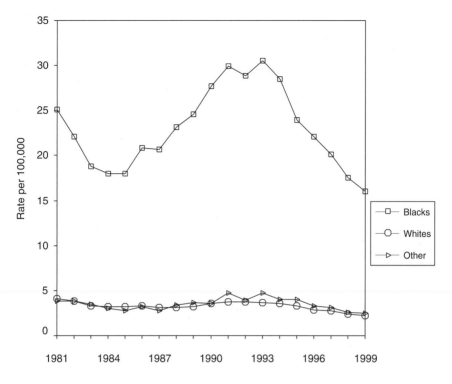

FIGURE 3-3 Firearm-related murder victimization rates by race, 1981-1999.
SOURCE: National Vital Statistics System data compiled using Web-based Injury Statistics Query and Reporting System (WISQARS). National Center for Health Statistics (2002).

matically than other age groups between 1985 and 1999. Adolescent victimization rates surpassed the rates for those 25 and older by 1990 and did not fall back below the rate for persons in their late 20s until 1998.

Blacks have been at high risk of victimization by firearm-related homicide. Figure 3-3 indicates that in 1999, for example, non-Hispanic blacks accounted for 51 percent of the firearm-related homicide victims, while representing only 13 percent of the total population (Bureau of Justice Statistics, 2002a). The firearm-related homicide victimization rate was 16.64 per 100,000 for non-Hispanic blacks, 6.19 for Hispanics, 1.53 for non-Hispanic whites, and 2.60 for other races. Blacks were also disproportionately affected by the rise and fall of firearm homicides in the 1980s and 1990s.[10]

---

[10]Race is presented in the figure regardless of Hispanic ethnicity, since Hispanic ethnicity is not available in the Web-based Injury Statistics Query and Reporting System (WISQARS) prior to 1990.

Offenders

Young males are an even larger percentage of firearm-related homicide offenders than homicide victims. For example, cumulative data from the FBI's Supplementary Homicide Reports (SHR) for the years 1976 to 1999 reveal that males committed 90 percent of all firearm-related homicides (Bureau of Justice Statistics, 2002a). In 1999, 56 percent of the 10,969 offenders who used firearms to commit murder were between 14 and 24 years old. The rate of handgun murders by persons under age 18 nearly quadrupled from 1985 to 1993, and rates for 18- to 24-year-olds more than doubled, while homicides by persons over 24 declined steadily from 1985 on. The highest concentrations of recent involvement in handgun homicides have been among young blacks; the homicide offense rate among blacks ages 18 to 24 tripled between 1984 and 1993, while the combined offense rates for young whites and Hispanics did not begin to increase until 1987 and even then accounted for a relatively small proportion of the subsequent rise and fall in the handgun homicide rate (Blumstein, 2000).

Historically, firearm homicide rates have been higher than the national average in the southern states, about average in the mid-Atlantic and north central regions, and below average in the New England, mountain, and west north central states (Bureau of Justice Statistics, 2002a). Larger cities (more than 100,000) have had higher homicide and firearm homicide rates than smaller cities, towns, or rural areas.

Firearms and Nonfatal Injuries

Aggravated Assault

Assaults are the most common type of nonfatal firearm injury in the United States, but firearms are not the most common method of nonfatal assault. Figure 3-4 shows trends in the rates of aggravated assault by firearm involvement. According to the UCR, the aggravated assault rate more than quadrupled from 1964 to 1992 and has been declining just as steeply since then.[11] Nonfirearm-related assaults accounted for 72 percent of the overall rise from 1964 to 1992 and 57 percent of the overall decline from 1992 to 2000; firearms were involved in only 18 percent of assaults in 2000; and assaults using blunt objects constituted the largest share of offenses.

---

[11]Recent trends in aggravated assault rates have dropped much more dramatically between 1993 and 2000 according to the NCVS than the UCR—53 versus 27 percent, respectively (Maguire and Pastore, 2002: Table 3.120; Rennison, 2001: Table 8).

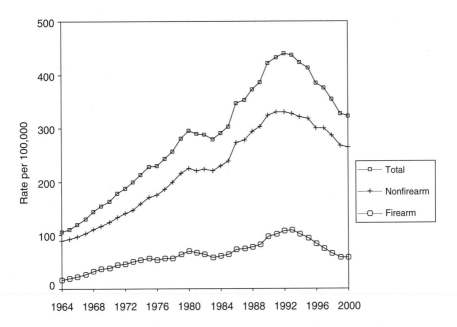

FIGURE 3-4 Rates of aggravated assault by firearm involvement.
SOURCES: Calculated from Zawitz (2001); Maguire and Pastore (2002).

Robberies

In 2000, the NCVS and the UCR provided similar estimates for 157,623 firearm-related robberies in the United States—157,623 (NCVS) and 166,807 (UCR)—remarkably consistent estimates given the methodological and coverage differences between the two data sources. For all weapon categories besides firearms the NCVS reports higher estimates than the UCR. The close correspondence on firearms therefore suggests that most firearm-related robberies are reported to the police. The NCVS data indicate that 90 percent of firearm-related robberies in 2000 were committed with a handgun.

Figure 3-5 presents rates of robbery stratified by firearm involvement for the years 1974 to 2000. The robbery rate rose and fell several times before reaching its peak of 271.9 per 100,000 in 1991; the rate then decreased by nearly half to 144.6 per 100,000 in 2000. Firearms robberies accounted for 24 percent of the rise from 1974 to 1991 and 39 percent of the decline from 1991 to 2000. Like the trends for aggravated assault and in contrast to the trends for murder, the robbery rate was not much influenced by the rates of offenses committed with firearms.

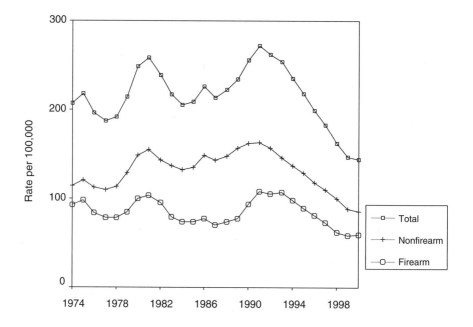

FIGURE 3-5 Rates of robbery by firearm involvement.
SOURCES: Calculated from Zawitz (2001); Maguire and Pastore (2002: Table 3.120); U.S. Census Bureau (2001a, 2001b, 2002).

Rape and Sexual Assaults

According to the NCVS, 84 percent of the rapes and sexual assaults reported in 2000 were committed without a weapon. There were an estimated 6,550 firearm-related rapes or sexual assaults in 2000; these constituted less than 3 percent of NCVS-reported rapes.

Firearms and Self-Harm

Historically, the number of successful suicides in the United States has far exceeded the number of homicides. In 1999, the number of suicides was nearly double the number of murders. In contrast, nonfatal injuries resulting from suicide attempts are much less common than injuries caused by violent assaults, regardless of weapons used. In this section, we describe the patterns and trends for death and nonlethal injuries resulting from self-inflicted, firearm-related harm.

Suicide

In 1999, there were 29,199 suicides in the United States—57 percent of them involving the use of a firearm. Males of all ages are at higher risk of suicide; in 1999, males committed 14,479 (87 percent) of firearm-related suicides. Whites are at higher risk of suicide than blacks, but the suicide rate for young black males has been rising and by 1999 was nearly the same as the suicide rate for young white males. Figure 3-6 shows the number and rate of firearm-related suicides per 100,000 by five-year age groupings for 1999. As the figure shows, more firearm-related suicides were committed by those 35 to 39 years old than any other five-year age grouping, although those 80 to 84 years old committed suicide at the highest rate, 13.7 per 100,000.

The total suicide rate has remained relatively constant in the United States, but the proportion of suicides committed with a firearm increased steadily from the 1960s to the early 1990s before beginning a moderate decline. The age distribution of suicides over this period also changed, with a rise in suicide among the young and the old and a small decline among working-age adults. Figure 3-7 shows trends in the suicide rate

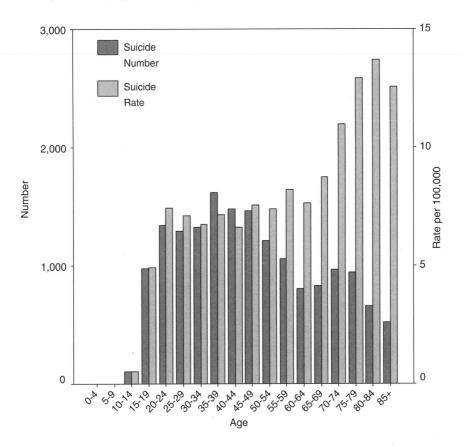

FIGURE 3-6 Number and rate of firearm-related suicides, 1999.

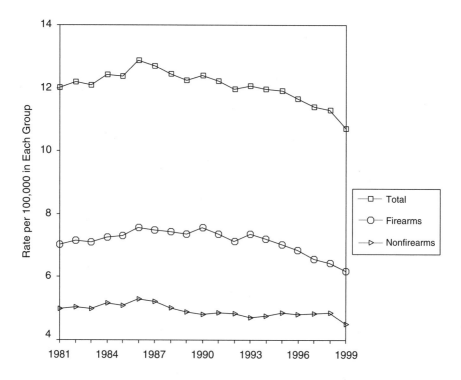

FIGURE 3-7 Suicide rates by firearm involvement.

stratified by firearm involvement from 1981 to 1999. Between 1986 and 1990, the firearm suicide rate plateaued at a rate of about 7.56 per 100,000; since then, firearm suicides have fallen by 18 percent to 6.19 per 100,000 in 1999.

Trends by race are presented in Figure 3-8. As the figure shows, whites have dominated the overall trend in firearm suicides. The firearm-related suicide rate for whites increased 9 percent from 1981 to a two-decade peak in 1990 before declining 19 percent over the past decade. For blacks, a similar pattern occurred, although the peak rate was in 1994. The rate for other races combined was relatively stable until 1994, then declined somewhat.

Trends by age are presented in Figure 3-9. Persons age 75 and older had the highest rates of firearm-related suicide during the previous two decades. The period from 1981 to 1990 saw the greatest change among this age group, increasing 48 percent to 16.37 per 100,000. Then, from 1990 to 1999, the firearm-related suicide rate for this age group decreased 21 percent to 13.05 per 100,000. Trends for

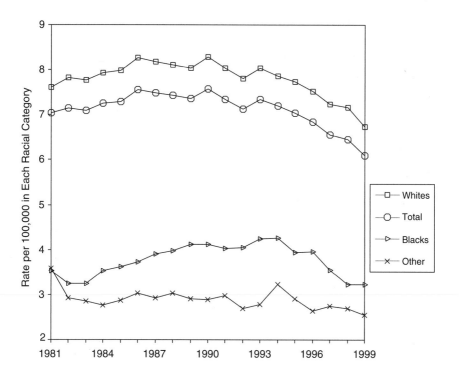

FIGURE 3-8 Suicide rates by race, 1981-1999.

persons ages 15 to 24 showed similar patterns, increasing until 1994, then declining to the present. By contrast, firearm-related suicide rates for those ages 25 to 74 have been declining steadily since the early 1980s. The rates for children ages 0 to 14 have remained relatively stable, increasing slightly from 1981 to 1990, then declining to the 1981 rate by 1999.

Nonfatal Self-Harm

In 2000, there were only 3,016 nonfatal firearm-related injuries recorded by the NEISS—about 4 percent of all reported self-injuries. Because NEISS only records self-injury events that are screened in an emergency department, and because firearm injuries may be more likely to be treated in an emergency department than other kinds of self-injuries, the actual fraction of nonlethal self-injuries that occur by firearm is likely to be even lower. Furthermore, rates of nonfatal firearm-related injuries have been declining since 1993 (Gotsch et al., 2001).

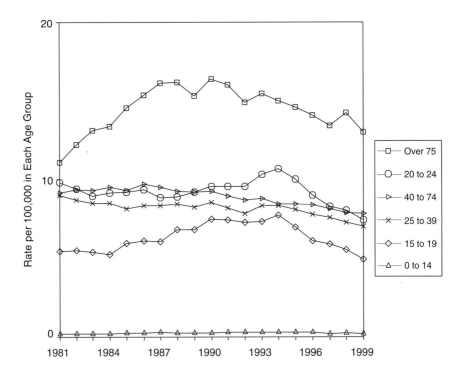

FIGURE 3-9 Firearm-related suicides by selected age groupings, 1981-1999.

Firearms and Accidents

Firearm-related accidental deaths represent a small fraction of all firearm-related deaths, but unintentional injuries represent a sizable proportion of all nonfatal injuries resulting from firearms—behind only the number caused by violent assaults.

In 1999 there were 824 firearm-related accidental deaths—less than 1 percent of the 97,860 total accidental deaths for that year—corresponding to an accidental firearm-related death rate of 0.30 per 100,000.

Rates of firearm-related accidental deaths have been declining since the mid-1960s (Ikeda et al., 1997; Frattaroli et al., 2002). Since 1981, the firearm-related accidental death rate has declined 63 percent from 0.83 to 0.30 per 100,000. The male rate of firearm-related accidental deaths is much higher than the female rate. In 1999, males accounted for 88 percent of accidental firearm-related deaths; however, both males and females have contributed roughly proportionally to the declining trend. In 1999, the fatal accident rate for blacks (0.47 per 100,000) was somewhat higher than the rate for whites (0.30 per 100,000). There are also substantial differences in trends in the rate firearm-related accidental deaths by age group. Although firearm-related accidental death rates have been on a downward trend for other age groups since the mid-1960s, rates for 15- to 24-year-olds rose from 1987 to 1993 and then declined.

4

Interventions Aimed at Illegal Firearm Acquisition

irearms are bought and sold in markets, both formal and informal. To some observers this suggests that one method for reducing the burden of firearm injury is to intervene in these markets so as to make it more expensive, inconvenient, or legally risky to obtain firearms for criminal use. As guns become more expensive to acquire or hold, it is hypothesized that criminals will reduce the percentage of their criminal careers in which they are in possession of a gun. However, the pervasiveness of guns and the variety of legal and illegal means of acquiring them suggests the difficulty of keeping firearms from people barred by law from possessing them. The goals of this chapter are to provide a systematic analytic framework linking interventions to the outcomes of interest and to describe what is known about the effectiveness of those interventions. We also suggest a research agenda that addresses the major unanswered questions.

Market-based interventions intended to reduce criminal access to guns include taxes on weapons and ammunition, tougher regulation of federal firearm licensees, limits on the number of firearms that can be purchased in a given time period, gun bans, gun buy-backs, and enforcement of laws against illegal gun buyers or sellers. Other interventions that may have market effects—for example, storage requirements (such as trigger locks or the placement of firearms in secure containers) and mandating new technologies that personalize guns so only lawful owners can fire them—are dealt with in detail elsewhere in the report. While these new technologies may make new guns less attractive relative to older secondhand guns and thus reduce the attractiveness of guns in aggregate to offenders, the potential market effects are probably secondary to other mechanisms by which these interventions may lower firearms injuries, such as preventing children from accidentally hurting themselves or others (see Chapter 8).

Little is known about the potential effectiveness of a market-based approach to reducing criminal access to firearms. Arguments for and against such an approach are based largely on speculation rather than research evidence. There is very little of an analytic or evaluative nature currently available in the literature on market interventions. Even on most descriptive topics (e.g., gun ownership patterns, types of guns used in crimes), there are only a few studies, often not well connected, that have been adequately summarized in existing papers (e.g., Braga et al., 2002; Hahn et al., 2005).

We begin with a brief discussion of legal and illegal firearms commerce, followed by a summary of what is known about the methods by which offenders acquire guns. We then present an analytic framework to understand the effects of specific interventions on gun markets. The next section reviews the literature evaluating various interventions. The final section presents the committee's views about high-priority research activities. The relationship of firearms acquisition and markets to suicide is quite different and is discussed in the chapter on suicide.

We note that the interventions discussed here may impose costs on legitimate users of firearms. A waiting period law inconveniences hunters and others who use firearms in legitimate fashion. In addition to delays, the system may generate errors, causing unnecessary embarrassment or worse. Some interventions putatively have no such effects and may even facilitate the activities of legitimate owners; for example, gun buy-backs can only help by providing another outlet for individuals wishing to dispose of existing weapons with minimal inconvenience. No research has explored these effects, although they may be important in forming attitudes toward gun control proposals.

HOW OFFENDERS OBTAIN FIREARMS

Legal and Illegal Firearms Commerce

In the United States, there are some 258 million privately owned firearms, including nearly 70 to 90 million handguns (Police Foundation, 1996; see also Table 3-2). Some 4.5 million new firearms, including about 2 million handguns (Bureau of Alcohol, Tobacco, and Firearms, 2000b) and about 2 million secondhand guns, are sold each year in the United States (Police Foundation, 1996). Legal firearms commerce consists of transactions made in the *primary* firearms market and in the largely unregulated *secondary* firearms market. Acquisitions (other than theft) of new and secondhand firearms from federal firearms licensees (FFLs), whether conducted properly or not, form the primary market for firearms (Cook et al.,

1995). Retail gun stores sell both new and secondhand firearms and, in this regard, resemble automobile sales lots. FFLs are required to ask for identification from all prospective gun buyers and to have them sign a form indicating that they are not prohibited from acquiring a firearm; the FFL must also initiate a criminal history background check of all would-be purchasers. FFLs are also required to maintain records of all firearms transactions, report multiple sales and stolen firearms to the Bureau of Alcohol, Tobacco, and Firearms (BATF), provide transaction records upon request to BATF; when they go out of business, they are required to transfer their records to BATF.

A privately owned gun can be transferred in a wide variety of ways not involving FFLs, such as through classified ads in newspapers, gun magazines, and at gun shows (which include both licensed and unlicensed dealers). Transfers of secondhand firearms by unlicensed individuals form the secondary market, for which federal law does not require transaction records or criminal background checks of prospective gun buyers (Cook et al., 1995). Using household survey data, Cook and Ludwig (1997) estimate that about 2 million transactions per year (30-40 percent of all gun transactions) occur in the secondary market. Primary and secondary firearms markets are closely linked because many buyers move from one to the other depending on relative prices and other terms of the transaction (Cook and Leitzel, 1996).

Since states vary greatly in their requirements on secondary firearms market transfers (see, e.g., Peters, 2000), another way to think about firearms commerce is to distinguish between regulated and unregulated transfers. In Massachusetts, for example, all firearms transfers must be reported to the state police, and secondary markets can be regulated through inspection of these transfer records (Massachusetts General Laws, Chapter 140). In neighboring New Hampshire, however, sales of guns by private citizens are not recorded, and even legitimate transfers in the secondary market cannot be monitored. In this report we use the primary/secondary distinction because it is standard, but regulation is probably the critical distinguishing feature.

Figure 4-1 presents a conceptual scheme of the flow of firearms to prohibited persons developed by Braga and his colleagues (2002). Through theft, firearms can be diverted to criminals and juveniles at any stage of commerce. Guns can be stolen from manufacturers, importers, distributors, licensed dealers, and private citizens. Cook et al. (1995) estimated that some 500,000 guns are stolen each year. This estimate, derived from National Crime Victimization Survey data for the years 1987 to 1992, suggests that 340,700 thefts occurred annually in which one or more guns were stolen; separate data from North Carolina suggest that on average 1.5 guns are stolen per theft (Cook et al., 1995). This figure is also consistent with a

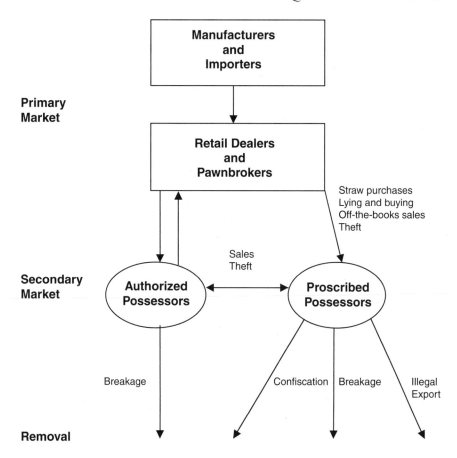

FIGURE 4-1 Firearms flows.
SOURCE: Braga et al. (2002).

similar estimate calculated for the Police Foundation (Cook and Ludwig, 1997), which used data from a telephone survey of a nationally representative sample of 2,568 adults in which those who were gun owners reported firearms theft and the number of firearms stolen per theft. Braga et al. (2002) also identify three broad mechanisms through which criminal consumers acquire firearms from licensees without theft: straw purchase, "lying and buying," and buying from a dealer who is willing to ignore regulations. A straw purchase occurs when the actual buyer, typically someone who is too young or otherwise proscribed, uses another person to execute the paperwork. Lying and buying refers to prohibited persons (e.g., felons and juveniles) who purchase firearms directly by showing false identification and lying about their status. And in some cases the seller is knowingly involved and may disguise the illegal transaction by falsifying the paper record of sale or reporting the guns as stolen.

The available research evidence suggests that gun-using criminals go through a number of guns during the course of their short careers. The population of active street criminals is characterized by brief careers (typically 5 to 10 years) and many interruptions through incarceration and injury (National Research Council, 1986). Each year a substantial fraction of current offenders are released from prison and may have to acquire new weapons in order to continue their criminal career; others will have just begun their careers and must obtain guns from somewhere. Survey research on criminally active populations suggests that gun offenders buy, steal, borrow, sell, and otherwise exchange guns quite frequently (Wright and Rossi, 1994; Sheley and Wright, 1993).

Young offenders have been noted as active in illegal markets both as sellers and buyers of guns through their informal networks of family, friends, and street sources. Using data from self-administered questionnaires completed by 835 male inmates in six correctional facilities in four states between November 1990 and February 1991, Sheley and Wright (1993) found that 86 percent of juvenile inmates had owned at least one firearm at some time in their lives, 51 percent reported having personally dealt with many guns before being incarcerated, and 70 percent felt that they could get a gun "with no trouble at all" upon release. Wright and Rossi (1994) found that 75 percent of incarcerated adult felons had owned at least one firearm at some time in their lives and, for those who did report ownership, the average number of guns owned prior to their current incarceration was approximately six. For incarcerated felons who reported stealing at least one gun, 90 percent also reported that they had sold or traded a stolen gun at least once in the past, and 37 percent had done so many times.

It is also important to recognize that guns have value in exchange as well as in use. Based on interviews with youth offenders, Cook and his colleagues (1995) suggest that guns were valuable commodities for youth to trade for services, money, drugs, or other items such as video games, VCRs, phones, and fax machines.

Guns are not costly when compared with other durable goods but may constitute a large asset in the portfolio of drug users or of youth. The retail prices of guns vary greatly based on the type, manufacturer, model, caliber, and age. For example, the suggested retail price of a new high-quality 9mm semiautomatic pistol is about $700, while a secondhand low-quality one can retail for as little as $50 (Fjestad, 2001). The proximate source of a gun can also influence its price for prohibited persons. Sheley and Wright's (1995) survey research suggests that juveniles paid less for guns acquired from informal and street sources than for guns acquired through normal retail outlets, such as gun stores and pawnshops: 61 percent of the juvenile inmates and 73 percent of the high school students who acquired their guns from a retail outlet paid more than $100, while only 30 percent of the juvenile inmates and 17 percent of the high school students who acquired their most recent gun from an informal or street source paid more than $100 (Sheley and Wright, 1995:49). We do not know whether this is driven by differences in the quality of the guns purchased or in the costs of distribution in the two sectors.

Gun Sources

There are three main types of evidence on the origins of guns for criminals and juveniles: survey research, BATF firearms trace data, and BATF firearms investigation data. Each provides different insights into the means by which offenders acquire firearms.

Survey Research

A number of inmate surveys have documented the wide variety of sources of guns available to criminals and youth. Table 4-1 summarizes some of the basic findings from three of the most widely cited of these surveys. Precise patterns are sometimes difficult to discern because different definitions and questions are used to elicit similar information. Nevertheless, survey research has documented a wide variety of sources of guns and methods of firearm acquisition used by criminals and youth. Guns referenced in these surveys come from a variety of sources, including family members, friends, the black market, and direct theft.

Wright and Rossi's (1994) 1992 survey of 1,874 convicted felons serving time in 11 prisons in 10 states throughout the United States, for example, revealed a complex market of both formal and informal transactions, cash and noncash exchange, and new and used handguns. Felons reported acquiring a majority of their guns from nonretail, informal sources. Only 21 percent of the respondents obtained the handgun from a retail outlet, with other sources including family and friends (44 percent) and the street (that is, the black market), drug dealers, and fences (26 percent). Moreover, the majority of handguns were not purchased with cash. Of the surveyed felons, 43 percent acquired their most recent handgun through a cash purchase, while 32 percent stole their most recent handgun. The remainder acquired their most recent handgun by renting or borrowing it, as a gift, or through a trade. Finally, almost two-thirds of the most recent handguns acquired by felons were reported as used guns, and one-third were reported as new guns. Illicit firearms markets dealt primarily in secondhand guns and constituted largely an in-state, rather than out-of-state, market.

TABLE 4-1 Sources and Method of Handgun Acquisition by Criminals

Study	Measure	Method of Firearm Acquisition as Reported by Prison Inmates	Source of Firearm as Reported by Prison Inmates
Bureau of Justice Statistics (1993)	Handgun possessed by inmate	27% retail purchase 9% direct theft	31% family/friends 28% black market/fence 27% retail outlet
Wright and Rossi (1994)	Most recent handgun—incarcerated felons	43% cash purchase 32% direct theft 24% rent/borrow, trade, or gift Estimated 40-70% directly or indirectly through theft	44% family and friends 26% black market/fence 21% retail outlet
Sheley and Wright (1993)	Most recent handgun—incarcerated juveniles	32% straw purchase 12% theft	90% from friend, family, street, drug dealer, drug addict, house or car

Results from a 1991 Bureau of Justice Statistics (BJS) survey of some 2,280 handgun-using state prison inmates support Wright and Rossi's observation that the illicit firearms market exploited by criminals is heavily dominated by informal, off-the-record transactions, either with friends and family or with various street sources (Bureau of Justice Statistics, 1993). The 1991 survey found that only 27 percent of the inmates who used a handgun in crime that led to their incarceration reported they obtained the handgun by purchase from a retail outlet. In contrast to the Wright and Rossi (1994) findings, the BJS survey found that only 9 percent of inmates who used a handgun in a crime had stolen it. More recently, Decker and colleagues' (1997) analysis of arrestee interview data (i.e., the Arrestee Drug Abuse Monitoring Survey) revealed that 13 percent of arrestees admitted to having a stolen gun. Among juvenile males, one-quarter admitted to theft of a gun (Decker et al., 1997).

Sheley and Wright's (1993) survey of high school students and incarcerated juveniles suggested that informal sources of guns were even more important to juveniles.[1] More than 90 percent of incarcerated juveniles obtained their most recent handgun from a friend, a family member, the street, a drug dealer, or a drug addict, or by taking it from a house or car (Sheley and Wright, 1993:6). Sheley and Wright (1995) found that 12 percent of juvenile inmates had obtained their most recent handgun by theft and 32 percent of juvenile inmates had asked someone, typically a friend or family member, to purchase a gun for them in a gun shop, pawnshop, or other retail outlet. When juveniles sold or traded their guns, they generally did so within the same network from which they obtained them—family members, friends, and street sources (Sheley and Wright, 1995).

BATF Firearms Trace Data

BATF firearms trace data, described in Chapter 3, have been used to document that firearms recovered by law enforcement have characteristics suggesting they were illegally diverted from legitimate firearms commerce to criminals and juveniles (see, e.g., Zimring, 1976; Kennedy et al., 1996; Wachtel, 1998; Cook and Braga, 2001). Trace data, reflecting firearms recovered by police and other law enforcement agencies, have revealed that a noteworthy proportion of guns had a "time to crime" (the length of time from the first retail sale to recovery by the police) of a few months or a few years. For example, Cook and Braga (2001) report that 32 percent of traceable handguns recovered in 38 cities participating in BATF's Youth

---

[1]In addition to the incarcerated juvenile sample described above, Sheley and Wright also surveyed 758 students enrolled at 10 high schools in 5 large cities that were proximate to the juvenile correctional facilities they surveyed between 1990 and 1991.

Crime Gun Interdiction Initiative (YCGII) were less than 3 years old. Cook and Braga (2001) also report that only 18 percent of these new guns were recovered in the possession of the first retail purchaser, suggesting that many of these guns were quickly diverted to criminal hands. Recovered crime guns are relatively new when compared with guns in public circulation. Pierce et al. (2001) found that guns manufactured between 1996 and 1998 represented about 14 percent of guns in private hands, but they accounted for 34 percent of traced crime guns recovered in 1999.

Wright and Rossi (1994) found that criminals typically use guns from within-state sources, whereas the 1999 YCGII trace reports suggest that the percentage of crime guns imported from out of state is closely linked to the stringency of local firearm controls. While 62 percent of traced YCGII firearms were first purchased from licensed dealers in the state in which the guns were recovered (Bureau of Alcohol, Tobacco, and Firearms, 2000c), this fraction was appreciably lower in northeastern cities with tight control—for example, Boston, New York, and Jersey City—where less than half of the traceable firearms were sold at retail within the state. A noteworthy number of firearms originated from southern states with less restrictive legislation, for example, Virginia, North Carolina, Georgia, and Florida (Bureau of Alcohol, Tobacco, and Firearms, 2000c).

Moreover, by examining the time-to-crime of out-of-state handguns in the trace data, Cook and Braga (2001) concluded that the process by which such handguns reach criminals in these tight-control cities is not one of gradual diffusion moving with interstate migrants (as suggested by Blackman, 1997-1998, and Kleck, 1999); rather, the handguns that make it into these cities are imported directly after the out-of-state retail sale. In contrast, Birmingham (AL), Gary (IN), Houston (TX), Miami (FL), New Orleans (LA), and San Antonio (TX), had at least 80 percent of their firearms first sold at retail in the state in which the city was located (Bureau of Alcohol, Tobacco, and Firearms, 2000c). Kleck (1999) attempts to explain the interstate movement of crime guns by simply observing that, according to the U.S. Census Bureau, 9.4 percent of the United States population moved their residence across state lines between 1985 and 1990. These migration patterns, however, do not necessarily explain the big differences in import and export patterns across source and destination states as well as the overrepresentation of new guns that show up in tight-control cities from other loose-control states.

BATF Investigation Data

While analyses of BATF trace data can document characteristics of crime guns that suggest illegal diversions from legitimate firearms commerce, trace data analyses cannot describe the illegal pathways through

TABLE 4-2 Volume of Firearms Diverted Through Trafficking Channels

Source	N(%)	Total Guns	Mean	Median
Firearms trafficked by straw purchaser or straw purchasing ring	695 (47%)	25,741	37.0	14
Trafficking in firearms by unregulated private sellers[a]	301 (20%)	22,508	74.8	10
Trafficking in firearms at gun shows and flea markets	198 (13%)	25,862	130.6	40
Trafficking in firearms stolen from federal firearms licensees	209 (14%)	6,084	29.1	18
Trafficking in firearms stolen from residence	154 (10%)	3,306	21.5	7
Firearms trafficked by federal firearms licensees, including pawnbroker	114 (8%)	40,365	354.1	42
Trafficking in firearms stolen from common carrier	31 (2%)	2,062	66.5	16

[a]As distinct from straw purchasers and other traffickers.
NOTE: N = 1,470 investigations. Since firearms may be trafficked along multiple channels, an investigation may be included in more than one category. This table excludes 60 investigations from the total pool of 1,530 in which the total number of trafficked firearms was unknown.
SOURCE: Adapted from Bureau of Alcohol, Tobacco, and Firearms (2000d).

which crime guns travel from legal commerce to its ultimate recovery by law enforcement. BATF also conducts numerous investigations both in the course of monitoring FFL and distributor compliance with regulations and following detection of gun trafficking offenses. Analyses of BATF firearms trafficking investigation data provide insights on the workings of illegal firearms markets (see, e.g., Moore, 1981; Wachtel, 1998). To date, the most representative look at firearms trafficking through a comprehensive review of investigation data was completed by BATF in 2000. This study examined all 1,530 investigations made between July 1996 and December 1998 by BATF special agents in all BATF field divisions in the United States[2] (Bureau of Alcohol, Tobacco, and Firearms, 2000d). They involved the diversion of more than 84,000 guns. As indicated in Table 4-2, the study revealed a variety of pathways through which guns were illegally diverted to criminals and juveniles.

---

[2]This does not include simple Armed Career Criminal or Felon in Possession cases.

The BATF study found that 43 percent of the trafficking investigations involved the illegal diversion of 10 guns or fewer but confirmed the existence of large trafficking operations, including two cases involving the diversion of over 10,000 guns. Corrupt FFLs accounted for only 9 percent of the trafficking investigations but more than half of the guns diverted in the pool of investigations. Violations by FFLs in these investigations included "off paper" sales, false entries in record books, and transfers to prohibited persons. Nearly half of the investigations involved firearms trafficked by straw purchasers, either directly or indirectly. Trafficking investigations involving straw purchasers averaged a relatively small number of firearms per investigation but collectively accounted for 26,000 guns. Firearms were diverted by traffickers at gun shows and flea markets in 14 percent of the investigations, and firearms stolen from FFLs, residences, and common carriers were involved in more than a quarter of the investigations.

Interpreting the Data

Braga et al. (2002) suggest that the three sources of data on illegal gun markets are not directly comparable but broadly compatible. Each data source has its own inherent limitations and, as such, it is difficult to credit the insights provided by one source over another source.

None of the three sources of data contradicts the hypothesis that stolen guns and informal transfers (as opposed to transfers from legitimate sources) predominate in supplying criminals and juveniles with guns. However, they also clearly suggest that licensed dealers play an important role and that the illegal diversion of firearms from legitimate commerce is a problem. In their review of these three sources of data, Braga and his colleagues (2002) suggest that, in the parlance of environmental regulation, illegal gun markets consist of both "point sources"—ongoing diversions through scofflaw dealers and trafficking rings—and "diffuse sources"—acquisitions through theft and informal voluntary sales. As in the case of pollution, both point sources and diffuse sources are important (see also Cook and Braga, 2001). Braga and his colleagues (2002) also speculate that the mix of point and diffuse sources differs across jurisdictions depending on the density of gun ownership and the strictness of gun controls.

ANALYTIC FRAMEWORK

General Model

Real interventions in gun markets tend to target particular types of firearms or sources. If policy raises the difficulty (cost, time, risk) of obtaining a particular type of gun or using a particular type of source, the effect might be mitigated by criminals' substitution across types of guns or sources. The following framework is helpful for organizing what is known, and what we would like to know, about whether access interventions can reduce harms from criminal gun use.

There are many types of guns; the term "type" encompasses both the literal firearm type (e.g., handguns versus long guns) and the source by which it is acquired (e.g., retail purchase, private sale, theft, loan, and other types of firearm transfers).[3] Furthermore, there are many types of individuals (legal possessors, juveniles, convicted felons and other persons prohibited from legal gun possession). Restrictions aim at reducing firearm possession or use by some of those groups. For analyzing the effects of these restrictions, consumer demand theory provides a useful conceptual framework, in which the use of each type of gun by each type of individual depends on the total cost that individual incurs in acquiring or retaining that gun. This generates a specific volume of use (possession or purchase) by each type of individual for each type of weapon. When the difficulty felons face in acquiring new guns rises, for example because of a targeted intervention, we assume that new gun use will decline among felons; whether that decline is substantial can be determined only empirically. Use of other kinds of guns may rise.

We use the term "cost" as broader than the money required for purchase of the item. Nonmonetary costs may be particularly important for gun acquisition by offenders, compared with purchases of unregulated legal goods; these costs include the time required to locate a reliable source or obtain information about prices, the risk of arrest by police (and sanction by a court), and the risk of violence by the seller. These are potentially important in any illicit market and have received some attention in the context of drug markets (Caulkins, 1998; Moore, 1973).

To make clear how this framework operates, consider an intervention that raises the costs criminals face to obtain new guns. The direct or "own" effect of this intervention is to reduce criminals' demand for new guns. Yet this is not the end of the story. The total effect of the policy intervention is the sum of the "own effect" and a "cross-effect" reflecting criminals' substitution of used guns for new ones as new guns become more costly. Even if the own effect is negative, the cross-effect might be sufficiently positive to render the overall effect close to zero.

---

[3]For discussion purposes, we are dramatically simplifying the large variety of guns available to consumers. Guns vary by type (revolvers, semiautomatic pistols, derringers, rifles, and shotguns), caliber and gauge (e.g., .22, .38, 9mm, .45, 12 gauge, 20 gauge, and dozens of other bullet calibers and shotgun gauges), and manufacturers (e.g., Smith & Wesson, Sturm Ruger, Colt, Glock, Sig Sauer, Lorcin, Bryco, and hundreds of other manufacturers). There is ample evidence suggesting that criminal consumers seem to prefer certain types of guns.

The patterns of substitution among sources may be different for different types of potential buyers. Adults without felony convictions or other disqualifications can presumably choose between buying new guns from retailers and used guns from legal private sellers. Juveniles, by contrast, cannot buy from retailers or law-abiding dealers in used guns. However, they can conceivably substitute by obtaining guns from a number of sources outside legal commerce, such as residential theft, informal transfers through their social networks, and scofflaw dealers; as one source becomes more difficult, youth may obtain more from another.

This framework is limited to an assessment of effects on the quantities of guns owned, which is not the final outcome of interest. Rather, it is crime or violence that ultimately interests policy makers. Whether changing the number and characteristics of firearms in the hands of persons of a given type increases harm is an additional question that requires different data and is considered at the end of the chapter.

We classify potential market interventions in two dimensions: market-targeted (primary or secondary) and supply or demand side programs. For example, consider police undercover purchases from unlicensed dealers. These aim to shift the supply curve in secondary markets by increasing the perceived risk of sale; dealers will be less willing to sell to unknown buyers and will charge a higher price when they do. Whether this has an influence on criminal possession of guns depends on many factors, such as the share of purchases that are made from nonintimate dealers and the price elasticity of demand (i.e., how much an increase in the price affects the purchase and retention of guns). Other interventions are focused on reducing demand, for example, taxes on FFL sales (primary market) and increasing sentences for purchasing from unlicensed dealers (secondary market).

Demand

What determines the demand for guns? Offenders acquire firearms for a variety of reasons: self-protection, a means for generating income, a source of esteem and self-respect, and a store of value. For example a rise in violence in a specific city may shift the demand curve up because of the increased return to self-protection. We assume that the demand for guns for criminal purposes is negatively related to the price and other costs of acquisition; there is no research on the elasticity with respect to either price or any other cost component that would allow quantification of the importance of this effect. Note that individuals make two kinds of acquisition decisions, active and passive; passive refers to holding rather than selling a valuable asset. Most market interventions aim only at the acquisition decision; retention is affected only indirectly, in that an increase in the value of a gun may lead to a greater willingness to sell to others.

Individual demand has an important time dimension to it, which makes inconvenience of acquisition a potentially valuable goal for an intervention. The value of a gun is partly situation-dependent; a perceived insult or opportunity to retaliate against a rival may make a firearm much more valuable if acquired now rather than in a few hours, when the opportunity or the passion has passed. Analytically and empirically that is a substantial complication; individuals are now characterized not only by their general risk of using a firearm for criminal purposes but also by their time-specific propensity of such use. This also allows for the possibility of positive effects from interventions that merely reduce the fraction of time an offender has a firearm.

Supply

The factors affecting the supply of firearms to offenders are comparably numerous. Guns used in crimes (crime guns) are obtained both from the existing stock in private hands (purchase in secondhand markets, theft, gifts) and from new production (sales by and thefts from FFLs, wholesalers, or manufacturers). In the aggregate these sources can be thought of as constituting a supply system; a higher money price will generate more guns for sale to high-risk individuals. Supply side interventions aim to shift the supply curve up, so that fewer guns are available at any given money price.

It may be useful to conceptualize each supply curve as independently determined. The factors that affect the costs of providing firearms through thefts (whether from households or stores) are likely to be distinct from those affecting provision of the same weapons through straw purchases. Raising penalties for stealing guns or expanding the burglary squad will raise the risk compensation (i.e., price) needed to induce burglars to undertake a given volume of gun theft. Those same measures are unlikely to have much effect on the risks faced in straw purchase transactions, which will be raised for example by tougher enforcement of FFL record-keeping requirements. While we will refer to a single supply curve for firearms to offenders, it is the sum of a number of components.

Markets may also be places; that is the guiding principle of much antidrug policing, since there are specific locations at which many sales occur on a continuing basis. It is unclear whether places are important for gun acquisition. Gun purchases are very rare events when compared with drug purchases; a few per year versus a few per week for those most active in the market (Koper and Reuter, 1996). The low frequency of gun purchases has two opposing effects. On one hand, it reduces the attraction to a seller of being in a specific place, since there will be a long period with no purchases but with potential police attention. On the other hand, buyers are less likely to be well informed because of the low rate of purchase and may be willing to pay a substantial price premium to obtain a gun more rapidly, thus increasing the value of operating in a location that is known to be rich in firearms acquisition opportunities.

Gun shows are potential specific places where criminals acquire guns. Gun shows may be especially attractive venues for the illegal diversion of firearms due to the large number of shows per year, the size of the shows, the large volume of transactions, and the advertising and promotion of these events. Gun shows provide a venue for large numbers of secondary market sales by unlicensed dealers; they are exempted from the federal transaction requirements that apply to licensed dealers who also are vendors at these events. The Police Foundation (1996) estimated, from the National Survey of Private Gun Ownership, that gun shows were the place of acquisition of 3.9 percent of all guns and 4.5 percent of handguns. The 1991 BJS survey of state prison inmates suggests that less than 1 percent of handgun using inmates personally acquired their firearm at a gun show (Bureau of Justice Statistics, 1993). However, these data did not determine whether a friend, family member, or street dealer purchased the gun for the inmate at a gun show. While it is not known what proportion of crime guns come from gun shows or what proportion of gun show dealers act criminally, research suggests that criminals do illegally acquire guns at these venues through unlicensed dealers, corrupt licensed dealers, and straw purchasers (Braga and Kennedy, 2000). Certain states specifically regulate firearms sales at gun shows; otherwise, there have been no systematic attempts to implement place-based interventions to disrupt illegal transactions at gun shows.

Note that the market is partly a metaphor. For example, many guns are acquired through nonmarket activities, gifts or loans from friends with no expectation of a specific payment in return. These may take place "in the shadow" of the market, so that the terms are influenced by the costs of acquiring guns in formal transactions; when guns are more expensive to acquire in the market, owners are more reluctant to lend them. However there is no empirical basis for assessing how close these links are. An additional complication is that guns are highly differentiated and there is no single price. No agency or researcher has systematically collected price data over a sufficient length of time to determine the correlation of prices across gun types over time and thus whether they are appropriately treated as a single market or even a set of linked markets.

Using the Framework

One value of this approach (demand, supply, and substitution) is in developing intermediate measures of whether an intervention might influence the desired outcome. For example, intensified police enforcement against sellers in the informal market (through "buy-and-bust" stings), even though affecting the firearms market for offenders, may not be a large enough intervention to produce detectable changes in the levels of either violent crimes or violent crimes with firearms, given the noisiness of these time series and lags in final effects. However, if this enforcement has not affected the money price or the difficulty of acquisition in the secondary market, then it almost certainly has not had the intended effects; thus a cost measure provides a one-sided test. The ADAM (Arrestee Drug Abuse Monitoring) data system provided a potential source of such data at the local level.

Table 4-3 presents a list of hypothesized effects of the major interventions discussed in this chapter. This is more in the nature of a heuristic than a precise classification or prediction. It distinguishes between the two classes of markets and the two forms of acquisition cost (monetary and nonmonetary) in each market. Note again that the principal market for offenders is conceptualized as illegal diversions from retail outlets, such as convicted felons personally lying and buying or using false identification to acquire guns, straw purchasers illegally diverting legally purchased guns, and corrupt licensed dealers falsifying transaction paperwork or making off-the-book sales. The secondary market includes all other informal firearms transfers, such as direct theft, purchases of stolen guns from others, loans or gifts from friends and families, and unregulated sales among private sellers.

TABLE 4-3 Intermediate Effects of Market Interventions

Outcomes

	Primary Market for Offenders		Secondary Market for Offenders	
	Price	Acquisition Difficulty	Price	Acquisition Difficulty
Intervention				
Regulating federal firearms licensees	+	+		
Limiting gun sales	+	+		
Screening gun buyers		+		
Buy-back programs			+	
Sell and bust			−	+
Buy and bust			+	+

NOTE: In cells with no entry, we assume no discernible effect.

SUBSTITUTION

Suppose for the sake of discussion that policy interventions can raise the difficulty faced by some individuals in obtaining some types of guns. The question of whether such interventions reduce gun use (or crime or violence) depends on how readily the potential buyers could substitute alternative weapons or sources for those targeted by policy.

In our framework, the existing studies, summarized in the section on how offenders obtain firearms, describe the distribution of guns across acquisition sources for a particular type of buyers (felons or youthful offenders). These surveys cannot provide an estimate of the total number of guns held by the population of offenders.

Although the studies are conducted on nonrandom convenience samples of inmates, they show fairly consistently that many guns are stolen or borrowed, rather than purchased in the primary market. Many guns are obtained through informal networks. The fact that criminals acquire guns from a variety of sources suggests substitution. Indeed, some (see, e.g., Kleck, 1999; Wright and Rossi, 1994; Sheley and Wright, 1995) have taken these studies to suggest that substitution possibilities are so pervasive that interventions cannot control the amount of gun use or ensuing harm. Some observers draw similar inferences from the fact that many guns are stolen from the large stock of guns available to steal.

Our framework, though simple, suggests that there are limits to what one can infer about substitution from these data. First, the existing studies combine survey responses of inmates from a variety of cities. The fact that inmates from various places, taken collectively, get their guns from different sources does not mean that any particular criminal or criminals in any particular city have ready access to all these alternatives. Cities may differ in terms of the sources of guns. Furthermore, even if persons of a particular type in a locale obtain their guns through different channels, this does not imply that each person has a variety of channels if deprived of the channel he or she currently uses.

Another finding in the literature concerns the vintage of guns used in crime. Vintage enters the framework through type: new and old guns may be seen as different types with particular policy relevance because there are different interventions for each type. In spite of the vast numbers of used guns that could be stolen and then transferred to criminals, the trace data suggest that a disproportionate fraction of crime guns are quite new, although, as noted in Chapter 2, it cannot be determined how well the trace data represent the total population of crime guns. In our framework, we can interpret this information to mean that criminals favor new guns over used guns, given current acquisition costs; this reflects in part the fact that new guns lack a potential liability from use in a previous crime that is unknown to the current purchaser. Again, it is only information on the distribution of types of guns used by criminals. Since criminals use new guns, some observers have taken this information to indicate that interventions targeting new guns can reduce crime. This is a possible but not a necessary consequence. If both new and old guns are available to criminals, and criminals are observed using new guns, we can infer that criminals prefer new guns to old ones, given the respective prices and difficulties of obtaining the two types of guns. But this fact provides no information about whether criminals would substitute old guns for new ones if they faced increased difficulty of getting new ones.

That different criminals get their guns from a variety of sources—and that many guns used in crime are recent guns—provides little evidence about whether interventions would affect the volume of gun use. This is information about the types of guns used, not about the volume of, or harm caused by, guns. By itself, these findings are consistent with any level of substitution. Suppose that, when local rules are loose, some criminals get guns locally while others get them from elsewhere. The locale then adopts tight rules and suppose that all guns seized thereafter turn out to be nonlocal. That is consistent with either of two contradictory stories. In one, the restriction is totally effective and those who were purchasing local firearms can find none. In the other, there is full substitution; all the local buyers are able to find nonlocal sources without much increase in cost. Any inference requires information about the change in the tendency for the targeted type of individual to purchase other guns relative to those targeted with restrictions. In the language of our framework, we need to know the effects of the restriction on costs and of own costs and other prices on the tendencies for each type of person to buy guns.

INTERVENTIONS TO REDUCE CRIMINAL ACCESS TO FIREARMS

This section summarizes the existing literature on the effects of different kind of access interventions. We do not include taxes on firearms or ammunition because there are no evaluations of either kind of tax.

Regulating Gun Dealers

As already noted, criminals can acquire guns in the primary market by personally making illegal purchases, arranging straw purchases, and by finding corrupt FFLs willing to ignore transfer laws. The available research evidence reveals that a very small number of FFLs generate a large number of crime gun traces (Pierce et al., 1995; Bureau of Alcohol, Tobacco, and Firearms, 2000b). Assuming it is possible to categorize dealers by risk of diversion per weapon, this concentration of crime gun traces suggests an opportunity to reduce the illegal supply of firearms to criminals by focusing limited regulatory and investigative resources on the relatively small group of high-risk dealers. In theory, this approach would increase the cost of guns to criminals by restricting their availability through retail outlets. However, in order for this approach to be effective in reducing gun violence, there must be limited substitution from regulated primary markets to unregulated secondary markets.

In their analysis of trace data contained in BATF's Firearm Tracing System, Pierce et al. (1995) found that nearly half of all traces came back to only 0.4 percent of all licensed dealers. However, the concentration of trace data may simply reflect the very high concentration of firearms sales among FFLs. In California, the 13 percent of FFLs with more than 100 sales during 1996-1998 accounted for 88 percent of all sales (Wintemute, 2000). While handgun trace volume from 1998 was strongly correlated with handgun sales volume at the level of the individual dealer and highly concentrated among high-volume dealers, Wintemute (2000) also found that trace volume varied substantially among dealers with similar sales volumes, suggesting that guns sold by certain dealers were more at risk for generating crime guns than others. However, as Braga and his colleagues (2002) point out, Wintemute did not determine whether this variation was greater than could be explained by chance alone. It is possible that the variation of traces among dealers with similar trace volume was not significantly different from what would be expected from a normal distribution of crime gun traces among dealers.

The findings are important nonetheless. Even if only some high-volume dealers are high risk, the fact that most crime weapons come from high-volume dealers suggests that concentration of regulatory resources on this relatively small population may lead to more efficient enforcement, unless there is substitution across dealers by size category.

Due to concern that some FFLs were scofflaws who used their licenses to supply criminals with guns, the Clinton administration initiated a review of licensing procedures that led to their tightening (Bureau of Alcohol, Tobacco, and Firearms, 2000b). In 1993 and 1994, federal law was amended to provide more restrictive application requirements and a hefty increase in the licensing fee, from $30 to $200 for three years. After these provisions were put into place, the number of federal licensees declined steadily from 284,117 in 1992 to 103,942 in 1999 (Bureau of Alcohol, Tobacco, and Firearms, 2000b). With the elimination of some 180,000 dealers, BATF regulatory and enforcement resources became less thinly spread. In 2000, BATF conducted focused compliance inspections on dealers who had been uncooperative in response to trace requests and on FFLs who had 10 or more crime guns (regardless of time-to-crime) traced to them in 1999 (Bureau of Alcohol, Tobacco, and Firearms, 2000a). The inspections disclosed violations in about 75 percent of the 1,012 dealers inspected. While the majority of the discrepancies were resolved during the inspection process, some 13,271 missing guns could not be accounted for by 202 licenses, and 16 FFLs each had more than 200 missing guns. More than half of the licensees had record-keeping violations only. The focused compliance inspections identified sales to more than 400 potential firearms traffickers and nearly 300 potentially prohibited persons, resulting in 691 referrals sent to BATF agents for further investigation (Bureau of Alcohol, Tobacco, and Firearms, 2000a). This reinforces the impression that a relatively small number of dealers systematically violate rules in ways that allow for leakage of guns to prohibited persons.

In a recent paper, Koper (2002) examined the effects of the nearly 70 percent reduction in FFLs following the 1993 and 1994 federal licensing reforms on the availability of guns to criminals. Using a data base of all active gun dealers in summer 1994 and the number of BATF gun traces to each dealer since 1990, Koper examined whether "dropout" dealers were more likely to be suppliers of crime guns than were "survivor" dealers. He concluded that it was not clear whether guns sold by the dropout dealers had a higher probability of being used in crime or moved into criminal channels more quickly when compared with active dealers. This study, however, used national BATF firearms trace data from 1990 through 1995, before the adoption of comprehensive tracing practices in most major cities and prior to BATF nationwide efforts to encourage law enforcement agencies to submit guns for tracing (Cook and Braga, 2001; Bureau of Alcohol, Tobacco, and Firearms, 2000c). National trace data from this time period are not representative of guns recovered by law enforcement, so it is difficult to interpret the findings of Koper's analysis of the impact of federal licensing reforms on the availability of guns to criminals.

Some states and localities have imposed additional regulations on gun dealers. In 1993, North Carolina found that only 23 percent of dealers also possessed its required state license (Cook et al., 1995). Noncomplying dealers were required to obtain a state license or forfeit their federal license. Alabama also identified FFLs who did not possess the required state license; 900 claimed not to know about the state requirements and obtained the license; another 900 reported that they were not currently engaged in the business of selling firearms; and 200 more could not be located (Cook et al., 1995). Alabama officials scheduled the licenses for these 1,100 dealers for cancellation. The Oakland (CA) Police Department worked with BATF to enforce a requirement for all licensed dealers to hold a local permit that required dealers to undergo screening and a criminal background check (Veen et al., 1997). This effort caused the number of license holders in Oakland to drop from 57 to 7 in 1997. Officials in New York found that only 29 of 950 FFLs were operating in compliance with local ordinances. In cooperation with BATF, all local license applications were forwarded to the New York Police Department, which assumed responsibility for screening and inspections. The increased scrutiny reduced the number of license hold-ers in New York from 950 to 259 (Veen et al., 1997).

These state-level and local initiatives have not been rigorously evalu-ated to determine whether they have affected criminal access to guns and rates of gun misuse.

Limiting Gun Sales

Federal law requires FFLs to report multiple firearms sales to BATF. A few states, including Virginia, Maryland, and California, have passed laws that limit the number of guns that an individual may legally purchase from FFLs within some specified time period. Underlying this intervention is the idea that some individuals make straw purchases in the primary market and then divert these guns to proscribed persons or others planning to do harm. Trace data analyses conducted by BATF suggest that handguns that were first sold as part of a multiple sale are more likely than others to move rapidly into criminal use (Bureau of Alcohol, Tobacco, and Firearms, 2000c). If multiple sales were limited, then the volume of new guns avail-able to criminals might decline. In the language of supply and demand, this is a supply-side intervention aimed at raising the price of new guns to criminals. In principle this sort of intervention holds promise. However, in order for this intervention to work—in the sense of reducing violence—not only must the intervention make it more difficult for criminals to get new guns but also the substitution possibilities must be limited; that is, compa-rably harmful guns cannot be available from comparably accessible sources.

In July 1993, Virginia implemented a law limiting handgun purchases by any individual to no more than one during a 30-day period. Prior to the passage of this law, Virginia had been one of the leading source states for guns recovered in northeast cities including New York, Boston, and Wash-ington, DC (Weil and Knox, 1996). Using firearms trace data, Weil and Knox (1996) showed that during the first 18 months the law was in effect, Virginia's role in supplying guns to New York and Massachusetts was greatly reduced. For traces initiated in the Northeast, 35 percent of the firearms acquired before one-gun-a-month implementation took effect and 16 percent purchased after implementation were traced to Virginia dealers (Weil and Knox, 1996). This study indicates a change in the origin of traced crime guns following the change in the law. In this sense, the law change had an effect. However, the law may have been undermined by a substitu-tion from guns first purchased in Virginia to guns first purchased in other states.[4] An important question not addressed by this study is whether the

---

[4]The Virginia legislature may nonetheless have achieved its goal of reducing the role of the state in the interstate illegal gun trade.

law change affects the ultimate outcome of interest—the quantity of criminal harm committed with guns—or even the intermediate questions of the law's effects on the number of guns purchased or owned.

Screening Gun Buyers

Enacted in 1994, the Brady Handgun Violence Prevention Act required FFLs to conduct a background check on all handgun buyers and mandated a one-week waiting period before transferring the gun to the purchaser. A total of 32 states were required to implement the provisions of the Brady act. The remaining states[5] and the District of Columbia were exempted because they already required a background check of those buying handguns from FFLs. In 1998, the background check provisions of the Brady act were extended to include the sales of long guns and the waiting period requirement was removed when, as mandated by the initial act, it became possible for licensed gun sellers to perform instant record checks on prospective buyers. The policy intent was to make gun purchases more difficult for prohibited persons, such as convicted felons, drug addicts, persons with certain diagnosed mental conditions, and persons under the legal age limit (18 for long rifles and shotguns, 21 for handguns). In 1996, the prospective purchasers with prior domestic violence convictions were also prohibited from purchasing firearms from FFLs.

Theoretically, by raising the cost of acquisition, this procedure reduces the supply of guns to would-be assailants and to some persons who might commit suicide. Several BJS studies have demonstrated that Brady background checks have created obstacles for prohibited persons who attempt to purchase a gun through retail outlets (Bureau of Justice Statistics, 1999, 2002). The Bureau of Justice Statistics (2002) reported that, from the inception of the Brady act on March 1, 1994, through December 31, 2001, nearly 38 million applications for firearms transfers were subject to background checks and some 840,000 (2.2 percent) applications were rejected. In 2001, 66,000 firearms purchase applications were rejected out of about 2.8 million applications (Bureau of Justice Statistics, 2002). Prospective purchasers were rejected because the applicant had a felony conviction or indictment (58 percent), domestic violence misdemeanor conviction or restraining order (14 percent), state law prohibition (7 percent), was a fugitive from justice (6 percent), or some other disqualification, such as having a drug addiction, documented mental illness, or a dishonorable discharge (16 percent) (Bureau of Justice Statistics, 2002).

---

[5]The 19 remaining states include: California, Connecticut, Delaware, Florida, Illinois, Indiana, Iowa, Maryland, Massachusetts, Missouri, Nevada, New Jersey, New York, Ohio, Oklahoma, Oregon, South Carolina, South Dakota, and Virginia.

These figures suggest the possibility that the Brady act might be effective in screening prohibited purchasers from making gun purchases from FFLs. Based on descriptive studies revealing heightened risks of subsequent gun offending, some researchers suggest extending the provisions of the Brady act to a wider range of at-risk individuals, such as persons with prior felony arrests (Wright et al., 1999) and misdemeanor convictions (Wintemute et al., 1998). Wright et al. (1999) compared the gun arrest rates of two groups in California. The first consisted of persons who were denied purchases because they had been convicted of a felony in 1977. The second was purchasers who had a prior felony arrest in 1977 but no conviction. Even though the former group would reasonably be labeled as higher risk, they showed lower arrest rates over the three years following purchase or attempt to purchase. It is important to recognize that the group of convicted felons who attempt to purchase through legal channels may be systematically lower risk than the entire felony population, precisely because they did attempt to use the prohibited legitimate market; the finding is suggestive rather than conclusive

Wintemute et al. (1998) also recognize that extending the provisions of the Brady act would greatly complicate the screening process. Moreover, while this policy seems to prevent prohibited persons from making gun purchases in the primary market, the question remains what, if any, effect it has on purchases in the secondary market, on gun crimes, and on suicide.

Using a differences-in-differences research design and multivariate statistics to control for state and year effects, population age, race, poverty and income levels, urban residence, and alcohol consumption, Ludwig and Cook (2000) compared firearm homicide and suicide rates and the proportion of homicides and suicides resulting from firearms in the 32 states affected by Brady act requirements (the treatment group) compared with the 19 states and the District of Columbia (the control group) that had equivalent legislation already in place. Ludwig and Cook (2000) found no significant differences in homicide and suicide rates between the treatment and control groups, although they did find a reduction in gun suicides among persons age 55 and older in the treatment states. This reduction was greater in the treatment states that had instituted both waiting periods and background checks relative to treatment states that only changed background check requirements. The authors suggest that the effectiveness of the Brady act in reducing homicides and most suicides was undermined by prohibited purchasers shifting from the primary market to the largely unregulated secondary market.

While the Brady act had no direct effect on homicide rates, it is possible that it had an indirect effect, by reducing interstate gun trafficking and hence gun violence in the control states that already had similar laws. Cook and Braga (2001) document the fact that criminals in Chicago (a high control jurisdiction) were being supplied to a large extent by illegal gun trafficking from south central states, in particular Mississippi, and that a modest increase in regulation—imposed by the Brady act—shut down that pipeline. However, this large change in trafficking channels did not have any apparent effect in gun availability for violent acts in Chicago, as the percentage of homicides with guns did not drop after 1994 (Cook and Braga, 2001). Moreover, the authors found that the percentage of crime handguns first purchased in Illinois increased after the implementation of the Brady act, suggesting substitution from out-of-state FFLs to in-state FFLs once the advantage of purchasing guns outside Illinois had been removed.

Gun Buy-Backs

Gun buy-back programs involve a government or private group paying individuals to turn in guns they possess. The programs do not require the participants to identify themselves, in order to encourage participation by offenders or those with weapons used in crimes. The guns are then destroyed. The theoretical premise for gun buy-back programs is that the program will lead to fewer guns on the streets because fewer guns are available for either theft or trade, and that consequently violence will decline. It is the committee's view that the theory underlying gun buy-back programs is badly flawed and the empirical evidence demonstrates the ineffectiveness of these programs.

The theory on which gun buy-back programs is based is flawed in three respects. First, the guns that are typically surrendered in gun buy-backs are those that are least likely to be used in criminal activities. Typically, the guns turned in tend to be of two types: (1) old, malfunctioning guns whose resale value is less than the reward offered in buy-back programs or (2) guns owned by individuals who derive little value from the possession of the guns (e.g., those who have inherited guns). The Police Executive Research Forum (1996) found this in their analysis of the differences between weapons handed in and those used in crimes. In contrast, those who are either using guns to carry out crimes or as protection in the course of engaging in other illegal activities, such as drug selling, have actively acquired their guns and are unlikely to want to participate in such programs.

Second, because replacement guns are relatively easily obtained, the actual decline in the number of guns on the street may be smaller than the number of guns that are turned in. Third, the likelihood that any particular gun will be used in a crime in a given year is low. In 1999, approximately 6,500 homicides were committed with handguns. There are approximately 70 million handguns in the United States. Thus, if a different handgun were used in each homicide, the likelihood that a particular handgun would be used to kill an individual in a particular year is 1 in 10,000. The typical gun buy-back program yields less than 1,000 guns. Even ignoring the first two points made above (the guns turned in are unlikely to be used by criminals and may be replaced by purchases of new guns), one would expect a reduction of less than one-tenth of one homicide per year in response to such a gun buy-back program. The program might be cost-effective if those were the correct parameters, but the small scale makes it highly unlikely that its effects would be detected.

In light of the weakness in the theory underlying gun buy-backs, it is not surprising that research evaluations of U.S. efforts have consistently failed to document any link between such programs and reductions in gun violence (Callahan et al., 1994; Police Executive Research Forum, 1996; Rosenfeld, 1996).

Outside the United States there have been a small number of buy-backs of much larger quantities of weapons, in response to high-profile mass murders with firearms. Following a killing of 35 persons in Tasmania in 1996 by a lone gunman, the Australian government prohibited certain categories of long guns and provided funds to buy back all such weapons in private hands (Reuter and Mouzos, 2003). A total of 640,000 weapons were handed in to the government (at an average price of approximately $350), constituting about 20 percent of the estimated stock of weapons. The weapons subject to the buy-back, however, accounted for a modest share of all homicides or violent crimes more generally prior to the buy-back. Unsurprisingly, Reuter and Mouzos (2003) were unable to find evidence of a substantial decline in rates for these crimes. They noted that in the six years following the buy-back, there were no mass murders with firearms and fewer mass murders than in the previous period; these are both weak tests given the small numbers of such incidents annually.

Banning Assault Weapons

In 1994, Congress enacted the Violent Crime Control and Law Enforcement Act, which banned the importation and manufacture of certain military-style semiautomatic "assault" weapons and ammunition magazines capable of holding more than 10 rounds (National Institute of Justice, 1997). Assault weapons and large-capacity magazines manufactured before the effective date of the ban were grandfathered and thus legal to own and transfer. These guns are believed to be particularly dangerous because they facilitate the rapid firing of high numbers of shots. While assault weapons and large-capacity magazines are used only in a modest fraction of gun crimes, the premise of the ban was that a decrease in their use may reduce gunshot victimization, particularly victimizations involving multiple wounds or multiple victims (Roth and Koper, 1997).

A recent evaluation of the short-term effects of the 1994 federal assault weapons ban did not reveal any clear impacts on gun violence outcomes (Koper and Roth, 2001b). Using state-level Uniform Crime Reports data on gun homicides, the authors of this study suggest that the potential impact of the law on gun violence was limited by the continuing availability of assault weapons through the ban's grandfathering provision and the relative rarity with which the banned guns were used in crime before the ban. Indeed, as the authors concede and other critics suggest (e.g., Kleck, 2001), given the nature of the intervention, the maximum potential effect of the ban on gun violence outcomes would be very small and, if there were any observable effects, very difficult to disentangle from chance yearly variation and other state and local gun violence initiatives that took place simultaneously. In a subsequent paper on the effects of the assault weapons ban on gun markets, Koper and Roth (2001a) found that, in the short term, the prices of assault weapons in both primary and legal secondary markets rose substantially at the time of the ban, and this may have reduced the availability of the assault weapons to criminals. However, this increase in price was short-lived as a surge in assault weapon production in the months prior to the ban and the availability of legal substitutes caused prices to fall back to nearly preban levels. The ban is also weakened by the ease with which legally available guns and magazines can be altered to evade the intent of the ban. The results of these two studies should be interpreted with caution, since any trends observed in the relatively short study time period (24-month follow-up period) are unlikely to predict long-term trends accurately.

District of Columbia Handgun Ban

Bans on the ownership, possession, or purchase of guns are the most direct means available to policy makers for reducing the prevalence of guns. The District of Columbia's Firearms Control Regulations Act of 1975 is the most carefully analyzed example of a handgun ban. This law prohibited the purchase, sale, transfer, and possession of handguns by D.C. residents other than law enforcement officers or members of the military. Note, however, that individuals who had previously registered handguns prior to the passage of this law were allowed to keep them under this law. Long guns were not covered by the ban.[6]

One would expect the passage of the District's handgun ban to have little impact on the existing stock of legally held handguns but to greatly reduce the flow of new handguns to law-abiding citizens. Over time, the number of legally held handguns will decline. It is less clear how the illegal

---

[6]For a more detailed discussion of the law and the politics surrounding its passage, see Jones (1981).

possession of guns will be affected. The flow of new guns to the illegal sector may be reduced to the extent that legal guns enter the illegal sector through resale or theft from the legal stock in the District. Theory alone cannot determine whether this handgun ban will reduce crime and violence overall. One would expect that the share of crimes in which guns are used should decline over time if the handgun ban is effective.

The empirical evidence as to the success of the Washington, DC, handgun ban is mixed. Loftin et al. (1991) used an interrupted-time-series methodology to analyze homicides and suicides in Washington, DC, and the surrounding areas of Maryland and Virginia before and after the introduction of the ban. They included the suburban areas around Washington, DC, as a control group, since the law does not directly affect these areas. Using a sample window of 1968-1987, they report a 25 percent reduction in gun-related homicides in the District of Columbia after the handgun ban and a 23 percent reduction in gun-related suicides. In contrast, the surrounding areas of Maryland and Virginia show no consistent patterns, suggesting a possible causal link between the handgun ban and the declines in gun-related homicide and suicide. In addition, Loftin et al. (1991) report that nongun-related homicides and suicides declined only slightly after the handgun ban, arguing that this is evidence against substitution away from guns toward other weapons.

Britt et al. (1996), however, demonstrate that the earlier conclusions of Loftin et al. (1991) are sensitive to a number of modeling choices. They demonstrate that the same handgun-related homicide declines observed in Washington, DC, also occurred in Baltimore, even though Baltimore did not experience any change in handgun laws.[7] Thus, if Baltimore is used as a control group rather than the suburban areas surrounding DC, the conclusion that the handgun law lowered homicide and suicide rates does not hold. Britt et al. (1996) also found that extending the sample frame an additional two years (1968-1989) eliminated any measured impact of the handgun ban in the District of Columbia. Furthermore, Jones (1981) discusses a number of contemporaneous policy interventions that took place around the time of the Washington, DC, gun ban, which further call into question a causal interpretation of the results.

In summary, the District of Columbia handgun ban yields no conclusive evidence with respect to the impact of such bans on crime and violence. The nature of the intervention—limited to a single city, nonexperimental, and accompanied by other changes that could also affect handgun homicide—make it a weak experimental design. Given the sensitivity of the results to alternative specifications, it is difficult to draw any causal inferences.

---

[7]Britt et al. (1996) do not report results for suicide.

SUMMARY

We have documented what is known about how people obtain firearms for criminal activities and identified the weaknesses of existing evaluations of interventions. There is not much empirical evidence that assesses whether attempts to reduce criminal access to firearms will reduce gun availability or gun crime. Most research has focused on determining whether prohibited persons illegally obtain firearms from legitimate commerce (legal primary and secondary markets) or whether crime guns are stolen or acquired through informal exchanges. Current research evidence suggests that illegal diversions from legitimate commerce are important sources of guns and therefore tightening regulations of such markets may be promising. There also may be promising avenues to control gun theft and informal transfers (through problem-oriented policing, requiring guns to be locked up, etc.). We do not yet know whether it is possible to actually shut down illegal pipelines of guns to criminals or what the costs of such a shutdown would be to legitimate buyers. Answering these questions is essential.

We also provide an analytic framework for assessing interventions. Since our ultimate interest is in the injuries caused using guns and not how guns are obtained, the key question involves substitution. In the absence of the pathways currently used for gun acquisition, could individuals have obtained alternative weapons with which to wreak equivalent harm?

Substitution has many dimensions; time, place, and quality are just some of them. For example, that crime guns tend to be newer than guns generally indicates that criminals prefer new guns, even though old guns are generally as easy to get and are cheaper. This may be strictly consumer preference, or it may be to avoid being implicated, through ballistics imaging, in other crimes in which the gun was used. Would offenders currently using newer guns use older guns—or any guns—if access to newer guns became more limited? If particular dealers account for a disproportionate share of crime weapons, then we are left with yet another version of the substitution question: Would the criminals have obtained other guns, with similar harmful effects, from other sources, including other FFLs? How long would this process of substituting from new to old or from one source to another take?

What data are needed to determine the extent of substitution among firearms? Much could be learned from individual-level data from a general population survey on the number of guns owned by length of time, along with detailed individual characteristics of the individual (age, demographic characteristics, psychiatric history, other high-risk behaviors), along with type of gun owned (if any) and the method of acquisition (retail purchase, legal purchase of used gun, illegal purchase of stolen gun, borrowed through informal network). In addition, one would want measures of the availability of firearms of each type to potential buyers of each type in each locale. For adults without criminal records, for example, there are established, observable prices of new guns at retail outlets. Similarly, there are active markets in used guns, for which there are (at least in principle) prices. The prices are individual specific in the sense that, for example, juveniles and felons cannot purchase guns at Wal-Mart.[8] In effect, they face an infinite price of guns through this channel.

Beyond this information one would also need a source of exogenous variation on the difficulty of obtaining guns through different channels. While guns available to legal buyers through retail outlets have literal prices, the measures of the difficulty of gun acquisition through some other channels are prices only in a metaphorical sense. When a city undertakes an intervention at a particular point in time, for example to make it more difficult for juveniles to get guns from interstate traffickers in new guns, then (provided that the policy has some effect), it is as if the price of guns to juveniles has risen. Provided that the timing of the intervention is independent of the time pattern of local gun use, we could treat it as an exogenous increase in the metaphorical price of a gun to juveniles; money prices may fall as other costs rise because this increase in nonmoney costs shifts the demand curve down. What happens to the tendencies for juveniles to obtain guns; do they substitute purchases of guns stolen from homes for the new guns they had previously purchased from traffickers? Is the substitution complete? That is, is the volume of juvenile gun use as high in the presence of the intervention as it was in the absence of the intervention?

The biggest potential problem with this framework, however, is the assumption of an exogenous intervention. No real intervention is likely to be exogenous; that is, unrelated to changes in gun crimes. It might be more realistic to think about exogeneity conditional on some specified set of covariates, but the prospects for finding consensus on the correct set of covariates to credibly maintain this independence assumption are unknown. Alternatively, researchers may be forced to rely on other methodological approaches and data.

The committee has not attempted to identify specific interventions, research strategies, or data that might be suited for studying market interventions, substitution, and firearms violence. The existing evidence is of limited value in assessing whether any specific market-focused firearm restrictions would curb harm. **Thus, the committee recommends that work be started to think carefully about the prospects for achieving "conditional exogeneity," the kinds of interventions and covariates that are likely to**

---

[8]We ignore for the moment corrupt agents at retail outlets, viewing them as the equivalent of straw purchasers.

satisfy this independence requirement, how one could gather the data, the potential for building in evaluation at the stage of policy change, and other possible research and data designs. Future work might begin by considering the utility of emerging data systems, described in this report, for studying the impact of different market interventions, This type of effort should be take place in collaboration with a group of survey statisticians, social scientists, and representatives from the Bureau of Justice Statistics and the National Institute of Justice.

5

The Use of Firearms to Defend Against Criminals

While a large body of research has considered the effects of firearms on injury, crime, and suicide, far less attention has been devoted to understanding their defensive and deterrent effects. Firearms are used to defend against criminals. For example, the presence of a gun may frighten a criminal away, thereby reducing the likelihood of loss of property, injury, or death.

In this chapter, we consider what is known about the extent and nature of defensive gun use (DGU). Over the past decade, researchers have attempted to measure the prevalence of defensive gun use in the population. This measurement problem has proved to be quite complex, with some estimates suggesting just over 100,000 defensive gun uses per year and others suggesting 2.5 million or more defensive gun uses per year.

A primary cause of this uncertainty is the disagreement over the definition of defensive gun use—in particular, whether it should be defined as a response to victimization or as a means to prevent victimization from occurring in the first place. There is also uncertainty regarding the accuracy of survey responses to sensitive questions and the related problems of how to effectively measure defensive gun use, the types of questions that should be asked, and the methods of data collection. These disagreements over definition and measurement have resulted in prevalence rates that differ by a factor of 22 or more. While even the smallest of the estimates indicates that there are hundreds of defensive uses every day, there is much contention over the magnitude and the details.

Since answers to this debate precede any serious investigation into other related questions, we focus our attention on summarizing and evaluating the DGU estimates from the various gun use surveys. We find that fundamental problems in defining what is meant by defensive gun use may be a primary impediment to accurate measurement. Finally, after reviewing the literature that attempts to count the annual number of defensive gun uses in the United States, we then consider the small set of studies that evaluate the effectiveness of firearms for defense.

COUNTING DEFENSIVE GUN USES

How many times each year do civilians use firearms defensively? The answers provided to this seemingly simple question have been confusing. Consider the findings from two of the most widely cited studies in the field: McDowall et al. (1998), using the data from 1992 and 1994 waves of the National Crime Victimization Survey (NCVS), found roughly 116,000 defensive gun uses per year, and Kleck and Gertz (1995), using data from the 1993 National Self-Defense Survey (NSDS), found around 2.5 million defensive gun uses each year.

Many other surveys provide information on the prevalence of defensive gun use. Using the original National Crime Survey, McDowall and Wiersema (1994) estimate 64,615 annual incidents from 1987 to 1990. At least 19 other surveys have resulted in estimated numbers of defensive gun uses that are similar (i.e., statistically indistinguishable) to the results founds by Kleck and Gertz. No other surveys have found numbers consistent with the NCVS (other gun use surveys are reviewed in Kleck and Gertz, 1995, and Kleck, 2001a).

To characterize the wide gap in the estimated prevalence rate, it is sufficient to consider the estimates derived from the NSDS and recent waves of the NCVS. These two estimates differ by a factor of nearly 22. While strikingly large, the difference in the estimated prevalence rate should, in fact, come as no surprise. As revealed in Table 5-1, the two surveys are markedly different, covering different populations, interviewing respondents by different methods, using different recall periods, and asking different questions.

The NCVS is an ongoing annual survey conducted by the federal government (i.e., the Census Bureau on behalf of the Department of Justice) that relies on a complex rotating panel design to survey a representative sample of nearly 100,000 noninstitutionalized adults (age 12 and over), from 50,000 households. To elicit defensive gun use incidents, the survey first assesses whether the respondent has been the victim of particular classes of crime—rape, assault, burglary, personal and household larceny, or car theft—during the past six months, and then asks several follow-up questions about self-defense. In particular, victims are asked:

TABLE 5-1 Comparing Sampling Design of the NCVS and NSDS

	National Crime Victimization Survey	National Self-Defense Survey
Coverage	• Noninstitutionalized U.S. population, age 12 and over, each year since 1973 • Defensive gun use questions to victims (self-reported)	• U.S population, age 18 and over, with phones, 1993 • DGU questions to all respondents
Sample design	• Rotating panel design • Stratified, multistage cluster sample of housing units • Telephone and personal contacts	• One-shot cross-section • Stratified by region (South and West oversampled) • Random digit dialing
Sample size	Approximately 50,000 households and 100,000 individuals	4,997 individuals
Response rate	Approximately 95% of eligible housing units	61% of eligible numbers answered by human beings
Sponsorship	U.S. Census Bureau for U.S. Bureau of Justice Statistics	Research Network
Estimated defensive gun use	116,398 annual incidents using 1993-1994 data from redesigned survey	2,549,862 annual incidents

SOURCE: McDowall et al. (2000: Table 1). Used with kind permission of Springer Science and Business Media.

> Was there anything you did or tried to do about the incident while it was going on?

> Did you do anything (else) with the idea of protecting yourself or your property while the incident was going on?

Responses to these follow-up probes are coded into a number of categories, including whether the respondent attacked or threatened the offender with a gun.

The NSDS was a one-shot cross-sectional phone survey conducted by a private polling firm, Research Network, of a representative sample of nearly 5,000 adults (age 18 and over). The survey, which focused on firearms use, first assessed whether the respondent used a gun defensively during the past five years, and then asked details about the incident. In particular, respondents were first asked:

Within the past *five years*, have you yourself or another member of your household *used* a handgun, even if it was not fired, for self-protection or for the protection of property at home, work, or elsewhere? Please do *not* include military service, police work, or work as a security guard.

If the answer was yes, they were then asked:

Did this incident [any of these incidents] happen in the *past 12 months*?

The discrepancies in the prevalence estimates of defensive gun use can and should be better understood. Remarkably little scientific research has been conducted to evaluate the validity of DGU estimates, yet the possible explanations are relatively easy to categorize and study. The two surveys are either (1) measuring something different or (2) affected by response problems in different ways, or (3) both. Statistical variability, usually reflected by the standard error or confidence interval of the parameter, also plays some role but cannot explain these order of magnitude differences.

Coverage

Perhaps the most obvious explanation for the wide variation in the range of DGU estimates is that the surveys measure different variables. In the NSDS, for example, all respondents are asked the gun use questions. In contrast, the NCVS inquires only about use among persons who claim to be victims of rape, assault, burglary, personal and household larceny, and car theft. The NCVS excludes preemptive uses of firearms, uses that occur in crimes not screened for in the survey (e.g., commercial robbery, trespassing, and arson), and uses for crimes not revealed by respondents.[1]

McDowall et al. (2000) found some evidence that these differences in coverage play an important role. In an experimental survey that overrepresents firearms owners, 3,006 respondents were asked both sets of questions about defensive gun use, with random variation in which questions came first in the interview. By holding the survey sampling procedures constant (e.g., consistent confidentiality concerns and recall periods), the authors focus on the effects of questionnaire content. Overall, in this experiment, the NCVS survey items yielded three times fewer reports of defensive gun use than questionnaires that ask all respondents about defensive uses.

The McDowall et al. (2000) crossover experiment is informative and is exactly the type of methodological research that will begin to explain the sharp divergence in gun use estimates and how best to measure defensive gun use. There remains, however, much work to be done. The sample used

---

[1]It is well known, for example, that incidents of rape and domestic violence are substantially underreported in the NCVS (National Research Council, 2003).

in this survey is not representative, and the methods shed light on only one of the many competing hypotheses. Furthermore, this limited evidence is difficult to interpret. Even with a consistent sampling design, inaccurate reporting may still play an important role. For example, estimates from an NCVS type of question would be biased if victims were reluctant to report unsuccessful defensive gun use. Likewise, the estimates found using the NSDS-type survey would be biased if respondents report defensive gun uses based on mistaken perceptions of harmless encounters.

Even if we accept the notion of fully accurate reporting, or at least consistent inaccuracies across the surveys, details on the cause of these differences are especially important. If these discrepancies result because of incomplete reporting of victimization among the classes considered (e.g., rape and domestic violence) in the NCVS, then one must address the measurement error questions again. Certainly, we are interested in the behavior of all victims, not just those who self-report. If instead, the differences occur because the NSDS-type question includes preemptive uses, then the relevant debate might focus on which variable is of interest.

In any case, much of the confusion surrounding the debate seems to center on what is meant by defensive gun use. Self-defense is an ambiguous term that involves both objective components about ownership and use and subjective features about intent (National Research Council, 1993).[2] Whether one is a defender (of oneself or others) or a perpetrator, for example, may depend on perspective. Some reports of defensive gun use may involve illegal carrying and possession (Kleck and Gertz, 1995; Kleck, 2001b), and some uses against supposed criminals may legally amount to aggravated assault (Duncan, 2000a, 2000b; McDowall et al., 2000; Hemenway et al., 2000; Hemenway and Azrael, 2000). Likewise, protecting oneself against possible or perceived harm may be different from protecting oneself while being victimized.

Given this ambiguity, perhaps one of the more important and difficult problems is to develop a common language for understanding defensive and offensive gun use. Uniform concepts and a common language will serve to facilitate future survey work, guide scholarly discussions, and enhance understanding of the complex ways in which firearms are related to crime, violence and injury. More generally, a commonly understood language can also influence the development of firearms policy and violence policy more generally.

---

[2]This lack of a clear definition may also contribute to inaccurate response. If scholars who think about these issues have yet to come up with a clear definition for the behavior of interest, it may be unreasonable to rely on the accuracy of respondents whom, in some cases, may not understand or interpret the question as intended.

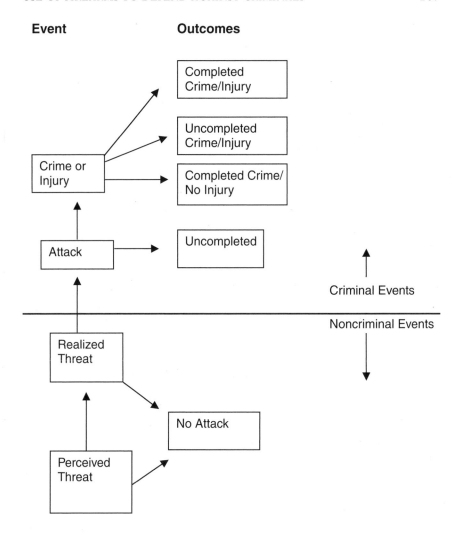

FIGURE 5-1 Stages and outcome of potential criminal encounters.
SOURCE: Adapted from Kleck (1997: Figure 7.1).

Although defining and measuring different types of gun use (both offensive and defensive) is not a simple matter, a typology similar to the one developed by Kleck may be a useful starting point (1997: Figure 7.1). Figure 5-1 provides a rough summary of the development of a violent or criminal encounter. Firearms and other weapons may be involved at different points in the development of a crime, from threats to realized crimes and injury. At each stage of a potentially threatening encounter, one may be interested in learning about the basic circumstances, about firearms use and other actions, about the intent of the respondent, and about outcomes. The relatively subjective nature of threats, which may or may not develop into criminal events, may justify placing these uses in a separate category (Kleck, 2001b:236). More generally, it would seem useful to distinguish between the more objective and subjective features of firearms use. Eliciting and interpreting relatively objective questions about whether and how one uses a gun may be relatively simple and lead to consensus on these basic matters. Eliciting and interpreting relatively subjective questions on intent may be much more complex and less amenable to consensus conclusions.[3]

Ultimately, researchers may conclude that it is impossible to effectively measure many aspects of defensive gun use. As noted above, counting crimes averted before the threat stage, and measuring deterrence more generally, may be impossible. Successful deterrence, after all, may yield no overt event to count. Imagine, for example, measuring defensive gun use for a person who routinely carries a handgun in a visible holster. How many times has this person "used a handgun, even it was not fired, for self-protection?" (i.e., the NSDS definition of defensive gun use). In this regard, much of the debate on the number of defensive gun uses may stem from an ill-defined question, rather than measurement error per se.

Response Problems in Firearms Use Surveys

Questions about the quality of self-reports of firearms use are inevitable. Response problems occur to some degree in nearly all surveys but are arguably more severe in surveys of firearm-related activities in which some individuals may be reluctant to admit that they use a firearm, and others may brag about or exaggerate such behavior.[4] If some sampled individuals give incorrect answers (inaccurate response) and others fail to answer the survey at all (nonresponse), investigators may draw incorrect conclusions from the data provided by a survey.

---

[3]A number of scholars have made explicit recommendations for collecting detailed narratives on the nature of the event. See, for example, recommendations made by Cook and Ludwig (1998), Smith (1997), and Kleck (2000). Hemenway and Azrael (2000) and Hemenway et al. (2000) collected and analyzed detailed narratives on gun use incidents that reveal that they are often complex and difficult to categorize.

[4]These same measurement problems were discussed in a report by the National Research Council (2001) that explored the data problems associated with monitoring illicit drug consumption.

Inaccurate Response

In fact, it is widely thought that inaccurate response biases the estimates of defensive gun use. Self-report surveys on possibly deviant behaviors invariably yield some false reports. Responses are miscoded, and respondents may misunderstand the questions or may not correctly remember or interpret the event. In addition to these unintentional errors, respondents may also exaggerate or conceal certain information.

The literature speculates widely on the nature of reporting errors in the firearms use surveys.[5] Some argue that reporting errors cause the estimates derived from the NCVS to be biased downward.[6] Kleck and Gertz (1995) and Kleck (2001a), for example, speculate that NCVS respondents doubting the legality of their behaviors or more generally fearing government intrusion may be inclined to provide false reports to government officials conducting nonanonymous interviews. Furthermore, Smith (1997) notes that NCVS respondents are not directly asked about firearms use but instead are first asked whether they defended themselves, and then they are asked to describe in what ways. Indirect questions may lead to incomplete answers.

Others argue that the estimates from the NSDS and other firearms use surveys are upwardly biased. Cook and Ludwig (1998), Hemenway (1997a), and Smith (1997), for example, suggest that the firearms use surveys do not effectively bound events that occur in prior interviews and thus may result in "memory telescoping." That is, respondents in the NSDS are more likely to report events that occurred prior to the observation window of interest. Furthermore, McDowall et al. (2000) speculate that preemptive uses recorded in the NSDS but not generally covered in the NCVS (which focuses on victims) are susceptible to a greater degree of subjectivity and thus inaccurate reporting.

A number of other general arguments have been raised as to why these surveys might be inaccurate. Some suggest that respondents may forget or conceal events that do not lead to adverse outcomes (Kleck and Gertz, 1995; Kleck, 2001a), while others suggest that respondents may exaggerate or conceal events due to social stigma. Some have even suggested that respondents may strategically answer questions to somehow influence the ongoing public debate (Cook et al., 1997). Finally, Hemenway (1997b) raises what amounts to a mechanical, rather than behavioral, concern

---

[5]See Kleck (2001a) for a detailed review of the various hypotheses about inaccurate reporting in gun use questionnaires.

[6]Kleck argues that the NCVS is well designed and uses state-of-the-art survey sampling techniques for measuring victimization, but for exactly those reasons it is not well designed for measuring defensive gun use.

regarding why the DGU estimates may be generally biased upward. For any rare event, in fact for any event with less than 50 percent probability, there are more respondents who can give false positive than false negative reports. Suppose, for example, in a sample of 1,000 respondents, the true prevalence rate is 1 percent; that is, 10 respondents used a gun defensively. Then 990 may provide false positive reports, while only 10 may provide false negative reports. Even small fractions of false positive reports may lead to substantial upward biases. Cook et al. (1997) further suggest that by focusing on victims, the NCVS reduces the scope of the false positive problem.

Although the rare events problem may be well known and documented in epidemiological studies of disease, it is uncertain whether this same phenomena affects inferences on defensive gun uses as well. People may have reasons to conceal or exaggerate defensive gun uses that may not apply when studying rare diseases. In fact, what is known about accurate reporting of other crime-related activities provides some evidence to the contrary. Validation studies on the accuracy of self-reports of illicit drug use among arrestees, for example, suggest that for this somewhat rare but illegal activity, the numbers of false reports of use are far less than the numbers of false reports of abstinence: self-reports of drug use are biased downward (Harrison, 1995).

Although theories abound, it is not possible to identify the prevalence of defensive gun use without knowledge on inaccurate reporting. Kleck and Gertz (1995) and others suggest that estimates from the NCVS are biased downward, arguing that respondents are reluctant to reveal information to government officials, and that indirect questions may yield inaccurate reports. Hemenway (1997a) and others suggest that estimates from the NSDS are biased upward, arguing that memory telescoping, self-presentation biases, and the rare events problem more generally lead the numbers of false positive reports to substantially exceed the numbers of false negative reports. It is not known, however, whether Kleck's, Hemenway's, or some other assumptions are correct. The committee is not aware of any factual basis for drawing conclusions one way or the other about reporting errors.

Nonresponse

While inaccurate response has received a great deal of speculative attention, the problem of nonresponse has hardly been noticed.[7] Nonresponse is a problem in survey sampling, but it is especially problematic in the firearms use phone surveys like the NSDS. Although not completely re-

---

[7]Both Duncan (2000b) and Hemenway (1997a) recognize the potential problems created by nonresponse in the firearms use surveys.

vealed by Kleck and Gertz (1995), the response rate in the NSDS appears to lie somewhere between 14 and 61 percent.[8] The response rate in the NCVS survey is substantially higher, at around 95 percent.

Survey data are uninformative about the behavior of nonrespondents. Thus, these data do not identify prevalence unless one makes untestable assumptions about nonrespondents. A simple example illustrates the problem. Suppose that 1,000 individuals are asked whether they used a firearm defensively during the past year but that 500 do not respond, so the nonresponse rate is 50 percent. If 5 of the 500 respondents used guns defensively during the past year, then the prevalence of defensive gun use among respondents is 5/500 = 1 percent. However, true prevalence among the 1,000 surveyed individuals depends on how many of the nonrespondents used a firearm. If none did, then true prevalence is 5/1,000 = 0.5 percent. If all did, then true prevalence is [(5 + 500)/1,000] = 50.5 percent. If between 0 and 500 nonrespondents used a firearm defensively, then true prevalence is between 0.5 and 50.5 percent. Thus, in this example, nonresponse causes true prevalence to be uncertain within a range of 50 percent.

Prevalence rates can be identified if one makes sufficiently strong assumptions about the behavior of nonrespondents. In the DGU literature, nonresponse is assumed to be random, thus implying that that prevalence among nonrespondents is the same as prevalence among respondents. The committee is not aware of any empirical evidence that supports the view that nonresponse is random or, for that matter, evidence to the contrary.

External Validity

A number of scholars have suggested that results from the NSDS and other firearms use surveys are difficult to reconcile with analogous statistics

---

[8]Kleck and Gertz report that 61 percent of contacts with persons for the NSDS resulted in a completed interview. Presumably, however, there were also many households in the original sampling scheme that were not contacted. For example, using data from the National Study of Private Firearms Ownership (NSPFO), a national phone survey designed to elicit information about firearms ownership and use, Cook and Ludwig (1998) report that 29,917 persons were part of the original sampling scheme, of which 15,948 were determined to be ineligible (phones not working, not residential, etc.), 3,268 were determined to be eligible, and the remaining 10,701 were unknown (e.g., no answer, answering machine, busy, etc.). Of the 3,268 that were known to be eligible, 2,568 provided complete interviews, for a response rate of 79 percent among contacted households. The 10,701 with unknown eligibility status must also be accounted for. If none of these households was actually eligible, than the true response rate would be 79 percent. If, however, all of these are eligible, then the true rate would be 18 percent [2,568/(10,701 + 3,268)]. Thus, the response rate in the NSPOF lies between 18 and 79 percent. If the response rates are consistent across the two surveys, the lower bound response rate for the NSDS would be 14 percent [(0.61/0.79)*0.18].

on crime and injury found in other data. For example, Hemenway (1997a) points out that results from the NSDS imply that firearms are used defensively in every burglary committed in occupied households and in nearly 60 percent of rapes and sexual assaults committed against persons over 18 years of age; that defensive gun users thought they wounded or killed offenders in 207,000 incidents, yet only 100,000 people are treated in emergency rooms for nonfatal firearms injuries; and that hundreds of thousands of persons almost certainly would have been killed if they had not used a firearm defensively, implying that nearly all potentially fatal attacks are successfully defended against (Cook and Ludwig, 1998). Cook and Ludwig (1998), Hemenway (1997a), and others argue that these and other similar comparisons lead to "completely implausible conclusions" and go on to suggest that these inconsistencies "only buttress the presumption of massive overestimation" of defensive gun uses in the NSDS (Hemenway, 1997a:1444).

Although potentially troubling, the strong conclusion drawn about the reliability and accuracy of the DGU estimates seems premature. In some cases, it may be that the comparison statistic is subject to error. The reported prevalence of rape in the NCVS, for example, is believed to be biased substantially downward (National Research Council, 2003). More importantly, however, evidence on the apparent biases of the estimated incident rates, wounding rates, and counts of averted injuries does not directly pertain to the accuracy of the DGU estimates. Kleck and Gertz (1995), in fact, note that victimization estimates drawn using the NSDS, a survey designed to measure firearms use rather than victimization, are subject to potential reporting errors in unknown directions. Cook and Ludwig (1998) find evidence of reporting errors of crime in the firearms use surveys, with many respondents reporting that crime was involved on one hand, yet that no crime was involved on the other. Likewise, questions about whether a respondent thought he wounded or killed the offender and those eliciting subjective information on what would have happened had a gun not been used are also subject to substantial reporting biases. As noted by Kleck and Gertz (1998), respondents may be inclined to "remember with favor their marksmanship" and may tend to exaggerate the seriousness of the event.

In addition to invalid response errors, sampling variability may also play an important role in these conditional comparisons. Inferences drawn from the relatively small subsamples of persons who report using firearms defensively (N = 213 in the NSDS) are subject to high degrees of sampling error. Using data from the National Study of Private Firearms Ownership, a survey similar to the NSDS, Cook and Ludwig (1998), for example, estimate that firearms were used defensively in 322,000 rapes (rape, attempted rape, sexual assault) but report a 95 percent confidence interval of

[12,000 to 632,000].[9] The lower bound interval estimate would imply that firearms are used defensively in less than 3 percent of all rapes and sexual assaults (Kleck, 2001a).

Replication and Recommendations

As indicated above, the estimated numbers of defensive gun uses found using the NSDS have been reproduced (i.e., are statistically indistinguishable) in many other surveys. Kleck (2001a:270) suggests that replication provides ample evidence of the validity of the findings in the NSDS survey:

> The hypothesis that many Americans use guns for self-protection each year has been repeatedly subjected to empirical test, using the only feasible method for doing so, survey of representative samples of the populations. The results of nineteen consecutive surveys unanimously indicate that each year huge numbers of Americans (700,000 or more) use guns for self-protection. Further, the more technically sound the survey, the higher the defensive gun use estimates. The entire body of evidence cannot be rejected based on the speculation that all surveys share biases that, on net, cause an over estimation of defensive gun use frequency because, ignoring fallacious reasoning, there is no empirical evidence to support this novel theory. At this point, it is fair to say that no intellectually serious challenge has been mounted to the case for defensive gun use being very frequent.

Certainly, the numerous surveys reveal some phenomena. In light of the differences in coverage and potential response errors, however, what exactly these surveys measure remains uncertain. Ultimately, the committee found no comfort in numbers: the existing surveys do not resolve the ongoing questions about response problems and do not change the fact that different subpopulations are queried. Mere repetition does not eliminate bias (Rosenbaum, 2001; Hemenway, 1997a).

However, the committee strongly agrees with the main sentiment expressed by Kleck and others. Evidence from self-reported surveys will invariably be subject to concerns over reporting errors and other biases. Still, we can hope to have a greater degree of confidence in the survey results by relying on replications and survey sampling experiments that serve to effectively reduce the degree of uncertainty about the true prevalence rate. The objective of these experiments should be consistency of results in a variety of sampling designs. Replications and experiments should disrupt aspects of the original study to check whether the prevalence estimate is reproduced or altered under different survey designs. Effective replications will vary the

---

[9]Kleck and Gertz (1995) do not report confidence intervals for these conditional estimates.

nature of the potential biases in order to explicitly reduce, rather than increase, the prospects of reproducing the original results (Rosenbaum, 2001).

These ideas are not new to this controversial literature. McDowall et al. (2000) do exactly this type of experimental evaluation by holding certain factors constant—namely, the sampling methodology—but varying the content of the questionnaire. Other similar experiments or replications or both could be used to vary the nature of memory telescoping, social presentation bias, and other plausible factors that might influence reporting behaviors. In fact, Cook and Ludwig (1998), Smith (1997), Kleck (2000), and many others make numerous recommendations for experiments or replications.

The committee strongly believes that these types of studies can and should be undertaken. Without reliable information, researchers will continue to be forced to make unsubstantiated assumptions about the validity of responses and thus about the prevalence of defensive gun use.

The committee recommends a systematic and rigorous research program to (1) clearly define and understand what is being measured, (2) understand inaccurate response in the national use surveys, and (3) develop methods to reduce reporting errors to the extent possible. Well-established survey sampling methods can and should be brought to bear to evaluate the response problems. Understanding response will be useful for not only explaining the striking gap in DGU estimates but, more importantly, understanding defensive gun use.

EFFICACY OF SELF-DEFENSE WITH A FIREARM

Accurate measurement on the extent of firearms use is the first step for beginning a constructive dialogue on how firearms are used in American society. Invariably, however, attention will turn to the more important and difficult questions about the consequences of using a firearm for self-defense. How effective are firearms at preventing injury and crime? Would gun users have been better off (on average) using alternative defensive strategies? How does the efficacy of self-defense vary by circumstance (e.g., abilities of victim and perpetrator, location of crime, weaponry)?

Answering these questions is essential for evaluating the costs and benefits of firearms to society. For example, if using a firearm defensively is no more effective than basic avoidance techniques, then defensive gun use would have no relative benefit. In contrast, if firearms are more effective at resisting crime and injury than alternative methods, then civilian ownership and the use of firearms may play a vital role in the nation's ability to deter and fight crime. Of course, the benefits of defensive gun use must ultimately be weighed against the potential costs that may arise if firearms are involved in the final stages of violent criminal encounters: defensive gun use may lead to relatively higher risks of injury and death to victims or offend-

TABLE 5-2 Probability of Injury and Loss Among Victims by Means of Self-Protection

| Method | Robbery | | Assault |
	Injury	Loss	Injury
With gun	12.8	15.2	27.9
All self-protection	34.0	52.8	58.1
No self-protection	23.6	83.6	55.2
All incidents	30.2	69.9	57.4

SOURCE: Adapted from Kleck (2001b:289, Table 7.1).

ers. Finally, both the benefits and costs must be evaluated within the context of offender weaponry. If criminals were not armed, would firearms be more or less useful for protecting potential victims? If the efficacy of self-defense depends on the number of firearms in society, then partial equilibrium analyses that hold offender weaponry fixed may not answer the right questions.

Empirical Evidence

While the literature on self-defense has been preoccupied with the basic measurement questions, a handful of studies assess the efficacy of defensive gun use.[10] Using data from the NCVS, Kleck (2001b) compares the probability of injury and crime by different defensive actions. The results, summarized in Table 5-2, suggest that respondents who use firearms are less likely to be injured and lose property than those using other modes of protection. For example, while the overall rate of injury in robbery is 30.2, only 12.8 percent of those using a firearm for self-protection were injured. Ziegenhagen and Brosnan (1985) draw similar conclusions about the efficacy of armed (although not firearm) resistance when summarizing 13 city victim surveys. Using a multivariate regression analysis, Kleck and DeLone (1993) confirm these basic cross-tabular findings.[11] Defense with a firearm is associated with

---

[10]A number of studies use samples of data collected from crimes reported to police. Police records are presumed to understate resistance in general and defensive gun use in particular (Kleck, 2001a; Kleck and DeLone, 1993). More importantly, these surveys cannot reveal successful forms of resistance that are not reported to the police at all.

[11]The committee is not aware of other multivariate analyses of the effects of resistance with a firearm on crime and injury. Researchers have, however, evaluated the effects of armed resistance. Using data from the NCVS, Kleck and Sayles (1990) conclude that rapes are less likely to be completed if the victim uses armed resistance. Lizotte (1986) draws similar conclusions using data from city victim surveys.

fewer completed robberies and less injury. Two forms of self-defense, namely using force without a weapon and trying to get help or attract attention, are associated with higher injury rates than taking no self-protective action.

The results suggest interesting associations: victims who use guns defensively are less likely to be harmed than those using other forms of self-protection. Whether these findings reflect underlying causal relationships or spurious correlations remains uncertain. Much of the existing evidence reports simple bivariate correlations, without controlling for any confounding factors. Kleck and DeLone (1993) rely on multivariate linear regression methods that implicitly assume that firearms use, conditional on observed factors, is statistically independent of the unobserved factors influencing the outcomes, as would be the case in a classical randomized experiment.[12] Is this exogenous selection assumption reasonable? Arguably, the decisions to own, carry, and use a firearm for self-defense are very complex, involving both individual and environmental factors that are related to whether a crime is attempted, as well as the outcomes of interest.[13] The ability of a person to defend himself or herself, attitudes toward violence and crime, emotional well-being, and neighborhood characteristics may all influence whether a person uses a firearm and the resulting injury and crime. Thus, in general, it is difficult to be confident that the control variables account for the numerous confounding factors that may result in spurious correlations. Furthermore, the committee is not aware of any research that considers whether the finding is robust to a variety of methodological adjustments. Without an established body of research assessing whether the findings are robust to the choice of covariates, functional form, and other modeling assumptions, it is difficult to assess the credibility of the research to date.

The most obvious and fundamental limitation, however, is that the data on defensive gun uses are, as described above, potentially error ridden. Without reliable information on the prevalence of defensive gun use, researchers are forced to make implausible and unsubstantiated assumptions about the accuracy of self-reported measures of resistance. For example, Kleck, one of the most vocal critics of DGU estimates derived from the NCVS, assumes these data are fully accurate when measuring the efficacy of resistance (Kleck, 2001b; Kleck and DeLone, 1993).

---

[12]Kleck and DeLone (1993) account for basic demographic characteristics of the victim (e.g., race, gender, age, income, and education) and some details on the event (e.g, whether the offender had a gun).

[13]Not only does the potential of unobserved factors create biases of unknown magnitude, but it is also difficult to determine the direction of these biases. If, as suggested by the National Research Council (1993:266), persons who use firearms were better prepared in general to defend against crime, then the estimated associations would be biased upward. In contrast, if firearms are used in more dangerous situations, then the estimated associations would be biased downward (Kleck, 2001b:292).

The response problems described above, however, cannot be ignored. To the contrary, these measurement problems may lead to substantial biases in unknown directions. If, for example, respondents are inclined to report being victimized when a crime is "successful" but conceal unsuccessful crimes, the estimated efficacy of resistance will be biased downward. In contrast, if respondents, concerned about being perceived as inept, are inclined to report successful forms of resistance but conceal ineffective forms, the estimated efficacy of self-defense will be biased upward. Without better information on the nature and extent of response problems, it is impossible to know whether and how the estimated associations between defensive gun use, crime, and injury are biased. If, as Kleck and Gertz (1995) suggest, the NCVS misses over 2 million defensive uses per year, then biases caused by reporting errors may be substantial.

Subjective Assessments

Subjective assessments on the efficacy of defensive gun use have been elicited in both the NCVS and the NSDS. Data from the 1994 NCVS, for example, reveal that 65 percent of victims felt that self-defense improved their situation, while 9 percent thought that it worsened their situation (Kleck, 2001a). More direct counterfactual questions were asked in the NSDS survey, in which respondents who reported using a firearm were asked (Kleck and Gertz, 1995:316):

> If you had *not* used a gun for protection in this incident, how likely do you think it is that you or someone else would have been *killed*? Would you say almost certainly not, probably not, might have, probably would have, or almost certainly would have been killed?

Nearly half of respondents perceived that someone might, probably, or almost certainly would have been killed.

Although intriguing, these assessments are of limited value. Certainly, there are obvious concerns about inaccurate reporting associated with subjective questions. Victims may be inclined to view their actions as effective regardless and may exaggerate counterfactual outcomes. Even if victims report truthfully, the existing questionnaires provide little guidance. What does a respondent mean when he states that someone might have been killed? Are all respondents using consistent criteria to interpret these questions?

Firearms and Fatalities

A number of researchers have attempted to infer the defensive utility of firearms by examining the firearms deaths that occur in or near the victim's home. Both Kellermann and Reay (1986) and Rushforth et al. (1974) compare fatalities caused by self-defense and other motivations. Both studies find that people using guns in self-defense account for a small fraction of fatalities in the home. Kellermann and Reay find that there were nearly 5 times as many homicides and 37 times as many suicides as perpetrators killed in self-defense. They go on to conclude, "The advisability of keeping a firearm in the home for protection must be questioned." Rushforth et al. (1974) found similar results and drew similar conclusions.

Although the facts are in no doubt, the conclusions do not seem to follow. Certainly, effective defensive gun use need not ever lead the perpetrator to be wounded or killed. Rather, to assess the benefits of self-defense, one needs to measure crime and injury averted. The particular outcome of an offender is of little relevance. It might be, as Kleck (2001b) suggests, that the ratio of firearm-caused fatalities to fatalities averted because of defensive gun use is a more relevant comparison. Answering this question, however, requires researchers to address the fundamental counterfactual questions regarding the effects of both defensive and offensive uses of firearms that have been the subject of much of this report and have generally proved to be elusive. Simple death counts cannot answer these complex questions.

Case-control sampling schemes matching homicide victims to non-victims with similar characteristics have also been used to infer whether owning a firearm is a risk factor for homicide and the utility of firearms for self-defense (see Chapter 7 for a discussion of the case-control methodology). Kellermann et al. (1993) found that persons who had a firearm in the home were at a greater risk for homicide in their home than persons who did not have a firearm (adjusted odds ratio of 2.7). Cummings et al. (1997) found that persons who purchased a handgun were at greater risk for homicide than their counterparts who had no such history (adjusted odds ratio of 2.2).

In light of these findings, Kellermann et al. (1993) ultimately conclude that owning firearms for personal protection is "counterproductive," (p. 1087) and that "people should be strongly discouraged from keeping guns in the home" (p. 1090). This conclusion rests on the implicit assumption that the decision to own a firearm is random or exogenous with respect to homicide in the home (after controlling for various observed factors, including whether a household member has been hurt in a fight, has been arrested, or has used illicit drugs). Cummings and his colleagues (1997) do not draw such strong causal conclusions, but instead simply describe the observed positive association between firearms and homicide.

In the committee's view, the exogenous selection assumption and the resulting conclusions are not tenable. While these observed associations between firearms ownership and homicide may be of interest, they do little to reveal the impact of firearms on homicide or the utility of firearms for self-defense. As noted by the authors, even small degrees of misreporting on ownership by either the cases or the controls can create substantial biases in the estimated risk factors (see Kleck, 1997, for an illustration of these biases). A more fundamental inferential problem arises from the fact that ownership is not likely to be random with respect to homicide or other forms of victimization. To the contrary, the decision to own a firearm may be directly related to the likelihood of being victimized. People may, for instance, acquire firearms in response to specific or perceived threats, and owners may be more or less psychologically prone toward violence. Thus, while the observed associations may reflect a casual albeit unspecified pathway, they may also be entirely spurious. As Kellermann and his colleagues note (1993:1089), "it is possible that reverse causation accounted for some of the association we observed between gun ownership and homicide."

6

Right-to-Carry Laws

This chapter is concerned with the question of whether violent crime is reduced through the enactment of *right-to-carry-laws,* which allow individuals to carry concealed weapons.[1] In all, 34 states have right-to-carry laws that allow qualified adults to carry concealed handguns. Proponents of these laws argue that criminals are deterred by the knowledge that potential victims may be carrying weapons and therefore that the laws reduce crime. However, it is not clear a priori that such deterrence occurs. Even if it does, there may be offsetting adverse consequences. For example, increased possession of firearms by potential victims may motivate more criminals to carry firearms and thereby increase the amount of violence that is associated with crime. Moreover, allowing individuals to carry concealed weapons may increase accidental injuries or deaths or increase shootings during arguments. Ultimately, it is an empirical question whether allowing individuals to carry concealed weapons generates net social benefits or net social costs.

The statistical analysis of the effects of these laws was initiated by John Lott and David Mustard (1997) and expanded by Lott (2000) and Bronars and Lott (1998) (hereinafter referred to simply as Lott). Lott concludes that the adoption of right-to-carry laws substantially reduces the prevalence of violent crime. Many other researchers have carried out their own statistical analyses using Lott's data, modified versions of Lott's data, or expanded

---

[1]The laws are sometimes called *shall-issue* laws because they require local authorities to issue a concealed-weapons permit to any qualified adult who requests one. A qualified adult is one who does not have a significant criminal record or history of mental illness. The definition of a nonqualified adult varies among states but includes adults with prior felony convictions, drug charges, or commitments to mental hospitals.

data sets that cover the more recent time period not included in the original analysis.[2]

Because the right-to-carry issue is highly controversial, has received much public attention, and has generated a large volume of research, the committee has given it special attention in its deliberations. This chapter reviews the existing empirical evidence on the issue. We also report the results of our own analyses of the data. We conclude that, in light of (a) the sensitivity of the empirical results to seemingly minor changes in model specification, (b) a lack of robustness of the results to the inclusion of more recent years of data (during which there are many more law changes than in the earlier period), and (c) the imprecision of some results, it is impossible to draw strong conclusions from the existing literature on the causal impact of these laws. Committee member James Q. Wilson has written a dissent that applies to Chapter 6 only (Appendix A), and the committee has written a response (Appendix B).

DESCRIPTION OF THE DATA AND METHODS

Researchers studying the effects of right-to-carry laws have used many different models. However, all of the analyses rely on similar data and methodologies. Accordingly, we do not attempt to review and evaluate each of the models used in this literature. Instead, we describe the common data used and

---

[2]Two other general responses to Lott's analysis deserve brief mention. First, some critics have attempted to discredit Lott's findings on grounds of the source of some of his funding (the Olin Foundation), the methods by which some of his results were disseminated (e.g., some critics have claimed, erroneously, that Lott and Mustard, 1997, was published in a student-edited journal that is not peer reviewed), and positions that he has taken on other public policy issues related to crime control. Much of this criticism is summarized and responded to in Chapter 7 of Lott (2000). The committee's view is that these criticisms are not helpful for evaluating Lott's data, methods, or conclusions. Lott provides his data and computer programs to all who request them, so it is possible to evaluate his methods and results directly. In the committee's view, Lott's funding sources, methods of disseminating his results, and opinions on other issues do not provide further information about the quality of his research on right-to-carry laws.

A second group of critics have argued that Lott's results lack credibility because they are inconsistent with various strongly held a priori beliefs or expectations. For example, Zimring and Hawkins (1997:59) argue that "large reductions in violence [due to right-to-carry laws] are quite unlikely because they would be out of proportion to the small scale of the change in carrying firearms that the legislation produced." The committee agrees that it is important for statistical evidence to be consistent with established facts, but there are no such facts about whether right-to-carry laws can have effects of the magnitudes that Lott claims. The beliefs or expectations of Lott's second group of critics are, at best, hypotheses whose truth or falsehood can only be determined empirically. Moreover, Lott (2000) has argued that there are ways to reconcile his results with the beliefs and expectations of the critics. This does not necessarily imply that Lott is correct and his critics are wrong. The correctness of Lott's arguments is also an empirical question about which there is little evidence. Rather, it shows that little can be decided through argumentation over a priori beliefs and expectations.

focus on the common methodological basis for all of them. In particular, we use the results presented in Tables 4.1 and 4.8 of Lott (2000) to illustrate the discussion. We refer to these as the "dummy variable" and "trend" model estimates, respectively. Arguably, these tables, which are reproduced in Table 6-1 and Table 6-2, contain the most important results in this literature.

Data

The basic data set used in the literature is a county-level panel on annual crime rates, along with the values of potentially relevant explanatory variables. Early studies estimated models on data for 1977-1992, while more recent studies (as well as our replication exercise below) use data up to 2000. Between 1977 and 1992, 10 states adopted right-to-carry laws.[3] A total of 8 other states adopted right-to-carry laws before 1977. Between 1992 and 1999, 16 additional states adopted such laws.

The data on crime rates were obtained from the FBI's Uniform Crime Reports (UCR). Explanatory variables employed in studies include the arrest rate for the crime category in question, population density in the county, real per capita income variables, county population, and variables for the percent of population that is in each of many race-by-age-by-gender categories. The data on explanatory variables were obtained from a variety of sources (Lott, 2000: Appendix 3).

Although most studies use county-level panels on crime rates and demographic variables, the actual data files used differ across studies in ways that sometimes affect the estimates. The data set used in the original Lott study has been lost, although Lott reconstructed a version of the data, which he made available to other researchers as well as the committee. This data set, which we term the "revised original data set," covers the period 1977-1992.[4] More recently, Lott has made available a data set covering the

---

[3]There is some disagreement over when and whether particular states have adopted right-to-carry laws. Lott and Mustard, for example, classify North Dakota and South Dakota as having adopted such laws prior to 1977, but Vernick and Hepburn (2003) code these states as having adopted them in 1985. Likewise, Lott and Mustard classify Alabama and Connecticut as right-to-carry states adopting prior to 1977, yet Vernick codes these states as not having right-to-carry laws. See Ayres and Donohue (2003a:1300) for a summary of the coding conventions on the adoption dates of right-to-carry laws.

[4]There are 3,054 counties observed over 16 years in the revised original data. In the basic specifications, there are a number of sample restrictions, the most notable of which is to drop all counties with no reported arrest rate (i.e., counties with no reported crime). This restricts the sample to approximately 1,650 counties per year (or approximately 26,000 county-year observations). In specifications that do not involve the arrest rate, Lott treats zero crime as 0.1 so as not to take the log of 0. Black and Nagin (1998) further restrict the sample to counties with populations of at least 100,000, which limits the sample to 393 counties per year. In some regressions, Duggan (2001) and Plassmann and Tideman (2001) estimate models that include data on the over 2,900 counties per year with nonmissing crime data.

period 1977-2000 that corrects acknowledged errors in data files used by Plassmann and Whitley (2003). We term this file the *"revised new data set."* [5] We make use of both of these data sets in our replication exercises.

Dummy Variable Model

For expository purposes it is helpful to begin by discussing the dummy variable model without "control" variables.[6] The model (in Lott, 2000: Table 4.1) allows each county to have its own crime level in each category. Moreover, the crime rate is allowed to vary over time in a pattern that is common across all counties in the United States. The effect of a right-to-carry law is measured as a change in the level of the crime rate in a jurisdiction following the jurisdiction's adoption of the law. Any estimate of a policy effect requires an assumption about the "counterfactual," in this case what would have happened to crime rates in the absence of the change in the law. The implicit assumption underlying this simple illustrative dummy variable model is that, in the absence of the change in the law, the crime rate in each county would, on average, have been the county mean plus a time-period adjustment reflecting the common trend in crime rates across all counties.

Dummy variable models estimated in the literature are slightly more complicated than the above-described model. First, they typically include control variables that attempt to construct a more realistic counterfactual. For example, if crime rates vary over time with county economic conditions, then one can construct a more credible estimate of what would have happened in the absence of the law change by including the control variables as a determinant of the crime rate. Most estimates in the literature use a large number of control variables, including local economic conditions, age-gender population composition, as well as arrest rates.

Second, some estimates in the literature model the time pattern of crime differently. In particular, some studies allow each region of the country to have its own time pattern, thereby assuming that in the absence of the law change, counties in nearby states would have the same time pattern of crime rates in a crime category. We term this the "region-interacted time pattern model," in contrast to the "common time pattern" dummy variable model above.

---

[5]These data were downloaded by the committee from www.johnlott.org on August 22, 2003.

[6]This no-control model is often used as a way to assess whether there is an association between the outcome (crime) and the law change in the data. The committee estimates and evaluates this model below (see Tables 6-5 and 6-6, columns 2 and 3).

Mathematically, the common time pattern dummy variable model takes the form

$$(6.1) \quad Y_{it} = \sum_{t=1977}^{1992} \alpha_t YEAR_t + \beta X_{it} + \delta LAW_{it} + \gamma_i + \varepsilon_{it} \ ,$$

where Y_{it} is the natural logarithm of the number of crimes per 100,000 population in county i and year t, $YEAR_t = 1$ if the year is t and $YEAR_t = 0$ otherwise, X_{it} is a set of control variables that potentially influence crime rates, $LAW_{it} = 1$ if a right-to-carry law was in effect in county i and year t and $LAW_{it} = 0$ otherwise, γ_i is a constant that is specific to county i, and ε_{it} is an unobserved random variable. The quantities α_t, β, and δ are coefficients that are estimated by fitting the model to data. The coefficient δ measures the percentage change in crime rates due to the adoption of right-to-carry laws. For example, if $\delta = -0.05$ then the implied estimate of the adoption of a right-to-carry law is to reduce the crime rate by 5 percent. The coefficients α_t measure common time patterns across counties in crime rates that are distinct from the enactment of right-to-carry laws or other variables of the model.

The vector X_{it} includes the control variables that may influence crime rates, such as indicators of income and poverty levels; the density, age distribution, and racial composition of a county's population; arrest rates; and indicators of the size of the police force. The *county fixed effect* γ_i captures systematic differences across counties that are not accounted for by the other variables of the model and do not vary over time. The values of the parameters α_t, β, and δ are estimated separately for each of several different types of crimes. Thus, the model accounts for the possibility that right-to-carry laws may affect different crimes differently.

Trend Model

While the dummy variable model measures the effect of the adoption of a right-to-carry law as a one-time shift in crime rates, one can alternatively estimate the effect as the change in time trends. The following trend model, which generated the results in Lott's Table 4.8, allows right-to-carry laws to affect trends in crime:

$$(6.2) \quad Y_{it} = \sum_{t=1977}^{1992} \alpha_t YEAR_t + \beta X_{it} + \delta_B YRBEF_{it} + \delta_A YRAFT_{it} + \gamma_i + \varepsilon_{it}$$

In this model, $YRBEF_{it}$ is a variable equal to 0 if year t is after the adoption of a right-to-carry law and the number of years until adoption if year t precedes adoption. $YRAFT_{it}$ is 0 if year t precedes adoption of a right-to-carry law and is the number of years since adoption of the law otherwise. The other variables are defined as in Model 6.1. The effect of adoption on the trend in crime is measured by $\delta_A - \delta_B$.

The interpretation of the "trend" model is slightly complicated, since the model already includes year effects to accommodate the time pattern of crime common across all counties. To see what this model does, consider a more flexible model with a series of separate dummy variables, for each number of years prior to—and following—the law change for adopting states (see the figures illustrating the section later in the chapter called "Extending the Baseline Specification to 2000"). Thus, for example, a variable called *shall_issue_minus_1* is 1 if the observation corresponds to a county in a state that adopts the law in the following year, 0 otherwise. Similarly, *shall_issue_plus_5* is 1 if the observation corresponds to a county in a state that adopted five years ago, 0 otherwise. And so on.

The coefficient on each of these variables shows how adopting states' time patterns of crime rates move, relative to the national time pattern, surrounding the respective states' law adoption. Note that the time pattern in question is not calendar time but rather time relative to local law adoption, which occurs in different calendar years in different places.

The trend model in equation 6.2 constrains the adopting states' deviations to fall on two trend lines, one for years before and one for years after adoption. Thus, the model restricts the yearly movements in the deviations to fall on trend lines with break points at the time of law adoption.

STATISTICAL ANALYSES OF RIGHT-TO-CARRY LAWS

In this section, we review the basic empirical findings on the effects of right-to-carry laws. We begin with a discussion of Lott's original estimates of Models 6.1 and 6.2 and the committee's efforts to replicate these findings. We then discuss results from other studies that estimate the effects of right-to-carry laws on crime.

Lott's Results

Table 6-1 (first row) displays Lott's estimates from Model 6.1. Lott finds that where they have been adopted, right-to-carry laws have reduced homicide by about 8 percent, rapes by about 5 percent, and aggravated assaults by about 7 percent (Lott, 2000:51). Lott also finds that adoption of right-to-carry laws may increase the rates of nonviolent property crimes (burglary, larceny, auto theft). In theory, this is possible, as criminals substitute away from crimes that involve contact with victims toward crimes that do not involve encounters with victims.

Rows 2 and 3 of Table 6-1 report the results of the committee's replication of these estimates. In row 2, we use the *revised original data set* and Lott's computer programs. The committee was unable to replicate Lott's estimate of the reduction in the murder rate, although the estimates are

TABLE 6-1 Dummy Variable Model with Common Time Pattern, Original and Revised Data[a]

	Sample	Years	Violent Crime	Murder	Rape
1. Lott (2000)	Original 1992	1992	−4.9%	−7.7%	−5.3%
2. Committee replication	Revised 1992[b]	1992	−4.91	−7.30	−5.27
SE			(0.98)**	(1.57)**	(1.22)**
3. Committee replication	Revised 2000[c]	1992	−1.76	−9.01	−5.38
SE			(1.07)	(1.70)**	(1.33)**

[a]The regressions use the covariates and specification from the original Lott and Mustard (1997) models that do not control for state poverty, unemployment, death penalty execution rates, or regional time trends. The controls include the arrest rate for the crime category in question (AOVIOICP), population density in the county, real per capita income variables (RPCPI RPCUI RPCIM RPCRPO), county population (POPC), and variables for the percentage of the population that is in each of many race x age x gender categories (e.g., PBM1019 is the percentage of the population that is black, male, and between ages 10 and 19). The "no

close and consistent with the conclusion that right-to-carry laws reduce the incidence of murder. Through communication with Lott, the committee learned that the data used to construct Table 4.1 of Lott (2000) were lost and that the data supplied to the committee are a reconstruction and not necessarily identical to the original data.

Row 3 displays estimates using the *revised new data set* restricted to period 1977-1992. The estimates from these revised data are substantially different from those originally reported by Lott (2000). In the dummy variable model, the magnitude of the estimated reduction in the rates of violent crime and aggravated assault was reduced, the estimated reduction in the murder rate increased, and the sign of the estimated effects of right-to-carry laws on robbery reversed. Moreover, the effects of right-to-carry laws on violent crime are no longer statistically significantly different from zero at the 5 percent significance level. Finally, the estimated increase in the rates of all property crimes increased substantially.

Table 6-2 presents estimates of the trend model. The first row displays Lott's estimates. Lott finds the passage of right-to-carry laws to be associated with changes in the crime trend. He finds a 0.9 percent reduction in the annual rate of growth of violent crime overall, and a 0.6 percent reduction in the rate of growth of property crimes. Row 2 of Table 6-2 shows the committee's attempt to replicate Lott's results using the *revised original data set*. The committee was unable to replicate most of the results in Lott's Table 4.8. Through communication with Lott, the committee learned that

Aggravated Assault	Robbery	Property Crimes	Auto Theft	Burglary	Larceny
–7.0%	–2.2%	2.7%	7.1%	0.05%	3.3%
–7.01 (1.14)**	–2.21 (1.33)	2.69 (0.72)**	7.14 (1.14)**	0.05 (0.76)	3.34 (0.89)**
–5.60 (1.25)**	1.17 (1.45)	5.84 (0.76)**	10.28 (1.24)**	4.12 (0.83)**	6.82 (0.82)**

controls" specification" includes county fixed effects, year dummies, and the dummy for whether the state has a right-to-carry law.

   [b]Using Lott's reconstruction of his original 1977-1992 data.

   [c]Using the revised new data set, which contains observations, 1977-2000, even though the estimates in this row use data only through 1992.

NOTE: All samples start in 1977. SE = standard error. Standard errors are in parentheses, where * = significant at 5% and ** = significant at 1%.

this is because there are many misprints in Table 4.8. Nonetheless, Lott's and the committee's results have the same signs for all crimes except aggravated assault. Row 3 displays estimates using the *revised new data set* restricted to the period 1977-1992. These new results tend to show larger reductions in the violent crime trends than those found using the revised original data.

Other Statistical Evaluations of Right-to-Carry Laws

Researchers have estimated the effects of right-to-carry laws using Lott's or related data and models. Many of these studies have found that the use of plausible alternative data, control variables, specifications, or methods of computing standard errors, weakens or reverses the results. Tables 6-3 and 6-4 display estimates from selected studies that illustrate variability in the findings about the effects of right-to-carry laws. The committee does not endorse particular findings or consider them to provide better estimates of the effects of right-to-carry laws than do Lott's results. Moreover, the committee recognizes that several independent investigators have used alternative models or data to obtain results that are consistent with Lott's. These investigators include Bartley and Cohen (1998) and Moody (2001). We focus on the conflicting results in this section because they illustrate a variability of the findings that is central to the committee's evaluation of their credibility.

TABLE 6-2 Trend Model with Common Time Pattern, 1977-1992[a]

	Sample	Years	Violent Crime	Murder	Rape
1. Lott (2000)	Original 1992	1992	−0.9%	−3.0%	−1.4%
2. Committee replication SE	Revised 1992[b]	1992	−0.50 (0.41)	−4.25 (0.65)**	−1.37 (0.51)**
3. Committee replication SE	Revised 2000[c]	1992	−2.15 (0.39)**	−3.41 (0.62)**	−3.37 (0.48)**

[a]The regressions use the covariates and specification from the original Lott and Mustard (1997) models that do not control for state poverty, unemployment, death penalty execution rates, or regional time trends. The controls include the arrest rate for the crime category in question (AOVIOICP), population density in the county, real per capita income variables (RPCPI RPCUI RPCIM RPCRPO), county population (POPC), and variables for the percentage of the population that is in each of many race × age × gender categories (e.g., PBM1019 is the percentage of the population that is black, male, and between ages 10 and 19).

Control Variables and Specification

The most common modifications to Lott's original analyses of right-to-carry laws has been to assess the sensitivity of the findings to variation in the control variables or the specification of the model. Lott's basic model relies on dozens of controls, but concerns have been raised that some controls may be missing, others may be unnecessary, and still others may be endogenous (that is, related to the unobserved determinates of county crime rates).

Duggan (2001), for example, raises concerns that county-level control variables may not be precisely measured on an annual basis and that the arrest rate control variable, which includes the crime rate in the denominator, may bias the estimates. In response to these concerns, Duggan estimated a simple dummy variable model that controls only for year and county fixed effects.[7] Duggan drops all other covariates from the model. When estimated on all county-year observations with nonmissing crime

---

[7]Duggan also changed the coding of the dates of adoption of right-to-carry laws, although this had only a minimal effect on the estimates. According to Duggan (2001) and others (see, for example, Ayres and Donohue, 2003a), there is an inconsistency in the coding used by Lott and Mustard. Duggan finds that in 8 of the 10 right-to-carry states, the adoption date is defined as the year the law was passed, but in 2 states, Florida and Georgia, the adoption date is set to the calendar year after the law was passed. Lott, in personal communications, maintains that the dates are coded correctly. The committee does not take a stand on which coding is correct.

Aggravated Assault	Robbery	Property Crimes	Auto Theft	Burglary	Larceny
−0.5%	−2.7%	−0.6%	−0.1%	−0.3%	−1.5%
0.46	−2.72	−0.69	−0.31	−1.58	−0.11
(0.48)	(0.56)**	(0.30)*	(0.48)	(0.32)**	(0.37)
−2.63	−3.02	−1.13	0.25	−1.80	−0.84
(0.45)**	(0.53)**	(0.27)**	(0.45)	(0.30)**	(0.30)**

[b]Using Lott's reconstruction of his original 1977-1992 data.

[c]Using the revised new data set, which contains observations, 1977-2000, even though the estimates in this row use data only through 1992.

NOTE: All samples start in 1977. SE = standard error. Standard errors are in parentheses, where * = significant at 5% and ** = significant at 1%.

data, this reduced the magnitude of the estimated reduction in the rates of murder and aggravated assault, and it reversed the signs of the estimated effects of right-to-carry laws on rape, robbery, and all violent crime. That is, according to Duggan's estimates, adoption of right-to-carry laws increases the frequencies of rape, robbery, and violent crime as a whole. Moreover, Duggan found there is no statistically significant effect of right-to-carry laws on violent crimes (at the 5 percent significance level).

Other researchers have varied the specification of the model, allowing for the effects of right-to-carry laws to be more heterogeneous. Black and Nagin (1998), for example, estimated a dummy variable model in which the effects of right-to-carry laws are allowed to vary among states (that is, the coefficient δ is allowed to take different values for different states). Plassmann and Tideman (2001) estimate a nonlinear Poisson regression model with a restricted set of covariates, but otherwise similar to Model 6.1. Ayres and Donohue (2003a) combined Models 6.1 and 6.2, thereby obtaining a hybrid model in which adoption of right-to-carry laws can affect both the level and the trend of crime. The results from these analyses, which vary the way in which right-to-carry laws can effect crime, are highly variable, with some suggesting that the laws increase crime, others suggesting that they decrease crime, and many being statistically insignificant.

In Black and Nagin (1998), for example, only Florida has a statistically significant decrease in the murder rate following adoption of a right-to-carry law, and only West Virginia has a statistically significant increase in

TABLE 6-3 Summary of Selected Studies: Dummy Variable Model (percentage) (shaded cells indicate a positive coefficient)

Source	Modification	Violent Crime	Murder	Rape
Lott (2000)	Original specification and data	−5*	−8*	−5*
Moody	Unweighted	−6*	−4*	−5*
	State-level analysis	−11	15	−22*
Duggan[a]	County and time effects only	−1	−6	3
	All counties	0	−1	6
Black and Nagin	Large counties		−9*	−4
	Exclude Florida		−1	1
	Florida		−27.7*	−17*
	Georgia		−5.2	−5
	Idaho		−21	−10
	Maine		7.2	4
	Mississippi		5.4	32*
	Montana		−36.7	−97*
	Oregon		−5.9	4
	Pennsylvania		−8.9	4
	Virginia		3.9	−8
	West Virginia		72*	−29*
Plassmann and Tideman	No control for arrest rate		−7*	−6*
	All counties		−2	−5
	Count model (Poisson)		−11*	−4*
	Florida		−24*	−16*
	Georgia		−8*	−16*
	Idaho		−6	10*
	Maine		1	−2
	Mississippi		5	11*
	Montana		−7	−4
	Oregon		−10*	−2
	Pennsylvania		−5	14*
	Virginia		8*	−3
	West Virginia		5	−1
Ayres and Donohue (2003a)	State trends	0	−9*	−2
	1977-1997 data	2	0	3
	State level analysis			
	State and time effects only	−3	−8	−1
	1977-1999 data	9*	−2	6*
Plassmann and Whitley[a,b]	Regional trend + others			
	1977-2000 data	−3	−6*	−7*
Ayres and Donohue (2003b)[a,b]	Regional trends + other controls			
	1977-2000 corrected data	0	−4	−5

Aggravated Assault	Robbery	Property Crimes	Auto Theft	Burglary	Larceny
-7*	-2	3*	7*	0	3*
-9*	-1	3*	3	1	4*
-18*	-10	1	-9	4	3
-6	4	6*	9*	8*	5
-5	10	7*	11*	10*	5
-7*	-3				
-6*	-5				
-7	7				
-4	8				
-31*	-64*				
-52*	-33*				
-45*	10				
-71*	-14				
-17*	-4				
7*	-5				
-16*	-12				
-3	9				
	-1				
	2				
	6*				
	-3*				
	1				
	-41*				
	-22*				
	25*				
	-27*				
	-48*				
	-14*				
	-5*				
	-9*				
3	-8	-1*	-1*	-4*	1
7*	0	-1	4	1	4
-10	-5	7*	9*	9*	7*
4*	16*	16*	23*	14*	16*
-2	-5	4	9*	0	6
1	-3	6*	11*	2	8*

continued

TABLE 6-3 Continued

Source	Modification	Violent Crime	Murder	Rape
	Standard errors			
Lott (2000)	Unadjusted standard errors	0.98	1.57	1.22
Duggan	State clustered standard errors	2.31	2.95	2.32
Helland and Tabarrok	Placebo standard errors	4.9	6.4	5.6

[a]Uses clustered sampling standard errors.
[b]Added covariates for state poverty, unemployment, death penalty execution rates, and regional time trends.

TABLE 6-4 Summary of Selected Studies: Trend and Hybrid Variable Model (shaded cells indicate a positive coefficient)

Source	Modification	Violent Crime	Murder	Rape
Lott (2000)	Original specification and data	2*	–3*	–1*
Lott (2000)[a]	1977-1996	–2*	–2*	–3*
Ayres and Donohue (2003a)	Hybrid model: Level	7*	3	7*
	Trend	–2*	–5*	–3*
	1977-1997 data: Level	0	7*	6*
	Trend	–2*	–4*	–3*
Plassmann and Whitley[a,b]	Regional trend + others 1977-2000 data	–1	–2	–3*
Ayres and Donohue (2003b)[a,b]	Regional trends + other controls 1977-2000 corrected data	0	–2	–2

[a]Added covariates for state poverty, unemployment, death penalty execution rates, and regional time trends.
[b]Standard errors adjusted for state clustering.

its murder rate. The estimated changes in the murder rates of other states that adopted right-to-carry laws are sometimes positive (three cases) and sometimes negative (five cases) and are not statistically significantly different from zero. Black and Nagin also report variations in the directions and statistical significance of changes in the rates of rape and aggravated assault. They report no statistically significant increases in robberies, but only 2 of the 10 states that adopted right-to-carry laws had statistically signifi-

Aggravated Assault	Robbery	Property Crimes	Auto Theft	Burglary	Larceny
1.14	1.33	0.72	1.14	0.76	0.89
2.77	3.34	1.89	2.59	2.29	2.27
6.6	7.5	5.1	6.5	5.7	5.7

NOTES: Shaded cells indicate a positive coefficient estimate and * indicates the estimate is statistically significant at the 5% significance level. Unless otherwise noted, the standard errors are not adjusted for state-level clustering. Exceptions: Duggan, Plassmann and Tideman, Ayres and Donohue.

Aggravated Assault	Robbery	Property Crimes	Auto Theft	Burglary	Larceny
–1*	–3*	–1*	0*	–2*	0
–3*	–3*	–2*	–3*	–1*	–2*
10*	–3	0	0	–3	0
–2	–1	0	0	0	1
6*	4	–1	9*	4*	5*
–3*	–4*	0	–2*	–3*	–2*
–2	–3*	0	0	–2	–1
–1	–2	0	0	–1	0

NOTES: Shaded cells indicate a positive coefficient estimate and * indicates the estimate is statistically significant at the 5% significance level. Unless otherwise noted, the standard errors are not adjusted for state-level clustering. Exceptions: Duggan, Plassmann and Tideman, Ayres and Donohue.

cant decreases. In summary, according to Black and Nagin, adoption of a right-to-carry law may increase, decrease, or have no discernible effect on the crime rate depending on the crime and the state that are involved.[8]

---

[8]To avoid selection problems associated with using counties with positive crime rates, Black and Nagin also restricted their analysis to counties with populations of 100,000 or more. This was done to mitigate a possible bias arising from Lott's use of the arrest rate as an explanatory variable. The arrest rate is the number of arrests divided by the number of crimes

Plassmann and Tideman (2001) document similar variability in the estimates. To account for the fact that county-level crime data include a large number of observations for which the outcome variable equals zero, Plassmann and Tideman estimate a nonlinear count data model. Using data from all counties with reported crime figures, the resulting estimates on murder and rape are consistent with Lott's findings, but the sign of the estimated effect of right-to carry laws on robbery is reversed. Furthermore, when the effects of right-to-carry laws are allowed to vary among states, Plassmann and Tideman found that adoption of a right-to-carry law may increase, decrease, or have no effect on the crime rate depending on the crime and state that are involved. Consider, for example, murder. Right-to-carry laws are estimated to have a statistically significant decrease in the murder rate in Florida, Georgia, and Oregon following adoption of a right-to-carry law. Virginia has a statistically significant increase in its murder rate. The changes in the murder rates of other states that adopted right-to-carry laws are not statistically significantly different from zero. Plassmann and Tideman conclude by noting the fragility in the estimated effects of right-to-carry laws: "While this ambiguous result is somewhat discouraging, it is not very surprising. Whenever the theoretically possible and in practice plausible effects of public policy are ambiguous, it can be expected that the effects of such a policy will differ across localities that are clearly different from each other" (p. 797).

Finally, the added flexibility of the hybrid model estimated by Ayres and Donohue (2003a) produces estimation results that are different from Lott's.[9] The results found when using the revised original data (1977-

---

and is undefined in counties that report no crimes of the types analyzed. Therefore, these counties are not included in Lott's analysis. Because the denominator of the arrest rate variable contains the dependent variable in Lott's models, it is possible that dropping no-crime counties biases the results of his analysis. Nearly all of the low-crime counties have populations below 100,000. Therefore, use of only counties with larger populations largely overcomes the problem of missing arrest rate data without creating a bias.

Lott (1999:8-9; 2000:142-143), however, has argued that Black's and Nagin's results are unreliable because they eliminated 85 percent of the counties in the nation (all the counties with populations of less than 100,000). In particular, they used only one county in West Virginia. Lott (2000: Table 4.9) presents his own estimation results according to which his findings are largely unaffected by disaggregating the right-to-carry effect by state. However, Lott does not report the details of his analysis or the statistical significance levels of his estimates. Moreover, his response does not explain why Black and Nagin found statistically significant increases in some crime rates for some states following passage of right-to-carry laws.

[9]The committee takes no position on whether the hybrid model provides a correct description of crime levels or the effects of right-to-carry laws. The important feature of the hybrid model is that it nests Models 6.1 and 6.2.

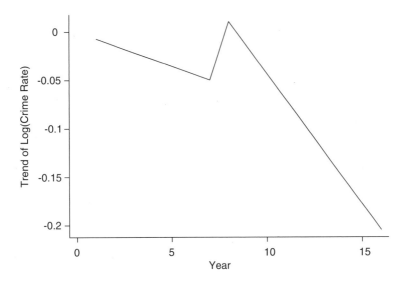

FIGURE 6-1 Trend in the logarithm of the violent crime rate.

1992) are illustrated in Figure 6-1, which shows the "relative trend" in the logarithm of the violent crime rate obtained from the Ayres and Donohue model for a hypothetical county in which a right-to-carry law is adopted in year 8. The relative trend is the difference between the crime trend in the adopting county and the trend in a nonadopting county with the same values of the explanatory variables X. According to the figure, adoption of the law increased the level of violent crime but accelerated a decreasing (relative) trend. Ayres and Donohue obtained similar results for rape and aggravated assault. For murder, the shift in the level is not statistically significant, but there is a statistically significant downward shift in the trend. There is no statistically significant effect on either the level or the trend for robbery and property crimes. Ayres and Donohue also report estimates from an expanded data set that includes the years 1977-1999. The results found using these data, which are reported in Table 6-4, are similar.

Updated Sample Endpoint

Several researchers, including Lott, have assessed whether the basic findings from Models 6.1 and 6.2 continue to hold when using more recent data. In the epilogue to the second edition of his book, Lott (2000: Table 9.1) analyzes data covering the period 1993-1996. Plassmann and Whitley (2003) use data through 2000. In addition to updating the data, these researchers also change the model specification. In particular, these analyses include additional covariates (i.e., state poverty, unemployment and death penalty execution rates) and allow for region-interacted time patterns, as opposed to a common time trend used in the original Lott models (Lott 2000:170).

With these new models and the updated sample endpoints, Lott found that the basic conclusions from the trend model are robust to the additional years of data covering the periods 1977-1996. Likewise, Plassmann and Whitley (2003) found that when the data are updated to cover the period 1977-2000, the trend model estimates of the effects of right-to-carry laws on crime continue to be negative, but only the estimates for rape and robbery are statistically significant. In the dummy variable model, Plassmann and Whitley found negative coefficient estimates for the right-to-carry coefficient for each violent crime category and positive coefficients for each of the property categories.

Ayres and Donohue (2003b), however, document a number of errors in the data used by Plassmann and Whitley, and Lott's revised new data correct these errors. Plassmann, in communications with the committee, has agreed that the changes to these data are appropriate. Using the revised new data, the committee exactly replicated the results reported by Ayres and Donohue (2003b).

In particular, Ayres and Donohue (2003b) found that rerunning the dummy variable model regressions using the corrected data reduced the magnitude of the estimated reduction in the rates of violent crime, murder, rape, and robbery, and it reversed the sign of the estimated effects of right-to-carry laws on aggravated assault. Moreover, none of the negative estimates is statistically significant, while effects for larceny, auto theft, and property crime overall are positive and significant. Likewise, the changes in the crime trends are generally small in absolute value, and none of the changes is significantly different from zero (see Table 6-4).[10]

Maltz and Targonski (2002) do not update the data but instead assess the quality of the county crime data used in the empirical research on right-to-carry laws. In particular, they note that not all police jurisdictions report their crime levels to the FBI and argue that there is systematic underreporting in the UCR. Maltz and Targonski (2002:298) conclude that "county-level crime data, as they are currently constituted, should not be used, especially in policy studies." However, Maltz and Targonski do not estimate the magnitude of the effects of underreporting on the results obtained by Lott and others. Thus, it is not known whether correcting for underreporting, if it were possible, would change any of the results.

---

[10]Both Ayres and Donohue (2003b) and Plassmann and Whitley (2003) use standard errors that account for state clustering.

Lott and Whitley (2002: Figure 5) report estimates of the effects of right-to-carry laws that are obtained by dropping from the data counties with large fractions of missing UCR reports. Lott's and Whitley's figure shows estimated trends in crime levels before and after adoption of right-to-carry laws, and they claim that these trends support the conclusion that adoption of right-to-carry laws reduces crime. The committee disagrees. According to Figure 5b of Lott and Whitley (2002), the murder rate peaks and begins to decrease at an accelerating rate approximately 5 years before the adoption of right-to-carry laws. Aggravated assault decreases prior to adoption and then increases for approximately 3 years following adoption before starting to decrease again (Figure 5e). Adoption has no effect on rape (Figure 5c). The rate of violent crimes as a whole decreases up to the time of adoption and then remains unchanged until approximately 3 years after adoption before beginning a steeper decline (Figure 5a). Among violent crimes, only robbery displays a decrease immediately following adoption (Figure 5d). However, this followed a period during which the robbery rate first increased and then remained constant for approximately 5 years. In summary, the committee concludes that it is at least possible that errors in the UCR data may account for some of Lott's results.

Standard Errors

A final point that has been argued in the literature is that conventional standard errors reported by Lott and others are not appropriate. The statistical analyses of dummy variable and trend models are conducted using a county-year pair as the unit of analysis. Right-to-carry laws, however, almost always vary only at the state level. Consequently, some investigators believe that treating the county-level observations as if they are statistically independent may lead to estimates of the standard errors that underestimate their true magnitude. These investigators make adjustments for state-level clustering that inflate their standard errors. For example, the standard error for the dummy variable model estimate of the effect of right-to-carry laws on violent crime increases from 0.98 when reporting the unadjusted standard error, to 2.31 when estimating clustered sampling standard errors (Duggan, 2001), to 4.9 when using the methods advocated by Helland and Tabarrok (2004) (see Table 6-3). The fact that the adjustments in most cases greatly increase the standard errors is a reason for concern. Once the standard errors have been adjusted for clustering, very few of the point estimates, in any of the models, using any of the data sets, are statistically different from zero.

However, investigators reporting cluster-adjusted standard errors do not formally explain the need for these adjustments. These adjustments, in fact, are not supported in the basic models specified in Equations 6.1 and

6.2. Instead, those who argue for presenting clustered standard errors often cite Moulton (1990) as the source of their belief that adjustments are needed. Moulton considered a model in which there is an additive source of variation (or additive effect) that is the same for all observations in the same cluster. He showed that ignoring this source of variation leads to standard errors that are too low. Investigators who make clustering corrections usually consider the counties in a state to constitute one of Moulton's clusters and appear to believe that the absence of state-level additive effects in their models causes standard errors to be too low. The models estimated in this literature, including those of Lott and his critics, typically contain county-level fixed effects (the constants γ_i in equations 6.1 and 6.2). Every county is always in the same state, so, any state-level additive effect simply adds a constant to the γ_i's of the counties in that state. The constant may vary among states but is the same for all counties in the same state. The combined county- and state-level effects are indistinguishable from what would happen if there were no state-level effects but each γ_i for the counties in the same state were shifted by the same amount. Therefore, state-level effects are indistinguishable from county-level effects. Any state-level effects are automatically included in the γ_i's. There is no need for adjustments for state-level clustering.

Other observationally equivalent but different models can support the use of adjusted standard errors. If, for example, the effects of right-to-carry laws (or other explanatory variables) vary across states, then the assumption of independence across counties would be incorrect. Adjustments to the standard errors can allow for uncertainty arising from the possibility that the coefficients of variables in the model that are not allowed to vary across states, in fact, vary randomly across states. The adjustments made by Duggan and Plassmann and Whitley, for example, can be used to correct estimated standard errors for this possibility (see Wooldridge, 2003).

These alternative models have not been discussed in the literature or by the committee. Thus, it is not clear whether the models that would support using clustered-sampling-adjusted standard errors are appropriate to evaluate the effects of right-to-carry laws. At the most basic level, researchers need to assess whether models that support clustering are of interest.[11] If, for example, coefficients can vary randomly among states, Models 6.1 and 6.2 reveal the mean coefficients. In other words, if different states have different coefficients, then researchers estimate an average over states. It is

---

[11]There are also important technical issues to consider. For example, a commonly used method for making these corrections is reliable only when the number of "clusters" (here states) is large, and there is reason to think that the 50 states do not constitute a large enough set of clusters to make these methods reliable.

not clear why anyone should care about this average, which is not related in any obvious way to (for example) nationwide benefits of right-to-carry laws. If coefficients vary among states, then it may be much more useful to estimate the coefficients for each state. It is entirely possible that the effects of right-to-carry laws vary among states, even after controlling everything else that is in the model. If they do, it may be much more useful to know which states have which coefficients, to see the magnitude of the variation, and to have a chance of finding out whether it is related to anything else that is observable. Of course, a number of the studies summarized above have varied Lott's model by allowing the effect of right-to-carry laws to differ by states (see, for example, Black and Nagin, 1998, and Plassmann and Tideman, 2001). A model in which coefficients are estimated separately for each state does not require adjustment of standard errors.

In summary, whether adjustment of standard errors is needed depends on the details of the effects that are being estimated and the model that is used to estimate them. These issues have not been investigated in studies of right-to-carry laws to date. Adjusted standard errors are not needed for Models 6.1 and 6.2. The precision of estimates from these models should be evaluated using unadjusted standard errors.

COMMITTEE'S ANALYSIS: ARE THE ESTIMATES ROBUST?

This section presents the results of the committee's own analysis of Lott's revised new data covering the period 1977-2000. The purpose of the analysis is to clarify and illustrate some of the causes of the conflicting results. The committee has not attempted to form our own estimates of the effects of right-to-carry laws. Rather, our analysis is directed toward gaining a better understanding of the fragility of the estimates. We begin by illustrating the sensitivity of the findings to extending the sample period to cover the years 1993-2000. We then demonstrate that the basic qualitative results are sensitive to variations in the explanatory variables. In all cases, we use the *revised new data set*. There is a consensus that these revised data, covering the periods 1977-2000, are correct.

Horowitz discusses this problem in further detail and provides a statistical explanation for the fragility in the estimates in Appendix D. This appendix describes two fundamental sources of difficulty in causal inference that are especially relevant to studies of right-to-carry laws. One is the difficulty of choosing the right explanatory variables for a statistical model. The second is the difficulty of estimating the relation among crime rates, a large number of potential explanatory variables, and the adoption of right-to-carry laws. Even if the correct explanatory variables were known, it would be hard to specify a model correctly, especially in high dimensional settings with many explanatory variables. The committee drew on some of

TABLE 6-5 Dummy Variable Model with Common Time Pattern, 2000 Data

	Years	Controls[a]	Violent Crime	Murder	Rape
0. Committee replication	1992[b]	Yes	−1.76	−9.01	−5.38
SE			(1.07)	(1.70)**	(1.33)**
1. Comm estimate w/ covariates	2000	Yes	4.12	−8.33	−0.16
SE			(0.71)**	(1.05)**	(0.83)
2. Comm estimate w/o covariates	1992[b]	No	−0.12	−1.22	1.39
SE			(1.29)	(2.65)	(2.24)
3. Comm estimate w/o covariates	2000	No	12.92	−1.95	17.91
SE			(0.78)**	(1.48)	(1.39)**

[a]The regressions use the covariates and specification from the original Lott and Mustard (1997) models that do not control for state poverty, unemployment, death penalty execution rates, or regional time trends. The controls include the arrest rate for the crime category in question (AOVIOICP), population density in the county, real per capita income variables (RPCPI RPCUI RPCIM RPCRPO), county population (POPC), and variables for the percentage of the population that is in each of many race × age × gender categories (e.g., PBM1019 is the percentage of the population that is black, male, and between ages 10 and 19). The "no

these ideas in our deliberations but did not adopt them in total as part of our consensus report. This statistical argument is presented to stimulate further discussion and dialogue on these issues.

Extending the Baseline Specification to 2000

Extending the sample to cover the period 1977-2000 provides an important test of the robustness of the estimates for two reasons. First, the number of observations from states with right-to-carry laws in effect more than triples when the additional years are included. Second, 16 additional states enacted right-to-carry laws during the period 1993-1999, thereby providing additional data on the effects of these laws.

Another reason for the importance of the extended data is that aggregate crime trends differ greatly between the periods 1977-1992 and 1993-1997. The first period was one of rising crime, especially in large urban areas, which tend to be in states that did not adopt right-to-carry laws during 1977-1992. The period 1993-1997 was one of declining crime. Any differences in estimation results between the 1977-1992 and 1977-1997

Aggravated Assault	Robbery	Property Crimes	Auto Theft	Burglary	Larceny
−5.60	1.17	5.84	10.28	4.12	6.82
(1.25)**	(1.45)	(0.76)**	(1.24)**	(0.83)**	(0.82)**
3.05	3.59	11.48	12.74	6.19	12.40
(0.80)**	(0.90)**	(0.52)**	(0.78)**	(0.57)**	(0.55)**
−4.17	9.18	8.47	11.98	8.53	8.56
(1.54)**	(2.17)**	(0.79)**	(1.48)**	(0.94)**	(0.93)**
12.34	19.99	21.24	23.33	19.06	22.58
(0.90)**	(1.21)**	(0.53)**	(0.85)**	(0.61)**	(0.59)**

controls" specification includes county fixed effects, year dummies, and the dummy for whether the state has a right-to-carry law.

[b]Using the revised new data set, which contains observations, 1977-2000, even though the estimates in this row use data only through 1992.

NOTE: All samples start in 1977. SE = standard error. Standard errors are in parentheses, where * = significant at 5% and ** = significant at 1%.

data constitute evidence of model misspecification (e.g., because the model cannot account for the change in the aggregate crime trend) and raise the possibility (although do not prove) that the estimated effects of right-to-carry laws are artifacts of specification errors. This is a particularly important concern because states that pass right-to-carry laws are not representative of the nation as a whole on important dimensions (e.g., percentage rural) that are correlated with rising crime in the 1977-1992 period and falling crime in the years 1993-2000.

The first row of Table 6-5 reports the results of extending the dummy variable model (6.1) to the new data covering the period 1977-2000. The specifications estimated are identical to the original model, with the only difference being that the number of years has been expanded. Compared with the model estimated on the original (1977-1992) sample period (see Table 6-5, Row 0), the results have now changed rather substantially. Only the coefficient on murder is negative and significant, while seven coefficients are positive and significant (violent crime overall, aggravated assault, robbery, property crime overall, auto theft, burglary, and larceny). The dummy variable results that were apparent with the earlier data set and

TABLE 6-6 Trend Model with Common Time Pattern, 2000 Data

	Years	Controls[a]	Violent Crime	Murder	Rape
0. Committee replication	1992[b]	Yes	−2.15	−3.41	−3.37
SE			(0.39)**	(0.62)**	(0.48)**
1. Comm estimate w/ covariates	2000	Yes	−0.95	−2.03	−2.81
SE			(0.18)**	(0.26)**	(0.20)**
2. Comm estimate w/o covariates	1992[b]	No	−1.41	−1.52	−3.45
SE			(0.47)**	(0.97)	(0.82)**
3. Comm estimate w/o covariates	2000	No	−0.62	0.12	−2.17
SE			(0.17)**	(0.32)	(0.30)**

[a]The regressions use the covariates and specification from the original Lott and Mustard (1997) models that do not control for state poverty, unemployment, death penalty execution rates, or regional time trends. The controls include the arrest rate for the crime category in question (AOVIOICP), population density in the county, real per capita income variables (RPCPI RPCUI RPCIM RPCRPO), county population (POPC), and variables for the percentage of the population that is in each of many race x age x gender categories (e.g., PBM1019 is the percentage of the population that is black, male,

earlier sample periods almost completely disappear with the extension of the sample to 2000. The committee views the failure of the original dummy variable model to generate robust predictions outside the original sample as important evidence of fragility of the model's findings.[12]

These results are also substantially different from those found when using the expanded set of control variables first adopted by Lott (2000: Table 9.1). As described above, Ayres and Donohue (2003b) estimate a dummy variable model using the revised new data (see Table 6-3). As in Lott (2000, Table 9.1) and Plassmann and Whitley (2003), they modify the original specification to include additional covariates (i.e., state poverty, unemployment, and death penalty execution rates) and region-interacted time patterns, as opposed to a common time trend used in the original Lott models (Lott 2000:170). These seemingly minor adjustments cause sub-

---

[12]In light of the variability in the estimates, statistical tests might aid in determining whether particular specifications can be rejected by the data. It is not possible to test empirically whether a proposed set of explanatory variables is the correct one. It is possible to test for specification, given a set of controls (see Horowitz, Appendix D). None of the models examined by the committee passes a simple specification test (i.e., Ramsey's 1969 RESET test).

Aggravated Assault	Robbery	Property Crimes	Auto Theft	Burglary	Larceny
−2.63 (0.45)**	−3.02 (0.53)**	−1.13 (0.27)**	0.25 (0.45)	−1.80 (0.30)**	−0.84 (0.30)**
−1.92 (0.20)**	−2.58 (0.22)**	−0.01 (0.13)	−0.49 (0.19)*	−2.13 (0.14)**	−0.73 (0.13)**
−2.02 (0.57)**	−0.44 (0.79)	−1.33 (0.29)**	1.62 (0.54)**	−2.50 (0.34)**	−1.27 (0.34)**
−0.65 (0.20)**	−0.88 (0.26)**	−0.81 (0.11)**	0.57 (0.19)**	−1.99 (0.13)**	−0.71 (0.13)**

and between ages 10 and 19). The "no controls" specification includes county fixed effects, year dummies, and th dummy for whether the state has a right-to-carry law.

bUsing the revised new data set, which contains observations, 1977-2000, even though the estimates in this row use data only through 1992.

NOTE: All samples start in 1977. SE = standard error. Standard errors are in parentheses, where * = significant at 5% and ** = significant at 1%.

stantial changes to the results. For example, right-to-carry laws are estimated to decrease murder by about 4 percent using the revised specification, but about 8 percent using the original specification. The estimated effects for the eight other crime categories decrease between 2 and 6 points when moving from the original to the revised specification.

We also estimate the trend model extending the sample to 2000 (row 1, Table 6-6). Relative to the estimates in row 0 (using only data to 1992), the estimates are mostly smaller but remain negative and statistically significant. Thus, the trend specification continues to show reductions in the rate of growth of crime following right-to-carry passage.

To explore why the updated dummy variable and trend models give conflicting results, we do two things. First, we estimate a more flexible year-by-year specification, a variant of Model 6.1, the dummy variable model. Second, we reanalyze the trend model (Model 6.2) by varying the number of years after the law's adoption to estimate its effects on crime. In each of these cases, we use the revised new Lott data through 2000 and we include the original controls used by Lott and Mustard (1997). In each of these cases, except for sampling variability, the changes should not affect the results if the trend model in equation 6.2 is properly specified.

In the first exercise, we replace the right-to-carry dummy with a series of dummies for each of the possible numbers of years prior to—and following—adoption. We summarize the estimated coefficients in three figures. These figures show the estimated coefficients normalized on the year of adoption and multiplied by 100 (so the y-axis is a percentage), and the associated 95 percentage confidence intervals.[13] The vertical line marks the adoption year, while the horizontal line marks 0.

Figure 6-2 shows the time pattern of coefficients from the violent crime model. For years preceding adoption, violent crime is increasing in ultimately adopting states (relative to the national time pattern). Following adoption, the increase relative to trend continues, reverses, then reverses twice again. For property crimes, in Figure 6-2, the upward trend for years prior to adoption continues following adoption.

Figure 6-3 and Figure 6-4 show graphs for individual violent and property crime categories, respectively. The obvious striking feature of these figures is that the big reductions in crime occur roughly 9 years after adoption. Otherwise, the postadoption estimates are generally small and sometimes positive and are, in general, both statistically insignificant and statistically indistinguishable from the preadoption estimates. The trend model essentially fits a line with constant slope through the postadoption portions of these graphs, and the line's slope is affected by years long after adoption. These time patterns raise serious questions about whether the reductions in crime documented in the trend model are reasonably attributed to the change in the law.

In the second exercise, to further explore the sensitivity of the trend model estimates, we reestimate the baseline trend model (Model 6.2) using revised new Lott data on the period 1977-2000. Table 6-7, row 1, repeats the estimates from Table 6-6, row 1 which includes all years for all states, regardless of the amount of time elapsed since the law change. Subsequent rows include observations that occur certain numbers of years after the law change. (Row 2, labeled "6 years," includes the year of the law change and the 5 following years, and so on.) These estimates show that including 5 years or fewer reverses the signs of the estimated effects of right-to-carry laws on murder and property crime (from negative to positive) and reduces the magnitude of the estimated reduction in the rates of rape, aggravated assault, robbery, and violent crime. Moreover, there are fewer statistically significant changes in crime trends. One needs to include at least 6 years following the prelaw-change period to find statistically significant reductions in the violent crime and murder trends.

The trend results rely on changes in crime trends occurring long after the law changes, again raising serious questions about whether one can

---

[13]That is, we subtract the year 0 coefficient from each year's coefficient.

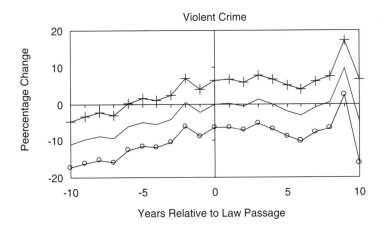

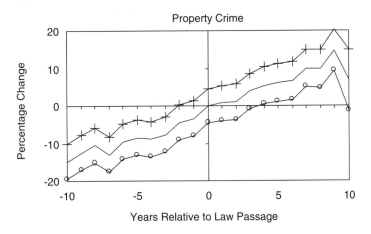

FIGURE 6-2 Year-by-year estimates of the percentage change in aggregate crime (normalized to adoption date of right-to-carry law, year 0).
—— Estimate, —o— bottom of 95% confidence interval (CI), —+—Top of 95% CI

sensibly attribute the estimates from trend models in the literature to the adoption of right-to-carry laws.

Are the Results Sensitive to Controls?

The final two rows of Table 6-5 present two sets of results obtained by the committee when estimating models identical to those of Model 6.1, but excluding socioeconomic and demographic controls. We include only the

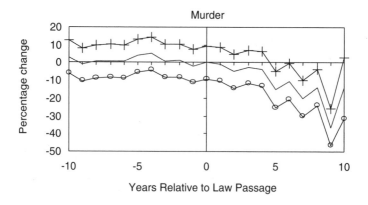

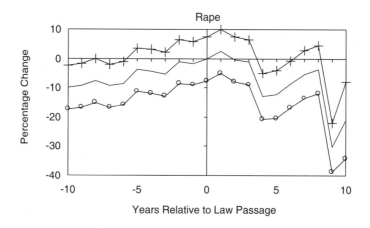

FIGURE 6-3 Year-by-year estimates of the percentage change in disaggregate violent crimes (normalized to adoption date of right-to-carry law, year 0).
—— Estimate, —ⵔ— bottom of 95% confidence interval (CI), ╂—Top of 95% CI

right-to-carry variable, year dummies, and county fixed effects. These estimates tell us how crime has changed in states that have adopted the right-to-carry laws before and after the law change, relative to national time patterns in crime. It is important to stress that the committee is not arguing that excluding all socioeconomic and demographic covariates is an appropriate method of identifying the effects of right-to-carry laws. Rather, we are simply assessing whether such laws are associated with a decline in the level of crime. If not, then detecting the effect, if any, of right-to-carry laws

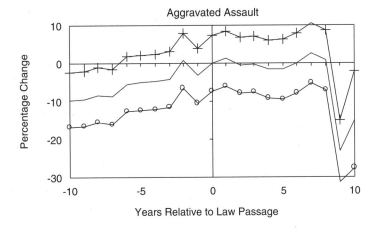

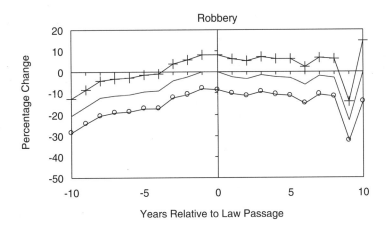

requires controlling for appropriate confounding variables and thereby reliance on a model such as those used by Lott and others.

The results without controls are quite different. Using the earlier sample period and the new data, one finds three negative coefficients, only one of them statistically significant. When the sample is extended to 2000, only one of nine coefficients is negative, and it is insignificantly different from zero. For example, the violent crime coefficient with controls is 4.1 percent, while it is 12.9 percent without controls. These results show that states that

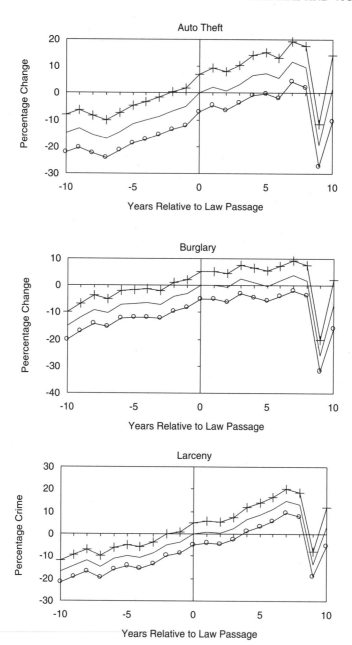

FIGURE 6-4 Year-by-year estimates of the percentage change in disaggregate property crimes (normalized to adoption date of right-to-carry law, year 0).
—— Estimate, —o— bottom of 95% confidence interval (CI), —+—Top of 95% CI

passed right-to-carry laws did not on average experience statistically significant crime declines relative to states that did not pass such laws.

There are two points to make about the no-controls results. First, the no-controls results provide a characterization of the data that shows that, if there is any effect, it is not obvious in the dummy variable model. What do estimates from that model mean? The model says that crime rates differ across counties and, moreover, that they change from one year to the next in the same proportionate way across all counties in the United States. Over and above this variation, there is a one-time change in the mean level of crime as states adopt right-to-carry laws. So these estimates indicate that, for the period 1977-1992, states adopting right-to-carry laws saw roughly no change in their violent crime rates and 8.5 percent increases in their property crime rates, relative to national time patterns. Estimating the model using data to 2000 shows that states adopting right-to-carry laws saw 12.9 percent increases in violent crime—and 21.2 percent increases in property crime—relative to national time patterns. The first-blush evidence provided by these no-controls models is thus not supportive of the theory that right-to-carry laws reduce crime.

A final lesson to draw from the no-controls dummy variable results is that the results are sensitive to the inclusion of controls. That is, whether one concludes that right-to-carry laws increase or decrease crime based on models of this sort depends on which control variables are included. Such laws have no obvious effect in the model without controls (and therefore no clear level effect in the raw data). Moreover, as demonstrated above, seemingly minor changes to the set of control variables substantially alter the estimated effects. Given that researchers might reasonably argue about which controls belong in the model and that the results are sensitive to the set of covariates, the committee is not sanguine about the prospects for measuring the effect of right-to-carry laws on crime. Note that this is distinct from whether such laws affect crime. Rather, in our view, any effect they have on crime is not likely to be detected in a convincing and robust fashion.

Estimates from the trend model are less sensitive to the inclusion of controls. While the no-control point estimates displayed in the third and fourth rows of Table 6-6 are smaller than in the model with controls, most of these estimates are negative and statistically significant. The trend model without controls shows reductions in violent and property crime trends following the passage of right-to-carry laws for both sample endpoints. For murder, however, the results are positive when using the 2000 endpoint, negative when using the 1992 endpoint, and statistically insignificant in both cases.

TABLE 6-7 Trend Model with Varying Postlaw Change Durations

	Years	Controls[a]	Violent Crime	Murder	Rape
1. Baseline comm estimate[b] from row 1 of Table 6-6	2000	Yes	−0.95	−2.03	−2.81
SE			(0.18)**	(0.26)**	(0.20)**
2. 6 years	2000	Yes	−0.97	−1.11	−2.90
SE			(0.29)**	(0.42)**	(0.33)**
3. 5 years	2000	Yes	−0.65	0.05	−2.45
SE			(0.35)	(0.50)	(0.40)**
4. 4 years	2000	Yes	−0.27	0.48	−0.74
SE			(0.44)	(0.63)	(0.50)

[a]The regressions use the covariates and specification from the original Lott and Mustard (1997) models that do not control for state poverty, unemployment, death penalty execution rates, or regional time trends. The controls include the arrest rate for the crime category in question (AOVIOICP), population density in the county, real per capita income variables (RPCPI RPCUI RPCIM RPCRPO), county population (POPC), and variables for the percentage of the population that is in each of many race × age × gender categories (e.g., PBM1019 is the percentage of the population that is black, male, and between ages 10 and 19).

CONCLUSIONS

The literature on right-to-carry laws summarized in this chapter has obtained conflicting estimates of their effects on crime. Estimation results have proven to be very sensitive to the precise specification used and time period examined. The initial model specification, when extended to new data, does not show evidence that passage of right-to-carry laws reduces crime. The estimated effects are highly sensitive to seemingly minor changes in the model specification and control variables. No link between right-to-carry laws and changes in crime is apparent in the raw data, even in the initial sample; it is only once numerous covariates are included that the negative results in the early data emerge. While the trend models show a reduction in the crime growth rate following the adoption of right-to-carry laws, these trend reductions occur long after law adoption, casting serious doubt on the proposition that the trend models estimated in the literature reflect effects of the law change. Finally, some of the point estimates are imprecise. Thus, the committee concludes that with the current evidence it is not possible to determine that there is a causal link between the passage of right-to-carry laws and crime rates.

Aggravated Assault	Robbery	Property Crimes	Auto Theft	Burglary	Larceny
−1.92	−2.58	−0.01	−0.49	−2.13	−0.73
(0.20)**	(0.22)**	(0.13)	(0.19)*	(0.14)**	(0.13)**
−1.06	−1.88	0.11	1.40	−1.13	0.33
(0.32)**	(0.36)**	(0.21)	(0.31)**	(0.23)**	(0.22)
−0.83	−1.63	0.28	1.83	−0.77	0.36
(0.39)*	(0.43)**	(0.25)	(0.37)**	(0.27)**	(0.26)
−0.34	−1.36	0.44	2.03	−0.47	0.31
(0.49)	(0.55)*	(0.32)	(0.47)**	(0.35)	(0.33)

[b]Using the revised new data set, for the full available time period (1977-2000).
NOTES: All samples start in 1977. All estimates use the trend model. Rows 2 through 4 of this table restrict the sample to include only years falling fixed numbers of years past the law change. For example, row 2 includes all the prelaw-change years, the year of the law change (year 0), plus 5 additional years, for a total of 6 years after the prelaw-change period. SE = standard error. Standard errors are in parentheses, where * = significant at 5% and ** = significant at 1%.

It is also the committee's view that additional analysis along the lines of the current literature is unlikely to yield results that will persuasively demonstrate a causal link between right-to-carry laws and crime rates (unless substantial numbers of states were to adopt or repeal right-to-carry laws), because of the sensitivity of the results to model specification. Furthermore, the usefulness of future crime data for studying the effects of right-to-carry laws will decrease as the time elapsed since enactment of the laws increases.

If further headway is to be made on this question, new analytical approaches and data sets will need to be used. For example, studies that more carefully analyze changes in actual gun-carrying behavior at the county or even the local level in response to these laws may have greater power in identifying the impact of such laws. Surveys of criminals or quantitative measures of criminal behavior might also shed light on the extent to which crime is affected by such laws.

7

Firearms and Suicide

While much attention surrounding the debate over firearms has focused on criminal violence in general, and homicide in particular, suicide is the most common cause of firearm-related death in the United States (National Center for Health Statistics, 2003; see Table 3-3). Do guns increase the lethality or frequency of suicide attempts? A large body of literature links the availability of firearms to the fraction of suicides committed with a gun. Yet, a central policy question is whether changes in the availability of firearms lead to changes in the overall risk of suicide.

Despite the clear associations between firearms and gun suicide, answering this broader question is difficult. Box 7-1 sketches out a conceptual framework describing various mechanisms by which firearms may be associated with rates of suicide. The fundamental issue is the degree to which a suicidal person would simply switch to using other methods if firearms were less available. On one hand, if substitutes were easily enough available, then gun restrictions might change the typical method of suicide yet have no effect on the overall risk of suicide at all. On the other hand, there are at least two mechanisms by which guns might directly cause an increase in the risk of completed suicide. First, guns may provide a uniquely efficient method of self-destruction so that access to a gun could lead to a higher rate of completed suicide. It is often stated, for example, that easy access to firearms could increase the rate of completed suicide among persons with transient suicidal feelings because such access might increase the likelihood of an attempt with a lethal outcome. Second, the induction hypothesis proposes that the le-

BOX 7-1
Conceptual Framework

Why might firearms access be associated with rates of suicide?

Direct Causality: Firearms might directly increase the risk of suicide. The instrumentality hypothesis proposes that if guns were inherently more lethal than other methods, then access to a gun could lead to a higher rate of completed suicide. The method selection or induction hypothesis proposes that firearms might be preferred over other methods because their quickness and effectiveness might decrease some of the other "costs" of a suicide attempt.

Spurious Correlation: Firearms might be associated with suicide but have no direct effect. Instead, there may be unmeasured confounders associated with both access to firearms and the propensity to commit suicide. In this case, if substitutes were easily enough available, gun access restrictions might reduce the incidence of gun suicide yet have no effect on the overall risk of suicide. Two examples highlight this possibility:

- **Reverse Causality**: The risk of suicide might increase or decrease the likelihood of gun ownership. On one hand, some persons who are planning to commit suicide may seek out a gun specifically for this purpose (Cummings et al., 1997b; Wintemute et al., 1999). On the other hand, family members might remove firearms from the home of someone who has made suicide attempts in the past.
- **Other Confounders**: Finally, there could be unmeasured and confounding "third factors" associated with both suicide risk and gun ownership, which could lead to an apparent (but noncausal) association between guns and suicide. Individual-level confounders might include propensities for social isolation and mistrust of others. For example, if persons who are prone to own guns because of their mistrust of others were also at greater risk for suicide, whether or not they owned guns, there could be a noncausal statistical association between gun ownership and suicide. Community-level confounders could also explain a link between gun ownership and suicide risk. For example, high levels of "social capital" might be associated with lower rates of defensive gun ownership, as well as with higher levels of social support for individuals at risk for suicide (Hemenway et al., 2001). Defensive gun use may also be correlated with particular cultural attitudes toward mental health services and individual problem-solving strategies; for accidental historical reasons or for specific cultural reasons, communities with higher levels of defensive gun ownership might also be communities that invest less heavily in "safety net" public services or with less access to mental health services.

thality of a gun might itself increase the likelihood of a suicide attempt among gun owners: persons who would prefer the efficiency of a gun would be less likely to make an attempt if a gun were not available. Ultimately, it is an empirical question whether access restrictions lead to substantial reductions in the rates of suicide.

In this chapter we review studies of the relationship between household gun ownership and the risk of suicide.[1] We review both studies that assess the relationships at aggregated geographic levels and those that look at the relationship between access and suicide at the level of the individual or household. Many studies conducted at aggregate levels rely on proxy measures of gun ownership; because these are so widely used, we devote special attention to discussing the pros and cons of using proxies for household gun ownership in ecological studies. Many individual-level studies of suicide use retrospective, case-control study designs; because the strengths and limitations of such a study design may be unfamiliar to some readers, we also discuss this methodology in some detail, with an explanation of the measures of association used in case-control studies presented in an appendix to the chapter. We then summarize the handful of studies that have evaluated the effects of specific gun laws on suicide. The final section presents the committee's conclusions.

ECOLOGICAL STUDIES OF GUN OWNERSHIP
AND THE OVERALL RISK OF SUICIDE

The great majority of research on suicide and gun ownership has been "ecological," in which the unit of observation is the community rather than the individual, comparing measures of household gun ownership rates to the rates of completed suicide. In some cases, the comparisons are allowed to vary over time; in all cases, comparisons are made across several geographic regions. Ecological studies of gun ownership and suicide in the United States are summarized in Table 7-1.

Cross-Sectional Associations

Almost all ecological studies using cross-sectional data, both within the United States and across countries, have found that both gun suicide rates and the fraction of suicides committed with a gun are higher in geographic areas with a higher prevalence of household gun ownership. This association has been reported by investigators across the spectrum of the gun control debate. It has been found across cities, states, regions, and nations (Kleck and Patterson, 1993; Azrael et al., 2004; Killias, 2001), and it contrasts with the more variable association between gun ownership rates and the fraction of homicides committed with a gun.

---

[1]Studies were identified using various search engines, by a search for book chapters and unpublished studies identified through personal communication with researchers in the field, and by review of the reference lists of previous publications. A particular effort was made to find studies in the firearms policy literature, reviewed for other chapters of this volume, which may have examined suicide as a secondary focus of the investigation.

However, the most important policy question is not whether gun access increases the risk of gun suicide, but whether gun access increases the *overall* risk of suicide. Many cross-sectional studies have reported a positive, bivariate association between gun ownership rates and overall suicide rates across cities, states, and regions of the United States, but the relationship is much smaller and less precise than the association between gun ownership rates and gun suicide rates. The association between gun ownership and overall suicide also appears to be sensitive to the details of the measures and the statistical models being used.

U.S. Studies

Several ecological studies by Birckmayer and Hemenway (2001) and by Miller et al. (2002a, 2002c) have focused on age-specific suicide rates by region and state. Their gun ownership measures include survey estimates of handgun and overall gun ownership from the GSS and, as a proxy measure, the fraction of suicides committed with a firearm. Before controlling for other social variables, Birckmayer and Hemenway find a positive association between regional GSS-reported rates of gun ownership and age-specific rates of suicide in every age group. After controlling for divorce, education, unemployment, urbanization, poverty, and alcohol consumption, they find a modest positive association between gun ownership and suicide risk for youth ages 15 to 24 (b = .35, 95% confidence interval .05 to .65) and for adults age 65 and over (b = .62, 95% C.I. .40-.84), but *not* for working-age adults between ages 25 and 64. Subsequent studies from the same research group use other model specifications, with varying results. For example, Miller et al. (2002a) do not incorporate control variables; they find a positive association between gun ownership and overall suicide rates in all age groups (incidence rate ratio 1.14; 95% CI 1.01-1.24) and a negative association between gun ownership and nongun suicide (IRR .87, 95% CI .77-.97) that is more pronounced for persons 45 years and older, suggesting greater substitution among methods in older age groups.

Duggan (2003) undertook a similar age-specific analysis, using subscriptions to the gun magazine *Guns & Ammo* as his proxy for gun ownership. Like Miller et al., Duggan did not include other covariates in his regression models and, like Miller et al., he found a positive and significant bivariate association between gun ownership and suicide across states. But Duggan also found a significant *positive* association between gun magazine subscription and *nongun* suicide for youth ages 10 to 19. The association between the gun proxy and nongun suicide shifts from positive to negative between ages 20 and 69 and becomes negative and statistically significant for persons over age 69. He concludes that the positive association between gun magazine subscriptions and nongun suicide among youth is evidence

TABLE 7-1 Ecological Studies of Associations Between Firearms
Prevalence and Suicide in the United States

Source	Unit of Analysis	Gun Measure	Subjects; Strata
Duggan (2003)	50 states 1996	Proxy: *Guns & Ammo*	10 yr. age groups
Hemenway and Miller (2002)	9 regions 1988-1997	Survey: GSS (household handgun ownership)	
Miller et al. (2002b)	9 regions 50 states 1988-1997	Survey: GSS, BRFSS Proxy: Cook index, FS/S (adult only)	Children 5-14
Miller et al. (2002c)	9 regions 50 states 1988-1997	Survey: GSS, BRFSS Proxy: Cook index , FS/S	Adult women
Miller et al. (2002a)	9 regions 50 states 1988-1997	Survey: GSS, BRFSS Proxy: Cook index, FS/S	10-yr. age groups
Birckmayer and Hemenway (2001)	9 regions 1979-1994	GSS	10-yr age groups
Azrael et al. (2004)	9 regions 50 states 1994-1998	Survey: GSS, BRFSS, HICRC Proxies: FS/S, UFDR, *Guns & Ammo*, NRA membership	

ORDER CARD
(Customers in North America Only)

Use this card to order additional copies of **Firearms and Violence**. All orders must be prepaid. Please add $4.50 for shipping and handling for the first copy ordered and $0.95 for each additional copy. If you live in CA, DC, FL, MD, MO, TX, or Canada, add applicable sales tax or GST. Prices apply only in the United States, Canada, and Mexico and are subject to change without notice.

___ I am enclosing a U.S. check or money order.

___ Please charge my VISA/MasterCard/American Express account.

Number: _____

Expiration date: _____

Signature: _____

FOUR EASY WAYS TO ORDER

- **Electronically:** Order from our secure website at: www.nap.edu
- **By phone:** Call toll-free 1-888-624-8422 or (202) 334-3313 or call your favorite bookstore.
- **By fax:** Copy the order card and fax to (202) 334-2451.
- **By mail:** Return this card with your payment to NATIONAL ACADEMIES PRESS, 500 Fifth Street NW, Washington, DC 20001.

All international customers please contact National Academies Press for export prices and ordering information.

Firearms and Violence

PLEASE SEND ME:

Qty.	Code	Title	Price
___	FIRVIO	Firearms and Violence	$47.95

	Subtotal	___
	Shipping	___
	Tax	___
	Total	___

Please print.

Name _____

Address _____

City _____ State _____ Zip Code _____

9124

NATIONAL ACADEMY PRESS

Publisher for The National Academies

National Academy of Sciences ◆ National Academy of Engineering ◆ Institute of Medicine ◆ National Research Council

Leading the World in Science, Technology, and Health

Visit our web site at

www.nap.edu

Use the form on the reverse of this card to order additional copies, or order online and receive a 20% discount.

Control Variables	Results: Guns and Gun Suicides	Results: Guns and Nongun Suicides	Results: Guns and Overall Suicides
None	all ages +	10-19: + 20-69: 0 70+: −	all ages +
Major depression, suicidal thoughts, and urbanization, OR education, OR unemployment, OR alcohol consumption	+	−	+
Poverty, education, urbanization	+	0	+
Poverty, urbanization	+	BRFSS:+ Others: 0	+
None	all ages +	<45: 0 45+: −	all ages +
Divorce, education, unemployment, urbanization	15-24: + 25-44: 0 45-84: +	0	15-24: + 25-64:0 65+: +
None	+	n/a	n/a

continued

TABLE 7-1 Continued

Source	Unit of Analysis	Gun Measure	Subjects; Strata
Kaplan and Geling (1998)	9 regions 1989-1991	Survey: GSS	Sex × race
Kleck and Patterson (1993)	170 U.S. cities	OLS proxy: gun crimes IV proxy: gun sport	
Sloan et al. (1990)	2 cities 1985-1987	Registry: handguns Proxies: Cook index Strictness of gun laws	Two age groups, race, sex
Lester (1989)	48 states 1980	Proxy: gun magazines	
Lester (1988a)	6 (of 7) Australian states	Survey-household gun ownership	
Lester (1988b)	9 regions 1970	Survey Proxy: gun laws	
Lester (1987a)	48 states 1970	Proxies: gun laws, UFDR Proxy: Cook index	
Duggan (2003)	50 states	Proxy: guns ammo sales rate	All ages

Control Variables	Results: Guns and Gun Suicides	Results: Guns and Nongun Suicides	Results: Guns and Overall Suicides
None	+	Male:- Female: 0	n/a
Community traits: race, sex, age unemployment rate, poverty, income, home ownership, college enrollment, transience, population change, divorce, place of worship, etc.	+	0	OLS: + IV: 0
None	+	-	0
None	+	0	+
None	0	-	0
% black, median age, % urban, divorce rate	+	0	0
None	+	UFDR:- Other: 0	0
State, year fixed effects	0	0	0

continued

TABLE 7-1 Continued

Source	Unit of Analysis	Gun Measure	Subjects; Strata
Mathur and Freeman (2002)	48 states	Gun dealers per capita	Adolescent suicide (15-19)
Azrael et al. (2004)	9 regions 50 states	Survey: GSS Proxy: FS/S	
Clarke and Jones (1989)	Entire United States	Survey: Gallup poll, GSS	Type of gun

NOTES: +, - indicate positive or negative effect (respectively), statistically significant at p < .05; 0 indicates not significant.

BRFSS = Behavioral Risk Factor Surveillance System; GSS = General Social Survey; FS/S = ratio of firearm suicide/total suicides; Cook Index = mean of firearm suicide/total suicide and firearm homicide/total homicide; HICRC = Harvard Injury Control Research Center; UFDR

for an omitted variable, because any plausible causal effect of gun ownership should be independent of, or negatively associated with, the nongun suicide rate. There are several other possible explanations for Duggan's results; most obviously, it may be that *Guns & Ammo* subscribers are not representative of all gun owners; his arguments about confounding would also have been strengthened by the inclusion of some observable covariates. All the same, both Miller's and Duggan's results support the view that different gun proxies may yield different results, and all of the age-stratified studies suggest that instrumentality effects, substitution, and omitted variables may be playing different roles at different ages.

The most comprehensive effort to control for confounding factors was published a decade ago. Kleck and Patterson (1993) undertook a cross-sectional study of the effect of firearms prevalence on crime rates and firearm-related fatalities in 170 U.S. cities. Although the study did not consider differences by age, the models included a set of 38 control variables previously identified as predictors of violence rates. Like other investigators, these authors found that higher levels of the proxy for gun owner-

Control Variables	Results: Guns and Gun Suicides	Results: Guns and Nongun Suicides	Results: Guns and Overall Suicides
State, year fixed effects FLFP, divorce, alcohol consumption family & cohort size	Not stated	Not stated	+
Regional fixed effects	+	Not stated	Not stated
None	Handgun + All guns: 0	n/a	All guns: 0 Handgun: +

= unintentional firearm death rate; FLFP = female labor force participation; OLS = ordinary least squares; IV = instrumental variable (two-stage least squares); NRA = National Rifle Association.

When only one result is listed in column, all gun measures gave similar results. When reported results include models both with and without covariates, only results with covariates are presented.

ship predicted higher rates of suicide ($b = .132$, $p < .05$). Kleck and Patterson also found evidence that there might be a different association between suicide risk and sporting gun ownership and suicide risk and defensive gun ownership. In particular, they found no significant effect of sporting gun ownership on the risk of suicide.

International Studies

Like the U.S. studies, the existing cross-national surveys have looked for an association between rates of household gun ownership, overall suicide rates, and the fraction of suicides committed with a gun. And, like the U.S. studies, cross-national studies have found a consistent association between gun ownership and the fraction of suicides committed with a gun across countries; but in contrast to the U.S. studies, the cross-national surveys do not reveal a consistent association between gun ownership and *overall* suicide rates.

Although gun ownership rates in the United States are much higher than in most other developed countries, the rates of suicide in the United States rank in the middle. Killias (1993), Killias (2001), and Johnson et al. (2000) found that reported rates of household gun ownership were strongly correlated with the fraction of suicides committed with a gun in each country (Spearman's rho = .79 to .92, p < .001). But the cross-country correlations between household gun ownership and overall rates of suicide have proven to be smaller and statistically imprecise (Spearman's rho .25, p = .27) (Killias, 2001). Likewise, in an often-cited study, Sloan et al. (1990) compared the rates of gun and nongun suicides in Seattle, Washington, with suicide rates in Vancouver, British Columbia, between 1985 and 1987; they found higher rates of gun ownership are associated with higher rates of gun suicide, lower rates of nongun suicide, and no significant difference in the overall suicide rate between the two cities (relative risk .97, 95% CI .87 to 1.09).

Associations Between Gun Ownership and Suicide Rates Across Time

The fraction of suicides in the United States that are committed with a firearm has increased from just over 35 percent in the 1920s to about 60 percent in the 1990s. Four studies have attempted to link this change in the fraction of gun suicides with changes in gun ownership across time.

Three of these four studies have found positive associations between proxies for gun ownership and the fraction of suicides committed with a gun, but only one study, focusing on youth suicide, found an association between gun ownership and overall suicide rates. Clarke and Jones (1989), examined the national prevalence of household gun ownership reported in polls by Gallup and the National Opinion Research Center between 1959 and 1984, comparing these reports with aggregate U.S. suicide rates over the same period. This study found a positive association between the fraction of households owning a handgun and the fraction of suicides committed with a gun (b = .68, p = .001), but no association between household gun ownership and overall risk of suicide (b = .04, p = .85). Azrael et al. (2004) also report a strong linear association between individual and household rates of gun ownership within regions and the fraction of suicides committed with a gun between 1980 and 1998, with cross-sectional beta coefficients ranging from .55 (for individual handgun ownership) to 1.02 (for household gun ownership of any kind), and an inter-temporal coefficient between FS/S and household gun ownership of .905 (s.e. = .355). They did not report the association between gun ownership and overall risk of suicide. Mathur and Freeman (2002) used state-level per capita gun dealership rates to predict adolescent suicide rates from 1970 to 1997. After controlling for state and year fixed effects and number of other observed covariates (e.g., divorce rates, per capital alcohol consumption, female labor force participation, family size, and cohort size), Mathur and Freeman found that increases in gun dealerships per capita predicted increases in the overall youth suicide rate. Finally, Duggan (2003) used two decades of gun magazine sales with controls for state and year fixed effects to explain the trends in suicide rates across all age groups. Duggan found no association between magazine subscription rates and either gun suicide or overall suicide rates across time (b = .046, s.e. = .064, and b = .004, s.e. = .051, respectively).

Assessment of Ecological Studies

Overall, the body of ecological studies has firmly established that firearms access is positively associated with gun suicide, but the association between firearm access and overall suicide is less certain.

In particular, gun suicide rates are strongly correlated with gun prevalence across space and possibly across time, in the United States and across countries. Likewise, many ecological studies do report a cross-sectional association between gun ownership rates and *overall suicide* rates in the United States. However, gun ownership rates do not seem to explain overall suicide trends across countries or across time in the United States. Moreover, the results seem to vary according to the firearm measure used, the age group being studied, and the covariates included.

To further improve our understanding of the effects of firearms on suicide, researchers need to be increasingly sensitive to the possibility of confounding factors and substitution. Moreover, these ecological studies introduce two additional problems that must be considered. First, the analyses are conducted at the aggregate level, rather than at the individual level, and second, direct measures of access to firearms are often not available, thus forcing researchers to rely on proxies. We consider each of these issues in turn.

Substitution and Confounders

As with all empirical analyses, researchers and policy makers must be sensitive to unobserved confounders when attempting to draw causal inferences (see Box 7-1). To what extent would suicidal persons substitute other methods if firearms were less available? Unmeasured and confounding factors associated with both suicide risk and gun ownership might lead to a spurious association between guns and suicide. For example, if persons who are prone to own guns because of their mistrust of others were also at greater risk for suicide, whether or not they owned guns, there could be a noncausal statistical association between gun ownership and suicide. Likewise, high levels of "social capital" might be associated with lower rates of defensive gun ownership and lower suicide rates (Hemenway et al., 2001). Neighborhood levels of gun ownership could even conceivably be affected by neighborhood suicide rates: suicide rates might contribute to a community's perceived level of violence, whether people are aware of making such a link or not.

This concern is not unique to ecological studies, but has been generally ignored in this literature. There have been few systematic efforts to explore or model possible confounders of the association between gun ownership and suicide risk. Two studies by Hemenway and associates are suggestive. First, Hemenway et al. (2001) investigated the hypothesis that persons who live in communities with higher levels of mutual trust may be at lower risk of suicide (because of increased social support), and lower risk of gun ownership and less likely to own firearms (because of decreased motivation for defensive gun ownership). They found that, across U.S. states, lower levels of mutual trust and civic engagement, as reported on the General Social Survey and on the Needham Lifestyle Survey, were associated with a higher fraction of suicides committed with a gun. This study did not examine the association between social capital, firearm ownership, and overall suicide rates. Hemenway and Miller (2000) investigated the hypothesis that regions with higher rates of firearm ownership were characterized by higher rates of major depression, which is known to be an important independent risk factor for suicide. They found that the cross-sectional, regional association between firearm ownership and suicide rates was not explained by differences in the regional prevalence of major depression and serious suicidal thoughts.

Proxy Measures of Ownership

Research linking firearms to suicide (and violence more generally) is limited by the lack of detailed information on firearms ownership (see Chapter 2). The existing surveys cannot be used to link ownership to outcomes of interest and, for that matter, cannot generally be used to draw inferences about ownership in more precise geographic areas (e.g., counties) that are often of interest in ecological studies. The GSS, which collects individual and household information on firearms ownership over time, is representative of the nine census regions and the nation as whole. Other surveys—the Behavioral Risk Factor Surveillance System (BRFSS) and the Harvard Injury Control Research Center Survey (HICRC)—collect information on gun ownership prevalence rates representative of individual states in certain years.[2]

---

[2]The BRFSS included firearm ownership questions in the 1992-1995 surveys conducted in 21 states. The HICRC can be used to draw inferences on ownership by states in 1996 and 1999.

TABLE 7-2 Correlation Coefficient Between a Proxy and Gun Ownership Rates

Proxy	GSS N = 9 regions	BRFSS N = 21 states	HICRC N = 48 states
FS/S	0.93	0.90	0.81
FH/H	0.52	0.19	0.02
Guns & Ammo	0.75	0.67	0.51

NOTE: GSS = Generalized Social Survey; BRFSS = Behavioral Risk Factor Surveillance Survey; HICRC = Harvard Injury Control Research Center.
SOURCE: Azrael et al. (2004: Table 3). Used with kind permission of Springer Science and Business Media.

As a result of these limitations, many ecological studies evaluating the relationship between firearms and suicide (and homicide) rely on proxies of ownership, rather than direct measures. Proxies have included the fraction of homicides committed with a firearm (FH/H), the fraction of suicides committed with a firearm (FS/S), subscription rates to *Guns & Ammo* (*G&A*), and other similar measures.[3]

The primary advantage of these proxies, as opposed to survey information, is that they can be readily computed at state, county, and other finer geographic levels. The disadvantage is that the proxy is not the variable of interest; ownership is. Thus, except in very particular circumstances, proxy measures result in biased estimates of the relationships of interest.

Several studies have explicitly evaluated different proxy measures of ownership. These assessments generally involve computing a correlation coefficient between the proxy and self-reported ownership measures from the GSS or other surveys.[4] Azrael et al. (2004), for example, systematically assess a number of commonly used proxies. Their basic results using the GSS and other ownership surveys are displayed in Table 7-2. The fraction of suicides committed with a firearm has the highest correlation among all of the measures considered, ranging from 0.81 in the state level data to 0.93 when using ownership data from the nine census regions. The fraction of homicides committed with a firearm has the lowest correlations, and *G&A* subscription rates lie between the two.

---

[3]See Azrael et al. (2001) for a summary of the different proxy measures used in the literature.

[4]These correlations are computed using both geographic and time-series variation in the ownership and proxy measures. Duggan (2003), in addition to comparing the *G&A* proxy to the GSS data, also uses other indicators that are thought to be highly correlated with ownership, such as the location of gun shows and community characteristics thought to be associated with ownership.

Given this evidence, Azrael et al. conclude that "FS/S is a superior proxy measure for cross-section analysis, easily computed from available data for state and large local jurisdictions and valid against survey based estimates" (p. 50). They also find, using similar methods, that FS/S is a useful proxy for measuring intertemporal variation in ownership. This finding appears to share some consensus. Many other researchers have also accepted FS/S as the best and in fact a nearly ideal proxy for studying the cross-sectional relationship between firearms and violence. One notable exception is Duggan (2003), who argues that the FS/S is a poor proxy for studying suicide, even in cross-sectional analyses.

After reviewing the existing evidence, the committee urges more caution in using FS/S as a proxy for gun ownership. As Duggan points out, the most obvious statistical problems concern the circularity of using FS/S as a proxy in a study of suicide, but the properties of FS/S in other kinds of studies (e.g., homicide) have also not yet been well described.

There are three basic problems with the existing analysis of proxies of firearms access. First, there is the problem of the accuracy of self-reported measures of firearm access, the standard against which the proxies are being compared. The effects of nonresponse and erroneous response in the surveys of firearms ownership, and random sampling errors more generally, have not been investigated. Certainly, response errors alone—as described both in Chapters 2 and 5—may result in biased estimates of the true prevalence of gun ownership. Moreover, if persons who are at risk for attempting suicide are less likely to participate in a household survey than other persons, then household surveys may not reflect the true relationship between gun ownership and method choice among persons who are actually at risk of attempting suicide. Existing research does not yet shed much light on these possible biases.

Second, there is the problem of aggregation bias in the correlation analysis. The primary reason for using a proxy is that more direct gun ownership data may not be available at the appropriate level of aggregation. But even if the proxy is highly correlated with observed ownership rates at one geographic level, it need not be correlated with gun ownership in smaller areas or in subgroups of the population. To explore this possibility, the committee reexamined the correlation between FS/S and gun ownership levels using the individual GSS survey responses aggregated to the 100 primary sampling units rather than the 9 census regions. In this case, we estimated the correlation between the percentage of suicides committed with a firearm and ownership levels to be 0.646 for firearms of any type and 0.639 for handguns, substantially less than the correlations reported by Azrael et al. (2004).

A similar problem is presented in Figure 7-1, which displays the relationship between FS/S and household gun ownership by age and gender.

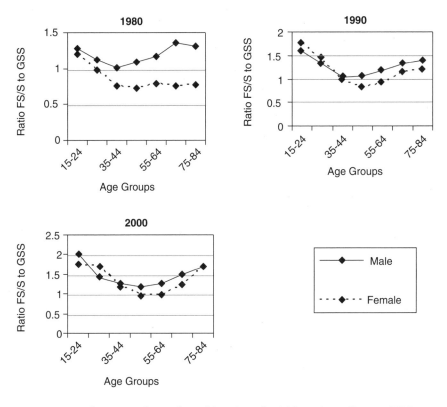

FIGURE 7-1 Changing relationship of fraction of suicides using a firearm (FS/S) to household gun ownership (GSS) in the US by age and sex.

This figure shows that the relationship between FS/S and household gun ownership (as reported in the GSS) varies by age and gender and appears to have changed between 1980 and 2000; for example, the difference in patterns of association between males and females has diminished substantially. Such changes suggest that the relationship between FS/S and other measures of gun ownership may be influenced by a number of social, political, and cultural factors that are not yet understood.

   Third, even if the estimated correlation coefficients are valid, it is not clear how this confirms (or refutes) the utility of such a proxy as a measure of gun ownership. To the contrary, except in very specific circumstances, regressions with proxies result in biased estimators.[5] Under the best cir-

---

[5]Maddala (1992) and Wooldridge (2000) illustrate the biases created by proxies measures in linear mean regression models.

cumstances, proxies reveal the sign but not the magnitude of the relation-ship of interest (Krasker and Pratt, 1986; Maddala, 1992). Azrael et al. (2004) attempt to provide some insight into this scale problem by running a simple linear regression of the form:

$$PREV = \beta_0 + \beta_1 FS/S + U,$$

where PREV is the true ownership rate, FS/S is the observed proxy, β_0 and β_1 are unknown coefficients, and U is a mean zero unobserved random variable, conditional on FS/S. The estimated slope coefficient is near unity, suggesting that a one-unit increase in FS/S implies a one-unit increase in the expected prevalence rate. The authors take this result, coupled with the strong cross-sectional correlation coefficients, as evidence supporting the idea that the FS/S proxy leads to (nearly) unbiased estimators of both the sign and the magnitude of the relationships of interest.

This logic, however, could be misleading. In the classical omitted vari-able model described by Wooldridge (2000:284-286), a unit coefficient on β_1 is sufficient. In other models, however, unbiased estimators may not exist. It is difficult to assess whether these conditions result in an unbiased estimator since Azrael et al. (2004) do not clearly describe the model they have in mind.[6] This problem becomes particularly important when FS/S is being used as a proxy in the study of suicide, and it seems to be an impor-tant source of misunderstanding. For example, Miller et al. (2002a, 2002c) assess the potential biases created by the FS/S proxy in the study of suicide, using statistical simulations. These authors claim to demonstrate that FS/S is not, by construction, correlated with the overall suicide rate, so that FS/S may be appropriately used as a measure of gun ownership in such a study. However, they do not explicitly describe their statistical model, and their description of the Monte Carlo simulation does not provide enough infor-mation to understand much about what was done. Furthermore, it is not

---

[6]No one, as far as we can tell, has investigated the actual linear or nonlinear shape of the relation between FS/S and gun ownership. Furthermore, Azrael et al. do not consider issues associated with the statistical error of the model. Suppose instead that we consider another linear model, in which the gun suicide rate is a function of the gun ownership prevalence: $FS/S = g_0 + g_1 PREV + V$, with V being a mean zero unobserved random variable, conditional on PREV (see, for example, Duggan, 2003). Indeed, this model may be more plausible if one believes that gun ownership is a causal factor in firearm-related suicides. And, if this were correct, then in models of the relation between suicide and the FS/S proxy, the explanatory variable (FS/S) would be correlated with the regression "error," a well-known cause of bias in regression analysis. In any case, the two models are not the same and do not have the same implications for the effects of using FS/S as a proxy. In the first model, the measurement errors are mean-independent of the proxy but not of the variable of interest, prevalence. In the second model, the measurement errors are independent of prevalence but not of the proxy.

obvious why the simulation is at all relevant: the basic finding that proxies create biases is an analytical result that cannot be resolved by a simulation. It is very easy to create other plausible simulations that lead to substantial correlations between FS/S and suicide and, more importantly, substantial biases in the estimated relations of interest.

In Box 7-2, for example, we present the results of a simulation conducted by the committee. In this Monte Carlo simulation, we study the relation between the suicide rate and FS/S as a proxy for gun ownership, but we derive very different results than those reported by Miller et al. (2002a, 2002c). In particular, we find a negative association between the suicide rate and FS/S: in this simulation, if FS/S is a good proxy for ownership, gun owners are *less* likely than nonowners to commit suicide.

This exercise illustrates at least two things: (1) the design of the Monte Carlo simulation matters and (2) having suicide-related variables on both sides of the regression can produce perverse results. In the end, the biases created by proxy measures are application specific. Duggan (2003), for example, highlights the potential problems caused by using FS/S as an explanatory variable in a model whose dependent variable is also suicide-related. As demonstrated in the simulation above, unobserved factors associated with

---

BOX 7-2
Monte Carlo Experiment

There is not enough information available from the published Monte Carlo design (Miller et al., 2002a, 2002b) to enable someone to replicate it. However, the committee did a Monte Carlo experiment that implied quite different results. The Monte Carlo simulates a study of the relation between the suicide rate and FS/S as a proxy for gun ownership. Let Z1, Z2, and Z3 denote unobserved independent standard normal variables, and let

FS = 10 + Z1;
NFS = 6 + Z2;
FS/S = FS/(FS + NFS);
POP = 50 + Z3; and
RATE = (FS +NFS)/POP,

where FS is the number of firearm suicides, NFS is the number of nonfirearm suicides, POP is the population size, and RATE is the total suicide rate for the population. With 1,000 replications, this design gave a mean value of FS/S in the neighborhood of 0.6 (similar to the fraction of suicides currently committed with a firearm in the United States). The correlation coefficient of FS/S and RATE was –0.29. The linear regression of RATE on FS/S gave a slope coefficient of –0.18 with a t-statistic of 9.6. So, according to this simulation, there is a negative association between the suicide rate and FS/S. In other words, if FS/S is a good proxy for ownership, gun owners are less likely than nonowners to commit suicide.

the measure of gun and nongun suicide (e.g., measurement error) may lead to purely spurious correlations between suicide and FS/S. Since suicide, S, is on both sides of the estimated equation, the implicit model is often a complicated, nonlinear relation between S and FS, not the linear model that is assumed in the literature. These issues may or may not be problematic when using FS/S to estimate the relationship between gun ownership and homicide.

Another important issue is how the proxy affects inference from specific models that may include other explanatory variables. This depends, among other things, on how true firearms prevalence and FS/S are related to the other observed and unobserved explanatory variables. These issues are complicated, and most of them have not been recognized, much less investigated, in the suicide and firearms literature.

Ecological Bias

All empirical studies face difficulties with making causal inferences, but ecological studies face special sources of bias in dealing with exposures and confounders. These difficulties arise because of the aggregation of observations and because the data on exposures, confounders, and outcomes are from different sources. At the most basic level, the data on firearms ownership in these studies may not come from the persons who committed suicide. Thus, ecological studies cannot establish whether there is a relation between gun ownership by an individual or household and suicide by that individual or member of the household. This may seem like a small problem in the case of gun suicide; after all, the victims of a gun suicide have undeniably achieved access to a gun. But community-level rates of gun ownership may not reflect the rates of gun ownership among highly suicidal persons. If, for example, the relationship between gun access and gun suicide varies by age and sex or by psychiatric disorder, then the aggregate association may reflect differences in the prevalence of suicidal states among persons of different age and sex or psychiatric disorder in the population, rather than differences in access to firearms. The geographical level of aggregation in state-level or regional ecological studies may be so high that there is no way of knowing whether the gun homicides or gun suicides occurred in the same areas with high levels of gun ownership.

Thus, even if FS/S is found to be a valid proxy for state-level gun prevalence, something that is not yet established, ecological studies may lead to biased inferences. The proxy is not a substitute for good data on household-level ownership or even ownership at a smaller level of aggregation by age, sex, or geography. Rather, better individual-level studies exploring the relationship between gun ownership and suicide may be needed in order to further understanding of the overall relationship between firearms and the risk of suicide.

INDIVIDUAL-LEVEL STUDIES OF THE ASSOCIATION
BETWEEN FIREARMS AND SUICIDE

Most individual-level studies use case-control or response-based study designs to study rare events, such as completed suicide. However, the strengths and weaknesses of this study design are not well understood by investigators outside the public health community, and in order to clarify the controversy surrounding some of these studies, it may be helpful to describe the most important features of the case-control study design. Studies of the rates and determinants of illness or behaviors can be classified as retrospective or prospective. Prospective studies usually select people on the basis of exposure and determine how many persons with the exposure, compared with persons without exposure, develop a certain outcome. In contrast, retrospective studies usually start by choosing persons according to whether an illness or behavior has already developed and seek to find the phenomena that might be associated with the development of the outcome. Intuitively, it makes sense that if one is studying a rare outcome, then a prospective design is inefficient because it may take a very large sample or a very long time to accumulate enough occurrences. In this case, the case-control sampling design is beneficial because it oversamples the behavior or outcome of interest.

To investigate suicide, for example, a case-control study might select as cases those persons who have committed suicide, and then randomly select as controls a certain predetermined number of subjects from the same population who did not commit suicide. The study design would seek to establish an association between the outcome (suicide) and an exposure (such as firearms or depression) by noting the proportions of cases and controls that have been exposed to the possible risk factor.

There are a number of important advantages to the case-control method that explain its common use in epidemiology. Because the outcomes have already happened, case-control studies require no costly follow-up waiting for the outcome to develop. Because case-control studies oversample the outcome of interest, they also require smaller samples sizes than prospective studies of comparable power; for this reason, the case-control sampling scheme is often the only feasible way to collect the information of interest. For example, although suicide is the most common cause of firearm-related deaths in the United States, the overall suicide rate is approximately 11 suicides per 100,000 persons per year. Very few prospectively collected data sets would be large enough to draw precise inferences about completed suicide.

Feasible and efficient as the case-control design may seem, it also suffers from important limitations arising from the nonrandom selection of cases or controls and from misclassification of the outcome or exposure.

For example, case-control studies are particularly susceptible to recall bias—a bias resulting from differential recall among case respondents compared with control respondents. The likelihood of recall bias may be directly influenced by the respondent's motivation to explain the illness (or outcome) itself. In a study of suicide, the victim's past history of depression might be more salient to the relatives of a person who has committed suicide compared with the relatives of a control subject, so that case-control studies of completed suicide might overstate the risk of psychopathology or of gun ownership among persons who have committed suicide, compared with controls.

Furthermore, relatives may follow a "stopping rule": once the family has found a "sufficient" explanation for the occurrence of the suicide—whether it is a gun in the home or psychopathology—they may be less likely to admit the presence of other, less socially acceptable risk factors; such ascertainment bias can lead to the underreporting of co-morbidity among risk factors and could explain reports of a greater frequency of gun ownership among suicides with no reported history of psychopathology. In the case of gun suicides, ascertainment bias may also arise because the outcome itself provides evidence of access to a gun. For example, family members are not always aware that firearms are kept in the home. If a subject has killed himself with a gun, family members would not be able to deny the gun's existence, even if they have first learned of its existence because the suicide has occurred. In contrast, the relatives of a living control subject may not know with certainty whether a gun is present in the household (Ludwig et al., 1998). Family awareness of suicidal risks could lead them to take steps to prevent the suicide of family members known to be at risk. In this case, the absence of firearms would be a sign of appropriate family responsiveness, and a nonexperimental study design would be unable to distinguish the protective effects of gun removal from the protective effects of other steps that the family may have undertaken at the same time.

Other limitations of case-control studies include nonrandom selection of cases or controls; it is often difficult to design a sample selection procedure that ensures that controls are, in fact, representative of the same population from which the cases were drawn. Even if the data are accurate and the sampling scheme is well defined, case-control studies, like other nonexperimental study designs, have a limited ability to distinguish causal from noncausal connections. In the case of firearms, individuals who own guns might have unobserved attributes that are associated with increased suicide risk, or, just as important, some individuals may seek to purchase guns because of a specific plan to commit suicide. These possibilities have very different implications from the point of view of preventive intervention.

Finally, the parameter reported in many case-control studies, termed the odds ratio, is often not the parameter of interest for policy. Presumably, policy makers are interested in the expected number of lives saved or lost because of firearms or other factors. The odds ratio, which is roughly the suicide probability with firearms divided by the suicide probability without firearms, can translate into many or few lives, depending on the suicide probabilities that are involved. Thus, a large odds ratio does not necessarily translate into a large number of lives, and a small odds ratio does not necessarily translate into a small number of lives. To see the problem, consider two populations, one in which the suicide probability conditional on owning a firearm is 0.02 per person per year and the suicide probability conditional on not owning a firearm is 0.01 per person per year, and another in which these two probabilities are 0.0002 and 0.0001, respectively. The odds ratio and the relative risk are the same in both scenarios, but if guns are causal, then removal of guns from the population might avert 0.01 deaths per person per year in the first scenario, but only 0.0001 deaths per person per year in the second. Policy makers would usually like to know the attributable risk, which can be defined as the difference between the incidence of the outcome among the exposed and the incidence of the outcome among the unexposed. For the odds ratio or relative risk to inform policy, it must therefore be considered in light of additional information. The appendix to this chapter provides a detailed discussion of the measures of association in case-control designs, illustrating the strengths and weaknesses of the odds ratio as a measure of association and explaining the information needed to estimate attributable risk.

Psychological Autopsy Studies

A number of studies have now been published that compare the prevalence of firearms in the homes of suicide victims with the prevalence of firearms in the homes of living controls; these studies, most of which make use of a "psychological autopsy" case-control design, are summarized in Table 7-3. Psychological autopsy studies are retrospective studies using interviews with relatives, neighbors, coworkers, or other close contacts of a deceased person (or of a living control subject) seeking to reconstruct the presence or absence of behavioral or psychological risk factors that may have predisposed the death. All of the studies that the committee reviewed have found a positive association between household gun ownership and suicide risk, although the magnitude of the estimated association varies. Although more recent studies have used better data collection strategies and more appropriate study samples (e.g., Conwell et al., 2002; Beautrais et al., 1996), the earlier studies suffer from methodological problems—ranging from sample selection problems to measurement bias, small samples, and

TABLE 7-3 Psychological Autopsy Studies of Firearm Prevalence
and Suicide

Source	Cases N	Controls n
Conwell et al. (2002)	Older adult suicides N = 86	Community controls n = 86
Shah et al. (2000)	Adolescent gun suicides N = 36	School-selected controls n = 36
Brent et al. (1999)	Adolescent suicides N = 140[a]	Community controls n = 131
Bailey et al. (1997)	Female homicides and suicides in the home N = 123 suicides; 143 homicides[a]	Community controls n = 266 pairs
Beautrais et al. (1996)	Suicides N = 197	Community controls n = 1,028 normal controls
Brent et al. (1994)	Adolescent suicides with affective disorder N = 63[a]	Community controls with affective disorder n = 23

Gun Measure	Covariates, Matching Factors	Result: Gun Access and Overall Suicide Risk
Firearm in home	Education, living situation, psychiatric illness	+: any gun, handgun 0: long gun
	Matching: age, race, sex, county of residence	
Firearm in the home	Previous mental health problems, alcohol use, conduct disorder	n/a: no information about overall suicide
	Matching: age, sex, school	(although gun is + associated with risk of gun suicide)
Firearm in the home	Psychiatric diagnosis, family history, life stressors, history of abuse	+: any gun
	Matching by sex; age, race, county of origin, socioeconomic status	
Firearm in the home	Mental illness; history of domestic violence; alcohol use, alcohol problems, prior arrest; illicit drug use; home security	+: any gun
	Matching: neighborhood, sex, race, age	
Firearm in the home	Age, gender, ethnicity, psychiatric diagnosis	0: gun not associated with overall risk of suicide (although gun is associated with risk of gun suicide)
Firearm in the home	Psychiatric diagnosis, family history, stressful life events, past treatment	+: any gun, handgun 0: not long gun
	Matching: age, sex, county of origin, socioeconomic status	

continued

TABLE 7-3 Continued

Source	Cases N	Controls n
Bukstein et al. (1993)	Adolescent suicides with substance abuse N = 23[a]	Community controls with substance abuse

n = 12 |
| Brent et al. (1993a) | Adolescent suicides

N = 67[a] | Community controls

n = 67 |
| Brent et al. (1993b) | Adolescent suicides N = 67[a] | Community controls without psychiatric disorder n = 38 |
| Kellermann et al. (1992) | Suicides in the home

N = 438[b] | Community controls

n = 438 |
| Brent et al. (1991) | Adolescent suicides

N = 47[a] | Inpatient controls

n = 94 47 attempters, 47 never-suicidal |
| Brent et al. (1988) | Adolescent suicides N = 27 | Inpatient controls n = 56 |

[a]Overlapping samples, western Pennsylvania.

Gun Measure	Covariates, Matching Factors	Result: Gun Access and Overall Suicide Risk
Firearm in the home	Psychiatric diagnosis, family history, stressful life events, past treatment Matching: age, race, sex, socioeconomic status, county of residence	+: any gun, handgun 0: not long gun 0: not gun storage
Firearm in the home	Psychiatric diagnosis Matching: age, sex, socioeconomic status, county of origin	+: any gun, handgun •particularly when no psychiatric disorder is present
Firearm in the home	Psychiatric diagnosis, family history, stressful life events Matching: age, sex, county of origin, socioeconomic status	+: any gun, loaded gun •particularly when no psychiatric disorder is present
Firearm in the home	Alcohol use, illicit drug use, domestic violence, living alone, education, previous hospitalization due to alcohol, current psychiatric medication. Matching: age, race, sex, neighborhood	+: any gun •particularly when no psychopathology is reported
Firearm in the home	Psychiatric diagnosis, family history; female headed household, treatment history Matching: age, sex, county of origin	+: any gun 0: Not gun storage
Firearm in the home	Precipitants, psychiatric diagnosis, family history, exposure to suicidal contact	+: any gun

[b]Overlapping samples, King County, Washington, and Shelby County, Tennessee.

failure to control for possible confounders—which raise doubts about the reliability and interpretation of the findings that have been reported to date.

By far the largest psychological autopsy studies of guns and suicide, homicide, and unintentional injury have been conducted by Kellerman et al. (1992, 1993, 1998; Bailey et al., 1997). Their 1992 study of firearms and suicide is representative of their approach. Cases occurred in King County, Washington, and Shelby County, Tennessee, and were selected for study if the suicide took place in or near the home of the victim, regardless of method of suicide used; out of 803 suicides occurring during the study period, 565 occurred in the home and 238 occurred elsewhere. Cases were matched with living controls of the same race, sex, and age range and residing in the same neighborhood; the team sought to interview proxy respondents for both cases and controls, but 50 percent of the control interviews were conducted with the (living) subjects themselves. The structured interviews screened for substance abuse, domestic violence, legal problems, current medications, and history of depression, as well as the presence or absence of a gun in the home, but the protocols did not make formal psychiatric diagnoses. The odds ratio associated with firearms ranked fifth among the seven variables that were included in the final conditional-logistic regression analysis; the seven measures, along with their adjusted odds ratios, included psychotropic medication prescribed (35.9), previous hospitalization due to drinking (16.4), active use of illicit drugs (10.0), lives alone (5.3), gun kept in household (4.8), failure to graduate from high school (4.1), and drinks alcohol (2.3). The adjusted odds ratio for gun access had a 95 percent confidence interval of 2.7 to 8.5. Guns were a stronger risk factor for suicide among the 63 case subjects with no history of depression or mental illness (odds ratio 32.8; 95 percent confidence interval 4.6 to 232.8). According to the proxy informants, only 3 percent of suicides in the sample had purchased a gun within two weeks before death.

This team's focus on suicide in the home would have been appropriate for a study of unintentional injuries. However, the element of intention leads to an important difference between a study of "suicide and guns in the home" (which would be the usual policy question) and a study of "guns and suicide in the home" (which is what the research group elected to study), because it is likely that decisions about method and location of suicide are made together. This means that a study of gun access in a study restricted to suicides that take place in the home may be no more informative than a study of bridge access in a study restricted to suicides that take place from a bridge.

The possibly biased sample selection strategy, as well as other problems in the execution of the study and reporting of results, provoked a storm of attacks on the research team, the federal funding agency, and the medical journal in which the reports were published. It is difficult to determine the degree of bias that was actually introduced in these studies by the sample selection strategy. However, one does learn that 58 percent of suicides taking place in the victim's home occurred by firearm, as did 46 percent of suicides not in the home. An informal calculation using assumptions that are favorable to the investigators suggests that omission of suicides taking place outside of the home may have led to an overstatement of the true relative risk by about 20 percent.[7] There are other problems with the execution of this study that may have actually led to biases of larger magnitude. For example, after eliminating the suicides that occurred outside the home, the investigators collected complete data for only 360 of 565 eligible cases, so that the final results were based on only 64 percent of the sample of suicides in the home and only 40 percent of the total suicide sample.

Several psychological autopsy studies have now focused on the risk of suicide among adolescents. There are three important reasons for selecting adolescents as a population for special scrutiny. First, suicide is the third leading cause of death among adolescents; if reducing access to firearms were a feasible way to reduce adolescent suicide, this would have great public health importance. Second, it is likely that "impulsive" suicides are more common among the young, so that studies of youth suicide may generalize to the type of suicide for which preventive efforts seem most promising. And third, studies of adolescent suicide are less susceptible to problems of reverse causality: because adolescents under the age of 18 are not allowed to pur-

---

[7]We do not have enough information to calculate a matched odds ratio, but an unmatched ratio can give a rough idea of the possible sampling bias. The investigators tell us that 65 percent of case subjects had guns in their home, compared with 41 percent of matched controls. This basic information implies an unmatched odds ratio for suicides in the home of $2.67 = (65/35)/(41/59)$.

How might the results change if we consider all suicides, not just those in the home? There were 238 suicides occurring outside the home during the observation period; 109, or about 45.8 percent of these suicides were committed with a firearm (compared to 57.7 percent among suicides occurring in the home). We do not know the fraction of these suicide victims who owned firearms. Assume, however, that that gun suicide probability by ownership status does not depend on whether the suicide occurs inside or outside the home. Then, from Kellerman et al., we know that 86 percent of suicidal owners used a gun and 6 percent of suicidal nonowners used a gun. Using the law of total probability, we know that the fraction of suicides committed with a firearm (0.458) can be decomposed into a weighted average of the fraction committed by owners (0.86) and nonowners (0.06), where the weights depend on the unknown fraction of owners. This implies that about 50 percent of out-of-home victims owned firearms, and that 60 percent of all victims owned firearms. Under these assumptions, the unmatched odds ratio comparing total suicides with control group equals $2.16 = (60/40)/(41/59)$; if out-of-home suicides had been included in the sample, the crude odds ratio might have been reduced by nearly 20 percent. The results are clearly sensitive to the assumption that the rates of gun suicide by ownership do not vary by the location of the suicide. If instead, one-quarter of suicidal nonowners used a gun (rather than 6 percent), the odds ratio would equal approximately 1.83, about 31 percent less than that reported by the authors.

chase long guns or handguns in any state, an association between household gun ownership and adolescent suicide cannot be attributed to the adolescent's suicidal plan. Six overlapping studies have been published by Brent and colleagues based on cases of adolescent suicide occurring in western Pennsylvania. The most recent report includes all of the adolescent suicides that have been investigated by this research team and can serve as a summary of the studies to date. Subjects were a consecutive series of 140 adolescent suicide victims from western Pennsylvania and 131 community controls who were matched to the group of suicide victims on age, race, gender, county of origin, and socioeconomic status. Family members were interviewed using a structured protocol concerning the circumstances of the suicide, stressors, and current and past psychopathology; parents were also interviewed regarding family history of psychopathology and availability of a firearm (Brent et al., 1999). Like Kellerman and his colleagues, this research group found an association between family gun ownership and the risk of suicide, with an odds ratio of 3.0 (with a 95 percent confidence interval = 1.3-6.8) for older adolescents and 7.3 (with a 95 percent confidence interval = 1.3-40.8) for younger adolescents. They found that firearms in the home appeared to be a stronger risk factor among subjects with no diagnosable psychiatric disorder.

The results that have been reported from these U.S. studies contrast with a large case-control study from New Zealand, reported by Beautrais and colleagues in 1996. This study compared a consecutive series of 197 persons of all ages who died by suicide, 302 individuals who made medically serious but nonlethal suicide attempts, and 1,028 randomly selected community controls. Suicide attempts by gunshot accounted for 13.3 percent of suicides and only 1.3 percent of serious but nonlethal suicide attempts. Access to a firearm was strongly associated with an increased risk that gunshot would be chosen as the method of suicide or suicide attempt (odds ratio = 107.9; 95 percent confidence interval 24.8 to 469.5), but this access was associated with a much smaller, and statistically nonsignificant increase in the overall risk of suicide (odds ratio = 1.4; 95 percent confidence interval = 0.96 to 1.99).

How can one reconcile the very different estimates from the United States and New Zealand? The Beautrais and Kellerman confidence intervals do not overlap, but of course one interpretation of the overall literature is that the estimate lies somewhere in the range between Beautrais, Brent, and Kellerman, with possible differences in effect size by age group and country. The U.S. and New Zealand studies together seem to suggest an odds ratio that may be above one, but is not much larger than two, if one thinks effects in the two countries are likely to be similar. However, the effects in the two countries may differ for reasons that we do not yet understand.

One possibility is that the cultural correlates of gun ownership are different in New Zealand and in the United States, and that, in one or both countries, some of the association between household gun ownership and the risk of suicide is explained by an unobserved characteristic of the families or social networks of suicidal persons. This interpretation is supported by two individual-level studies based on the National Longitudinal Study on Adolescent Health (called AddHealth), which found that adolescents who reported that they had access to a gun in their homes also reported higher rates of nonlethal suicidal thoughts and behaviors (Resnick et al., 1997; Borowsky, et al., 2001). These results may reflect reporting bias on the part of the adolescents (if suicidal adolescents are more likely to admit, or even brag about, the presence of a gun), familial transmission of a mood disorder (if a single heritable trait increases the likelihood that a parent will own a gun, and that an adolescent will experience suicidal thoughts), or correlates of particular parenting styles or family constellations (if parents who are more likely to own a gun are also more likely to have a distant or rejecting relationship with an adolescent child). However, they indicate that the association between household gun ownership and risk of suicide may be due to factors beyond the relative lethality of firearms.

Risk of Suicide Among Recent Gun Purchasers

Another way to clarify the causal relationship between suicidal intention and gun ownership is to study the risk of suicide among recent gun purchasers. Two record linkage studies have done this by using state gun registration systems to compare the risk of suicide among gun purchasers with the risk of suicide in a general population. Both of these studies suggest that a small but significant fraction of gun suicides are committed within days to weeks after the purchase of a handgun, and both also indicate that gun purchasers have an elevated risk of suicide for many years after the purchase of the gun. The first study, by Cummings et al. (1997a), linked the membership list of a large health maintenance organization (HMO) in Washington State with state handgun registration records and state death certificates. Cases were HMO members who died of suicide or homicide between 1980 and 1992; for each case subject, five control subjects matched by age, sex, and zip code were randomly selected from the HMO membership list. For each case and control subject, family members were identified, and computerized records of handgun purchasers in Washington State were searched for the first occurrence of a handgun purchase from 1940 until the case's date of death. About 52.7 percent of the suicides were committed with a gun; 24.6 percent of persons who committed suicide had a history of a handgun purchase by themselves or a family member, compared with 15.1 percent of controls, with an adjusted relative risk of 1.9 (95 percent confidence interval 1.4 to 2.5). About 3.1 percent of suicide victims or their family members had purchased a first handgun within a year of the suicide, compared with 0.7 percent of controls. After the first year, the relative risk of suicide persisted, but at a much lower level; the median interval from first handgun purchase to suicide with a gun was 10.7 years.

The second study, by Wintemute et al. (1999), reported similar findings in a population-based study of individuals purchasing handguns in California in 1991. This study did not investigate the risk of suicide among the family members of gun purchasers, but the changes in suicide risk over time were presented in more detail. Age and sex-standardized mortality ratios for handgun purchasers were compared with the mortality of the general adult population of California. The risk of suicide in the first week after purchase was 57 times the risk of suicide in the general population, and the risk within the first year was 4.31 times the risk of suicide of the general population. The rates of suicide by firearm within the first six years after handgun purchase are presented graphically in Figure 7-2.

Taken together, these two studies provide strong evidence that some guns are indeed purchased for the purpose of carrying out a planned suicide, but this seems to represent only a small fraction of completed suicides: handguns purchased within the past year were used in about 5 percent of suicides in California, and about 3 percent of suicides in the Washington HMO. However, the focus on legal handgun purchases provides only a lower-bound estimate of the fraction of gun purchases that have occurred

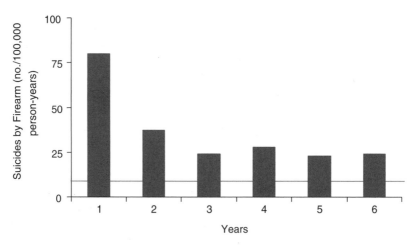

FIGURE 7-2 Rates of suicide by firearm during the six years after purchase among persons who purchased in California in 1991.
NOTE: The horizontal line indicates the age- sex-adjusted average annual rate of suicide by firearms in California for 1991-1995 (10.7 per 100,000 persons per year).
SOURCE: Adapted from Wintemute et al. (1999).

for the purpose of suicide, and both studies concern the purchase of handguns in states with gun registration laws, so they do not indicate how many guns might be purchased for the purpose of suicide if gun registration did not occur. The most important limitation is that these studies do not indicate whether handgun purchasers would have substituted other methods of suicide if a gun were not available, and do not measure other factors, such as history of substance abuse, psychiatric illness, criminal activity, or domestic violence, which might explain or modify a link between gun ownership and propensity for suicide.

Assessment of Individual-Level Studies

All of the individual-level studies reviewed here have found a strong association between gun access and the likelihood that a suicide, if it occurs, will take place by means of a gun. There is also strong evidence that some guns are specifically purchased for the purpose of suicide, suggesting that some individuals definitely prefer a firearm to commit suicide, if suicide is their intention. But such reverse causality does not entirely explain the link between gun access and overall risk of suicide, because several studies have found that adolescents (who are not eligible to purchase guns) are at higher risk of suicide if they live in a home with a gun.

It is not yet clear if the individuals who used a gun to commit suicide would have committed suicide by another method if a gun had not been available. Overall, the U.S. studies have consistently found that household gun ownership is associated with a higher *overall* risk of suicide, but the estimate of such an association was significantly smaller in a study from New Zealand. Although reverse causality cannot explain the association between guns and risk of suicide for adolescents, it remains possible that some other heritable or environmental family trait links the likelihood of gun ownership and suicide. For example, several studies have found that adolescents with access to firearms in their homes are also more likely to report *thoughts* of suicide, suggesting that it may be some unobserved characteristic of gun-owning families in the United States that places such adolescents at higher risk.

Next Steps

Despite these concerns with the existing literature, it is the committee's view that individual level studies in general, and case-control studies in particular, have been underutilized in this literature. All empirical research in this area must be cognizant of the potential for substitution and confounders, but individual-level study designs allow researchers to avoid the biases introduced by aggregation and proxy measures of ownership and are particularly well suited to the exploration of "third variables" that could explain the link between firearms and suicide in the United States.

WHAT DIFFERENCE COULD A GUN LAW MAKE?

While suicide has rarely been the basis for public support of the passage of specific gun laws, suicide prevention may be the unintended by-product of such laws. For example, federal ownership standards that have been set by the Brady Handgun Violence Prevention Act might reduce the risk of gun suicide among several high-risk groups, including persons with a history of violent behavior, substance abuse, and severe mental disorder. Gun storage laws might reduce the risk of suicide among children and adolescents; gun buy-backs might reduce the stock of infrequently used guns that might be used for suicide, and cooling off periods could reduce the use of guns in suicides motivated by transient suicidal states. But gun policies could also increase the risk of suicide. For example, mental health advocates have opposed the creation of registries of persons with a history of mental illness, arguing that the stigma of appearing in a state-sponsored registry could lead some persons to refuse needed mental health treatment, thus increasing rather than decreasing the risk of a lethal outcome.

Tables 7-4, 7-5, and 7-6 summarize studies of the effects of specific gun laws. Several cross-sectional and time-series studies do report a decline in firearm suicides in response to gun control legislation, but so far there is little evidence for an effect on the overall risk of suicide.

Cross-Sectional Studies of Gun Laws and Suicide

We identified 14 cross-sectional studies of the association between strictness of gun control laws and rates of suicide; these studies are summarized in Table 7-4. Overall, most studies found that stricter gun laws were associated with lower gun suicide rates. For example, 8 out of 9 studies found that states or cities with stricter gun control laws have lower rates of gun suicide. These studies have used a variety of methods for classifying the types and strictness of gun laws; it is worth noting that many of them compare the same geographic areas over the same time intervals, so they should not be regarded as independent samples. In general, laws restricting the buying and selling of firearms have been associated with lower rates of firearm suicide, but laws governing the right to carry firearms seem to have no association.

Lower gun suicide rates have sometimes been associated with higher nongun suicide rates, and the findings regarding overall suicide rates have been less consistent: 5 out of 11 studies found an association between stricter gun laws and overall rates of suicide, another 5 studies found no significant association, and 1 study produced mixed results.

Time Series Studies of Gun Laws and Suicide

A number of studies have described the trends in gun suicides in one or two local or national jurisdictions before and after the passage of a gun control law. Studies using one or two jurisdictions are summarized in Table 7-5; most of these studies have also been reviewed in previous chapters. These studies present conflicting findings about the association between gun laws and suicide, depending on the model specification and time period under study. For example, several reports by Rich et al. (1990), Carrington and Moyer (1994), Leenaars and Lester (1999), and Lester (2000) reach different conclusions about the trends in gun suicide and overall suicide and homicide in Canada before and after the passage of restrictive gun control laws in 1977, compared with trends in the United States over the same period of time.

Another notable example in this literature is the study by Loftin et al. (1991) evaluating the District of Columbia's Firearms Control Regulations Act of 1975. This study has been prominently cited as showing a significant decline in gun suicides following the institution of a ban on handguns. However, overall suicides, not gun suicides, are the policy question of interest, and the investigators did not report whether there were significant differences in the estimates of the trend in *overall* suicide rates. Other concerns about the Loftin study were raised in Chapter 5 in relation to homicide, and they are likely to apply to the results pertaining to suicide as well.

The overall problem with the interrupted time-series study design is that simple comparisons cannot distinguish the effects of passage of a gun law from the effects of a myriad of other factors that may be changing over the same period of time. We identified four studies, summarized in Table 7-6, that improve on this research design by using "difference-of-differences" methods across many jurisdictions to evaluate the effect of gun policies on suicide rates. These studies compare the differences in outcomes before and after the introduction of a new policy in the various jurisdictions in which such policies have been introduced, with the differences in the outcomes over the same period of time among otherwise similar jurisdictions that have not been exposed to a change in policy. By making comparisons within the same jurisdiction at multiple points of time and across many jurisdictions at any single point in time, investigators hope to control for unobserved characteristics of the jurisdiction that do not change over time and for unobserved time trends that may be shared across jurisdictions. As with the simpler interrupted time-series design, the validity of the results depends on many assumptions about how and when the law was implemented, how long it might take for the law to have a discernible effect on the use of firearms, how long such an effect might last, and about the presence or absence of other factors that might affect the suicide rate during the time when the gun law came into effect.

TABLE 7-4 Cross-Sectional Studies of Gun Laws and Suicide

Source	Units of Analysis	Gun Law
Kleck and Patterson (1993)	170 large cities, 1979-1981	10 types of law, or aggregate index
Yang and Lester (1991)	48 states, 1980	Strictness of state gun control laws (update of Sommers, 1984)
Boor and Bair (1990)	50 states, DC 1985	Three types of gun laws
Lester (1988c)	9 regions, 1970	Strictness of handgun control laws
Lester (1987a)	48 states, 1970	Strictness of handgun control laws
Lester and Murrell (1986)	48 states, 1960, 1970	Strictness of handgun control laws 1964-1970
Sommers (1984)		Nine types of laws
Medoff and Maggadino (1983)	50 states, 1970	(a) type of law (b) strictness of enforcement
DeZee (1983)	States 1978	Individual and aggregated gun laws

Controls and Strata	Results Gun Suicide	Results: Nongun Suicide	Results: Overall Suicide
% black, % male, median age, unemployment rate, poverty, income, home ownership, college enrollment, transience, population change, divorce, church membership, etc.	Index: decrease Permit: decrease Mental: decrease	Index: 0 Permit: 0 Mental: 0 Dealer decrease Other: 0	Index: 0 Mental: 0 Dealer decrease Other 0
Gun ownership: various proxies	Dealer: decrease Other: 0		
Unemployment, divorce	Decrease	Increase	Decrease
% male, % 35-64, % black, % urban, population density; % population change, divorce rate, crime rate, unemployment rate	n/a	n/a	Decrease
% black, median age, % urban, divorce rate	0	0	0
Gun ownership: Wright survey None	Decrease	0	0
None	Decrease	"Other" increase	Overall: decrease male: decrease female: 0
Divorce rate, unemployment rate	Wait: decrease Mental: decrease	n/a	n/a
White male suicide rates only: age, median income, unemployment rate, occupational prestige, % catholic, region	n/a	n/a	Decrease
% unemployed, % male, % youth, % white collar, % blue collar, % foreign born	n/a	n/a	0

continued

TABLE 7-4 Continued

Source	Units Of Analysis	Gun Law
Lester and Murrell (1982)	48 states 1960, 1970	Three types of gun laws
Lester and Murrell (1980)	States, 1959-1971 1969-1971	Strictness of gun laws in 1968
Murray (1975)	50 states, 1969	Seven types of gun laws, 1966
Geisel et al. (1969)	50 states; large cities, 1960, 1965	Weighted index, handgun laws

NOTE: Decrease/increase: gun law predicts fewer/more suicides; 0 = effect not significant at p =.05; n/a = not stated in report.

TABLE 7-5 Interrupted-Time-Series Studies of Gun Laws and Suicide

Source	Areas Compared	Time Periods Compared	Gun Law
Lester (2000)	Canada	1970-1996	1978 Bill C-51
Carrington (1999)	Canada	1969-1976; 1978-1985	1978 Bill C-51
Leenaars and Lester (1999)	Canada	1969-1976; 1978-1985	1978 Bill C-51
Cantor and Slater (1995)	Queensland (Australia)	1990-1991; 1992-1993	1992 Weapons Act
Carrington and Moyer (1994)	Ontario	1965-1977 1979-1989	1978 Bill C-51
Lester and Leenaars (1993)	Canada	1969-1976; 1978-1985	1978 Bill C-51

Controls and Strata	Results Gun Suicide	Results: Nongun Suicide	Results: Overall Suicide
None	Seller: decrease Buyer: decrease Carry: 0	n/a increase Buyer: increase Carry: 0	
None	n/a	n/a	Decrease
% unemployed, median education, % interstate migrants, % college grads, % white collar, median income, % foreign born, % young adult, log of population	n/a	n/a	0
Per capita income, median education, % male, police per capita, % nonwhite, population density, licensed hunters	Decrease	n/a	0

Change in Gun Suicide After Gun Law	Change in Nongun Suicide After Gun Law	Change in Overall Suicide After Gun Law
Decrease	Increase	Increase
Trend flattens for males	No change in trend for males	Trend flattens for males
Trend varies by age, sex	Trend varies by age, sex	Trend varies by age, sex
Trend varies by urban/rural, sex	Trend varies by urban/rural, sex	Trend varies by urban/rural, sex
Not significant	Trend downward	Trend downward
Decrease	Not significant	
		Not significant

continued

TABLE 7-5 Continued

Source	Areas Compared	Time Periods Compared	Gun Law
Snowdon and Harris (1992)	Australian states	1968-1979; 1980-1989	1980 gun law (South Australia)
Thomsen and Albrektsen (1991)	Denmark	1984-1985; 1986-1987	1986 law
Loftin et al. (1991)	DC vs. suburbs (a) mean monthly rates (b) ARIMA with age-standardized annual rates	1968-1976; 1977-1987	1976 handgun ban in DC
Rich et al. (1990)	Toronto	1973-1977; 1979-1983	1978 Bill C-51
Nicholson and Garner (1980)	DC vs. nation	Two selected years (1976; 1979)	1976 handgun ban in DC

NOTE: ARIMA = autoregressive, integrated, moving-average time series models.

In the first quasi-experimental study to examine effects of gun policy on adult suicide, Ludwig and Cook (2000) evaluated the impact of the 1994 Brady act in 32 "treatment" states that were directly affected by the act, compared with 19 "control" jurisdictions that had equivalent legislation already in place. The authors found a reduction in firearm suicides among persons age 55 and older of 0.92 per 100,000 (with a 95 percent confidence interval = −1.43 to −.042), representing about a 6 percent decline in firearm suicide in this age group. This decrease, however, was accompanied by an offsetting increase in nongun suicide, so that the net effect on overall suicide rates was not significant (−.54 per 100,000; with a 95 percent confidence interval = −1.27 to 0.19). Using a similar methodology, Reuter and Mouzos (2003) found no significant effect study of a large scale Australian gun buy-back program on total suicide rates.

Change in Gun Suicide After Gun Law	Change in Nongun Suicide After Gun Law	Change in Overall Suicide After Gun Law
Decrease (SA males)	Increase (S.A. males)	No difference
No change	Not stated	Decrease (not qualified)
(a) Decrease	(a) Not significant	(a) Decrease (not quantified)
(b) Not significant	(b) Not stated	(b) Not stated
Decrease	Increase-jumping	Not significant
Decrease	Not significant	Decrease

Two other studies have evaluated the effects of safe storage laws on child and adolescent suicide (see Chapter 8). Cummings et al. (1997a) evaluated the possible effect of state safe storage gun laws on child mortality due to firearms; they found an insignificant decline in gun suicides (rate ratio 0.81, with a 95 percent confidence interval = 0.66-1.01) and overall suicides (rate ratio 0.95, with a 95 percent confidence interval = 0.75-1.20) for children under age 15 in states that had instituted such a law. In a similar study, Lott and Whitley (2000) investigated the effects of safe storage laws introduced in various states between 1979 and 1996. They compared gun and nongun suicides among children in the age group most likely to be affected by the law, as well as gun suicides in the next older age group, which should have been unaffected by the law. Their models also controlled for state and year fixed effects and 36 other demographic variables. They, too, found some reduction in gun suicides among children in states with stricter gun storage laws, but no reduction of overall suicide rates.

TABLE 7-6 Quasi-Experimental Studies of Gun Laws and Suicide

Source	Areas and Time Period Compared	Gun Law	Population
Reuter and Mouzos	Australian states, 1979-1998	1996 gun buy-back	Whole population
Ludwig and Cook (2001)	50 states + DC 1985-1997	1994 Brady act	21-54 years 55+
Lott and Whitley (2000)	50 states + DC 1979-1996	Safe storage laws Other gun laws	Children and adolescents 0-19
Cummings, Grossman, Rivara, and Koepsell (1997a)	50 states + DC 1979-1994	Safe storage laws	Children under 15

SUMMARY AND RECOMMENDATIONS

The committee draws the following conclusions on the basis of the present evidence:

1.   States, regions, and countries with higher rates of household gun ownership have higher rates of gun suicide. There is also cross-sectional, ecological association between gun ownership and *overall* risk of suicide, but this association is more modest than the association between gun ownership and gun suicide; it is less consistently observed across time, place, and persons; and the causal relation remains unclear.

2.   The risk of suicide is highest immediately after the purchase of a handgun, suggesting that some firearms are specifically purchased for the purpose of committing suicide.

3.   Some gun control policies may reduce the number of gun suicides, but they have not yet been shown to reduce the overall risk of suicide in any population.

Change in Gun Suicide After Gun Law	Change in Nongun Suicide After Gun Law	Change in Overall Suicide After Gun Law
Continuation of of decreasing trend	Continuation of increasing trend	Increase
No significant difference	No significant difference	No significant difference
Decrease	No significant difference	No significant difference
Mixed: Decrease with higher age limits	Not stated	No significant difference
mixed (see text)	Not stated	No significant differences
No significant difference	No significant difference	No significant difference

There are several substantive differences between the research literature linking guns and crime and the research literature linking guns and suicide. First, there is a cross-sectional association between rates of household gun ownership and the number and fraction of suicides committed with a gun that appears to be much more consistent than, for example, the cross-sectional association between gun ownership and gun homicide. There also appears to be a cross-sectional association between rates of household gun ownership and *overall* rates of suicide, reported by investigators on both sides of the gun policy debate. However, the association is small, the findings seem to vary by age and gender, and results have been sensitive to model specifications, covariates, and measures used; furthermore, the association is *not* found in comparisons across countries. In the absence of a simple association between household gun ownership and crime rates within the United States, the literature on guns and crime has been forced to attend to some of the methodological problems of omitted variables and endogenous relationships inherent in studying complex social processes. The presence of a simple bivariate association between gun ownership and suicide may have prevented suicide investigators from pursuing study designs having a better hope of justifying a causal inference. The issue of substitution has been almost entirely ignored in the literature of guns and suicide.

Some of the problems in the suicide literature may also be attributable to the intellectual traditions of the injury prevention field, which has been strongly shaped by successes in the prevention of car crashes and other unintentional injuries. An unintentional injury prevention model can lead to misunderstandings when it is applied to the study of intentional injury; the investigation of intentional injury should take account of the complexities of preference, motivation, constraint, and social interaction among the individuals involved.

In addition to better addressing these fundamental problems associated with drawing causal inferences, this chapter has highlighted a number of other data and methodological obstacles. What sort of data and what sort of studies would be needed in order to improve the understanding of the association between firearms and suicide? Although some knowledge may be gained from further ecological studies, the most important priorities appear, to the committee, to be improved data systems, improved individual-level studies of the association between gun ownership and suicide, and a more systematic analysis of the effect of firearms laws and related interventions on the risk of suicide.

Proxy Measures of Gun Ownership

The association between gun ownership and gun suicide has led to recommendations for the use of the fraction of suicides committed with a firearm (FS/S) as a proxy for household gun ownership when direct measures are unavailable. This means that a better understanding of the relationship between firearms and suicide may also make a technical contribution to the study of firearms and crime. However, investigators should be aware of the biases that can be introduced by any proxy measures, and they are warned that particularly serious artifacts can be introduced if FS/S is used as a proxy for gun ownership when suicide is also the outcome of interest.

Data Systems

The absence of information about gun ownership has been a major stumbling block for ecological and individual-level studies of suicide as well as for studies of homicide and other gun-related crime. In order to better understand these associations, it would be useful to collect individual-level information about gun ownership in studies of suicidal behavior, as well as information about suicidal behavior in studies of legal and illegal gun use. Indeed, because FS/S should not be used as a proxy measure for gun ownership in ecological studies of suicide, the further understanding of the association between firearms and suicide will be particularly dependent on the availability of direct information about gun ownership. Potentially valuable state-level information could be made available through the regular inclusion of gun ownership questions in the Behavioral Risk Factor Surveillance System, and a better understanding of the possible linkage between household gun ownership and adolescent risk-taking might come from the regular inclusion of household gun ownership questions, in addition to the existing adolescent gun use questions, in the Youth Risk Behavior Surveillance System.

At the moment, the U.S. vital statistics system is the only source of nationally representative information about lethal self-injuries. This system sets important limitations on present knowledge. The proposed National Violent Death Reporting System, now being piloted in six states with funding from the Centers for Disease Control and Prevention, could provide more information about demographic background, intent, circumstances, precipitants, method of injury, and source of the firearm (in the case of gun suicides) than is presently available. In this regard, it may be a much more significant improvement for the study of suicide than for the study of homicide, for which similar national data systems are already available.

But there are potential problems that should be considered in the planning of such a system, which might affect the overall usefulness of the final result (see Chapter 2 for further details). Data systems that collect information about a series of cases (such as the recording of injuries or deaths) cannot be used without an appropriate comparison group to make valid inferences about the association between exposures and outcomes. Will the data be collected in a way that would permit such comparisons? This might be accomplished by using the injury surveillance system in the way that cancer registries are now used, as a source of cases for case-control or record-linkage studies of the risk factors for the designated outcome. Will the data system collect sufficiently complete and reliable information about relevant exposures? It would be helpful to develop the NVDRS system with several specific research questions in mind, to ensure that the system will actually be usable, and will actually be used.

Improved Individual-Level Studies

The committee recommends further individual-level studies of the link between firearms and both lethal and nonlethal suicidal behavior. It would be useful to have an ongoing, longitudinal study that determines both predictors of gun ownership and other known risk factors for suicidal thoughts, nonlethal suicidal behaviors, and completed suicide. Added detail about method choice and correlates of gun ownership would help to clarify the possible link between household gun ownership and intentional injury. In light of findings from previous case-control studies, sources of ascertainment bias, factors influencing impulsivity, and confounding and modifying factors other than psychiatric diagnosis should receive special attention. Several strategies might be used to overcome sources of reporting bias in psychological autopsy study designs. Administrative and medical records may be used to supplement individual interviews, and questionnaire designs and computer-assisted interview strategies developed to investigate sensitive topics, such as illegal drug use and adolescent sexual behavior, may serve as models.

Further Policy Studies

Suicide prevention has rarely been the basis for public support of the passage of specific gun laws, but effects on suicide rates could be an unintended by-product of such laws, and the effects of different firearms policy interventions on suicide remain poorly understood. **Thus, the committee recommends further studies of the link between firearms policy and suicide.**

APPENDIX
MEASURES OF ASSOCIATION IN CASE-CONTROL STUDIES

The odds ratio is the principal measure of association in a case-control study. One of the most useful features of the odds ratio, and the reason for its use in case-control study designs, is that it can be estimated from a response-based sampling design, even if the incidence of the exposure and outcome in the underlying population remain unknown.

Likelihood of Suicide and Gun Ownership

Suppose, for example, that one wishes to learn how the likelihood of suicide varies with gun ownership in a population of 1,000,000 persons for whom there were the following number of suicides among gun owners and nongun owners in the course of one year:

	Suicide = yes	Suicide = no	Total
Gun owner	A = 60	B = 399,940	A + B = 400,000
Not gun owner	C = 40	D = 599,960	C + D = 600.000
Total	A + C = 100	B + D = 999,900	1,000,000

In this population, the incidence of suicide among gun owners is A/(A+B), or 60 per 400,000 per year, and the incidence of suicide among nongun owners is C/(C+D), or 40 per 600,000 per year. To compare these two probabilities, we could calculate the relative risk, which can be defined as the incidence of the outcome in the exposed group divided by the incidence of the outcome in the unexposed group, namely:

$$\text{(1) RR} = \frac{\text{incidence of outcome in exposed group}}{\text{incidence of outcome in unexposed group}} = \frac{A/(A+B)}{C/(C+D)}$$

In our example, the relative risk of suicide among gun owners compared with nongun owners would be (60/400,000)/(40/600,000), which equals 2.25.

However, another relative measure of association is the odds ratio. The odds in favor of a particular event are defined as the frequency with which the event occurs, divided by the frequency with which it does not occur. In our sample population, the odds of suicide among gun owners were 60/399,940, and the odds of suicide among nongun owners were 40/599,960. The odds ratio can then be defined as the odds in favor of the outcome in the exposed group, divided by the odds in favor of the outcome in the unexposed group.

$$\text{(2) odds ratio} = \frac{\text{odds of outcome in exposed group}}{\text{odds of outcome in unexposed group}} = \frac{A/B}{C/D}$$

In our example, the odds ratio of suicide for gun owners relative to nongun owners would be (60/399,940) / (40/599,960), which is about 2.2502. As the outcome becomes more rare, (B) approaches (A + B) and (D) approaches (C + D), and the odds ratio approaches the risk ratio. As a rule of thumb, the odds ratio can be used as a direct approximation for the risk ratio whenever the incidence of the outcome falls below about 10 percent. This "rare outcome assumption" holds true in most studies of completed suicide. Although the rare outcome assumption is not required for the odds ratio to be a valid measure of association in its own right (Miettinen, 1976; Hennekens and Buring, 1987), the odds ratio does diverge from the risk ratio as the outcome becomes more common.

Of what use is this estimate? Why not just calculate the risk ratio directly? It turns out that the odds ratio has several attractive mathematical properties, but the most important property is that the ratio that we have just calculated as (a/b)/(c/d), is equivalent to (a/c)/(b/d). In our example, the odds ratio we calculated is therefore exactly equal to the ratio of gun owners to nonowners among the suicide victims (60/40) divided by the ratio of gun owners to nonowners among population members who have not committed suicide: (399,940/599,960). This sleight of hand means that the odds ratio of exposure, given the outcome, which is the measure of association obtained from a case-control study, can be used to estimate the odds ratio of the outcome, given exposure, which is usually the question of interest.

To see how this works, suppose that we now conduct a case-control study in the population in order to estimate the association between gun ownership and suicide. We might do this by selecting all 100 suicides that occurred during the study year, and by drawing a random sample of 100 control subjects who did not commit suicide during the study year. The results of the case-control study might be as follows:

	Outcome Present	Outcome Absent
Exposure Present	a = 60	b = 40
Exposure Absent	c = 40	d = 60
	a + c = 100 = total cases	b + d = 100 = total controls

Even though the control group in the case-control study now contains only 100 subjects, we have selected these subjects so that they are representative of the frequency of exposure to firearms in the population of nonsuicides from which the control sample was drawn. So the odds ratio for our case-control study is:

$$(3) \text{ odds ratio} = (a/c)/(b/d) = (60/40)/(40/60) \approx 2.25$$

Prospective studies can measure the frequency of the outcome among persons with different levels of exposure; retrospective case-control studies measure the frequency of exposure among persons with different levels of the outcome. But the symmetry of the odds ratio allows us to estimate the risk of the outcome, given exposure, from information about the odds of exposure, given the outcome.

Attributable Risk

In fact, by themselves, neither the odds ratio nor the risk ratio can assist policy makers who need to compare the number of occurrences that could be altered through intervention with the costs of the intervention. Policy makers would prefer to know the attributable risk, which can be defined as the difference between the incidence of the outcome among the exposed and the incidence of the outcome among the unexposed:

$$(4) \quad AR = A/(A+B) - C/(C+D).$$

To see the problem with the odds ratio and the relative risk, consider two populations, one in which the suicide probability conditional on owning a firearm is 0.02 per person per year and that conditional on not owning a firearm is 0.01 per person per year, and another in which these two probabilities are 0.0002 and 0.0001, respectively. The odds ratio and the relative risk are the same in both scenarios, but if guns are causal, then removal of guns from the population might avert 0.01 deaths per person per year in the first scenario, but only 0.0001 deaths per person per year in the second.

In a case-control study, this limitation can be overcome by using information from other sources. When a case-control study is population based—that is, when all or a known fraction of cases in a particularly community are identified and a random sample of unaffected individuals are selected as controls—or when information about the incidence of outcome and exposure are available from other sources, it is possible to calculate the incidence rates and attributable risk from the information derived from the study (see, for example, Manski and Lerman, 1977; Hsieh et al., 1985).

In our example, suppose that we already know that the cases represent all of the suicides occurring in the population in a given year, and suppose that we know the size of the population. We know, from the case-control study itself, that 40 percent of control households in random sample own firearms, and the study has revealed an odds ratio of (about) 2.25 to 1. The "rare outcome" assumption is satisfied, which simplifies the calculations; we can treat the odds ratio as a risk ratio and calculate incidence rates and attributable risks as follows:

The total incidence of suicide in the population is equal to the incidence of suicide among gun owners, times the probability of being a gun owner, plus the incidence of suicide among nongun owners, times the probability of not being a gun owner, i.e.:

$$(5.1) \quad 10/100,000 = (A/(A+B))(.40) + (C/(C+D))(.60)$$

A, B, C, and D are the unobserved "true" frequencies of events in the population. But from the risk ratio of 2.25 we also know that:

$$(5.2) \quad A/(A+B) = 2.25(C/(C+D))$$

So: $(5.3) \quad 10/100,000 = (2.25)(C/C+D)(.40) + (C/C+D)(.60)$
$$= (.90+.60)(C/C+D)$$
$$= (1.50)(C/C+D)$$

Therefore, the probability of suicide among nongun owners = $C/(C+D)$ = $(10/100,000)/(1.50) \approx 6.67$ per 100,000 persons per year; and the probability of suicide among gun owners = $(2.25)(C/C+D) = 15$ per 100,000 persons per year.

The attributable risk is the difference between the probability of suicide among gun owners, and the probability of suicide among nongun owners: $15 - 6.67 \approx 8.33$ suicides per 100,000 attributable to gun ownership. The interpretation of this attributable risk depends on the actual causal mechanism linking exposure and outcome. In our example, there would be about 8.33 suicides per 100,000 that might be preventable by restricting access to guns, if guns were to play a causal role in the risk of suicide.

implementation strategies lack structured evaluations and are not com-
ly informed by an appreciation of the limitations of children's develop-
tal stages.

Table 8-1 is a summary of the targeted populations, program design,
evaluations of 11 selected interventions. This selection has been based
he popularity of the program and whether the program has been peer-
uated using randomized control groups. Most of these programs are
ered on educating children themselves about firearms and violence or
ugh programs involving parents or health care providers. Other com-
ensive programs, such as those listed by the Office of Juvenile Justice
Delinquency Prevention (e.g., Boston Strategy to Prevent Youth Vio-
e) were not listed either because they incorporated suppression and

BLE 8-1 Firearms Prevention Programs

am	Developer, Sponsor and/or Publisher	Type of Program	Target Age or Grade
am	National Rifle Association	"Just say no"	Pre-K to grade 6
to nt m o	Brady Center to Prevent Gun Violence	Physician-directed parent education	Parents

8

Firearm Injury Prevention F

Th
mc
me

an
on
eva
cer
thr
pre
an
len

TA

Prog

Edc
Eag
Gun
Safe
Prog

I n this chapter we review the research on the effec
secondary, and tertiary programs for the preventior
Special attention is given to efforts to prevent the
youth. The first section summarizes behavioral interv
ward reducing firearms injury. The second part consi
about technological interventions aimed at preventing
both cases, the existing research is very limited.

BEHAVIORAL INTERVENTION

In this section we review two aspects of behavior
have been designed to prevent firearms injury: the str
ness of the program plans in each case and the qual
outcomes research data.

The prevention of firearms violence has been addr
ways, from legislative reform, to media campaigns, to
tions. Educational interventions are typically employe
with a focus on modifying the attitudes, knowledge,
vidual children. Other educational and media interve
parents and older youth with messages designed to i
edge of the dangers of firearms as well as methods to
storage. Most of these interventions are developed by
or organizations whose concern for violence—or the p
among the children leads them to be proactive. How
are rarely based on theoretical models or prelimina

prevention strategies for many types of violence, or they were designed specifically to deter illegal gun possession and use.

Outcome Measures

The impact of most of these types of behavioral interventions is measured in terms of changes in knowledge, attitudes, and behavior. Specific outcomes may include knowledge of the danger of guns and attitudes toward firearms and violence. Changes in behavior are detected by proximal and distal outcome measures for the individuals targeted. For example, if the program is designed to educate parents about firearms safety, a proximal behavior goal would be related to how a gun is stored in the home

Description of Program	Evaluation
Motivational program for children in pre-K through grade 1, with easy-to-understand rhymes; activity books for grades 2-6; 7-minute video, reward stickers, parent letter, instructor guides, in-service video. The message: If you see a gun, stop, don't touch it, leave the area, and tell an adult.	Hardy et al. (1996) evaluated a similar program and in posttest found no difference between children's behavior toward firearms in both treated and control groups. Of three programs evaluated (STAR and STOP, see below), Howard (2001) ranks the Eddie Eagle program the best based on educational material appropriate for developmental level and presentation appearance of printed material.
Kit prepares health care providers to talk with patients/clients and their families about the dangers of keeping a gun in the home. The fundamental goal is to assist the health care provider in incorporating gun violence prevention into routine injury prevention counseling.	Oatis et al. (1999) demonstrate in a pre- and post-randomized trial that there was not a statistically significant drop in gun ownership or improvement in gun storage after a practice-based intervention aimed to promote these behaviors.

continued

TABLE 8-1 Continued

Program	Developer, Sponsor and/or Publisher	Type of Program	Target Age or Grade
Straight Talk About Risks (STAR)	Brady Center to Prevent Gun Violence	Skills-building	Pre-K to grade 12
Safe Alternatives and Violence Education (SAVE)	San Jose Police Department (San Jose, CA)	Skills-building	Juvenile offenders ages 10-18
Options, Choices, and Consequences (Cops and Docs)	Roy Farrell, M.D., Washington Physicians for Social Responsibility	Shock	Grades 7 and 8
In a Flash	National Emergency Medicine Association	Shock	Middle school children (ages 10-14)

Description of Program	Evaluation
Straight talk about risks of firearm injury and death. Age-appropriate lessons help children identify trusted adults, deal with peer pressure, and recognize risks related to gun handling.	Using a randomized prospective study design with 600 students, the Education Development Center, Inc. (LeBrun et al., 1999) found STAR to be most effective for increasing gun safety knowledge and attitudes for children in grades 3-5 and only moderately effective for older children. Hardy (2002b) in a randomized control study (34 children ages 4 to 7) concludes that STAR-like programs are ineffective in deterring children's play with guns.
One-day, 6-hour violence awareness class for juvenile offenders and their parents.	Arredono et al. (1999) demonstrate in pretest and posttest evaluations that recidivism rates declined at 2-year follow-up, but no comparison group was used.
Doctor and police officer give a 2-hour presentation of medical, legal, and emotional consequences of gun violence; students are shown photos of gunshot victims whose injuries are the result of gang and domestic violence and suicide attempts.	Health Partners Research Foundation (1999) observes that program improves students' knowledge about guns but does not change attitudes and behaviors. Detailed information about this evaluation is not available.
20-minute video with graphic depiction and emotional impact of gun violence through interviews with children who have been paralyzed, disfigured, or blinded by gunshot wounds.	No evaluation of effectiveness as of 2002.

continued

TABLE 8-1 Continued

Program	Developer, Sponsor and/or Publisher	Type of Program	Target Age or Grade
Calling the Shots	Michael McGonigal, M.D., Regions Hospital, St. Paul, Minnesota	Shock	Juvenile offenders ages 15-17
The Living Classroom Foundation	The Living Classroom Foundation, Baltimore, MD, contact: John Dillow, Director of the Maritime Institute	Shock	Adjudicated middle school students with drug or gun offenses
Teens on Target (TNT)	Operated by Youth Alive! Oakland, CA	Peer-based education, intervention, and mentoring program	Urban youth at risk

Description of Program	Evaluation
Hospital-based 4-hour program. While children are being lectured on trauma resuscitation, a gunshot victim (teenage actor) is brought in, and children are asked to help resuscitate, but "patient" dies. Children are then directed to counselors to discuss their emotions and told that the situation was not real but a realistic rendering of what happens in emergency rooms every day	Health Partners Research Foundation (1999), in randomized treatment and control groups 2 weeks before and after the program, found that levels of discomfort with aggression increased after program. No changes in behavior around firearms were found in this evaluation.
The main purpose of this 9-week program is employment training and GED preparation. One section of one day is spent on gun violence prevention; students are shown a video depicting a violent scene of a juvenile shot in a drug dispute. After the video, children share personal experiences and think up behaviors that can prevent violent outcomes.	No evaluation of effectiveness as of 2002
Peers meet with youth who have been suspended from school for carrying weapons or engaging in destructive behavior. Peers also visit adolescents recovering from violent injuries who convince them not to retaliate.	The National Council on Crime and Delinquency (2001) conducted a randomized prospective study of the program assessing attitudes and behavior toward guns and truancy rates following completion of the program, but results are not yet available.

continued

TABLE 8-1 Continued

Program	Developer, Sponsor and/or Publisher	Type of Program	Target Age or Grade
Hands Without Guns	Office of Justice Programs, Education Fund to End Handgun Violence, Joshua Horwitz. Based in Washington, DC, but implemented in several U.S. cities	Peer-based education and outreach	Middle school and high school students
Child Development-Community Policing (CD-CP) Program	A collaborative effort by the New Haven, CT, Department of Police Services and the Child Study Center at the Yale University School of Medicine	Interrelated training and consultation focusing on sharing knowledge and developing ongoing collegial relationships between police and mental health workers.	Police officers and mental health professions

(locked, loaded, etc.), whereas the distal behavior goal might be to reduce the rare acts of gun violence involving children. If the program is designed to educate young children about firearms, then a proximal behavior goal would be avoidance of a nearby gun, and a distal behavior goal would be the reduction of child gun accidents.

Description of Program	Evaluation
Public health and education campaign aimed at providing a forum for youth encouraging them to develop their own constructive responses to gun violence.	Internal evaluation of the program (1999) reports that pre- and post-campaign surveys with a sample of 400 Washington, DC, students show that kids who could identify the program were less likely to carry guns than those who had never heard of the program.
Police supervisors spend 3 full days in training activities to become familiar with developmental concepts, patterns of psychological disturbance, methods of clinical intervention, and settings for treatment. 　　Mental health clinicians spend time with police officers in squad cars, at police stations, and on the street learning directly from officers about their day-to-day activities.	No evaluation of effectiveness as of 2002

The outcome data may come from a number of sources—self-report, proxy report (e.g., peers, teachers, parents) and direct observation using school records, and criminal records. Most of the programs described in this chapter assess children's knowledge or attitudes about firearms, and most used self-report and questionnaires to assess change in knowledge or attitudes.

A review of the literature reveals only one standardized measure of children's attitudes toward firearms and violence: the Attitudes Toward Guns and Violence Questionnaire (AGVQ), developed by Shapiro and his colleagues (1997) at the Applewood Centers in Cleveland, Ohio. The AGVQ demonstrates satisfactory internal consistency (Cronbach's alpha = .94) and concurrent validity, with 23 items relating to violence, guns, or conflict behavior answered on a 3-point Likert-type scale (disagree, not sure, agree). A factor analysis of the AGVQ revealed four factors associated with participants owning or wanting to own a gun: (1) aggressive response to shame: the belief that shame resulting from being insulted can be undone only through aggression; (2) comfort with aggression: general beliefs, values, and feelings about aggression and violence; (3) excitement: feelings of being excited and stimulated by guns; and (4) power/safety: feeling the need to carry a gun to be powerful and safe on the streets. Shapiro and his colleagues (1998), administering the AGVQ to 1,619 children and adolescents, found that the measure was useful for predicting gun ownership. Validity coefficients were lower for girls in elementary school.

Measuring *behavior* in the presence of firearms is more difficult and rarely done as part of the evaluation of firearm violence programs. When behavior is measured, one of two sources of information is typically obtained:

• Community-wide or school-wide measures of the consequences of gun-carrying or gun violence—for example, school suspensions, mortality and morbidity rates, arrest rates for firearm-related offenses, suicide attempts using firearms. The behaviors that firearm violence programs are typically designed to modify or prevent are often rare events (e.g., accidental firearm deaths), so from a program evaluation point of view it is difficult to assess the effectiveness of a program designed to keep something of low frequency from actually happening. This is because data must be collected from a large number of individuals and often over a long period of time to obtain adequate numbers for analysis.

• Program participants' description of their experiences around firearms through focus groups, class discussions, or questionnaires. Younger children may be asked if they have ever seen or touched a gun, and adolescents may be asked if they carry a gun or if they would use a gun in certain situations. While this information may be of interest, self-reports are subject to biases that may lead to underreporting, particularly when children and adolescents are asked about socially sensitive behaviors (Moskowitz, 1989).

The most direct outcome measure of behavior is an unobtrusive observation of children and adolescents when they encounter a gun. None of the firearms safety programs we discuss has actually utilized this method of evaluation, however, usually because of policy regulations at schools prohibiting even disabled firearms on campus. Nonetheless, direct observation may be the most accurate method of discerning what a child or adolescent would do when confronted with a firearm. Researchers who have directly observed children's behaviors around firearms following an intervention have found high rates of gun play (see Hardy et al., 1996; Hardy, 2002b).

The best evaluation of a firearm violence prevention program should assess its impact on knowledge, attitudes, *and* behavior from a variety of sources, particularly since these variables are not highly correlated. Inconsistencies between children's knowledge and behavior following participation in more general violence prevention programs is well documented (Arcus, 1995). Moreover, Wilson-Brewer and colleagues (1991) found in a survey of 51 programs that fewer than half claimed to reduce actual violence levels. Those that did claim to do so had limited empirical data to support their claims.

The correlation between children's knowledge about guns and the likelihood that they will handle a gun is less well studied. However, a recent study by Hardy (2002b) suggests that the two outcomes following a firearm violence prevention program are unrelated. In this study, 70 children ages 4 to 7 were observed in a structured play setting in which they had access to a semiautomatic pistol. Observers coded several behaviors, including gun safety statements ("Don't touch that!") and gun touching. Assuming that children who say "Don't touch that gun!" to another child have some knowledge that guns are dangerous (or for some other reason should not be touched), one might expect that these children would themselves not touch the guns. Nonetheless, 15 of the 24 children who made such comments in the study subsequently touched the gun themselves during the 10-minute interval.

Another way Hardy (2002b) assessed the correlation between firearms safety knowledge and behavior was to examine the relationship between a child's belief that a gun is real and his or her behavior around that gun. Again, however, the evidence suggests no significant relationship. Specifically, the children who correctly identified the real gun as such were no less likely to play with the gun ($n = 19$) than were children who believed the gun was a toy ($n = 16$). These findings were later replicated in a study with children ages 9 to 15 (Hardy, 2002a).

Study Design

Once the appropriate outcome measures are identified and operationally defined, program developers must decide on the design of the evaluation. Serious evaluations have the goal of excluding alternative explanations for the result; the goal is to ensure that any changes noted in the targeted knowledge, attitudes, and behaviors are due to the program and are not due to extraneous variables and events—environmental changes, developmental changes, practice effects, etc.

There are several steps that program developers can take so as to exclude such alternative explanations. First, depending on whether the program is individual-based, school-based or community-based, developers should identify the target population; for example, a school-based prevention program may be developed for grade schools, or a media-based campaign may be developed for rural communities. Next, the evaluation should be based on a sample of individuals, schools, or communities that are representative of the target population; otherwise the obtained results may depend in some unknown way on the sample and may not be generalizable to the population. For example, if the sample includes only grade schools with highly motivated teachers, then the results may not be generalizable to all grade schools. The key point is that the sample should be representative of an identified population; in the above example, the population is more accurately identified as grade schools with highly motivated teachers.

A second step that program developers can take to exclude alternative explanations is to assess the targeted knowledge, attitudes, and behaviors in a control or comparison group not exposed to the program. Ideally, the comparison group should differ from the treatment group only in the subsequent exposure to the program. Developers can compare baseline data concerning the knowledge, attitudes, or behaviors targeted for change to check that the groups do not differ in systematic ways prior to the intervention. Of course the comparison group and experimental group may differ in unmeasured ways. The ideal way to exclude alternative explanations, including explanations due to unmeasured differences between groups, is by random assignment of individuals or schools or communities to the experimental and comparison conditions. (See Weisburd and Petrosino, forthcoming; Flay, 2002; and Boruch et al., 2004, for discussions of the advantages of randomization in the field of criminology, for school-based prevention programs, and for place-based trials, respectively.) Randomized trials exclude alternative explanations for the estimated differences between the groups because, on average, randomization produces groups that differ only in terms of the prevention intervention. That is, the randomized trials produce defensible evidence because alternative explanations for outcome are spread evenly across the treatment and comparison groups. Even when we randomize to experimental and comparison conditions, it is useful to collect and compare baseline data concerning the knowledge, attitudes, or behavior(s) targeted for change to check that the groups do not, by chance, differ in systematic ways prior to the intervention.

Quality of the Research

Firearm violence prevention programs are disseminated widely in U.S. public school systems to children ranging in age from 5 to 18. Every day children are taught to say "no" to guns and violence by educators who use a variety of methods to get the message across, from depicting the deadly consequences of firearm violence, to building skills needed to resist peer pressure, to using peer educators to reach students at risk. On the surface, this primary prevention approach to reducing firearm deaths and injuries among children and adolescents appears to be a worthwhile venture. A closer examination of these programs, however, suggests that present educational efforts may *not* be effective at reducing the risk of firearm morbidity and mortality among children, and in fact may have the opposite effect for some youth.

Only a few firearm prevention programs have been evaluated for outcome measures of attitudes and behavior using at least some of the criteria listed above: pretest data and randomized experimental and control groups. One of these is Straight Talk about Risks (STAR), a Brady Center to Prevent Gun Violence program designed to educate children (in pre-K to grade 12) on the risks of handling a firearm. Younger children are taught to identify a trusted adult, obey rules, and solve problems without fighting. Lessons for older children center on understanding emotions that may lead to conflict, identifying mixed messages from the media, dealing with peer pressure, and learning about implications for victims of gun violence. Evaluations of STAR have produced mixed results. In a randomized prospective study design with 600 students, the Education Development Center, Inc. (LeBrun et al., 1999) found STAR to be most useful for increasing gun safety knowledge and attitudes for children in grades 3 to 5 and only moderately helpful for older children. However, in a small randomized control study of 70 preschool children (mean age 4.77 years), Hardy (2002b) concludes that STAR-like programs are ineffective in deterring children's play with guns.

Of the more than 80 other programs described at least briefly in the literature, few have been adequately evaluated as to their effectiveness. Those that have been evaluated provide little empirical evidence that they have a positive impact on children's knowledge, attitudes, and beliefs. The field of firearm violence prevention is in its infancy and thus can draw lessons from the related fields of injury, violence, and substance abuse prevention. These fields have experienced the same kinds of developmental issues. For example, substance abuse scientists recognize that care must be taken in devising preventive interventions. In the early stages of substance abuse prevention, prevention programs sometimes increased knowledge about where to get and how to use drugs and cigarettes (Glasgow et al., 1981; Goodstadt, 1978; Thompson, 1978). Similarly, simplistic efforts to educate children about firearms safety and violence are likely to be ineffective and may be potentially counterproductive. For young children, firearm violence prevention curricula may be insufficient to overcome their natural curiosity about guns, impulsivity, and inability to generate preventive strategies in dangerous situations. For older children, the lessons may be unlikely to alter their perceptions of invulnerability and overcome the influence of peer pressure. Moreover, the lessons may result in *increases* in the very behaviors they are designed to prevent, by enhancing the allure of guns for young children and by establishing a false norm of gun-carrying for adolescents.

In light of the lack of evidence, the committee recommends that existing and future firearm violence prevention programs should be based on general prevention theory and research and incorporate evaluation into implementation design. Theory—that is, education, psychological and sociological theories—can be used to formulate prevention programs. This is widely the case in the field of preventive interventions (see Flay, 2002). Prevention scientists use a sequence of studies to test the utility of the theories for prevention and aid in the further refinement of the prevention program (Flay and Best, 1982). These studies are conducted prior to wide-scale evaluation of the prevention program (Flay, 1986, 2002). Similarly, the ideas and theories underlying firearm violence prevention programs should be tested and refined by a sequence of studies. These studies may include structured laboratory observations—that is, researchers working closely with the schools and community groups can recruit a representative sample of children and adolescents and randomize the children to experimental and comparison conditions, collect pretest and posttest behavior, and structure an experimental setting to elicit the targeted behavior.

FIREARMS SAFETY TECHNOLOGY

Safety technologies have often been suggested as an alternative means of preventing injury and crime. Locking technology might be used to limit who can use a particular firearm. Protection technology might be used to shield vulnerable persons or reduce the lethality of weaponry. Sensor and tracking technology might be used to detect concealed weapons, provide situational awareness for law enforcement, detect lost or stolen firearms, limit when or where firearms can be discharged, or identify firearms that have been discharged. To varying degrees, these different classes of technologies are all being developed or considered by the National Institute of Justice, the Office of Science and Technology, and other public and private organizations.[1]

The potential of technology can be especially alluring. If widely adopted and effective, safety technologies may alter the rates of gun ownership, discharge, and mortality, as well as, more generally, the markets for weaponry and injury. The actual effects of a particular safety device on violence and injury, however, are difficult to predict. Even if perfectly reliable, technology that serves to reduce injury among some groups may lead to increased deviance or risk among others (Viscusi, 1992; Violence Policy Center, 1998; Leonardatos et al., 2001).

Many persuasive arguments have been made about the benefits and costs of different firearms safety technologies. Despite the rhetoric, however, there is almost no research that evaluates the efficacy and cost-effectiveness of different interventions. The numerous arguments on the potential benefits and costs of technology are largely speculative.

Locking Technology

To illustrate both the complexities of the issue and the lack of evidence, it is useful to consider what is known about locking devices, perhaps the most widely debated, studied, funded, and utilized firearms safety technology. From simple trigger locks and gun safes to more sophisticated personalized and "smart" guns, the promise of this technology is to reduce the unauthorized transfer and use of firearms.[2] Unauthorized transfers occur in households, for example, from a parent to a child, in seizures from victims to assailants, in thefts from residences, vehicles, and commercial places, and in illicit transfers on the secondary market.

Much of the interest in locking technologies stems from the desire to decrease the number of injuries and fatalities involving children. Children under the age of 18 are not, in general, legally allowed to possess a handgun. Yet each year, hundreds of children are fatally shot or injured in firearms accidents and suicides. Juveniles also use handguns in criminal activities, including the inner-city gang wars associated with the steep rise in the juvenile homicide rate during the late 1980s and the highly publicized

---

[1]See the Office of Science and Technology web page, http://www.ojp.usdoj.gov/nij/sciencetech/welcome.html, for more details.

[2]Basic safety technologies have been around and widely used for over a century. Smith and Wesson, for example, manufactured more than 500,000 guns with grip safeties between 1886 and 1940 (Teret and Culross, 2002). Mechanical locks are available commercially at negligible cost. More sophisticated personalized guns, however, are either not yet developed or not widely distributed.

mass school shootings in which, in many cases, the assailants obtained firearms from their own homes (National Research Council and Institute of Medicine, 2002).

While much of the attention and legislation regarding gun locks has focused on reducing juvenile fatalities, these locking technologies may also impact broader classes of unauthorized possession and discharge. The National Institute of Justice has been particularly interested in the potential of these technologies for reducing the handful of fatalities that occur each year when police officers are fatally shot with their own firearm. More generally, certain types of locking systems may decrease injuries that result from firearms seizures, theft, and illegal transfers on the secondary market.[3] While the specific numbers are unknown, the majority of criminals do not obtain handguns via licensed dealers, and a large fraction of violent handgun crimes are committed by proscribed users (see Chapter 5; Wright and Rossi, 1986; Pacific Research Institute for Public Policy 1997; Cook and Braga, 2001).

Locking technologies may also cause unintended injuries. In particular, locking devices may compromise the ability of authorized users to defend themselves. A lock may fail entirely or may take too much time for the weapon to be of use. In fact, Wirsbinski (2001) and Weiss (1996), in reviewing the engineering design of the different locks for the Sandia National Laboratories, concluded that the existing personalized locking technologies did not meet the reliability standards required for on-duty law enforcement officers.[4]

The interaction between gun safety technology and the behavior of users may also lessen the effectiveness of locking technologies. At the most basic level, authorized users may not lock their guns and unauthorized users may design ways to disable locks, access unlocked guns, or use different weaponry. Safety technology may also lead to less cautious behavior around firearms: authorized users may be careless in storing weapons, juveniles familiar with locked guns may not be cautious around unlocked guns, and so forth. Finally, these technologies may create new markets for firearms among consumers who otherwise would not be inclined to own a gun.

---

[3]Presumably, for locks to deter illegal transfers in the secondary market, the key must be maintained by a third party—for example, the authorized dealer—rather than the owner of the gun (Cook and Leitzel, 2002). This may be possible with some of the automated biomechanical technologies being developed (e.g., fingerprint technology) but may be more difficult with many of the manual technologies.

[4] Wirsbinski (2001) and Weiss (1996), and the New Jersey Institute of Technology (2001) evaluated the reliability of different locking technologies in laboratory settings. A workshop report of the National Academy of Engineering (2003) summarizes some of the key technological and practical barriers to developing personalized handguns.

To evaluate the effect of locking technologies on injury, a number of researchers have laid out conceptual models linking technology interventions to injury. These models suggest that the efficacy of personalization technology depends on the type and reliability of the technology, the extent to which these technologies are integrated into the stock of firearms, and the behavioral response of consumers and producers of firearms. Different sets of assumptions about the nature of these factors lead to different qualitative conclusions about the efficacy of safety technologies. Assuming they are unreliable, not widely used, or result in unintended behavioral responses, many conclude that locking devices may increase injury (see, for example, Violence Policy Center, 1998; Leonardatos et al., 2001). Others, under different sets of assumptions, conclude that these technologies may decrease crime and injury (see, for example, Cook and Leitzel, 2002; Teret and Culross, 2002). It is not known, however, which assumptions are correct. Thus, without credible empirical evidence, the realized effects of different safety technologies are impossible to assess.

In the absence of direct empirical evidence, a number of researchers have appealed to the lessons learned from other product safety innovations and legislation, especially automobile safety technologies. These analogies, however, ultimately do not answer the question at hand—namely, how firearms safety technologies impact injury. While a review of the product safety literature is beyond the scope of this report, it seems clear that (1) the efficacy of product safety innovations varies by product and (2) there are ongoing and controversial debates on the effects of some of the most well-known innovations, including seat belts. In fact, scientists have long warned that safety innovations can lead to offsetting behavioral responses. Auto safety innovations may lead to increased recklessness (Peltzman, 1975); child safety caps may lead to unsafe storage behaviors (Viscusi, 1984); and low-tar cigarettes may lead to increased smoking (Benowitz et al., 1983; Institute of Medicine, 2001). There is hardly consensus on the effects of product safety innovations on injury. Furthermore, in contrast to most other consumer products, firearms safety technology invariably reduces the effectiveness of the weapon. Firearms, after all, are designed to injure. Other safety devices do not generally impair the primary function of the product. Seatbelts, for example, do not reduce the effectiveness of automobiles, and safety caps do not reduce the effectiveness of medication.

Child Access Prevention Laws

Child access prevention (CAP) laws, sometimes referred to as "safe storage" or "gun owner responsibility" laws, make owners liable if a child uses an unlocked firearm. The first of these of laws was passed in Florida in 1989, and at least 17 other states and several cities have adopted similar provisions (Brady Campaign, 2002). State laws differ in what age children are covered, ranging from 12 to 18, in the penalty imposed, from civil to criminal liability, and what it means to safely store a gun. Effectively, however, CAP laws require gun owners with children to lock their firearms.

Two papers evaluate the effects of CAP laws on accidents, suicide, and crime. Lott and Whitley (2002), using the same basic data and methods as in the Lott and Mustard (1997) analysis of right-to-carry laws (see Chapter 6), conclude that CAP laws have no discernible effect on juvenile accidents or suicide, but they do result in a substantial increase in violent and property crime. In sharp contrast, Cummings et al. (1997) find that CAP laws reduce accidents and may reduce suicide and homicide among youth as well, although these are imprecisely estimated.[5] They conclude that during the five-year period from 1990 to 1994, these statutes prevented approximately 39 deaths of young children, and another 216 children might have lived had these laws been in effect in all states.

It is difficult to explain the conflicting estimates. Using state-level injury statistics, both analyses rely on interrupted-time-series designs that assume, after controlling for observed factors, that CAP laws were the only notable change in the environment. The formal models and specifications differ. Cummings et al. (1997) estimates a negative binomial count model with fixed state and time effects but an otherwise parsimonious specification of control variables. Lott and Whitley (2002) use Tobit and log-linear models with fixed state and time effects and a rich specification of 36 control variables to account for variation in demographics (e.g., age, race, income, education) and firearms laws. Lott and Whitley also evaluate different outcomes and assess the sensitivity of their findings more generally.

In both studies, it is unreasonable to assume that CAP laws were the only notable event that may have affected firearms related injury and crime. Time-series variation in crime is thought to be a highly complex process that depends on numerous economic, demographic, and social factors. Moreover, CAP laws and other local firearms legislation may be adopted in response to the local variation in the outcomes of interest. For example, a sharp increase in accidental injuries and fatalities spurred a Florida legislature that had previously turned down similar legislation to adopt the CAP law in 1989 (Morgan, 1989). If the 1988-1989 wave of accidental injuries would have naturally regressed back to some steady-state level, any observed correlations between Florida's CAP law and the injury rate would be spurious. Even if all the other factors that may influence injury or crime are time invariant, the dynamics that connect the law to the outcomes of inter-

---

[5]Webster and Starnes (2000), updating the Cummings et al. (1997) analysis, draw similar conclusions.

est are likely to be complex. The impact of a CAP law adopted in a particular place and time will almost certainly depend on how the law is enforced and advertised over time, how this affects storage practices over time, and how this in turn affects injury and crime over time.

The problems with this research are compounded due to the lack of detailed data on the law, on ownership and storage, and on outcomes. The data do not reveal information on the storage practices of particular households or in the aggregate or how the laws are implemented and enforced. The data do not link ownership to outcomes. Rather, we simply observe aggregate correlations between injury and crime, and CAP law legislation (see the discussion of ecological associations in Chapter 7). It is not known whether the observed associations reflect changes in the behavior of firearms owners, whether changes in accidents are associated with juvenile shooters, or whether changes in victimization are associated with crimes committed in households. A final data related concern is the possibility of changes in reporting behavior. Webster and Starnes (2000) suggest that whether a death is coded as an accident, a suicide, or a homicide is "likely to vary across place and time." If the coding behaviors change in response to the legislation, for example, if after the law is passed accidental shootings are more likely to be classified as suicides or homicides, then the observed empirical results may be due to coding changes rather than the law.

Thus, in the committee's view, until independent researchers can perform an empirically based assessment of the potential statistical and data related problems, the credibility of the existing research cannot be assessed.

Conclusions

In general, we find that the scientific bases for understanding the impact of different technologies on the rates of injury is sorely lacking. The existing research outlines a number of interesting hypotheses, but, in the end, the extent to which different technologies affect injury remains unknown.

We should note that this conclusion stands in contrast to a recently released report from the Institute of Medicine (2002). In particular, the report, *Reducing Suicide: A National Imperative*, recommends safety devices as an effective means of reducing injury associated with firearms. While this recommendation may (or may not) be justified for many reasons, we found no credible scientific evidence in the Institute of Medicine's report or elsewhere that demonstrates whether safety devices can effectively lower injury. Rather, the lack of research on this potentially important intervention is a major shortcoming in the body of knowledge on firearms. Without a much stronger research base, the benefits and harms of technology remain largely unknown.

Thus, the committee recommends that a sustained body of empirical research be developed to study the effects of different safety technologies on violence and crime. There are many obstacles to answering the key empirical questions, not the least of which is the lack of detailed individual-level data on firearms ownership, the use of safety devices and firearms, and the outcomes of interest that, in the case of accidents, are especially rare. Without better individual-level data, researchers will continue to be forced to rely on aggregated data that are subject to many different interpretations and strong assumptions that are rarely justified. Researchers may exploit the fact that many of these technologies have been used for over a century and, more recently, have been widely disseminated. Well-designed experimental evaluations that subsidize technologies in different locales may be an alternative approach to reveal the demand for these technologies as well as their effects on crime and violence.

9

Criminal Justice Interventions to Reduce Firearm-Related Violence

This chapter reviews the state of knowledge of the effectiveness of criminal justice interventions aimed at reducing deliberate or accidental injuries or deaths from firearms. The policies are: (1) gun courts, (2) enhanced sentences for criminal uses of firearms, and (3) problem-oriented policing to prevent firearm-related crimes. These interventions have had recent broad bipartisan support and are a major focus of the federal government's ongoing efforts to reduce firearm-related violence. In particular, over $500 million has been devoted to Project Safe Neighborhoods, a program designed to provide funds to hire new federal and state prosecutors, support investigators, provide training, and develop and promote community outreach efforts (for further details, see http://www.psn.gov/about.asp\). The research evidence, however, is mixed. In some cases, the committee found evidence that programs may be effective, in others the evidence suggests that programs may have negligible effects, and in others the evidence base is lacking.

GUN COURTS

Gun courts, which are descendants of the drug court movement of the 1990s, generally target particular types of offenders for quicker, and sometimes tougher, processing in community-based courts. Gun courts operate differently across jurisdictions but typically feature small caseloads, frequent hearings, immediate sanctions, family involvement, and treatment services. Little research has been conducted on the operations and crime prevention effectiveness of gun courts. Most available knowledge comes from the Office of Juvenile Justice and Delinquency Prevention's examination of a juvenile gun court operating in Jefferson County, Alabama.

The Jefferson County Juvenile Gun Court in Birmingham, Alabama, focuses on first-time juvenile gun offenders. Its core components include a 28-day boot camp, a parent education program, a substance abuse program, intensive follow-up supervision, and community service (Office of Juvenile Justice and Delinquency Prevention, 2002). Birmingham's juvenile gun court is administered as part of the family court and provides services to offenders and their families. The juvenile gun court seeks to provide swift consequences by reviewing incoming cases within 72 hours and trying them within 10 working days. The court also attempts to provide certain consequences by providing judges with the authority to impose mandatory detention of juvenile offenders, with judicial discretion as to whether juvenile cases are eligible for diversion. All offenders attend the 28-day boot camp, and the court can add more time to a youth's stay for various infractions. While the juveniles attend boot camp, parents attend an education program that includes training on improving youth-parent communication skills and discussions of the impact of firearm-related violence on victims, perpetrators, and families. Parents who fail to complete the program may be arrested and jailed. After the youths return from boot camp, they are required to participate in substance abuse classes for six weeks, take mandatory weekly drug tests during this time period, and perform community service work, such as neighborhood and graffiti cleanup. Probation officers and transition aides provide intensive follow-up supervision, and parental involvement is required throughout the adjudication process.

An evaluation of the Birmingham juvenile gun court compared the case processing records and recidivism rates for three groups of juvenile gun offenders: a group of Birmingham juveniles with limited prior offenses who participated in the gun court's core components, a group of Birmingham juveniles with prior offenses who received short juvenile correction commitments and did not receive after-care monitoring, and a comparison group of juveniles from a nearby city who did not participate in a gun court program (Office of Juvenile Justice and Delinquency Prevention, 2002). The evaluation revealed that the Birmingham gun court group had significantly lower levels of recidivism (17 percent) than the Birmingham nongun court group (37 percent) and the comparison group (40 percent). The evaluators also found that having a prior gun offense (common to youth in the nongun court groups) increased the odds of recidivism (Office of Juvenile Justice and Delinquency Prevention, 2002). The evaluation did not provide an estimate of the extent to which the differences among the groups in prior gun offending could account for some of the observed recidivism reductions.

ENHANCED SENTENCES FOR CRIMINAL USE OF FIREARMS

Sentencing Enhancements for Firearm-Related Crimes

Firearms sentence enhancement laws mandate minimum sentences or extra prison time for felonies committed with firearms. Unlike most gun control measures, enhanced prison penalties for firearm-related crimes have widespread support from all sides of the firearms policy debate. Firearms sentence enhancements do not affect the ability of law-abiding citizens to keep firearms for recreation or self-defense and have the potential to reduce firearm-related violence by incapacitating those who have been convicted of firearm-related crimes and deterring future firearms crimes. Although a recent rigorous research study suggests that sentence enhancements can result in modest crime reductions (Kessler and Levitt, 1999), the evidence on the effects of sentencing enhancements on firearm-related crime is less clear.[1]

In their examination of the case for a gun-emphasis policy in the prosecution of violent offenders, Cook and Nagin (1979) conclude that firearms use in robbery and assault deserves stiffer punishment because it increases the chance of the victim's death. In their analysis of case information, Cook and Nagin found that, while there was little difference in recidivism rates between gun users and those using other weapons in Washington, DC, criminals who used a gun in one crime were more likely to be rearrested for a firearm-related crime. Finally, they also found that, in Washington during the mid-1970s, there was little distinction in prosecution and sentencing between firearm-related crime defendants and other-weapon-related defendants when controlling for other characteristics of the case. Apparently, prosecutors had a "weapons" emphasis, but not a "gun" emphasis.

Several small-scale studies suggest that sentencing enhancements for firearm-related crimes might reduce some types of crimes. The results of these studies, however, are sometimes difficult to interpret. For example, McPheters and his colleagues (1984) used interrupted-time-series analyses to evaluate the effects of Arizona's 1974 firearms sentencing enhancement law. They found highly significant reductions in firearm-related robberies in Pima and Maricopa counties and no significant firearm-related robbery reductions in five southwestern cities outside Arizona that did not pass similar laws during the study time period used as controls. This impact on firearm-related robberies, however, may have been due to regression to the mean, as Arizona experienced a 75 percent increase in firearm-related robberies in the two years prior to the passage of the law (McPheters et al., 1984).

---

[1] Two National Research Council reports (1978, 1993) explicitly address the deterrent effects of penalties. Both conclude that the likely effects of manipulations of the severity of penalties are fairly small.

Loftin and McDowall (1981) examined the effects of a Michigan firearms law that required a 2-year mandatory sentence for felonies committed while in possession of a firearm on the certainty and severity of sentences and on the number of serious violent crimes in Detroit. A substantial media campaign announcing that "One With a Gun Gets You Two" preceded the law's going into effect in January 1977, and the Detroit prosecutor adopted a strict policy of not plea bargaining such cases down to lesser charges. Their examination of cases processed though the Detroit Recorder's Court between 1976 and 1978 found little change in the certainty or severity of sentences for firearm-related murders and armed robberies, but they did find that there was a significant increase in the expected sentence for firearms-related assault cases that could be attributed to the firearms law.

Similarly, in their examination of California's firearms sentencing enhancement law, Lizotte and Zatz (1986) found little difference in prison sentences given to firearm-related criminals in California, except when defendants had three or more prior arrests. Loftin and McDowall (1981) evaluated the crime control effects of the Michigan firearms law, again using time-series analysis, and found no significant reductions in armed robbery or firearm-related assaults in Detroit. They did find a significant reduction in firearm-related homicides but concluded that the overall results best fit a model in which the firearms law had no preventive effects on crime. A later analysis by Loftin et al. (1983) affirmed these conclusions.

The Florida Felony Firearm Law mandated a 3-year prison sentence for anyone possessing a firearm while committing or attempting to commit any of 11 specified felonies. Using time-series analysis models, Loftin and McDowall (1984) examined the effects of the October 1975 Florida firearms law on firearm-related homicides, armed robberies, and firearm-related assaults in Miami, Tampa, and Jacksonville. To reduce any historical effects, nonfirearm-related homicides, unarmed robberies, and knife assaults were used as control time series. Loftin and McDowall (1984) did not find any significant reductions in firearm-related crime in Jacksonville and Miami associated with the passage of the gun law. They did, however, find a significant decrease in firearm-related homicides and a significant increase in firearm-related assaults in Tampa. While they recommend further testing and examination of the data, Loftin and McDowall (1984) tentatively concluded that the Florida firearms law did not have a measurable deterrent effect on violent crime. In a later paper, McDowall et al. (1992) pooled the Detroit, Jacksonville, Tampa, and Miami time series with data collected from a study examining the effects of Pennsylvania's 1982 firearm sentencing enhancement law on violent crime in Pittsburgh and Philadelphia. They found that these two cities showed significant reductions in homicide associated with the passage of the law. The pooled results led McDowall and his colleagues (1992) to very different conclusions from the city-level studies. The authors found that mandatory sentencing laws significantly reduced the number of homicides, but the effects of mandatory sentencing laws on assaults and robberies were inconclusive.

Nationwide studies have not found any crime prevention effects associated with firearms sentence enhancements. Kleck (1991) conducted a cross-sectional analysis of 1980 data for 170 cities and found that the existence of a firearms sentence enhancement law was not related to homicide, assault, or robbery rates. However, as Marvell and Moody (1995) observe, cross-sectional designs are not suitable for studying short-term impacts, and it is difficult to be confident that the control variables account for the numerous differences between cities that may mask the laws' impacts. In an attempt to mitigate the methodological problems in earlier research studies, Marvell and Moody (1995) conducted a comprehensive evaluation of the effects of firearms sentence enhancements on crime and prisons. The authors conducted a pooled time-series, cross-sectional design analysis for nearly all states over a period of 16 to 24 years such that, for each state, the other states served as controls. They found little evidence to suggest that firearms sentencing enhancements had any effects on crime rates or firearms use. Moreover, the authors did not find any indication that these laws increased prison admissions or prison populations.

Raphael and Ludwig (2003) observe that Richmond's well-known Project Exile program to deter illicit carrying of firearms by convicted felons is essentially a firearms sentence enhancement initiative, as firearms offenders are diverted from state to federal courts. At the heart of Project Exile, all Richmond felon-in-possession cases are prosecuted in federal courts, with the defendants facing a mandatory five-year prison sentence if convicted. Project Exile also includes training for local law enforcement on federal statutes and search and seizure procedures, a public relations campaign to increase community involvement in fighting firearm-related crime, and a massive advertising campaign intended to send the message of zero tolerance for gun crime and to inform potential offenders of the swift and certain federal sentence (Raphael and Ludwig, 2003). Advocates of the program claim success based on a 40 percent decrease in Richmond firearm-related homicides between 1997 and 1998.

In their evaluation of Project Exile, Raphael and Ludwig (2003) found that the decline in Richmond firearm-related homicides would have been likely to occur even in the absence of the program. The authors revealed that nearly all of the reduction in Richmond firearm-related homicides associated with Project Exile may be attributable to an unusually high level of and increase in firearm-related homicide prior to the implementation of the program. They also found little statistical evidence of an impact between felon-in-possession convictions and city-level homicide rates. Their null finding is robust to a variety of methodological adjustments, including an analysis of omitted variable bias that uses juveniles, who are generally exempt from federal felon-in-possession charges, as an additional in-city control group. In his subsequent analysis of the Raphael-Ludwig data, Levitt (2003) suggests that the expectations of a large decrease in crime associated with Project Exile were probably unrealistic, given the small number of additional felon-in-possession convictions per year (roughly 80) and the small increase in total punishment in Richmond (240 extra person-years of imprisonment that would be associated with an estimated 2.5 percent reduction in crime in Richmond). Greenwood (2003) also speculates that Project Exile did not focus sufficiently on the most dangerous offenders associated with the bulk of firearm-related crime in Richmond.

Mandatory Penalties for Unlawful Carrying of Guns

Mandatory sentencing laws, which require a mandatory penalty for unlicensed or otherwise unlawful carrying of a firearm, seek to reduce gun use in unpremeditated crimes by deterring the casual carrying of firearms in public places. The best known example of laws that institute a mandatory penalty for unlawful carrying is the Massachusetts Bartley-Fox gun law.

The Massachusetts legislature enacted the Bartley-Fox gun law, which mandated a one-year minimum prison term for the unlicensed carrying of firearms and a two-year sentence for crimes committed while possessing a gun, to reduce the incidence of firearm-related crime as well as the illicit carrying of firearms (Beha, 1977). The amendment was adopted in July 1974 and became effective beginning in April 1975. Two months prior to the law's effective date, a concerted campaign was launched to characterize the impending consequences in the following terms, "If you are caught with a gun, you will go to prison for a year and nobody can get you out" (Pierce and Bowers, 1981:122).

While the mandatory sentence provision removed most judicial discretion in sentencing a defendant convicted of illegally carrying a gun, the defendant could in fact escape the 1-year sentence in a variety of ways (Deutsch and Alt, 1977). If someone was apprehended with a firearm on his person, the police could file a charge of illegal possession, which does not carry a mandatory minimum, rather than a charge of illegal carrying. Later in the process, prosecutors could also press for the lesser possession charge regardless of the initial police charge. Judges and juries could also find the defendant guilty of a lesser charge. As Zimring commented, "the one-year minimum will only invoke mandatory one-year jail terms for carrying without a license to the extent that police, prosecutors, and judges want it to produce such results. If there is strong resistance from any single link in this chain, the mandatory minimum can be avoided" (as quoted in Deutsch and Alt, 1977:545).

A series of studies examined the impact of the Bartley-Fox law on gun crime and the administration of justice in Boston. Beha (1977) examined the daily application of the Bartley-Fox law by police, prosecutors, and judges through simple before-after analyses of prosecutions for firearms violations and firearm-related crimes in Boston between 1974 and 1975. He analyzed two 6-month samples of all complaints relating to the illegal use, possession, or carrying of a firearm for 1974 and 1975 drawn from the dockets of Boston district courts and cross-checked against Boston Police Department records.

His analysis suggests that Bartley-Fox made it more likely for a prison sentence to be imposed in both firearm assault prosecutions and cases in which illegal carrying was the most serious charge, but the law did not affect the disposition of prosecutions for armed robbery and homicide. Beha (1977) also found that criminal justice officials did not systematically attempt to evade the mandatory sentence. In an analysis of yearly issuances of firearms identification cards and licenses to carry firearms between 1970 and 1975, Beha reported that the high degree of publicity attendant on the amendment's passage, some of which was inaccurate, increased citizen compliance with existing legal stipulations surrounding firearm acquisition and possession, some of which were not in fact addressed by the amendment. Using simple before-after analyses of percentage changes in reported crime rates between 1970 and early 1977, Beha notes that the law did not seem to affect armed robbery but produced definite reductions in firearm-related assaults and firearm-related assault-homicides. However, the total number of aggravated assaults remained constant over time, suggesting a shift from guns to less lethal weapons.

Other studies suggest that criminal justice practitioners may have hindered the implementation of the Bartley-Fox law. In interviews with Boston police officers, Carlson (1982) found that 89 percent of the officers interviewed reported becoming more selective about whom to frisk for weapons, as they did not want to arrest someone who was otherwise a law-abiding citizen. The National Institute of Justice also reports that, between 1974 and 1976, arrests in gun incidents decreased by 23 percent, while weapons seizures without arrest increased by 120 percent. While it is unclear whether the number of guns seized without arrest increased in tandem with all weapons seizures, these figures suggest that police may have made fewer gun-carrying arrests to evade the law.

Rossman et al. (1980) found that Bartley-Fox impeded the flow of cases through the criminal justice system, as defendants had no incentive to plead guilty. They found that the rate at which gun-carrying cases went to trial tripled, the conviction rate was halved, and the median time to disposition doubled. Dismissals and not-guilty verdicts doubled, suggesting that judges may have been avoiding the imposition of the mandatory sentence for some defendants. Rossman and his colleagues (1980) also found that, while a smaller fraction of gun-carrying defendants were convicted of felony gun-carrying, the fraction that received prison sentences did increase. These shifts in case processing and the discretionary actions of criminal justice practitioners in Massachusetts are common responses to the adoption of mandatory sentences (see, e.g., Alschuler, 1978).

Pierce and Bowers (1981) used interrupted-time-series techniques and multiple control group comparisons to examine the impact of Bartley-Fox on firearm-related and nonfirearm-related assaults, robbery, and homicide in Boston. They found a statistically significant reduction in gun assaults in March 1975, one month prior to the implementation of the Bartley-Fox law. The authors suggest that the vigorous publicity campaign influenced behavior before the law actually went into effect. The multiple control group comparison consisted of simple percentage change analyses of firearm-related crime rates in 1974 and 1975 for Boston relative to other New England cities, the United States without Massachusetts, the middle Atlantic states, the north central states, and selected cities within a 750-mile radius, including Washington, DC, Baltimore, New York, Philadelphia, Cleveland, and Detroit. Pierce and Bowers (1981) found that the law significantly reduced firearm-related assaults, but produced offsetting increases in nonfirearm-related armed assaults; there was some reduction in firearm-related robberies accompanied by a lesser increase in nonfirearm-related armed robberies; and firearm-related homicides were reduced with no increase in nonfirearm-related homicides. They conclude that the law, in the short term, may have deterred some individuals from carrying or using their firearms, but it did not prevent them from substituting alternative weapons.

Using similar methods, Deutsch and Alt (1977) analyzed police reports of firearm-related assaults, homicide (all types), and armed robbery (including other weapons) for the time period January 1966 through October 1975. The evaluation was designed to detect short-term impacts of the law, as it only included a six-month horizon after the enactment of the law. Deutsch and Alt found a statistically significant 18 percent decrease in gun assaults and a statistically significant 20 percent decrease in armed robberies, but no statistically significant changes in homicide incidents. Hay and McCleary (1979) reanalyzed Deutsch and Alt's data and suggest that the stochastic components of the time series were not specified correctly and the postintervention time series was too short to permit an accurate specification of the intervention component. Hay and McCleary suggest that the Deutsch and Alt findings are inconclusive. In a rejoinder, Deutsch (1979) critiques the ARIMA model specification choices made by Hay and McCleary in their reanalysis and comments that their research was "wrought with inconsistencies, inaccuracies, and half truths" (p. 327).

In their analysis of the Deutsch and Alt data, Berk and his colleagues (1979) conclude that the law reduced armed robbery, had mixed effects on firearm-related assaults, and had no effects on homicides. In his later analysis, Deutsch (1981) expanded the time series through September 1977 and found that the Bartley-Fox law produced significant reductions in homicide, firearm-related assaults, and armed robbery. The broader methodological lesson learned from this exchange was that identifying appropriate models for evaluation purposes can be a very subjective exercise. As Kleck (1997) suggests, "Experts in [time series] modeling also commonly point out difficulties that even experienced practitioners have in specifying time series models. Specification is very much an art rather than a science, so that different researchers, using the same body of data, can make substantially different, even arbitrary, specification decisions, and, as a result, obtain sharply different results" (p. 354).

Indeed, with such dissimilar findings, it is difficult to specify the effects of the Bartley-Fox law on firearm-related crime. Collectively, this body of research seems to suggest a broad impact on gun crime in Boston. However, it is unclear whether the firearms sentencing enhancement or the mandatory sentence for illegal gun-carrying generated the impact. Kleck (1991) observes that, if one accepts that the Bartley-Fox law worked as a whole, it is risky to infer that other gun-carrying laws would also work, since it may have been a unique constellation of factors in the Boston setting that was responsible for the effect.

Conclusion

Punishment enhancements for firearm-related crimes seem to be justified in sentencing by seriousness considerations, since firearms use in violent crimes increases the likelihood of the victim's death (Cook and Nagin, 1979). Moreover, there is some evidence to suggest that there should be an incapacitation effect, since gun offenders usually persist in their choice of using a firearm in subsequent crimes (Cook and Nagin, 1979). However, the available research evidence on the deterrent effects of firearms sentencing enhancements on firearm-related crime is mixed, with city-level studies suggesting reductions in firearm-related homicides and possibly other types of firearm-related crime in urban settings (McDowall et al., 1992), as well as nationwide studies suggesting no crime prevention effects at the state level (Marvell and Moody, 1995).

The committee recommends more rigorous study of firearms sentencing enhancement laws at the city level. As Kleck (1997) suggests, state-level analyses suffer from aggregation bias, and lumping heterogeneous jurisdictions into one area could conceal potentially important causal effects at lower levels of aggregation. City-level studies need to engage more rigorous methods, such as pooled time-series, cross-sectional studies that allow the detection of short-term impacts while controlling for variation in violence levels both across different areas and different times.

PROBLEM-ORIENTED POLICING TO PREVENT FIREARM-RELATED CRIME

Problem-oriented policing may hold some promise for reducing firearm-related violence. Problem-oriented policing works to identify *why* things are going wrong and to frame responses using a wide variety of approaches. Using an iterative focus on problem identification, analysis, response, evaluation, and adjustment of the response, problem-oriented policing has been applied against a wide variety of crime, fear, and disorder concerns (Goldstein, 1990; Eck and Spelman, 1987; Braga et al., 1999). Our review emphasizes programs specifically aimed at reducing proscribed possession and firearm-related violence.[2] Problem-oriented policing programs to reduce firearm-related violence generally focus on reducing the illegal possession, carrying, and use of firearms in gun violence "hot spots" and among violent gun offenders.

While this section categorizes these types of police interventions by whether they are primarily focused on places or offenders, in practice these firearm-related crime prevention strategies overlap. For example, when the police are deployed to prevent gun violence in particular places, they often focus their attention on controlling the illegal gun behaviors of particular individuals in that location. When police efforts are focused on preventing gun violence by likely offenders, such as gang members, they sometimes focus their attention on places, such as gang turf and drug market areas frequented by these individuals. The distinction between a focus on offenders and a focus on places matters less than the idea that the police attempt to reduce crime and violence by strategically focusing on identifiable risks.

Policing Gun Violence Hot Spots

Place-oriented crime prevention strategies have begun to occupy a central role in police crime prevention research and policy (Eck and Weisburd, 1995). This idea developed from the hot-spots crime perspective, which suggests that crime does not occur evenly across urban landscapes; rather, it is concentrated in a relatively few places that generate more than half of all observed criminal events (Pierce et al., 1988; Sherman

---

[2]For a recent review of problem oriented policing in general, see National Research Council (2004).

et al., 1989; Weisburd et al., 1992). Even in the most crime-ridden neighborhoods, crime appears to cluster at a few discrete locations, and other areas are relatively crime free (Sherman et al., 1989). A number of researchers have argued that many crime problems can be reduced more efficiently if police officers focus their attention on these deviant places (Sherman, 1995; Weisburd, 1997). Sherman and Rogan (1995) suggest three mechanisms through which hot-spots patrol may reduce firearm-related crime in a targeted beat: firearms seized in high firearm-related crime areas may have had significantly higher risk of imminent firearms use in crimes; illegal gun carriers who are arrested may be more frequent gun users; and the visibility of the intensive patrols coupled with increased contacts with citizens may deter gun-carrying by those who are not checked by the police.

Much attention has focused on using place-based policing to reduce gun crime (Sherman, 2001). In this section, we review the evidence from the Kansas City Gun Project and its subsequent replications in Indianapolis and Pittsburgh. All three of these evaluations used place-oriented policing strategies to attempt to confiscate proscribed firearms and prevent crime in gun violence hot spots. We also briefly summarize the anecdotal evidence on the New York Street Crime Unit.

Kansas City Gun Project

The Kansas City Gun Project examined the gun violence prevention effects of proactive patrol and intensive enforcement of firearms laws via safety frisks during traffic stops, plain view searches and seizures, and searches incident to arrests on other charges (Sherman and Rogan, 1995). Over a 6-month period in 1992-1993, the targeted police patrols were conducted in a 10 × 8 block area of Kansas City with a homicide rate 20 times higher than the national average. Simple computer analyses of call and incident data were used to focus police interventions at hot-spot locations. A pair of two-officer cars, working overtime from 7 p.m. to 1 a.m. 7 days a week and not required to answer citizen calls for service, provided extra patrol in the targeted beat.[3] Data from the targeted area were compared with data from a beat with nearly identical numbers of drive-by shootings in 1991. The comparison beat received routine levels of police activities.

---

[3] The officers initiated a high volume of contact with the street population. During 29 weeks in 1992-1993, the directed patrols resulted in 1,090 traffic citations, 948 car checks, 532 pedestrian checks, 170 state or federal arrests, and 446 city arrests (Sherman and Rogan, 1995).

Comparing the differences in crime rates in the targeted and control communities both before and after the intervention, Sherman and Rogan (1995) assessed the impact of hot-spot policing on firearms seizures and crime. The evaluation concludes that proactive patrols focused on firearms recoveries resulted in a statistically significant 65 percent increase in firearms seizures (29 additional firearms seized) and a statistically significant 49 percent decrease in firearm-related crimes in the target beat area (83 fewer firearm-related crimes); firearms seizures and firearm-related crimes in the comparison beat area did not significantly change (Sherman and Rogan, 1995).[4] Furthermore, none of the contiguous beats showed significant increases in firearm-related crime, and two of the contiguous beats reported significant decreases in firearm-related crimes.

Indianapolis Directed Patrol Project

During a 90-day period beginning in July 1997, the Indianapolis Police Department (IPD) implemented a police strategy similar to the Kansas City program (McGarrell et al., 2001). The Indianapolis program tested the effects of two types of directed patrol strategies on firearm-related crime. In the north district, the IPD pursued a directed patrol strategy that sought to prevent firearm-related violence by focusing on suspicious activities and locations. In the east district, the IPD pursued a general deterrence strategy that attempted to prevent firearm-related violence by maximizing the number of vehicle stops in the targeted area. In contrast to the Kansas City study, police activities were not guided by computer analyses of hot-spot locations in either of the targeted areas. Finally, IPD officials worked closely before and during the intervention to secure community support and address concerns (McGarrell et al., 2001). IPD officers were trained to treat citizens with respect and to explain the reasons for the stop.

The evaluation used a pre-post design to determine the effects of the two strategies on firearm-related crime. Both target areas were compared with the same comparison district as well as to citywide crime trends. During the 90-day intervention period, the number of firearms seized in the east district increased by 50 percent, while the north district experienced a modest 8 percent increase (McGarrell et al., 2001). The number of firearms seized in the comparison area decreased by 40 percent. The evaluation revealed that there were statistically significant decreases in firearm-related crime, homicide, aggravated assault with a firearm, and armed robbery in the north district. No statistically significant changes in firearm-related crime were noted in the east district. The evaluation did not reveal any

---

[4]Sherman and Rogan (1995) estimated that there were at least 100,000 handguns in Kansas City.

evidence of immediate spatial displacement of firearm-related crime or significant diffusion of crime control benefits into surrounding areas. It is also
noteworthy that not a single citizen complaint was tied to the directed
patrol study (McGarrell et al., 2001).

Police Gun Suppression Patrols in Pittsburgh

Over a 14-week period beginning in July 1998, the Pittsburgh Police
Department focused on suppressing illegal guns on city streets through the
implementation of a special Gun Suppression Patrol program (Cohen and
Ludwig, 2003). Two patrol teams of four officers each were assigned to
separate police zones experiencing high rates of illegal gun activity. With
the aid of crime maps and activity reports on recent shots fired, the patrol
teams focused on high-risk times and high-risk places in targeted areas. The
patrol teams initiated citizen contacts through traffic stops and "stop and
talk" activities with persons on foot. These contacts were used as an opportunity to solicit information and investigate suspicious activities associated
with illegal carrying and use of guns. When warranted for officer safety
reasons (usually suspicious actions or demeanor), pat-downs for weapons
were conducted; when there was reasonable suspicion of criminal activity
and an arrest made, these searches sometimes escalated to more thorough
checks (Cohen and Ludwig, 2003).

The impact evaluation of the Pittsburgh program used a repeated-
differences model. Shots-fired calls for service and firearm-related injuries
in the two treatment zones were compared with those in the remaining four
police zones in Pittsburgh. The 6-week period between June 7 and July 18,
1998, served as the pre-period, and the 14 weeks between July 19 and
October 24 were the post-period. The evaluation found that shots-fired
calls for service from residents were reduced by more than 50 percent in one
target area, and gunshot injuries were down by nearly 70 percent in the
other target area, representing a reduction of 2.5 gunshot injuries weekly in
the latter target area (Cohen and Ludwig, 2003).

New York Police Department's Street Crime Unit

Beginning in 1994, the New York Police Department (NYPD) maintained a special Street Crime Unit that targeted firearm-related violence hot
spots and aggressively sought out sources of illegal firearms (Office of
Juvenile Justice and Delinquency Prevention, 1999). Between 1994 and
1997, the NYPD made 46,198 gun arrests and confiscated 56,081 firearms.
Nonfatal shootings declined by 62 percent between 1993 and 1997 and, in
1998, New York had only 633 homicides, its lowest since 1964 (Office of
Juvenile Justice and Delinquency Prevention, 1999). At the same time, the

aggressive policing tactics of the NYPD have been criticized as resulting in increased citizen complaints about police misconduct and abuse of force (Greene, 1999).[5] The aggressive gun-oriented policing strategies of the NYPD have not been formally evaluated.[6]

What Has Been Learned?

The evidence from the three targeted place-based firearm and crime suppression patrols is compelling. All three evaluations are well designed and all reveal the same qualitative conclusion, namely, increased firearms seizures, reductions in crime, and little if any displacement. Moreover, these findings are supported by the larger literature on actual randomized policing experiments, which show place-based policing interventions as having substantial crime control effects (see the National Research Council, 2004).

Despite these encouraging findings, there are several shortcomings in the research information that create uncertainty about the potential efficacy of place-based targeted firearms patrols. At the most basic level, the credibility of the quasi-experimental statistical model rests with whether the underlying comparison group is in fact comparable (Meyer, 1995). In particular, the methodology rests on an assumption that the only important difference between the targeted and control patrol areas is in the intervention. In fact, however, the targeted areas were not chosen at random and were not identical to the comparison patrols. Even if the groups are comparable, these evaluations cannot reveal whether the findings reflect a change from general to targeted policing or a change in resource allocation. In all three evaluations, additional resources were explicitly devoted to the targeted areas. The Kansas City program, for example, included both targeted interventions and additional nighttime patrols. Finally, the interventions were of limited duration and scope, focusing on particular areas at particular points in time. As such, the evaluations may not provide insight into the long-term, large-scale potential of these targeted interventions.

Will hot-spot policing have long-term deterrent effects on gun violence? To what extent will there be geographic substitution of violence? How long will it take criminals to adapt to the new system? Will other forms of crime and violence emerge as police change the focus of their efforts? These are important questions for policy officials who must make decisions about whether and how widely to implement such programs.

---

[5]Others suggest that the increase in the number of citizen complaints is unremarkable; the NYPD's broader "broken windows" policing strategy significantly increased the number of police-resident contacts, resulting in an overall decrease in the rate of citizen complaints per police-resident contact.

[6]Other aspects of the New York City policing practices in the 1990s have been evaluated. For a review of this literature, see National Research Council (2004).

Given the early success of these three modest interventions and given the consistency of the basic finding, it would seem worthwhile to learn more about the longer term impacts. **Thus, the committee recommends that a sustained and systemic research program be devoted to studying the impact of different place-based gun suppression patrol and targeted policing approaches in general.** These evaluations should focus on replicating the existing evidence in different settings, running experimental evaluations, and formalizing and estimating behavioral models of policing and crime. Additional evaluations should assess the longer term impacts, paying particular attention to issues of substitution, adaptation, and deterrence.

Policing Violent Gun Offenders

A small number of chronic offenders generate a disproportionate share of crime. In their seminal study of nearly 10,000 boys in Philadelphia, Wolfgang et al. (1972) revealed that the most active 6 percent of delinquent boys were responsible for more than 50 percent of all delinquent acts committed. The RAND Corporation's survey of jail and prison inmates in California, Michigan, and Texas revealed that, in all three states, the most frequent 10 percent of active offenders committed some 50 percent of all crimes and 80 percent of crimes were committed by only 20 percent of the criminals (Chaiken and Chaiken, 1982). Moreover, 1 percent of offenders committed crimes at the very high rate of more than 50 serious offenses per year (Rolph et al., 1981).

The observation that a small number of highly active offenders generates a large share of the crime problem is an important insight for law enforcement agencies with limited resources to prevent crime. Many serious urban crime problems, for example gang violence, are driven by groups of these criminally active individuals. Focusing criminal justice attention on a small number of high-risk offenders may be a promising way to control gun violence.

St. Louis Youth Firearm Suppression Program

The Firearm Suppression Program (FSP) sought parental consent to search for and seize the guns of juveniles (Rosenfeld and Decker, 1996). While this program was not explicitly focused on dangerous offenders, it represents a police program to prevent firearm-related violence by disarming a very risky population of potential gun offenders—juveniles. The program was operated by the St. Louis Metropolitan Police Department's Mobile Reserve Unit, which is a police squad dedicated to responding to pockets of crime and violence throughout St. Louis (Rosenfeld and Decker, 1996). Home searches were initiated on the basis of resident requests for police service, reports from other police units, and information gained from other investigations. As Rosenfeld and Decker describe, "an innovative feature of the program is its use of a 'Consent to Search and Seize' form to secure legal access to the residence. Officers inform the adult resident that the purpose of the program is to confiscate illegal firearms, particularly those belonging to juveniles, without seeking criminal prosecution. The resident is informed that she will not be charged with the illegal possession of a firearm if she signs the consent form" (p. 204). While it was operating, the program generated few complaints from the persons who were subjected to the search, but it received criticism from local representatives of the American Civil Liberties Union, who questioned the possibility of receiving real consent to search when a person is standing face-to-face with two police officers (Rosenfeld and Decker, 1996).

A key component of the program was to respond to problems identified by residents, and the success of the program was reliant on effective police-community relationships. By seeking and acquiring community input into the process of identifying and confiscating guns from juveniles, the St. Louis Metropolitan Police Department developed a model of policing gun violence that put a premium on effective communication and trust with the community not found in most problem-oriented policing projects. As Rosenfeld and Decker (1996) observe, the Firearm Suppression Program was also designed to send a clear message that juvenile firearms possession will not be tolerated by the police or the community because it places individuals at risk and threatens public safety. However, while this program gained national attention for its innovative approach and seemed to be a promising route to disarming juveniles,[7] the Mobile Reserve Unit underwent a series of changes that caused the program to be stopped and restarted several times; the subsequent incarnations did not take the same approach as the original program. A rigorous impact evaluation of the original Firearm Suppression Program was not completed.

Boston Gun Project and Operation Ceasefire

The Boston Gun Project was a problem-oriented policing enterprise expressly aimed at taking on a serious, large-scale crime problem—homicide victimization among young people in Boston. Like many large cities in the United States, Boston experienced a large, sudden increase in youth homicide between the late 1980s and early 1990s. The Boston Gun Project proceeded by: (1) assembling an interagency working group of largely line-level criminal justice and other practitioners; (2) applying quantitative and

---

[7]Rosenfeld and Decker (1996) note that the officers involved in the program seized 402 firearms in 1996 and, during the first quarter of 1996, seized 104 firearms.

qualitative research techniques to create an assessment of the nature of and dynamics driving youth violence in Boston; (3) developing an intervention designed to have a substantial, short-term impact on youth homicide; (4) implementing and adapting the intervention; and (5) evaluating the intervention's impact (Kennedy et al., 1996). The project began in early 1995 and implemented what is now known as the Operation Ceasefire intervention, which began in late spring 1996. While the Boston Gun Project initially focused on firearms and firearm-related violence, the focus evolved as it found that gangs and violent gang offending were central to Boston's youth gun violence problem. To trigger intervention, any serious violent offending by a gang (knives, blunt instrument beatings) was enough. In practice, however, it was mostly gun offending. Because much of the youth violence epidemic in the 1990s involved firearms and because the Boston Gun Project is cited as a highly effective way to reduce youth firearm-related violence, we devote attention to it in this report.

The project has been extensively described and documented (Kennedy et al., 1996; Kennedy et al., 1997; Kennedy, 1997). Briefly, a working group of law enforcement personnel, youth workers, and researchers diagnosed the youth violence problem in Boston as one of patterned, largely vendetta-like hostilities("beefs") among a small population of chronic criminal offenders, and particularly among those involved in some 60 loose, informal, mostly neighborhood-based groups (these groups were called "gangs" in Boston, but were not Chicago- or LA-style gangs, which are much larger and more formally organized). As this diagnosis developed, the focus of the project shifted from its initial framework of juvenile violence and firearm-related violence to gang violence. A central hypothesis of the working group was that a meaningful period of substantially reduced youth violence might serve as a firebreak and result in a relatively long-lasting reduction in future youth violence (Kennedy et al., 1996). The idea was that youth violence in Boston had become a self-sustaining cycle among a relatively small number of youth, with objectively high levels of risk leading to nominally self-protective behavior, such as gun acquisition and use, gang formation, tough street behavior, and the like: behavior that then became an additional input into the cycle of violence (Kennedy et al., 1996). If this cycle could be interrupted, a new equilibrium at a lower level of risk and violence might be established, perhaps without the need for continued high levels of either deterrent or facilitative intervention. The larger hope was that a successful intervention to reduce gang violence in the short term would have a disproportionate, sustainable impact in the long term.

The Operation Ceasefire "pulling-levers" strategy was designed to deter by reaching out directly to gangs, saying explicitly that violence would no longer be tolerated, and backing up that message by "pulling every lever" legally available when violence occurred (Kennedy, 1997). Simultaneously, youth workers, probation and parole officers, and later churches and other community groups offered gang members services and other kinds of help. The Operation Ceasefire working group delivered this message in formal meetings with gang members, through individual police and probation contacts with gang members, through meetings with inmates of secure juvenile facilities in the city, and through gang outreach workers and activist black clergy. The deterrence message was not a deal with gang members to stop violence. Rather, it was a promise to gang members that violent behavior would evoke an immediate and intense response. If gangs committed other crimes but refrained from violence, the normal workings of police, prosecutors, and the rest of the criminal justice system dealt with these matters. As described below, Operation Ceasefire also attempted to disrupt the illegal supply of firearms to youth by focusing enforcement attention on firearms traffickers.

The evaluation of Operation Ceasefire used a basic one-group time-series design to measure the effects of the intervention on youth homicide and other indicators of nonfatal serious violence in Boston. Braga et al. (2001a, 2001b) found that the Operation Ceasefire intervention was associated with a 63 percent decrease in monthly number of Boston youth homicides, a 32 percent decrease in monthly number of shots-fired calls, a 25 percent decrease in the monthly number of firearm-related assaults, and, in one high-risk police district given special attention in the evaluation, a 44 percent decrease in monthly number of youth firearm-related assault incidents. These reductions associated with Operation Ceasefire persisted when control variables, such as changes in Boston's employment trends, youth population, and citywide violence trends, were added to the regression models. Furthermore, the basic qualitative results also remained when youth homicide trends in Boston were compared with youth homicide trends in other large U.S. cities. Boston's significant youth homicide reduction was distinct when compared with youth homicide trends in most major U.S. and New England cities (Braga et al., 2001a, 2001b).[8]

The dramatic drop in the youth homicide rate in Boston and the associated analysis of Braga et al. (2001a, 2001b) are compelling. Youth homicides in Boston were reduced just after the adoption of Operation Ceasefire.[9] However, it is difficult to specify cause and effect. Braga and his

---

[8]Piehl et al. (1999) examined the youth homicide time series for exogenous structural breaks; these analyses suggest that the maximal break in the series occurred in June 1996—just after the Operation Ceasefire implementation date.

[9]Boston, like many other U.S. cities, experienced a sudden increase in firearm-related violence in 2001. Reported crimes involving firearms increased by over 10 percent between 2000 and 2001 and decreased moderately in 2002 (http://www.ci.boston.ma.us/police/pdfs/dec2003.pdf). McDevitt and his colleagues (2003) suggest that the Boston youth violence problems are dynamic, and the interventions designed to deal with youth violence need to be adjusted appropriately. Since 2001, Boston has been expanding Operation Ceasefire to deal with a wider range of violence problems.

colleagues compare youth homicide before and after the intervention. This type of methodology holds much appeal when an intervention is the only notable event occurring in the time period under study. Observational data from Boston, however, were not derived from an experimental evaluation. To the contrary, during this period of dramatic declines in youth crime throughout the country, there were potentially many levers being pulled in Boston, some controlled by the Operation Ceasefire group and some controlled by outside (and perhaps unobserved) forces. Furthermore, even if all of the determinants of violence except Operation Ceasefire were time invariant, the dynamics that connect enforcement to violence would be complex (these same issues are discussed in National Research Council, 2001). An activity undertaken at a specific place and time presumably does not generate an instant response in violence. And, to the extent that there is a response, it may merely reflect short-term acceleration in the rate of change but not in the steady-state levels in youth crime.

The existing research provides some insight into these potential statistical problems. Braga and his colleagues controlled for demographic shifts, drug market changes, and employment. Moreover, the evaluation shows that the Boston trend is very different from trends in other cities. Kennedy et al. (2001) provide an anecdotal account of the Boston story and Braga et al. (2001a, 2001b) survey the plausibility that other Boston interventions, most notably public health interventions, were associated with the sudden drop. Still, the primary evaluation does allow one to make direct links between key components of the intervention and the subsequent behavior of individuals subjected to the intervention. Many complex factors affect the trajectory of youth violence problems, and, while the there is a strong association between the youth homicide drop and the implementation of Operation Ceasefire, it is very difficult to specify the exact role it played in the reduction of youth homicide in Boston.

Supply-Side Programs

In addition to preventing gun violence amongst gangs, Boston's Operation Ceasefire interagency problem-solving group sought to disrupt the illegal supply of firearms to youth by systematically (Braga et al., 2001a: 199):

- Expanding the focus of local, state, and federal authorities to include intrastate trafficking in Massachusetts-sourced guns, in addition to interstate trafficking;
- Focusing enforcement attention on traffickers of those makes and calibers of guns most used by gang members, on traffickers of guns showing short time-to-crime, and on traffickers of guns used by the city's most violent gangs;

• Attempting restoration of obliterated serial numbers and subsequent trafficking investigations based on those restorations;

• Supporting these enforcement priorities through analysis of crime gun traces generated by the Boston Police Department's comprehensive tracing of crime guns and by developing leads through systematic debriefing of (especially) arrestees involved with gangs or involved in violent crime.

The Boston supply-side approach was implemented in conjunction with the pulling-levers demand-side strategy to reduce youth violence. The gun trafficking investigations and prosecutions followed the implementation of the pulling-levers strategy, so their effects on firearm-related violence could not be independently established (Braga et al., 2001a). However, the National Institute of Justice, in partnership with the Bureau of Alcohol, Tobacco, and Firearms, recently funded a demonstration program in Los Angeles to examine the effects of disrupting the illegal supply of firearms on the nature of the illegal market and on firearm-related violence (Tita et al., 2003). In addition to addressing the firearm-related violence problem in Los Angeles, this interagency law enforcement project was developed to provide other jurisdictions with guidance on how to analyze and develop appropriate problem-solving interventions to control illegal firearms markets.

Other Applications of the Pulling-Levers Focused Deterrence Approach

After the well-publicized success of Boston's Operation Ceasefire, a number of jurisdictions began experimenting with these new problem-solving frameworks to prevent gang and group-involved violence. Braga et al. (2002) detail the experiences of Minneapolis (MN), Baltimore (MD), the Boyle Heights section of Los Angeles (CA), Stockton (CA), and Indianapolis (IN) in tailoring the approach to fit their violence problems and operating environments. Although specific tactics sometimes varied across the cities, these programs implemented the basic elements of the original Boston strategy, including the pulling-levers focused deterrence strategy, designed to prevent violence by and among chronic offenders and groups of chronic offenders; the convening of an interagency working group representing a wide range of criminal justice and social service capabilities; and jurisdiction-specific assessments of violence dynamics, perpetrator and victim characteristics, and related issues such as drug market characteristics and patterns of firearms use and acquisition. All were facilitated by a close, more or less real-time partnership between researchers and practitioners. Basic pretest/posttest analyses from these initiatives revealed that these new approaches to the strategic prevention of gang and group-involved violence were associated with reductions in violent crime (Braga et al., 2002). To date, these replication studies are mostly descriptive in nature.[10]

What Has Been Learned?

While broad support for the pulling-levers approach may be justified for many reasons, the committee found modest scientific evidence that demonstrates whether these types of targeted policing programs can effectively lower crime and violence. Clearly, there was pronounced and important change in the youth homicide rate in Boston over the period of the intervention, some of which was arguably due to Operation Ceasefire, some due to secular changes in youth homicide, and some due to other (and perhaps unknown) factors. The particular effects of this intervention, however, are unknown. Furthermore, in the committee's view, the existing data and methods make it difficult to assess how Operation Ceasefire and other similar policing programs affect crime. Researchers cannot hope to credibly control for the many confounders that influence violence and crime using simple time-series comparisons. With similar policing programs being adopted in a number of other areas, there may be opportunities to combine data from these sites to provide more persuasive estimates. Invariably, however, researchers will be confronted with the fact that the programs were not randomly adopted, the trends in violence are influenced by a multitude of factors, and the dynamics of crime and violence are highly complex.

The lack of research on this potentially important intervention is an important shortcoming in the body of knowledge on firearms injury interventions. These programs are widely viewed as effective, but in fact knowledge of how, if at all, they reduce youth crime is limited. Without a much stronger research base, the benefits and harms of these policing interventions remain largely unknown. **The committee recommends that a sustained and systematic research program should be conducted to assess the effect of targeted policing aimed at high-risk offenders.** Additional insights might be gained by using observational data from different applications, especially if combined with thoughtful behavioral models of policing and crime. An alternative means of assessing the impact of these types of targeted policing interventions would be to run randomized experiments, similar in spirit to those described above. Using this framework, one might hope to disentangle the effects of the various levers and more generally assess the effectiveness of these targeted policing programs.

---

[10]McGarrell and Chermak (2003) recently completed an unpublished study of the Indianapolis pulling-levers intervention. Using time-series analyses, they found a 42 percent reduction in homicides associated with the implementation of the intervention and found that homicides were less likely to involve firearms, groups, and drugs.

References

CHAPTER 1

Azrael, D., P.J. Cook, and M. Miller
    2004   State and local prevalence of firearms ownership: Measurement, structure and trends. *Journal of Quantitative Criminology* 20(1):43-62.
Campbell, D.T., and J.C. Stanley
    1966   *Experimental and Quasi-Experimental Design for Research.* Skokie, IL: Rand McNally.
Centers for Disease Control and Prevention
    2001   Statistics Query and Reporting System (WISQARS). National Center for Injury Prevention and Control, Centers for Disease Control and Prevention (producer). Available: http://www.cdc.gov/ncipc/wisqars. [Accessed 10/10/02].
Cook, P.J.
    1991   The technology of personal violence. *Crime and Justice: A Review of Research* 14:1-71.
Cook, T.D., and D.T. Campbell
    1979   *Quasi-Experimentation: Design & Analysis Issues for Field Settings.* Boston, MA: Houghton Mifflin Co.
Duggan, M.
    2001   More guns, more crime. *Journal of Political Economy* 109(5):1086-1114.
Federal Bureau of Investigation
    2001   *Crime in the United States, 2000.* U.S. Department of Justice. Available: http://www.fbi.gov/ucr/00cius.htm. [Accessed 1/10/03].
Gardner, B.A., editor
    1999   *Black's Law Dictionary,* 7th edition. Eagan, MN: West Group.
Hardy, M.S.
    1997a The myth of millions of annual self-defense gun uses: A case study of survey overestimates of rare events. *Chance* 10(3):6-10.
    1997b Survey research and self-defense gun use: An explanation of extreme overestimates. *Journal of Criminal Law and Criminology* 87(4):1430-1445.

2002   Behavior oriented approaches to reducing youth gun violence. *The Future of Children*12(2):101-115.

Kaplan, M.S., and O. Geling
1998   Firearm suicides and homicides in the United States: Regional variations and patterns of gun ownership. *Social Science and Medicine* 45:1227-1233.

Kleck, G., and M. Gertz
1995   Armed resistance to crime: The prevalence and nature of self-defense with a gun. *Journal of Criminal Law and Criminology* 86(1):150-187.

Kleck, G., and E.B. Patterson
1993   The impact of gun control and gun ownership levels on violence rates. *Journal of Quantitative Criminology* 9:249-287.

Miller, M., D. Hemenway, and D. Azrael
2002   Household firearm ownership levels and homicide rates across U.S. regions and states, 1988-1997. *American Journal of Public Health* 92:1988-1993.

Monkkonen, E.J.
2001   *Murder In New York City.* Berkeley: University of California Press.

National Research Council
2001   *Informing America's Policy on Illegal Drugs: What We Don't Know Keeps Hurting Us.* Committee on Data and Research for Policy on Illegal Drugs, C.F. Manski, J.V. Pepper, and C.V. Petrie, eds. Committee on Law and Justice and Committee on National Statistics. Washington, DC: National Academy Press.

2002   *Scientific Research in Education.* Committee on Scientific Principles for Education Research. R.J. Shavelson and L. Towne, eds. Center for Education. Division of Behavioral and Social Sciences and Education. Washington, DC: The National Academies Press.

National Rifle Association
2002   Competitive Shooting Programs. Available: http://www.nrahq.org/compete/ [Accessed 10/12/02].

Robinson, W.S.
1950   Ecological correlations and behaviors of individuals. *American Sociological Review* 15:351-357.

U.S. Department of the Interior, Fish and Wildlife Service and U.S. Department of Commerce,
U.S. Census Bureau
2002   *2001 National Survey of Fishing, Hunting, and Wildlife-Associated Recreation.* Washington, DC: U.S. Government Printing Office.

Zimring, F., and G. Hawkins
1998   *The Citizen's Guide to Gun Control.* New York: Macmillan Publishing Company.

CHAPTER 2

Annest, J.L., and J.A. Mercy
1998   Use of national data systems for firearm-related injury surveillance. *American Journal of Preventive Medicine* 15(3S):17-30.

Azrael, D., P.J. Cook, and M. Miller
2004   State and local prevalence of firearms ownership: Measurement, structure and trends. *Journal of Quantitative Criminology* 20(1):43-62.

Biderman, A.D., and J.P. Lynch
1991   *Understanding Crime Incidence Statistics: Why the UVR Diverges from the NCS.* New York: Springer-Verlag.

Blackman, P.H.
   1999   The limitations of BATF firearms tracing data for policymaking and homicide
          research. *Proceedings of the Homicide Research Working Group Meetings, 1997
          and 1998.* Washington, DC: National Institute of Justice, U.S. Department of Jus-
          tice.
   2003   *Armed Citizens and Crime Control* (4 page leaflet). Fairfax, VA: National Rifle
          Association.
Bureau of Alcohol, Tobacco, and Firearms
   1997   *Crime Gun Trace Analysis Reports: The Illegal Firearms Market in 17 Communi-
          ties.* Washington, DC: U.S. Department of the Treasury.
   2000a *Crime Gun Trace Reports (1999): National Report.* Washington, DC: U.S. Depart-
          ment of the Treasury.
   2002b *Crime Gun Trace Reports (2000): National Report.* Washington, DC: U.S. Depart-
          ment of the Treasury.
Bureau of Justice Statistics
   1994   *Criminal Victimization.* Washington, DC: U.S. Department of Justice.
   2001   UCR and NIBRS Participation: Level of Participation by States as of August 2001.
          Retrieved from the World Wide Web at http://www.ojp.usdoj.gov/bis/nibrsstatus.
          htm. [Accessed 11/30/02].
Caspar, R.
   1992   Followup of nonrespondents in 1990. In C.F. Turner, J.T. Lessler, and J.C.
          Gfroerer, eds., *Survey Measurement of Drug Use: Methodological Studies.* DHHS
          Publication No. (ADM) 92-1929. Washington, DC: U.S. Department of Health
          and Human Services.
Congressional Research Service
   1992   *Assault Weapons: Military-Style Semi-Automatic Firearms Facts and Issues.* Report
          92-434. Washington, DC: U.S. Government Printing Office.
Cook, P.J.
   1991   The technology of personal violence: A review of the evidence concerning the im-
          portance of gun availability and use in violent crime, self defense, and suicide.
          Crime and Justice 14:1-71.
Cook, P.J., and A.A. Braga
   2001   Comprehensive firearms tracing: Strategic and investigative uses of new data on
          firearms markets. *Arizona Law Review* 43:277-309.
Decker, S.H., S. Pennell, and A. Caldwell
   1997   Illegal firearms: Access and use by arrestees. *NIJ Research in Brief* (January). Na-
          tional Institute of Justice. Washington, DC: U.S. Department of Justice.
Fagan, J., D. Wilkinson, and G. Davies
   2002   Social Contagion of Violence. Unpublished paper presented at the May 2002 meet-
          ing of the Committee to Improve Research and Data on Firearms, National Re-
          search Council, Washington, DC.
Gfroerer, J.T., J.C. Lessler, and T. Parsley
   1997   Studies of nonresponse and measurement error in the national household survey on
          drug abuse. In L. Harrison and Hughes, eds., *The Validity of Self-Reported Drug
          Use: Improving the Accuracy of Survey Estimates.* NIDA Research Monograph
          167: 273-295. Washington, DC: U.S. Department of Health and Human Services.
Hall, M.J., and M.F. Owings
   2000   *Hospitalizations for Injury: United States, 1996.* Advance Data from Vital and
          Health Statistics; no. 318 (August 9). National Center for Health Statistics,
          Hyattsville, MD.

Harrison, L., and A. Hughes
1997   *The Validity of Self-Reported Drug Use: Improving the Accuracy of Survey Esti-mates.* National Institute on Drug Abuse Research Monograph 167. Rockville, MD: National Institute on Drug Abuse.

Institute of Medicine
1999   *Reducing the Burden of Injury: Advancing Prevention and Treatment.* Washing-ton, DC: National Academy Press.

Jarvis, J.
1992   The National Incident-Based Reporting System and its application to homicide research. Pp. 81-85 in C. Block and R. Block, eds., *Questions and Answers on Lethal and Non-Lethal Violence.* Proceedings of the first annual Workshop of the Homicide Research Working Group. HV 6529. H668a 1992. Washington, DC: National Crime Prevention Council.

Kleck, G.
1991   *Point Blank: Guns and Violence in America.* New York: Aldine de Gruyter.
1999   BATF gun trace data and the role of organized gun trafficking in supplying guns to criminals. *Saint Louis University Public Law Review* 18:23-45.

Loftin, C., and J.A. Mercy
1995   Estimating the incidence, causes, and consequences of interpersonal violence for children and families. Pp. 192-213 in *Integrating Federal Statistics on Children: Report of a Workshop.* National Research Council and Institute of Medicine. Wash-ington, DC: National Academy Press.

MacKenzie, D., P. Baunach, and R. Roberg, eds.
1990   *Measuring Crime: Large Scale, Long Range Efforts.* Albany: State University of New York Press.

Maltz, M.D.
1999   *Bridging Gaps in Police Crime Data.* Discussion paper from the BJS Fellows Pro-gram. Bureau of Justice Statistics. BJS Clearinghouse (1 800 732-3277). Washing-ton, DC: U.S. Department of Justice.

Maltz, M.D., and J. Targonski
2002   A note on the use of county-level UCR data. *Journal of Quantitative Criminology* 18(2):297-318.

Miller, M., D. Azrael, and D. Hemenway
2001   Household firearm ownership and suicide rates in the United States. *Epidemiology* 13:517-524.

National Research Council
2001   *Informing America's Policy on Illegal Drugs: What We Don't Know Keeps Hurt-ing Us.* Committee on Data and Research for Policy on Illegal Drugs, C.F. Manski, J.V. Pepper, and C.V. Petrie, eds. Committee on Law and Justice and Committee on National Statistics. Washington, DC: National Academy Press.
2002   *Scientific Research in Education.* Committee on Scientific Principles for Education Research, R.J. Shavelson and L. Towne, eds. Center for Education, Division of Behavioral and Social Sciences and Education. Washington, DC: The National Academies Press.
2003   *Measurement Problems in Criminal Justice Research.* Committee on Law and Jus-tice, J.V. Pepper and C.V. Petrie, eds. Washington, DC: The National Academies Press.

Pierce, G.L., A.A. Braga, R.R. Hyatt, and S.C.S. Koper
2002   The Characteristics and Dynamics of Illegal Firearms Markets: Implications for a Supply-Side Enforcement Strategy. Working Paper. Center for Criminal Justice Policy Research, Northeastern University.

Poggio, E.C., S.D. Kennedy, J.M. Chaiken, and K.E. Carlson
  1985   *Blueprint for the Future of the Uniform Crime Reporting Program: Final Report of the UCR Study.* Bureau of Justice Statistics NCJ-98348. Washington, DC: U.S. Department of Justice.
Riedel, M.
  1999.   Sources of homicide data: A review and comparison. Pp. 75-95 in M.D. Smith and M. Zahn, eds., *Homicide: A Sourcebook of Social Research.* Thousand Oaks, CA: Sage.
Robinson, W.S.
  1950   Ecological correlations and the behavior of individuals. *American Sociological Review* 15:351-357.
Smith, T.W.
  1995   Trends in non-response rates. *International Journal of Public Opinion Research* 7:157-171.
Tourangeau, R., and M.E. McNeeley
  2003   Measuring crime and crime victimization: Methodological issues. In J.V. Pepper and C.V. Petrie, eds., *Measurement Problems in Criminal Justice Research.* Committee on Law and Justice, National Research Council. Washington, DC: The National Academies Press.
Wiersema, B., C. Loftin, and D. McDowell
  2000   A comparison of supplementary homicide reports and national vital statistics system homicide estimates for U.S. counties. *Homicide Studies* 4:317-340.
Zawitz, M.W., and K.J. Strom
  2000   *Firearm Injury and Death from Crime, 1993-97.* Bureau of Justice Statistics NCJ 182992. Washington, DC: U.S. Department of Justice.
Zimring, F.
  1975   Firearms and federal law: The Gun Control Act of 1968. *Journal of Legal Studies* 4:133-198.

CHAPTER 3

Alpers, P.
  2000   *Costa Rica: Diagnostico Armas de Fuego.* Max Loria for the Arias Foundation for Peace and Human Progress (translated by Greg Puley).
  2001   Harvard Injury Control Research Center and HELP networks. Arias Foundation for Peace and Human Progress, San José, Costa Rica.
Azrael, D., P.J. Cook, and M. Miller
  2004   State and local prevalence of firearms ownership: Measurement, structure and trends. *Journal of Quantitative Criminology* 20(1):43-62.
Barclay, G., C. Tavares, and A. Siddique
  2001   *International Comparisons of Criminal Justice Statistics 1999.* Research Development and Statistics Directorate, Home Office U.K.
Baumer, E.P., S.F. Messner, and R. Rosenfeld
  2002   *Homicide Rates and Support for Capital Punishment: A Multi-Level Analysis.* Annual Meeting of the Homicide Research Working Group, St. Louis, MO, May 30-June 2.
Bennett, W.J., J.J. DiIulio, and J.P. Walters
  1996   *Body Count: Moral Poverty and How to Win America's War Against Crime and Drugs.* New York: Simon & Schuster.

Blumstein, A.
    1995   Youth violence, guns, and the illicit-drug industry. *Journal of Criminal Law and Criminology* 86:10-36.
    2000   Disaggregating the violence trends. In A. Blumstein and J. Wallman, eds., *The Crime Drop in America*. New York: Cambridge University Press.
Blumstein, A., and D. Cork
    1996   Linking gun availability to youth gun violence. *Law and Contemporary Problems* 59:5-24.
Braga, A.
    2003   Serious youth gun offenders and the epidemic of youth violence in Boston. *Journal of Quantitative Criminology* 19(1):33-54.
Bureau of Alcohol, Tobacco, and Firearms
    2002   *Firearms Commerce in the United States* 2001-2002. Washington, DC: U.S. Department of the Treasury.
Bureau of Justice Statistics
    2002a   Homicide Trends in the U.S. Available: http://www.ojp.usdoj.gov/bjs/homicide/htm. [Accessed 1/10/03].
    2002b   *Criminal Victimization in the United States, 2000: Statistical Tables*. Washington, DC: U.S. Department of Justice.
Cohen, J., and G. Tita
    1999   Diffusion in homicide: Exploring a general method for detecting spatial diffusion processes. *Journal of Quantitative Criminology* 15:379-406.
Cook, P.J.
    1998   The epidemic of youth gun violence. In *Perspectives on Crime and Justice: 1997-1998 Lecture Series*. Washington, DC: National Institute of Justice.
    1998   The unprecedented epidemic in youth violence. Pp. 27-64 in M. Tonry and M.H. Moore, eds., *Youth Violence, Crime and Justice: A Review of Research*. Volume 24. Chicago: University of Chicago Press.
    2002   After the epidemic: Recent trends in youth violence in the United States. In M. Tonry and M.H. Moore, eds., *Crime and Justice: A Review of Research*. Volume 29. Chicago: University of Chicago Press.
Cork, D.
    1999   Examining space-time interaction in city-level homicide data: Crack markets and the diffusion of guns among youth. *Journal of Quantitative Criminology* 15:379-406.
Corzine, J., L. Huff-Corzine, and G.S. Weaver
    2000   Using federal firearms licenses (FFL) data as an indirect measurement of gun availability. In *Proceedings of the Homicide Research Working Group: 1999*. Washington, DC: Federal Bureau of Investigation.
Donohue, J.J., III, and S.D. Levitt
    2001   The impact of legalized abortion on crime. *Quarterly Journal of Economics* 116:379-420.
Duggan, M.
    2001   More guns, more crime. *Journal of Political Economy* 109(4):1086-1114.
Fox, J.A.
    1996   *Trends in Juvenile Violence: A Report to the United States Attorney General on Current and Future Rates of Juvenile Offending*. Washington, DC: Bureau of Justice Statistics.
    2001   *Uniform Crime Reports Supplementary Homicide Reports 1976-1999*. Produced by Northeastern University, College of Criminal Justice. Ann Arbor, MI: Inter-University Consortium for Political and Social Research.

Frattaroli, S., D.W. Webster, and S.P. Teret
  2002   Unintentional gun injuries, firearm design, and prevention: What we know, what we need to know, and what can be done. *Journal of Urban Health* 79:49-59.
Gotsch, K.E., J.L. Annest, J.A. Mercy, and G.W. Ryan
  2001   Surveillance for fatal and nonfatal firearm-related injuries—United States, 1993-1998. Centers for Disease Control and Prevention. *Morbidity and Mortality Weekly Report* 50(SS-2).
Grogger, J., and M. Willis
  2000   The emergence of crack cocaine and the rise in urban crime. *Review of Economics and Statistics* 82:519-529.
Harris Interactive
  2002   Harris Poll 2002.http://www.harrisinteractive.com/harris_poll/index.asp?PID=234. [Accessed 3/16/04].
Hemenway, D., and M. Miller
  2000   Firearm availability and homicide rates across 26 high-income countries. *Journal of Trauma* 49(6):3.
Ikeda, R.M., R. Gorwitz, S.P. James, K.E. Powell, and J.A. Mercy
  1997   *Fatal Firearm Injuries in the United States, 1962-1994.* Atlanta: Centers for Disease Control.
Kennedy, D.M., A.M. Piehl, and A. Braga
  1996   Youth violence in Boston: Gun markets, serious youth offenders, and a use-reduction strategy. *Law and Contemporary Problems* 59:147-196.
Killias, M.
  1993a International correlations between gun ownership and rates of homicide and suicide. *Canadian Medical Association Journal* 148(10):1721-1725.
  1993b Gun ownership, suicide, and homicide: An international perspective. In A. Alvazi del Frate, U. Zvekic, and J.J.M. van Dijk, eds., *Understanding Crime: Experiences of Crime and Crime Control.* Rome: UNICRI.
Kleck, G.
  1997   Carrying Guns for Protection: Results from the National Self-Defense Survey. Unpublished paper, School of Criminology and Criminal Justice, Florida State University.
Krug, E.G, K.E. Powell, and L.L. Dahlberg
  1998   Firearm-related deaths in the United States and 35 other high- and upper-middle income countries. *International Journal of Epidemiology* 7:214-221.
Land, K., and P. McCall
  2001   The indeterminacy of forecasts of crime rates and juvenile offenses. In *Juvenile Crime, Juvenile Justice.* Panel on Juvenile Crime: Prevention, Treatment, and Control, Committee on Law and Justice and Board on Children, Youth, and Families, National Research Council and Institute of Medicine. Washington, DC: National Academy Press.
Lester, D.
  1990   The availability of firearms and the use of firearms for suicide: A study of 20 countries. *Acta Psychiatrica Scandinavia* 81:146-147.
Maguire, K., and A.L. Pastore
  2002   *Sourcebook of Criminal Justice Statistics.* Available: http://www.albany.edu/sourcebook/. [Accessed 1/10/03].
Miller, M., D. Hemenway, and D. Azrael
  2002   Household firearm ownership levels and homicide rates across U.S. regions and states, 1988-1997. *American Journal of Public Health* 92:1988-1993.

National Center for Health Statistics

2002   Web-based Injury Statistics Query and Reporting System. Available: http://www.cdc.gov/ncipc/wisqars/default.htm. [Accessed 3/16/04].

National Research Council

1993   *Understanding and Preventing Violence.* Panel on the Understanding and Control of Violent Behavior, A.J. Reiss, Jr. and J. Roth, eds. Washington, DC: National Academy Press.

Rand, M.R., and C.M. Rennison

2002   True crime stories? Accounting for differences in our national crime indicators. *Chance* 15(2):47-51.

Rennison, C.M.

2001   *Criminal Victimization 2000: Changes 1999-2000 with Trends 1993-2000.* BJS National Crime Victimization Survey NCJ 187007. Washington, DC: U.S. Department of Justice.

Rosenfeld, R., T. Bray, and A. Egley

1999   Facilitating homicide: A comparison of gang-motivated, gang-affiliated, and nongang youth homicides. *Journal of Quantitative Criminology* 15:495-516.

Rosenfeld, R., S.F. Messner, and E.P. Baumer

2001   Social capital and homicide. *Social Forces* 80:283-309.

United Nations

2000   United Nations International Study on Firearms Regulations. Available: http://www.ifs.unvie.ac.at/~uncjin/firearms/Default.htm. [Accessed 12/12/02].

U.S. Census Bureau

2001a *Statistical Abstract of the United States: 2001*, Table 2. Available: www.census.gov/statab/www/. [Accessed 7/2/02].

2001b Time Series of National Population Estimates: April 1, 2000 to July 1, 2001. Table US-2001EST-01.Population Division. Available: http://eire.census.gov/popest/data/national/populartables/table01.php. [Accessed 11/01/02].

2002   Time Series of Intercensal State Population Estimates: April 1, 1990 to April 1, 2000. Table CO-EST2001-12-00.Population Division. Available: http://eire.census.gov/popest/data/counties/tables/CO-EST2001-12/CO-EST2001-12-00.php. [Accessed 11/01/02].

Wilson, J.Q.

2002   Crime: Public policies for crime control. In J.Q. Wilson and J. Petersilia, eds., *Crime*, 2nd edition. Oakland, CA: Institute for Contemporary Studies Press.

Wintemute, G.

2000   Guns and gun violence. Pp. 45-96 in A. Blumstein and J. Wallman, eds., *The Crime Drop in America.* Cambridge, UK: Cambridge University Press.

Zawitz, M.

2001   Estimated Firearm Crime. Available: http://www.ojp.usdoj.gov/bjs/glance/tables/guncrimetab.htm. [Accessed 10/01/02].

CHAPTER 4

Blackman, P.A.

1997- The limitations of BATF tracing for policy making and homicide. In *Proceedings*
1998   *of the Homicide Working Group.* Washington, DC: National Crime Prevention Council.

Braga, A.A., and D.M. Kennedy

2000   Gun shows and the illegal diversion of firearms. *Georgetown Public Policy Review* 6(1):7-24.

Braga, A.A., P.J. Cook, D.M. Kennedy, and M.H. Moore
2002   The illegal supply of firearms. In M. Tonry, ed., *Crime and Justice: A Review of Research*. Volume 29. Chicago: University of Chicago Press.

Britt, C., III, G. Kleck, and D.J. Bordua
1996   A reassessment of the DC gun law: Some cautionary notes on the use of interrupted time series designs for policy impact assessment. *Law & Society Review* 30:361-80.

Bureau of Alcohol, Tobacco, and Firearms
2000a *Commerce in Firearms in the United States*. Washington, DC: U.S. Department of the Treasury.
2000b *Crime Gun Trace Reports (1999): National Report*. Washington, DC: U.S. Department of the Treasury.
2000c *Following the Gun: Enforcing Federal Laws Against Firearms Traffickers*. Washington, DC: U.S. Department of the Treasury.
2000d *ATF Regulatory Actions: Report to the Secretary on Firearms Initiative*. Washington, DC: U.S. Department of the Treasury.

Bureau of Justice Statistics
1993   *Survey of State Prison Inmates, 1991*. Washington, DC: U.S. Department of Justice.
1999   *Presale Handgun Checks, the Brady Interim Period, 1994-1999*. Washington, DC: U.S. Department of Justice.
2002   *Background Checks for Firearms Transfers, 2001*. Washington, DC: U.S. Department of Justice.

Callahan, C.M., F.P. Rivara, and T.D. Koepsell
1994   Money for guns: Evaluation of the Seattle gun buy-back program. *Public Health Reports* 109:472-477.

Caulkins, J.
1998   The cost-effectiveness of civil remedies: The case of drug control interventions. *Crime Prevention Studies* 9:219-237.

Cook, P.J., and A.A. Braga
2001   Comprehensive firearms tracing: Strategic and investigative uses of new data on firearms markets. *Arizona Law Review* 43:277-309.

Cook, P.J., and J. Leitzel
1996   Perversity, futility, jeopardy: An economic analysis of the attack on gun control. *Law and Contemporary Problems* 59:91-118.

Cook, P.J., and J. Ludwig
1997   *Guns in America: Results of a Comprehensive Survey on Private Firearms Ownership and Use*. Washington, DC: Police Foundation.

Cook, P.J., S. Molliconi, and T. Cole
1995   Regulating gun markets. *Journal of Criminal Law and Criminology* 86:59-92.

Decker, S.H., S. Pennell, and A. Caldwell
1997   *Illegal Firearms: Access and Use by Arrestees*. Bureau of Justice Statistics. Washington, DC: U.S. Department of Justice.

Fjestad, S.P.
2001   *22nd Edition of the Blue Book of Gun Values*. Minneapolis, MN: Blue Book Publications.

Hahn, R.A., O. Bilukha, A. Crosby, M.T. Fullilove, and A. Liberman
2005   Firearms laws and the reduction of violence: A systematic review. Task Force on Community Preventive Services, E.K. Moscicki, S. Snyder, F. Tuma, and P.A. Briss. *American Journal of Preventive Medicine*. January.

Jones, E.D., III
    1981   The District of Columbia's Firearm Control Regulations Act of 1975: The toughest handgun control law in the United States—or is it? *Annals of the American Academy of Political and Social Science* 455:138-149.
Kennedy, D.M., A.A. Braga, and A.M. Piehl
    1996   Youth violence in Boston: Gun markets, serious youth offenders, and a use-reduction strategy. *Law and Contemporary Problems* 59:147-196.
Kleck, G.
    1999   BATF gun trace data and the role of organized gun trafficking in supplying guns to criminals. *Saint Louis University Public Law Review* 18:23-45.
    2001   Impossible policy evaluations and impossible conclusions: A comment on Koper and Roth. *Journal of Quantitative Criminology* 17(1):75-80.
Koper, C.S.
    2002   Federal legislation and gun markets: How much have recent reforms of the federal firearms licensing system reduced criminal gun suppliers? *Criminology and Public Policy* 1(2):151-178.
Koper, C.S., and P. Réuter
    1996   Suppressing illegal gun markets: Lessons learned from drug enforcement. *Law and Contemporary Problems* 59:119-146.
Koper, C.S., and J. Roth
    2001a   The impact of the 1994 federal assault weapon ban on gun violence outcomes: An assessment of multiple outcomes measures and some lessons for policy evaluation. *Journal of Quantitative Criminology* 17(1):33-74.
    2001b   The impact of the 1994 federal assault weapon ban on gun markets: An assessment of short-term primary and secondary market effects. *Journal of Quantitative Criminology* 18(3):239-266.
Loftin, C., D. McDowall, B. Wiersema, and T. Cottey
    1991   Effects of restrictive licensing of handguns on homicide and suicide in the District of Columbia. *New England Journal of Medicine* 325(23):1615-1620.
Ludwig, J., and P.J. Cook
    2000   Homicide and suicide rates associated with the implementation of the Brady Handgun Violence Prevention Act. *Journal of the American Medical Association* 284:585-591.
Moore, M.H.
    1973   Achieving discrimination on the effective price of heroin. *American Economic Review* 63:270-277.
    1981   Keeping handguns from criminal offenders. *Annals of the American Academy of Political and Social Science* 455:92-109.
National Institute of Justice
    1997   *Crack, Powder Cocaine and Heroin: Drug Purchase and Use Patterns in Six Cities* Washington, DC: U.S. Department of Justice.
National Research Council
    1986   *Criminal Careers and "Career Criminals."* Panel on Research on Criminal Careers, A. Blumstein, J. Cohen, J.A. Roth, and C.A. Visher, eds. Washington, DC: National Academy Press.
    2001   *Informing America's Policy on Illegal Drugs: What We Don't Know Keeps Hurting Us.* Committee on Data and Research for Policy on Illegal Drugs, C.F. Manski, J.V. Pepper, and C.V. Petrie, eds. Committee on Law and Justice and Committee on National Statistics. Washington, DC: National Academy Press.
Peters, R.
    2000   *Gun Control in the United States: A Comparative Survey of State Gun Laws.* New York: Open Society Institute.

Pierce, G.L., L. Briggs, and D. Carlson
   1995   *The Identification of Patterns in Firearms Trafficking: Implications for a Focused Enforcement Strategy.* Bureau of Alcohol, Tobacco, and Firearms. Washington, DC: U.S. Department of the Treasury.
Pierce, G.L., A.A. Braga, C. Koper, J. McDevitt, D. Carlson, J. Roth, and A. Saiz
   2001   *The Characteristics and Dynamics of Gun Markets: Implications for a Supply-Side Enforcement Strategy.* Final Report to the National Institute of Justice. Boston: Center for Criminal Justice Policy Research, Northeastern University.
Police Executive Research Forum
   1996   Gun buy-backs: Where do we stand and where do we go? In M.R. Plotkin, ed., *Under Fire: Gun Buy-Backs, Exchanges, and Amnesty Programs.* Washington, DC: Police Executive Research Forum.
Police Foundation
   1996   *Guns in America: Results of a Comprehensive National Survey on Firearms Ownership and Use.* Washington, DC: Police Foundation.
Reuter, P., and J. Mouzos
   2003   Australia's gun control: Massive buy-back of low risk guns. In J. Ludwig and P.J. Cook, eds., *Evaluating Gun Control.* Washington, DC: Brookings Institution.
Rosenfeld, R.
   1996   Gun buy-backs: Crime control or community mobilization? In M.R. Plotkin, ed., *Under Fire: Gun Buy-Backs, Exchanges, and Amnesty Programs.* Washington, DC: Police Executive Research Forum.
Roth, J., and C. Koper
   1997   *Impacts of the 1994 Assault Weapons Ban: 1994-1996.* Research in Brief. National Institute of Justice. Washington, DC: U.S. Department of Justice.
Sheley, J.F., and J.D. Wright
   1993   Motivations for gun possession and carrying among serious juvenile offenders. *Behavioral Sciences and the Law* 11:375-388.
   1995   *In the Line of Fire: Youth, Guns and Violence in Urban America.* New York: Aldine de Gruyter.
Taylor, B., N. Fitzgerald, D. Hunt, J. Reardon, and H. Brownstein
   2001   ADAM Preliminary Findings on Drug Use and Drug Markets: Adult Arrestees. National Institute of Justice. Available: http://www.adam-nij.net/files/2000_Preliminary_Findings.pdf.
Veen, J., S. Dunbar, and M. Stedman Ruland
   1997   *The BJA Firearms Trafficking Program: Demonstrating Effective Strategies to Control Violent Crime.* Bureau of Justice Assistance. Washington, DC: U.S. Department of Justice.
Wachtel, J.
   1998   Sources of crime guns in Los Angeles, California. *Policing: An International Journal of Police Strategies and Management* 21:220-239.
Weil, D.S., and R. Knox
   1996   Effects of limiting handgun purchases on interstate transfer of firearms. *Journal of the American Medical Association* 275:1759-1761.
Wintemute, G.J.
   2000   Relationship between illegal use of handguns and handgun sales volume. *Journal of the American Medical Association* 284:566-567.
Wintemute, G.J., C.M. Drake, J.J. Beaumont, M.A. Wright, and C. Parham
   1998   Prior misdemeanor convictions as a risk factor for later violent and firearm-related criminal activity among authorized purchasers of handguns. *Journal of the American Medical Association* 280:2083-2087.

Wright, J.D., and P. Rossi
  1994   *Armed and Considered Dangerous: A Survey of Felons and Their Firearms.* Expanded edition. Hawthorne, NY: Aldine de Gruyter.
Wright, M.A., G.J. Wintemute, and F. Rivara
  1999   Effectiveness of denial of handgun purchase to persons believed to be at high risk for firearm violence. *American Journal of Public Health* 89:88-90.
Zimring, F.E.
  1976   Street crime and new guns: Some implications for firearms control. *Journal of Criminal Justice* 4:95-107.

CHAPTER 5

Cook, P.J., and J. Ludwig
  1998   Defensive gun uses: New evidence from a national survey. *Journal of Quantitative Criminology* 14(2):111-131.
Cook, P.J., J. Ludwig, and D. Hemenway
  1997   The gun debate's new mythical number: How many defensive gun uses per year? *Journal of Policy Analysis and Management* 16(2):463-469.
Cummings, P., T.D. Koepsell, D.C. Grossman, J. Savarino, and R.S. Thompson
  1997   The association between purchase of a handgun and homicide or suicide. *American Journal of Public Health* 87(6):974-978.
Duncan. O.D.
  2000a   Gun use surveys: In numbers we trust? *Criminologist* 25(1):1-6.
  2000b   As Compared to What? Offensive and Defensive Gun Use Surveys, 1973-1994. National Institute of Justice, Working Paper 185056.
Harrison, L.D.
  1995   The validity of self-reported data on drug use. *Journal of Drug Issues* 25(1):91-111.
Hemenway, D.
  1997a   The myth of millions of annual self-defense gun uses: A case study of survey overestimates of rare events. *Chance* 10(3):6-10.
  1997b   Survey research and self-defense gun use: An explanation of extreme overestimates. *Journal of Criminal Law and Criminology* 87(4):1430-1445.
Hemenway, D., and D. Azrael
  2000   The relative frequency of offensive and defensive gun uses: Results from a national survey. *Violence and Victims* 15(5):257-271.
Hemenway, D., D. Azrael, and M. Miller
  2000   Gun use in the United States: Results from two national surveys. *Injury Prevention* 6:263-267.
Kellermann, A.L., and D.T. Reay
  1986   Protection or peril? An analysis of firearm-related deaths in the home. *New England Journal of Medicine* 314(24):1557-1560.
Kellermann, A.L., F.P. Rivara, N.B. Rushforth, J.G. Branton, D.T. Reay, J.T. Francisco, A.B. Locci, J. Prodzinski, B.B. Hackman, and G. Somes
  1993   Gun ownership as a risk factor for homicide in the home. *New England Journal of Medicine* 329(15):1084-1091.
Kleck, G.
  1997   *Targeting Guns.* New York: Aldine de Gruyter.
  2000   Research Agenda on Guns, Violence and Gun Control. Working Paper.

2001a   The frequency of defensive gun use: Evidence and disinformation. Chapter 6 in G. Kleck and D.B. Kates, eds., *Armed: New Perspectives on Gun Control*. New York: Prometheus Books.

2001b   The nature and effectiveness of owning, carrying and using guns for self-protection. Chapter 7 in G. Kleck and D.B. Kates, eds., *Armed: New Perspectives on Gun Control*. New York: Prometheus Books.

Kleck, G., and M.A. DeLone

1993   Victim resistance and offender weapon effects in robbery. *Journal of Quantitative Criminology* 9(1):55-81.

Kleck, G., and M. Gertz

1995   Armed resistance to crime: The prevalence and nature of self-defense with a gun. *Journal of Criminal Law and Criminology* 86(1):150-187.

1998   Carrying guns for protection: Results from the national self-defense survey. *Journal of Research in Crime and Delinquency* 35:193-224.

Kleck, G., and S. Sayles

1990   Rape and resistance. *Social Problems* 37:149-162.

Lizotte, A.J.

1986   Determinants of completing rape and assault. *Journal of Quantitative Criminology* 2:203-217.

Ludwig, J.

1998   Concealed-gun-carrying law and violent crime: Evidence from state panel data. *International Review of Law and Economics* 18(2):239-254.

McDowall D., and B. Wiersema

1994   The incidence of defensive firearm use by US crime victims, 1987 through 1990. *American Journal of Public Health* 84(12):1982-1984.

McDowall, D., C. Loftin, and B. Wiersema

1998   Estimates of the Frequency of Firearm Self-Defense from the Redesigned National Crime Victimization Survey. Violence Research Group Discussion Paper 20.

McDowall, D., C. Loftin, and S. Presser

2000   Measuring civilian defensive firearm use: A methodological experiment. *Journal of Quantitative Criminology* 16(2):1-19.

National Research Council

1993   *Understanding and Preventing Violence*. Committee on Law and Justice, A.J. Reiss and J. Roth, eds. Washington, DC: National Academy Press.

2001   *Informing America's Policy on Illegal Drugs: What We Don't Know Keeps Hurting Us*. Committee on Data and Research for Policy on Illegal Drugs, C.F. Manski, J.V. Pepper, and C.V. Petrie, eds. Committee on Law and Justice and Committee on National Statistics. Washington, DC: National Academy Press.

2003   *Measurement Problems in Criminal Justice Research*. Committee on Law and Justice, J.V. Pepper and C.V. Petrie, eds. Washington, DC: The National Academies Press.

Rosenbaum, P.R.

2001   Replicating effects and biases. *American Statistician* 55(3):223-227.

Rushforth, N.B., C.S. Hirsch, A.B. Ford, and L. Adelson

1974   Accidental firearm fatalities in a metropolitan county (1958-1974). *American Journal of Epidemiology* 100(6):499-505.

Smith, T.W.

1997   A call for truce in the DGU War. *Journal of Criminal Law and Criminology* 87(4):1462-1469.

Ziegenhagen, E.A., and D. Brosnan

1985   Victim response to robbery and crime control policy. *Criminology* 23:675-695.

CHAPTER 6

Ayres, I., and J.J. Donohue III
  2003a Shooting down the "more guns, less crime" hypothesis. *Stanford Law Review* 55:1193.
  2003b The latest misfires in support of the "more guns, less crime" hypothesis. *Stanford Law Review* 55:1371-1398.
Bartley, W.A., and M.A. Cohen
  1998 The effect of concealed weapons laws: An extreme bound analysis. *Economic Inquiry* 36(2):258-265.
Black, D.A., and D.S. Nagin
  1998 Do right-to-carry laws deter violent crime? *Journal of Legal Studies* 27:209-219.
Bronars, S., and J.R. Lott, Jr.
  1998 Criminal deterrence, geographic spillovers, and the right to carry concealed handguns. *American Economic Review* 88:475-479.
Donohue, J.J., III
  2002 Divining the Impact of State Laws Permitting Citizens to Carry Concealed Handguns. Unpublished manuscript, Stanford Law School.
Duggan, M.
  2001 More guns, more crime. *Journal of Political Economy* 109(4):1086-1114.
Helland, E., and A. Tabarrok
  2004 Using placebo laws to test "more guns, less crime." *Advances in Economic Analysis and Policy* 4(1):Article 1. http://www.bepress.com/bejeap/advances/vol4/iss1/art.
Lott, J.R., Jr.
  1999 More Guns, Less Crime: A response to Ayres and Donohue. Working paper no. 247, Program for Studies in Law, Economics and Public Policy, Yale Law School.
  2000 *More Guns, Less Crime: Understanding Crime and Gun-Control Laws.* Chicago: University of Chicago Press.
Lott, J.R., Jr., and D.B. Mustard
  1997 Crime, deterrence, and right-to-carry concealed handguns. *Journal of Legal Studies* 26(1):1-68.
Lott, J.R., Jr., and J.E. Whitley
  2002 A Note on the Use of County-Level UCR Data: A Response. Working paper.
Ludwig, J.
  1998 Concealed-gun-carrying law and violent crime: Evidence from state panel data. *International Review of Law and Economics* 18(2):239-254.
Maltz, M.D., and J. Targonski
  2002 A note on the use of county-level UCR data. *Journal of Quantitative Criminology* 18(2):297-318.
Moody, C.E.
  2001 Testing for the effects of concealed weapons laws: Specification errors and robustness. *Journal of Law and Economics* 44(3):799-813.
Moulton, B.R.
  1990 An illustration of a pitfall in estimating the effects of aggregate variables on micro units. *Review of Economics and Statistics* 72:334-338.
Olson, D.E., and M.D. Maltz
  2001 Right-to-carry weapon laws and homicide in large U.S. counties: The effect on weapon types, victim characteristics and victim offender relationships. *Journal of Law and Economics* 44(3):747-770.
Plassmann, F., and T.N Tideman
  2001 Does the right to carry concealed handguns deter countable crimes? Only a count analysis can say. *Journal of Law and Economics* 44(2:2):771-798.

Plassmann, F., and J.E. Whitley
  2003 Comments: Confirming more guns, less crime. *Stanford Law Review* 55:1313-1369.
Ramsey, J.B.
  1969 Tests for specification errors in classical linear least squares regression analysis. *Journal of the Royal Statistical Society* Series B 31(2):350-371.
Vernick, J., and L.M. Hepburn
  2002 State and federal gun laws: Trends for 1970-1999. In J. Ludwig and P.J. Cook, eds., *Evaluating Gun Policy: Effects on Crime and Violence.* Washington, DC: Brookings Institution Press.
Wooldrige, J.M.
  2003 *Introductory Econometrics: A Modern Approach.* Second ed. Mason, OH: Thomson Southwestern.
Zimring, F., and G. Hawkins
  1997 Concealed handguns: The counterfeit deterrent. *The Responsive Community* 7:46-60.

CHAPTER 7

Azrael, D., P.J. Cook, and M. Miller
  2004 State and local prevalence of firearms ownership: Measurement, structure and trends. *Journal of Quantitative Criminology* 20(1):43-62.
Bailey, J.E., A.L. Kellermann, G.W. Somes, J.G. Banton, F.P. Rivara, and N.P. Rushforth
  1997 Risk factors for violent death of women in the home. *Archives of Internal Medicine* 157:777-782.
Beautrais, A.L, P.R. Joyce, and R.T. Mulder
  1996 Access to firearms and the risk of suicide: A case control study. *Australian and New Zealand Journal of Psychiatry* 30:741-748.
Birckmayer, J., and D. Hemenway
  2001 Suicide and firearm prevalence: Are youth disproportionately affected? *Suicide and Life Threatening Behavior* 31(3):303-310.
Boor, M., and J.H. Bair
  1990 Suicide rates, handgun control laws, and sociodemographic variables. *Psychological Reports* 66:923-930.
Borowsky, I.W., M. Ireland, and M.D. Resnick
  2001 Adolescent suicide attempts: risks and protectors. *Pediatrics* 107(3):485-493.
Brent, D.A., M. Baugher, J. Bridge, J. Chen, and L. Beery
  1999 Age and sex-related risk factors for adolescent suicide. *Journal of the American Academy of Child and Adolescent Psychiatry* 38:1497-1505.
Brent, D.A., J.A. Perper, and C.J. Allman
  1987 Alcohol, firearms, and suicide among youth: Temporal trends in Allegheny County, Pennsylvania, 1960 to 1983. *Journal of the American Medical Association* 257:3369-3372.
Brent, D.A, J.A. Perper, C.J. Allman, G.M. Moritz, M. Wartella, and J.P. Zelenak
  1991 The presence and accessibility of firearms in the homes of adolescent suicides: A case-control study. *Journal of the American Medical Association* 266:2989-2995.
Brent, D.A., J. A. Perper, C.E. Goldstein, D.J. Kolko, M.J. Allan, C.J. Allman, and J.P. Zelenak
  1988 Risk factors for adolescent suicide: A comparison of adolescent suicide victims with suicidal inpatients. *Archives of General Psychiatry* 45:581-588.

Brent, D.A, J.A. Perper, G. Moritz, M. Baugher, J. Schweers, and C. Roth
  1993a Firearms and adolescent suicide: A community case-control study. *American Journal of Diseases of Children* 147:1066-1071.
  1994 Suicide in affectively ill adolescents: A case-control study. *Journal of Affective Disorders* 31(3):193-202.
Brent, D.A., J.A. Perper, G. Moritz, M. Baugher, and C. Allman
  1993b Suicide in adolescents with no apparent psychopathology. *Journal of the American Academy of Child and Adolescent Psychiatry* 32:494-500.
Bukstein, O.G., D.A. Brent, J.A. Perper, G. Moritz, M. Baugher, J. Schweers, C. Roth, and L. Balach
  1993 Risk factors for completed suicide among adolescents with a lifetime history of substance abuse: A case-control study. *Acta Psychiatrica Scandinavia* 88:403-408.
Cantor, C.H., and P.J. Slater
  1995 The impact of firearm control legislation on suicide in Queensland: Preliminary findings. *Medical Journal of Australia* 162:583-585.
Carrington, P.J.
  1999 Gender, gun control, suicide and homicide in Canada. *Archives of Suicide Research* 5:71-75.
Carrington, P.J., and S. Moyer
  1994 Gun control and suicide in Ontario. *American Journal of Psychiatry* 151:606-608.
Clarke, R.V., and P.R. Jones
  1989 Suicide and increased availability of handguns in the United States. *Social Science and Medicine* 28:805-809.
Conwell, Y., P.R. Duberstein, K. Connor, S. Eberly, C. Cox, and E.D. Caine
  2002 Access to firearms and risk for suicide in middle-aged and older adults. *American Journal of Geriatric Psychiatry* 10:407-416.
Cummings P., D.C. Grossman, F.P. Rivara, and T.D. Koepsell
  1997a State guns safe storage laws and child mortality due to firearms. *Journal of the American Medical Association* (October) 278(13):1084-1086.
Cummings, P., T.D. Koepsell, D.C. Grossman, J. Savarino, and R.S. Thompson
  1997b The association between the purchase of a handgun and homicide or suicide. *American Journal of Public Health* 87:974-978.
DeZee, M.R.
  1983 Gun control legislation: Impact and ideology. *Law and Policy Quarterly* 5:367-379.
Duggan, M.
  2003 Guns and suicide. Pp 41-67 in J. Ludwig and P. Cook, eds. *Evaluating Gun Policy: Effects on Crime and Violence*. Washington, DC: Brookings Institution Press.
Geisel, M.S., R. Roll, and R.S. Wettick
  1969 The effectiveness of state and local regulations of handguns. *Duke University Law Journal* 4:647-476.
Hemenway, D., and M. Miller
  2000 Firearm availability and homicide rates across 26 high income countries. *Journal of Trauma* 49:985-988.
  2002 The association of rates of household handgun ownership, lifetime major depression and serious suicidal thoughts with rates of suicide across U.S. census regions. *Injury Prevention* 8:313-316.
Hemenway, D., B.P. Kennedy, I. Kawachi, and R.D. Putnam
  2001 Firearm prevalence and social capital. *Annals of Epidemiology* 11:484-490.
Hennekens C.H., and J.E. Buring
  1987 *Epidemiology in Medicine*. Boston: Little, Brown & Co.

Hsieh, D., C.F. Manski, and D. McFadden
   1985   Estimation of response probabilities from augmented retrospective observations. *Journal of the American Statistical Association* 80:651-662.
Johnson, G.R., E.G. Krug, and L.B. Potter
   2000   Suicide among adolescents and young adults: A cross-national comparison of 34 countries. *Suicide and Life Threatening Behavior* 30:74-82.
Kaplan, M.S., and O. Geling
   1998   Firearm suicides and homicides in the United States: Regional variations and patterns of gun ownership. *Social Science Medicine* 46:1227-1233.
Kellermann, A.L, F.P, Rivara, G. Somes, D.T. Reay, J. Francisco, J.G. Banton, J. Prodzinski, C. Fligner, and B.B. Hackman
   1992   Special article: Suicide in the home in relation to gun ownership. *New England Journal of Medicine* 327:467-472.
Kellermann, A.L., et al.
   1993   Gun ownership as a risk factor for homicide in the home. *New England Journal of Medicine,* 329(15):1084-1091.
Kellermann, A.L., F.P. Rivara, R.K. Lee, J.G. Banton, P. Cummings, B.B. Hackman, and G. Somes
   1996   Injuries due to firearms in three cities. *New England Journal of Medicine* 335:1438-1444.
Kellermann, A.L., et al.
   1998   Injuries and deaths due to firearms in the home. *Journal of Trauma* 45 (2):263-267.
Killias, M.
   1993   International correlations between gun ownership and rates of homicide and suicide. *Canadian Medical Association Journal* 148:1721-1725.
   2001   Guns, violent crime, and suicide in 21 countries. *Canadian Journal of Criminology* 43:429-439.
Kleck, G.
   1997   *Targeting Guns.* New York: Aldine de Gruyter.
Kleck, G., and E.B. Patterson
   1993   The impact of gun control and gun ownership levels on violence rates. *Journal of Quantitative Criminology* 9:249-287.
Krasker, W.S., and J.W. Pratt
   1986   Bounding the effects of proxy variables on regression coefficients. *Econometrica* 54(3):641-656.
Leenaars, A.A., and D. Lester
   1999   Suicide notes in alcoholism. *Psychological Reports* 85:363-364.
Lester, D.
   1987a Availability of guns and the likelihood of suicide. *Sociology and Social Research* 71:287-288.
   1987b An availability-acceptability theory of suicide. *Activitas Nervosa Superior* 29:164-166.
   1988a State laws on suicide and suicide rates. *Psychological Reports* 62(1):134-139.
   1988b Restricting the availability of guns as a strategy for preventing suicide. *Biology and Society* 5:127-129.
   1988c Gun control, gun ownership, and suicide prevention. *Suicide and Life-Threatening Behavior* 18:176-180.
   1989   Gun ownership and suicide in the United States. *Psychological Medicine* 19:519-521.

2000   Gun availability and the use of guns for suicide and homicide in Canada. *Canadian Journal of Public Health* 91(3):186-187.

Lester, D., and A. Leenaars

1993   Suicide rates in Canada before and after the tightening of firearm control laws. *Psychological Reports* 72:787-790.

Lester, D., and M.E. Murrell

1980   The influences of gun control laws on suicidal behavior. *American Journal of Psychology* 137:121-122.

1982   The preventive effect of strict gun control laws on suicide and homicide. *Suicide and Life-Threatening Behavior* 12:131-140.

1986   The influence of gun control laws on personal violence. *Journal of Community Psychology* 14:315-318.

Loftin, C., D. McDowall, B. Wiersema, and T.J. Cottey

1991   Effects of restrictive licensing of handguns on homicide and suicide in the District of Columbia. *New England Journal of Medicine* 325:1615-1620.

Lott, J.R., Jr., and J.E. Whitley

2000   Safe Storage Gun Laws: Accidental Deaths, Suicides, and Crime. Working paper #237, Yale Law School, Program for Studies in Law, Economics, and Public Policy.

Ludwig, J., and P.J. Cook

2000   Homicide and suicide rates associated with implementation of the Brady Handgun Violence Prevention Act. *Journal of the American Medical Association* 284(5):585-591.

2001   The benefit of reducing gun violence: Evidence from contingent valuation survey data. *Journal of Risk and Uncertainty* 22(3):207-226.

Ludwig, J., P.J. Cook, and T. Smith

1998   The gender gap in reporting household gun ownership. *American Journal of Public Health* 88:1715-1718.

Maddala, G.S.

1992   *Introduction to Econometrics.* New York: Macmillan.

Manski, C.F., and S.R. Lerman

1977   The estimation of choice probabilities from choice based samples. *Econometrica* 45(8):1977-1988.

Markush, R.E., and A.A. Bartolucci

1984   Firearms and suicide in the United States. *American Journal of Public Health* 74:123-127.

Mathur, V.K., and D.G. Freeman

2002   A theoretical model of adolescent suicide and some evidence from U.S. data. *Health Economics* 11(8):695-708.

McKeown, R.E., C.Z. Garrison, S.P. Cuffe, J.L. Waller, K.L. Jackson, and C.L. Addy

1998   Incidence and predictors of suicidal behaviors in a longitudinal sample of young adolescents. *Journal of the American Academy of Child and Adolescent Psychiatry* 37(6):612-619.

Medoff, M.H., and J.P. Maggadino

1983   Suicides and firearm control laws. *Evaluation Review* 7:357-372.

Mietinnen, O.S.

1976   Estimability and estimation in case referent studies. *American Journal of Epidemiology* 103:226-235.

Miller, M., D. Azrael, and D. Hemenway

2001   Firearm availability and unintentional firearm deaths. *Accident Analysis and Prevention* 33:477-484.

2002a Firearm availability and unintentional firearm deaths, suicide and homicide among 5-14 year olds. *Journal of Trauma* 52(2):267-274.

2002b Household firearm ownership and suicide rates in the United States. *Epidemiology* 13:517-524.

2002c Firearm availability and suicide, homicide, and unintentional firearm deaths among women. *Journal of Urban Health* 79(1):26-38.

Murray, D.R.
1975 Handguns, gun control laws and firearm violence. *Social Problems* 23:81-92.

National Center for Health Statistics
2003 *National Vital Statistics Reports* 52(3).

Nicholson, R., and A. Garner
1980 *The Analysis of the Firearms Control Act of 1975*. Washington DC: U.S. Conference of Mayors.

Resnick, M.D., P.S. Bearman, R.W. Blum, K.E. Bauman, K.M. Harris, J. Jones, J. Tabor, T. Beuhring, R. Sieving, M. Shew, M. Ireland, L.H. Bearinger, and J.R. Udry
1997 Protecting adolescents from harm: Findings from the National Longitudinal Study on Adolescent Health. *Journal of the American Medical Association* 278(10):823-832.

Reuter, P., and J. Mouzos
2003 Australia's gun control: Massive buy-back of low risk guns. In J. Ludwig and P.J. Cook, eds., *Evaluating Gun Control*. Washington, DC: Brookings Institution.

Rich, C.L., J.G. Young, R.C. Fowler, J. Wagner, and A. Black
1986 San Diego suicide study: Young vs. old subjects. *Archives of General Psychiatry* 43:577-582.

1990 Guns and suicide: Possible effects of some specific legislation. *American Journal of Psychiatry* 147:342-346.

Shah, S., R.E. Hoffman, L. Wake, and W.M. Marine
2000 Adolescent suicide and household access to firearms in Colorado: Results of a case-control study. *Journal of Adolescent Health* 26:157-163.

Sloan, J.H., F.P. Rivara, D.T. Reay, J.A.J. Ferris, and A.L. Kellermann
1990 Firearm regulations and community suicide rates. A comparison of two metropolitan areas. *New England Journal of Medicine* 322:369-373.

Snowdon, J., and L. Harris
1992 Firearm suicides in Australia. *Medical Journal of Australia* 156:79-83.

Sommers, P.M.
1984 Letter to the editor. *New England Journal of Medicine* 310:47-48.

Thomsen, J.L., and S.B. Albrektsen
1991 An investigation of a pattern of firearm fatalities before and after introduction of new legislation in Denmark. *Medical Science and Law* 31:162-166.

Wintemute, G.J., C.A. Parham, J.J. Beaumont, M. Wright, and C. Drake
1999 Mortality among recent purchasers of handguns. *New England Journal of Medicine* 341:1583-1589.

Wooldridge, J.M.
2000 *Introductory Econometrics: A Modern Approach*. Cincinnati, OH: South-Western College Publishing.

Yang, B., and D. Lester
1991 The effect of gun availability on suicide rates. *Atlantic Economics Journal* 19:74.

CHAPTER 8

Arcus, M.
  1995   Family Life Education: What Works? Paper presented at the meeting of the National Council on Family Relations, November 18, Portland, OR.
Arredono, S., T. Aultman-Bettride, T.P. Johnson, et al.
  1999   *Preventing Youth Handgun Violence: A National Study for Trends and Patterns for the State of Colorado.* Boulder, CO: Center for the Study and Prevention of Violence.
Benowitz, N.L., S.M. Hall, R.I. Herning, P. Jacob, R.T. Jones, and A.L. Osman
  1983   Smokers of low-yield cigarettes do not consume less nicotine. *New England Journal of Medicine* 309(July 21):139-142.
Boruch, B., H. May, H. Turner, J. Lavenberg, A. Petrosino, D. de Moya, J. Grimshaw, and E. Foley
  2004   Estimating the effects of interventions that are deployed in many places: Place-randomized trials. *American Behavioral Scientist* 47(5):608-633.
Brady Campaign to Reduce Gun Violence
  2002   *Child Access Protection (CAP) Laws.* Available at: http://www.bradycampaign.org/facts/gunlaws/cap.asp. [Accessed 7/25/02].
Cook, P.J., and A. Braga
  2001   Comprehensive firearms tracing: Strategic and investigative uses of new data on firearms markets. *Arizona Law Review* 43(2):277-309.
Cook, P.J., and J.A. Leitzel
  2002   "Smart" guns: A technological fix for regulating the secondary market. *Contemporary Economic Policy* 20(1):38-49.
Cummings, P., D.C. Grossman, F.P. Rivara, and T.D. Koepsell
  1997   State gun safe storage laws and child mortality due to firearms. *Journal of the American Medical Association* 278:1084-1086.
Flay, B.R.
  1986   Efficacy and effectiveness trials (and other phases of research) in the development of health promotion programs. *Preventive Medicine* 15:451-474.
  2002   School-Based Randomized Trials for Evaluation Problem Behavior Prevention Programs. Prepared for Conference on Progress and Prospects for Place-based Randomized Trials, Rockefeller Foundation Study and Conference Center, Bellagio, Italy, November 11-15.
Flay, B.R., and J.A. Best
  1982   Overcoming design problems in evaluating health behavior problems. *Evaluation and the Health Professions* 5:43-69.
Glasgow, R.E., K.D. McCaul, V.B. Freeborn, and H.K. O'Neill
  1981   Immediate and long term health consequences information in the prevention of adolescent smoking. *Behavior Therapist* 4:15-16.
Goodstadt, M.
  1978   Alcohol and drug education: models and outcomes. *Health Education Monographs* 6:263-279.
Hardy, M.S.
  2002a Behavior-oriented approaches to reducing youth gun violence. *Future of Children* 12(2):101-115.
  2002b Teaching firearm safety to children: Failure of a program. *Journal of Developmental and Behavioral Pediatrics* 23(2):71-76.
Hardy, M.S., F.D. Armstrong, B.L. Martin, and K.N. Strawn
  1996   A firearm safety program for children: They just can't say no. *Journal of Developmental and Behavioral Pediatrics* 17:216-221.

Health Partners Research Foundation
1999   Calling the Shots: A Hospital Based Violence Prevention Program. Presented at the Centers for Disease Control Injury Prevention Forum, June 1999.

Howard, P.K.
2000   An overview of a few well-known national children's gun safety programs and ENA's newly developed program. *Injury Prevention* 27(5):485-488.
2001   An overview of a few well-known national children's gun safety programs and ENA's newly developed program. *Journal of Emergency Nursing* 27(5):485-488.

Institute of Medicine
2001   *Clearing the Smoke: Assessing the Science Base for Tobacco Harm Reduction.* Committee to Assess the Science Base for Tobacco Harm Reduction, Board on Health Promotion and Disease Prevention. K. Stratton, P. Shetty, R. Wallace, and S. Bondurant, eds. Washington, DC: National Academy Press.
2002   *Reducing Suicide: A National Imperative.* Committee on Pathophysiology and Prevention of Adolescent and Adult Suicide, Board on Neuroscience and Behavioral Health. S.K. Goldsmith, T.C. Pellmar, A.M. Kleinman, and W.E. Bunney, eds. Washington, DC: National Academy Press.

LeBrun, E., G. Naue, S. Naureckas, and M. Witwer
1999   *School-Based Curricula to Prevent Gun Violence: A Review and Call for Evaluation of Programs.* Chicago: Handgun Epidemic Lowering Plan (HELP) Network.

Leonardatos, C., P.H. Blackman, and D.B. Kopel
2001   Smart guns/foolish legislators: Find the right public safety laws, and avoiding the wrong ones. *Connecticut Law Review* 34(1):157-219.

Lott, J.R., Jr., and D.B.M. Mustard
1997   Crime, deterrence and right-to-carry concealed handguns. *Journal of Legal Studies* 26(1):1-68.

Lott, J.R., Jr., and J.E. Whitley
2002   Safe storage gun laws: Accidental deaths, suicide, and crime. *Journal of Law and Economics* 44(1):659-689.

Morgan, L.
1989   Lawmakers pass gun bill: Governor promises to sign. *St. Petersburg Times* June 21, p. 1A.

Moskowitz, J.M.
1989   Preliminary guidelines for reporting outcome evaluation studies of health promotion and disease prevention programs. In M.T. Braverman, ed., *Evaluating Health Promotion Programs: New Directions for Program Evaluation.* San Francisco: Jossey-Bass.

National Academy of Engineering
2003   *Owner-Authorized Handguns: A Workshop Summary.* Steering Committee for NAE Workshop on User-Authorized Handguns. Lance A. Davis and Greg Pearson, eds. Washington, DC: The National Academies Press.

National Council on Crime and Delinquency
2001   *Teens on Target Evaluation.* I. Arifuku, author. Oakland, CA: National Council on Crime and Delinquency.

National Research Council and Institute of Medicine
2002   *Deadly Lessons: Understanding Lethal School Violence.* Case Studies of School Violence Committee. Committee on Law and Justice and Board on Children, Youth, and Families. M.H. Moore, C.V. Petrie, A.A. Braga, and B.L. McLaughlin, eds. Washington, DC: National Academy Press.

New Jersey Institute of Technology
  2001   *Personalized Weapons Technology Project Progress Report with Findings and Recommendations*, Vol. I and II. April 15. Newark, NJ: New Jersey Institute of Technology.
Oatis, P.J., N.M. Fenn Buderer, P. Cummings, and R. Fleitz
  1999   Pediatrics practice based evaluation of the Steps to Prevent Firearm Injury program. *Injury Prevention* 5(1):48-52.
Office of Juvenile Justice and Delinquency Prevention
  1999   *Promising Strategies to Reduce Gun Violence*. Office of Juvenile Justice and Delinquency Prevention. Washington, DC: U.S. Department of Justice.
Pacific Research Institute for Public Policy
  1997   Problematic arguments for banning handguns. Pp. 31-49 in D.B. Kates and G. Kleck, eds., *The Great American Gun Debate: Essays on Firearms and Violence*. San Francisco: Pacific Research Institute for Public Policy.
Peltzman, S.
  1975   The effects of automobile safety regulation. *Journal of Political Economy* 83(2):677-725.
Shapiro, J.P., R.L. Dorman, W.M. Burkey, C.J. Welker, and J.B. Clough
  1997   Development and factor analysis of a measure of youth attitudes toward guns and violence. *Journal of Clinical Child Psychology* 26:311-320.
Shapiro, J.P., R.D. Dorman, C.J. Welker, and J.B. Clough
  1998   Youth attitudes toward guns and violence: Relations with sex, age, ethnic group, and exposure. *Journal of Clinical Child Psychology* 27:98-108.
Teret, S.P., and P.L. Culross
  2002   Product-oriented approaches to reducing youth gun violence. *Future of Children* 12(2):119-132.
Thompson, E.L.
  1978   Smoking education programs, 1960-1976. *American Journal of Public Health* 68:257.
Violence Policy Center
  1998   *False Hope of Smart Guns*. Available at: http://www.vpc.org/fact_sht/smartgun.htm. [Accessed 7/24/02].
Viscusi, W.K.
  1984   The lulling effect: The impact of child resistant packaging on aspirin and analgesic ingestions. *American Economic Review* 74(2):324-327.
  1992   *Fatal Tradeoffs: Public and Private Responsibilities for Risk*. New York: Oxford University Press.
Webster, D.W., and M. Starnes
  2000   Reexamining the association between child access prevention gun laws and unintentional shooting deaths of children. *Pediatrics* 106(4):1466-1469.
Weisburd, D., and A. Petrosino
  forth-   Randomized experiments. In Richard Wright, ed., *Encyclopedia of Criminology*.
  coming   Chicago: Fitzroy Dearborn.
Weiss, D.R.
  1996   Smart Gun Technology Project Final Report. SAND96-1131. May. Prepared by the Sandia National Laboratories for the U.S. Department of Energy. Available: www.prod.sandia.gov/cgi-bin/techlib/access-control.pl/1996/961131.pdf [Accessed 3/17/04].
Wilson-Brewer, R., S. Cohen, L. O'Donnell, and I. Goodman
  1991   Violence Prevention for Young Adolescents: A Survey of the State of the Art. Available from the ERIC Clearinghouse, ED356442; 800-443-3742.

Wirsbinski, J.W.
  2001 Smart Gun Technology Update. Sandia National Laboratories, Albuquerque, New
        Mexico.
Wright, J.D., and P.H. Rossi
  1986 *Armed and Considered Dangerous: A Survey of Felons and Their Firearms.* New
        York: Aldine de Gruyter.

CHAPTER 9

Alschuler, A.W.
  1978 Sentencing reform and prosecutorial power: A critique of recent proposals for
        "fixed" and "presumptive sentencing." *University of Pennsylvania Law Review*
        126(3):550-577.
Beha, J.A.
  1977 "And nobody can get you out:" The impact of a mandatory prison sentence for the
        illegal carrying of a firearm on the use of firearms and on the administration of
        criminal justice in Boston. *Boston University Law Review* 57:96-146, 289-333.
Berk, R., D. Hoffman, J.D. Roma, and H. Wong
  1979 Estimation procedures for pooled cross-sectional and time-series data. *Evaluation
        Quarterly* 3(2):385-411.
Blumstein, A.
  1995 Youth violence, guns and the illicit-drug industry. *Journal of Criminal Law and
        Criminality* 86:10-36.
Boston Police Department
  2002 *Crime Reduction Strategies: Firearms Crime.* Boston: Boston Police Department.
Braga, A.A., D.M. Kennedy, E.J. Waring, and A.M. Piehl
  2001a Problem-oriented policing, deterrence, and youth violence: An evaluation of
        Boston's Operation Ceasefire. *Journal of Research in Crime and Delinquency*
        38(3):195-225.
Braga, A.A., D.M. Kennedy, A.M. Piehl, and E.J. Waring
  2001b Measuring the impact of Operation Ceasefire. In *Reducing Gun Violence: The
        Boston Gun Project's Operation Ceasefire.* National Institute of Justice. Washing-
        ton, DC: U.S. Department of Justice.
Braga, A.A., D.M. Kennedy, and G. Tita
  2002 New approaches to the strategic prevention of gang and group-involved violence.
        In C.R. Huff, ed., *Gangs in America*, 3rd edition. Newbury Park, CA: Sage Publi-
        cations.
Braga, A.A., D.L. Weisburd, E.J. Waring, L.G. Mazerolle, W. Spelman, and F. Gajewski
  1999 Problem-oriented policing in violent crime places: A randomized controlled experi-
        ment. *Criminology* 37(3):541-580.
Carlson, K.
  1982 *Mandatory Sentencing: The Experiences of Two States.* National Institute of Jus-
        tice. Washington, DC: U.S. Department of Justice.
Chaiken, J., and M. Chaiken
  1982 *Varieties of Criminal Behavior.* Santa Monica, CA: RAND Corporation.
Cohen, J., and J. Ludwig
  2003 Policing crime guns. Pp. 217-239 in J. Ludwig and P. Cook, eds., *Evaluating Gun
        Policy: Effects on Crime and Violence.* Washington, DC: Brookings Institution
        Press.

Cook, P.J., and J.H. Laub
  1998   The unprecedented epidemic in youth violence. Pp. 27-64 in M. Tonry and M.H. Moore, eds., *Youth Violence. Crime and Justice: A Review of Research*. Volume 24. Chicago: University of Chicago Press.
Cook, P.J., and D. Nagin
  1979   *Does the Weapon Matter? An Evaluation of a Weapons-Emphasis Policy in the Prosecution of Violent Offenders*. Washington, DC: INSLAW.
Deutsch, S.J.
  1979   Lies, damn lies, and statistics: A rejoinder to the comment by Hay and McCleary. *Evaluation Review Quarterly* 3:315-328.
  1981   Intervention modeling: Analysis of changes in crime rates. In J.A. Fox, ed., *Methods in Quantitative Criminology*. New York: Academic Press.
Deutsch, S.J., and F.B. Alt
  1977   The effect of Massachusetts' gun control law on gun-related crimes in the city of Boston. *Evaluation Quarterly* 1:543-568.
Eck, J.E., and W. Spelman
  1987   *Problem-Solving: Problem-Oriented Policing in Newport News*. National Institute of Justice. Washington, DC: U.S. Department of Justice.
Eck, J.E., and D. Weisburd
  1995   Crime places in crime theory. In J. Eck and D. Weisburd, eds., *Crime and Place*. Monsey, NY: Criminal Justice Press.
Goldstein, H.
  1990   *Problem-Oriented Policing*. Philadelphia: Temple University Press.
Greene, J.A.
  1999   Zero tolerance: A case study of police practices and policies in New York City. *Crime and Delinquency* 45(2):171-181.
Greenwood, P.
  2003   Commentary on Raphael and Ludwig. Pp. 280-286 in J. Ludwig and P. Cook, eds., *Evaluating Gun Policy: Effects on Crime and Violence*. Washington, DC: Brookings Institution Press.
Hay, R.A., and R. McCleary
  1979   Box-Tiao time series models for impact assessment: A comment on the recent work of Deutsch and Alt. *Evaluation Quarterly* 3:277-314.
Kennedy, D.M.
  1997   Pulling levers: Chronic offenders, high-crime setting and a theory of prevention. *Valparaiso University Law Review* 31(2):449-484.
Kennedy, D.M., A.M. Piehl, and A.A. Braga
  1996   Youth violence in Boston: Gun markets, serious youth offenders, and a use-reduction strategy. *Law and Contemporary Problems* 59(1):147-197.
Kennedy, D.M., A.A. Braga, and A.M. Piehl
  1997   The (un)known universe: Mapping gangs and gang violence in Boston. In D. Weisburd and J.T. McEwen, eds., *Crime Mapping and Crime Prevention*. Monsey, NY: Criminal Justice Press.
  2001   Developing and implementing Operation Ceasefire. In *Reducing Gun Violence: The Boston Gun Project's Operation Ceasefire*. National Institute of Justice. Washington, DC: U.S. Department of Justice.
Kessler, D., and S. Levitt
  1999   Using sentence enhancements to distinguish between deterrence and incapacitation. *Journal of Law and Economics* 42:343-363.

Kleck, G.
  1991   *Point Blank: Guns and Violence in America.* New York: Aldine de Gruyter.
  1997   *Targeting Guns: Firearms and Their Control.* New York: Aldine de Gruyter.
Levitt, S.
  2003   Commentary on Raphael and Ludwig. Pp. 277-279 in J. Ludwig and P. Cook, eds.,
         Evaluating Gun Policy: Effects on Crime and Violence. Washington, DC: Brookings
         Institution Press.
Lizotte, A., and M. Zatz
  1986   The use and abuse of sentence enhancement for firearms offenses in California.
         Law and Contemporary Problems 49(1):199-221.
Loftin, C., and D. McDowall
  1981   "One with a gun gets you two:" Mandatory sentencing and firearms violence in
         Detroit. *Annals of the American Academy of Political and and Social Science*
         455:150-167.
  1984   The deterrent effects of the Florida felony firearm law. *Journal of Criminal Law
         and Criminology* 75(1):250-259.
Loftin, C., M. Heumann, and D. McDowall
  1983   Mandatory sentencing and firearms violence. *Law and Society Review* 17(2):287-
         318.
Marvell, T., and C. Moody
  1995   The impact of enhanced prison terms for felonies committed with guns. *Criminol-
         ogy* 33(1):247-281.
McDevitt, J., A.A. Braga, D. Nurge, and M. Buerger
  2003   Boston's Youth Violence Prevention Program: A comprehensive community-wide
         approach. In Scott H. Decker, ed., *Policing Gangs and Youth Violence.* Belmont,
         CA: Wadsworth Publishing Company.
McDowall, D., C. Loftin, and B. Wiersema
  1992   A comparative study of the preventive effects of mandatory sentencing laws for gun
         crimes. *Journal of Criminal Law and Criminology* 83:378-394.
McGarrell, E., and S. Chermak
  2003   Strategic Approaches to Reducing Firearms Violence: Final Report on the India-
         napolis Violence Reduction Partnership. Final report submitted to the National
         Institute of Justice. School of Criminal Justice, Michigan State University.
McGarrell, E.F., S. Chermak, A. Weiss, and J. Wilson
  2001   Reducing firearms violence through directed police patrol. *Criminology and Public
         Policy* 1:119-148.
McPheters, L., R. Mann, and D. Schlagenhauf
  1984   Economic response to a crime deterrence program: Mandatory sentencing for rob-
         bery with a firearm. *Economic Inquiry* 22(2):550-570.
Meyer, B.D.
  1995   Natural and quasi-experiments in economics. *Journal of Business and Economic
         Statistics* 13(2):151-162.
National Research Council
  1978   *Deterrence and Incapacitation: Estimating the Effects of Criminal Sanctions on
         Crime Rates.* Panel on Deterrence and Incapacitation, Alfred Blumstein, Jacqueline
         Cohen, and Daniel Nagin, eds. Washington, DC: National Academy Press.
  1993   *Understanding and Preventing Violence,* Volume 1. Panel on the Understanding
         and Control of Violent Behavior, Albert J. Reiss, Jr. and Jeffrey A. Roth, eds.
         Washington, DC: National Academy Press.

2001   *Informing America's Policy on Illegal Drugs: What We Don't Know Keeps Hurting Us.* Committee on Data and Research for Policy on Illegal Drugs, C.F. Manski, J.V. Pepper, and C.V. Petrie, eds. Committee on Law and Justice and Committee on National Statistics. Washington DC: National Academy Press.

2004   *Fairness and Effectiveness in Policing: The Evidence.* Committee to Review Research on Police Policy and Practices, W. Skogan and K. Frydl, eds. Washington, DC: The National Academies Press.

Office of Juvenile Justice and Delinquency Prevention
1999   *Promising Strategies to Reduce Gun Violence.* Washington, DC: U.S. Department of Justice.

2002   *Juvenile Gun Courts: Promoting Accountability and Providing Treatment.* Washington, DC: U.S. Department of Justice.

Piehl, A.M., S.J. Cooper, A.A. Braga, and D.M. Kennedy
1999   Testing for Structural Breaks in the Evaluation of Programs. Working paper #7226. Cambridge, MA: National Bureau of Economic Research.

Pierce, G.L., and W.J. Bowers
1981   The Bartley-Fox gun law's short-term impact on crime in Boston. *Annals of the American Academy of Political and Social Science* 455:120-137.

Pierce, G., S. Spaar, and L. Briggs
1988   *The Character of Police Work: Strategic and Tactical Implications.* Boston: Center for Applied Social Research, Northeastern University.

Raphael, S., and J. Ludwig
2003   Prison sentence enhancements: The case of Project Exile. Pp. 251-276 in J. Ludwig and P. Cook, eds., *Evaluating Gun Policy: Effects on Crime and Violence.* Washington, DC: Brookings Institution Press.

Rolph, J., J. Chaiken, and R. Houchens
1981   *Methods for Estimating the Crime Rates of Individuals.* Santa Monica, CA: RAND Corporation.

Rosenfeld, R., and S. Decker
1996   Consent to search and seize: Evaluating an innovative youth firearms suppression program. *Law and Contemporary Problems* 59(2):197-220.

Rossman, D., P. Froyd, G.L. Pierce, J. McDevitt, and W.J. Bowers
1980   Massachusetts' mandatory minimum sentence gun law. *Criminal Law Bulletin* 16(2):150-163.

Sherman, L.W.
1995   The police. In J.Q. Wilson and J. Petersilia, eds., *Crime.* San Francisco: ICS Press.

2001   Reducing gun violence: What works, what doesn't, what's promising. *Criminal Justice* 1(1):11-25.

Sherman, L.W., and D. Rogan
1995   Effects of gun seizures on gun violence: "Hot spots" patrol in Kansas City. *Justice Quarterly* 12(4):673-694.

Sherman, L.W., P. Gartin, and M. Buerger
1989   Hot spots of predatory crime: Routine activities and the criminology of place. *Criminology* 27(1):27-56.

Tita, G., K.J. Riley, G. Ridgeway, C. Grammich, A.F. Abrahamse, and P.W. Greenwood
2003   *Reducing Gun Violence: Results from an Intervention in East Los Angeles.* Prepared for the National Institute of Justice. Santa Monica, CA: RAND Corporation.

Weisburd, D.
1997   *Reorienting Criminal Justice Research and Policy: From the Causes of Criminality to the Context of Crime.* National Institute of Justice. Washington, DC: U.S. Department of Justice.

Weisburd, D., L. Maher, and L. Sherman
    1992   Contrasting crime general and crime specific theory: The case of hot spots of crime. *Advances in Criminological Theory* 4(1):45-69.
Wolfgang, M., R. Figlio, and T. Sellin
    1972   *Delinquency in a Birth Cohort*. Chicago: University of Chicago Press.

Appendix A

Dissent

James Q. Wilson

he thrust of Chapter 6 of the committee's report is that studies purporting to show a relationship between right-to-carry (RTC) laws and crime rates are fragile. Though I am not an econometrician, I am struck by the fact that most studies of the effect of policy changes on crime rates are fragile in this sense: Different authors produce different results, and sometimes contradictory ones. This has been true of studies of the effect on crime rates of incapacitation (that is, taking criminals off the street), deterrence (that is, increasing the likelihood of conviction and imprisonment), and capital punishment. In my view, committees of the National Research Council that have dealt with these earlier studies have attempted, not simply to show that different authors have reached different conclusions, but to suggest which lines of inquiry, including data and models, are most likely to produce more robust results.

That has not happened here. Chapter 6 seeks to show that fragile results exist but not to indicate what research strategies might improve our understanding of the effects, if any, of RTC laws. To do the latter would require the committee to analyze carefully not only the studies by John Lott but those done by both his supporters and his critics. Here, only the work by Lott and his coauthors is subject to close analysis.

If this analysis of Lott's work showed that his findings are not supported by his data and models, then the conclusion that his results are fragile might be sufficient. But my reading of this chapter suggests that some of his results survive virtually every reanalysis done by the committee.

Lott argued that murder rates decline after the adoption of RTC laws even after allowing for the effect of other variables that affect crime rates.

The committee has confirmed this finding as is evident in its Tables 6-1, 6-2, 6-5 (first row), 6-6 (first row), and 6-7 (first two rows). This confirmation includes both the original data period (1977-1992) used by Lott and data that run through 2000. In view of the confirmation of the findings that shall-issue laws drive down the murder rate, it is hard for me to understand why these claims are called "fragile."

The only exceptions to this confirmation are, to me, quite puzzling. Tables 6-5 and 6-6 suggest that RTC laws have no effect on murder rates when no control variables are entered into the equations. These control variables (which include all of the social, demographic, and public policies other than RTC laws that might affect crime rates) are essential to understanding crime. Suppose Professor Jones wrote a paper saying that increasing the number of police in a city reduced the crime rate and Professor Smith wrote a rival paper saying that cities with few police officers have low crime rates. Suppose that neither Jones nor Smith used any control variables, such as income, unemployment, population density, or the frequency with which offenders are sent to prison in reaching their conclusions. *If* such papers were published, they would be rejected out of hand by the committee for the obvious reason that they failed to supply a complete account of the factors that affect the crime rate. One cannot explain crime rates just by observing the number of police in a city any more than one can explain them just by noting the existence of RTC laws.

It is not enough to say that it is hard to know the right set of control variables without calling into question the use of economics in analyzing public policy questions. All control variables are based on past studies and reasonable theories; any given selection is best evaluated by testing various controls in one's equations.

In addition, with only a few exceptions, the studies cited in Chapter 6, including those by Lott's critics, do not show that the passage of RTC laws drives the crime rates up (as might be the case if one supposed that newly armed people went about looking for someone to shoot). The direct evidence that such shooting sprees occur is nonexistent. The indirect evidence, as found in papers by Black and Nagin and Ayres and Donohue [cited in Chapter 6], is controversial. Indeed, the Ayres and Donohue paper shows that there was a "statistically significant downward shift in the trend" of the murder rate (Chapter 6, page 135). This suggests to me that for people interested in RTC laws, the best evidence we have is that they impose no costs but may confer benefits. That conclusion might be very useful to authorities who contemplate the enactment of RTC laws.

Finally, the committee suggests that extending the Lott model to include data through 2000 may show no effect on RTC laws on murder rates if one analyzes the data on a year-by-year basis (Table 6-7, rows three and four). I wish I knew enough econometrics to feel confident about this argument, but I confess that at first blush it strikes me as implausible. To me, Lott's general argument is supported even though it is hard to assign its effect to a particular year. Estimating the effects of RTC laws by individual years reduces the number of observations and thus the likelihood of finding a statistically significant effect. It is possible that doing this is proper, but it strikes me that such an argument ought first to be tested in a peer-reviewed journal before it is used in this report as a sound strategy.

Even if the use of newer data calls into question the original Lott findings, a more reasonable conclusion is that Lott's findings depend on crime rate trends. The committee correctly notes that between 1977 and 1992 crime rates were rising rapidly while between 1993 and 1997 they were declining. Lott's original study was of the first time period. Suppose that his results are not as robust for the second period. The committee concludes that this shows that his model suffers from "specification errors" (page 141). Another and to me more plausible conclusion is that the effect of RTC laws on some crime rates is likely to be greater when those rates are rising than when they are falling. When crime rates are rising, public policy interventions (including deterrence, incapacitation, and RTC laws) are likely to make a difference because they create obstacles to the market and cultural forces that are driving crime rates up. But when crime rates are falling, such interventions may make less of a difference because they will be overwhelmed by market and cultural changes that make crime less attractive. This may or may not be a reasonable inference, but it is worthy of examination.

In sum, I find that the evidence presented by Lott and his supporters suggests that RTC laws do in fact help drive down the murder rate, though their effect on other crimes is ambiguous.

Appendix B
Committee Response to Wilson's Dissent

This response addresses Professor Wilson's dissent from one aspect of the committee report. It is important to stress at the outset that his dissent focuses on one part of one chapter of the report. Except for the effects of right-to-carry laws on homicide, the entire committee is in agreement on the material in Chapter 6 and the report overall. In particular, the committee, including Wilson, found that "it is impossible to draw strong conclusions from the existing literature on the causal impact" of right-to-carry laws on violent and property crime in general and rape, aggravated assault, auto theft, burglary, and larceny in particular.

The only substantive issue on which the committee differed is whether the existing research supports the conclusion that right-to-carry laws substantially reduce murder. The report suggests that the scientific evidence is inconclusive. Wilson disagreed, arguing that virtually every estimate shows a substantial and statistically significant negative effect of right-to-carry laws on murder.

While it is true that most of the reported estimates are negative, several are positive and many are statistically insignificant. In addition, when we use Lott's trend model but restrict the out years to five years or less (Table 6-7), the trends for murder become positive and those for other crimes remain negative. Therefore, the key question is how to reconcile the contrary findings or, conversely, how to explain why these particular positive, or negative, findings should be dismissed. Three sets of results discussed more fully in Chapter 6 provide support for the committee's conclusion: Published studies, the committee's analysis of control variables, and the committee's analysis extending the time period.

1. **Published studies.** There is no question that the empirical results on the effects of right-to-carry laws on murder (and other crimes) are sensitive to seemingly small variations in data and specification. Indeed, Wilson agrees that a few studies find positive effects of right-to-carry laws on murder. We cite four studies in Tables 6-3 and 6-4: Ayres and Donohue, Black and Nagin, Moody, and Plassmann and Tideman (cited in Chapter 6). There are almost certainly others not reported in these tables.

The rest of the committee and Wilson agree that fragility does not prove that the results of any specific paper are incorrect. However, some of the published results must be incorrect because they are inconsistent with one another. The important question, therefore, is whether the correct results can be identified. The rest of the committee thinks that they cannot. Contrary to Wilson's claim, the committee did assess the existing body of empirical literature on right-to-carry laws (see the section beginning on page 127 and Tables 6-3 and 6-4). As described in the report, all of the empirical research on right-to-carry laws relies on the same conceptual and methodological ideas (page 121). Relative to the basic models estimated by Lott, some researchers used data from more counties and some from fewer; some used hybrid linear models while others used nonlinear specifications; some provide state-specific estimates while most provide a single national estimate; some added control variables while others used relatively parsimonious specifications; and so forth. All of the studies described in the literature review made plausible cases for their choices of models and data. Wilson seems to argue that a careful evaluation of the literature would reveal which paper or papers obtained correct results, but he does not suggest the evaluation criteria. The rest of the committee does not think that application of any scientific criteria to existing papers would identify the effects of right-to-carry laws on crime.

2. **Committee control variable analysis.** Chapter 6 shows that when the trend and dummy variable models do not include demographic and socioeconomic covariates (but do include year and county dummy variables) the estimates are relatively small, positive in one case (Table 6-6, Row 3), and statistically insignificant in all cases. Contrary to Wilson's assertion, the chapter does not claim that this or any other specification is correct. Rather, this finding simply reveals that "detecting the effect, if any, of right-to-carry laws requires controlling for appropriate confounding variables." In light of the fragility revealed in the literature, the fundamental issue is which set of covariates is sufficient to identify the effects of right-to-carry laws on homicide and other crimes. The importance of controlling for the correct set of covariates is well known. In fact, much of the debate between Lott and his statistically oriented critics focuses on determining the correct set of control variables. Everyone (including Wilson and the rest of the committee) agrees that control variables matter, but there is disagree-

ment on the correct set. Thus, the facts that there is no way to statistically test for the correct specification and that researchers using reasonable specifications find different answers are highly relevant. Given the existing data and methods, the rest of the committee sees little hope of resolving this fundamental statistical problem.

Furthermore, the example of the relationship between crime rates and policing in the dissent raises another problem. The usual way one proceeds in research is to estimate the relationship between two variables and if a significant relationship is found controls are introduced to test the relationship. As the dissent notes, these controls are selected based on reasonable theories and research. In this case, the bivariate relationship (between right to carry laws and crime) is small, positive in one case, and insignificant in all. This is not like the hypothesized conflicting bivariate findings in Wilson's police example. Thus the selection of controls in the analysis of right-to-carry laws is as difficult as the committee contends

3. Committee trend model analysis. Wilson states that the trend model analysis in Table 6-7 estimates the effects of right-to-carry laws on a yearly basis, rather than a single trend.[1] This is incorrect. The estimates reported in Table 6-7 are found using Lott's trend model with restrictions on the number of postadoption years used in the analysis. If the model is correctly specified, this restriction should be inconsequential. However, we find substantial differences, especially for murder. In fact, when we restrict the number of postadoption years to five or fewer, the estimates switch from negative to positive. Thus, Model 6.2 appears to be misspecified. Moreover, despite Wilson's assertion, these types of sensitivity test are commonly used in peer-reviewed journals and are suggested by Rosenbaum (2001) as a way to assess the robustness of an empirical model. Of course, results like those reported in Chapter 6 might often lead a paper to be rejected from a peer-reviewed journal.

Wilson further suggests that Lott's findings may depend on the crime rate trends that changed dramatically over the course of the 1990s. All of the studies in this literature, however, attempt to control for trends in crime, and thus purport to reveal a time invariant effect of right-to-carry laws. If the effects vary by time, all of the existing models are misspecified.

In sum, we are encouraged that Professor Wilson agrees with the rest of the committee except for the specific conclusion regarding the effects of right-to-carry laws on murder. On this point, we find his arguments to be unconvincing and his summary of some parts of the chapter inaccurate. In our view the evidence on homicide is not noticeably different from that on other crimes evaluated in this literature and cannot be easily separated. If

---

[1]Contrary to Wilson's claim, the results in Table 6-7 all rely on models with covariates.

the effects of right-to-carry laws on violent and property crimes are ambiguous, as argued in Chapter 6, we see no reason why the same is not true of homicide. Professor Wilson may be correct on this matter—it is theoretically possible—but we maintain that the scientific evidence does not support his position.

REFERENCE

Rosenbaum, P.R.
  2001   Replicating effects and biases. *American Statistician* 55(3):223-227.

Appendix C

Judicial Scrutiny of Challenged Gun Control Regulations: The Implications of an Individual Right Interpretation of the Second Amendment

Scott Gast [*]

A s part of a divorce proceeding, Timothy Joe Emerson was enjoined by a court from taking any action to threaten or injure his wife. Several months after the imposition of this injunction, Emerson was indicted under a federal law prohibiting any person subject to such a court order from possessing a firearm.[1] Emerson challenged his indictment in part on the ground that this federal law violated his Second Amendment right to keep and bear arms.[2] To the surprise of many in the legal community, the United States Court of Appeals for the Fifth Circuit was sympathetic to his claim, holding that the Second Amendment does, in fact, protect an *individual's* right to keep and bear arms.[3]

Emerson's victory, however, was not unqualified. While the Fifth Circuit held that the Second Amendment protects an individual right, it explained that the right is not absolute:

---

[*]J.D., University of Virginia School of Law, 2002. The author would like to thank Professor Richard Bonnie for his thoughtful comments during the preparation of this paper. The author is currently an attorney at Covington & Burling in Washington, DC; the views expressed in this paper are his own.

[1]18 U.S.C. § 922(g)(8) provides in part that "It shall be unlawful for any person . . . who is subject to a court order that . . . restrains such person from harassing, stalking, or threatening an intimate partner of such person or child of such intimate partner or person, or engaging in other conduct that would place an intimate partner in reasonable fear of bodily injury to the partner or child . . . to ship or transport in interstate or foreign commerce, or possess in or affecting commerce, any firearm or ammunition."

[2]The Second Amendment provides, "A well regulated Militia, being necessary to the security of a free State, the right of the people to keep and bear Arms, shall not be infringed."

[3]*United States v. Emerson*, 270 F.3d 203, 264, reh'g denied, reh'g en banc denied, 281 F.3d 1281 (5th Cir. 2001), cert. denied, 536 U.S. 907 (June 10, 2002) (No. 01-8780).

Although, as we have held, the Second Amendment does protect individual rights, that does not mean that those rights may never be made subject to any limited, narrowly tailored specific exceptions or restrictions for particular cases that are reasonable and not inconsistent with the right of Americans generally to keep and bear their private arms as historically understood in this country.[4]

The court went on to hold that the deprivation of Emerson's right in this case was reasonable, finding "the nexus between firearm possession by the party so enjoined and the threat of violence, is sufficient, though likely barely so, to support the deprivation."[5]

The Fifth Circuit's decision in *Emerson* was significant as the first time a federal appellate court had recognized an individual right interpretation of the Second Amendment.[6] Shortly thereafter, in early 2003, several judges of the Ninth Circuit Court of Appeals, while ultimately adhering to that court's standing interpretation of the Second Amendment as guaranteeing a collective right, indicated their own affinity for the reasoning in *Emerson*.[7]

---

[4]Id. at 261.

[5]Id. at 264.

[6]The federal courts of appeals that have addressed the interpretation of the Second Amendment have favored (and, with the exception of the Fifth Circuit, still do favor) a collective right interpretation. See, e.g., *Silveira v. Lockyer*, 312 F.3d 1052, 1087 (9th Cir. 2002), reh'g en banc denied, 328 F.3d 567 (9th Cir. 2003) ("[W]e are persuaded that we were correct in *Hickman* [*v. Block*, 81 F.3d 98 (9th Cir. 1996)] that the collective rights view, rather than the individual rights models, reflects the proper interpretation of the Second Amendment."); *United States v. Napier*, 233 F.3d 394, 403 (6th Cir. 2000) ("It is well-established that the Second Amendment does not create an individual right."); *Gillespie v. City of Indianapolis*, 185 F.3d 693, 710 (7th Cir. 1999) (Second Amendment protection "inures not to the individual but to the people collectively, its reach extending so far as is necessary to protect their common interest in protection by a militia."); *United States v. Wright*, 117 F.3d 1265, 1273 (11th Cir. 1997), vacated in part on other grounds, *United States v. Wright*, 133 F.3d 1412 (11th Cir. 1998) ("The concerns motivating the creation of the Second Amendment convince us that the amendment was intended to protect only the use or possession of weapons that is reasonably related to a militia actively maintained and trained by the states."); *Love v. Pepersack*, 47 F.3d 120, 122 (4th Cir. 1995) ("[T]he Second Amendment preserves a collective, rather than individual, right."); *United States v. Hale*, 978 F.2d 1016, 1019 (8th Cir. 1992) ("[W]e cannot conclude that the Second Amendment protects the individual possession of military weapons.").

[7]Other courts of appeals have taken note of the Fifth Circuit's interpretation of the Second Amendment, without necessarily embracing it. See, e.g., *United States v. Price*, 328 F.3d 958, 961 (7th Cir. 2003) (acknowledging the Fifth Circuit's decision in Emerson, as well as the Attorney General's position outlined in his letter to the NRA, but concluding that "even were we inclined to, there is no need for us to wade into that Second Amendment quagmire because, although it espouses an individual rights approach to the Second Amendment, the Emerson court agrees with our conclusion that rights under the amendment can be restricted"); *United States v. Wilson*, 315 F.3d 972, 973 n.3 (8th Cir. 2003) (acknowledging the Emerson decision but noting that the Fifth Circuit "nonetheless upheld the constitutionality" of the challenged firearm law).

In *Nordyke v. King* (2003), a panel of three circuit judges wrote that, "if we were writing on a blank slate, we may be inclined to follow the approach of the Fifth Circuit in *Emerson*."[8] One judge went even further, writing a special concurrence to emphasize his view that the Ninth Circuit had gotten its interpretation of the Second Amendment wrong, and that the court should now embrace an individual right view of the Amendment.[9] Despite their disagreement with the earlier court decision, the judges acknowledged that they were bound by the precedent set in *Hickman v. Block* (1996)[10] to hold that the Second Amendment protects a collective right of the people of the state. Other judges on the Ninth Circuit were not as sympathetic to *Emerson*; on May 6, 2003, the full Ninth Circuit declined the opportunity to reconsider *Hickman* by rehearing en banc arguments in *Silveira v. Lockyer* (2003) another Second Amendment case[11] (the vote on rehearing came after the panel decision in *Nordyke*, which criticized *Silveira*, had been issued), but not without public dissent from several judges on the Second Amendment issue.[12] The Ninth Circuit's action leaves the Fifth Circuit alone—at least for the moment—among the federal appellate courts in maintaining an individual right view of the Second Amendment.

Growing support for an individual right interpretation of the Second Amendment has not been limited to the judicial branch of government. On May 17, 2001, United States Attorney General John Ashcroft wrote the executive director of the National Rifle Association's (NRA) Institute for Legislative Action to express his view that "the text and the original intent of the Second Amendment clearly protect the right of individuals to keep and bear firearms."[13] The Department of Justice put the Attorney General's words into action when it filed a brief in opposition to a grant of certiorari in *Haney v. United States* (2001).[14] In that case, the Tenth Circuit had held that 18 U.S.C. § 922(o), which prohibits the possession of machine guns, did not violate the Second Amendment, as that constitutional provision was intended only to preserve the effectiveness of state militias.[15] In its brief opposing Supreme Court review of the Tenth Circuit's decision, the Justice

---

[8]*Nordyke v. King*, 319 F.3d 1185, 1191 (9th Cir. 2003) (Alarcon, O'Scannlain, and Gould, JJ.).

[9]Id. at 1192-93 (Gould, J., concurring).

[10]81 F.3d 98 (9th Cir. 1996).

[11]*Silveira v. Lockyer*, 328 F.3d 567, 568 (9th Cir. 2003).

[12]See id. (Pregurson, J., dissenting); id. (Kozinski, J., dissenting); id. at 570 (Kleinfeld, J., dissenting); id. at 589 (Gould, J., dissenting).

[13]Letter from John Ashcroft, Attorney General, United States Department of Justice, to James Jay Baker, Executive Director, National Rifle Association, Institute for Legislative Action (May 17, 2001) (on file with author).

[14]264 F.3d 1161 (10th Cir. 2001); Brief for the United States in Opposition to Petition for Certiorari in *United States v. Haney*, No. 01-8272 (U.S., May 6, 2002).

[15]Haney, 264 F.3d at 1165.

Department acknowledged that "[t]he government agrees with petitioner that the Fifth Circuit's decision in *Emerson* reflects a sounder understanding of the scope of purpose of the Second Amendment than does the court of appeals' decision in the instant case."[16] Nevertheless, the government supported the decision of the appellate court that the federal law was a valid restriction on this individual right.[17]

The individual right interpretation has also received recent support in Congress. On July 15, 2003, United States Senator Orrin Hatch of Utah introduced the District of Columbia Personal Protection Act, which would repeal the District of Columbia's ban on firearm ownership and restrict the authority of the District's council to prohibit such ownership in the future. In introducing the measure, Senator Hatch noted that "this bill goes a long way toward restoring the constitutionally guaranteed right of Americans who reside in the District of Columbia to possess firearms."[18] His bill was introduced with 21 cosponsors.[19] In a similar vein, two public policy organizations filed separate lawsuits challenging the District of Columbia's handgun ban, arguing that it violates the Second Amendment.[20]

These developments are remarkable in that they signal an apparent momentum toward the widespread acceptance of an interpretation of the Second Amendment that protects an individual right to possess a firearm. If these developments continue and an individual right interpretation becomes accepted by the courts, another important question closely follows: assuming that individuals do have the constitutionally guaranteed right to keep

---

[16]Brief of the United States, supra note 14. In addition, in its opposition briefs in both the Haney and Emerson cases, the United States included as an appendix a November 9, 2001 memorandum from the Attorney General to all United States' Attorneys. In that memo, the Attorney General notes that, "In my view, the Emerson opinion, and the balance it strikes, generally reflect the correct understanding of the Second Amendment." Id.; Brief for the United States in Opposition to Petition for Certiorari in *United States v. Emerson*, No. 01-8780 (U.S. May 6, 2002).

[17]The United States Supreme Court has denied certiorari in Haney and in the Emerson case. *United States v. Haney*, 264 F.3d 1161 (10th Cir. 2001), cert. denied, 536 U.S. 907 (June 10, 2002); *United States v. Emerson*, 270 F.3d 203, (5th Cir. 2001), cert. denied, 536 U.S. 907 (June 10, 2002).

[18]149 Cong. Rec. S9425 (daily ed. July 15, 2003) (statement of Sen. Hatch).

[19]The original cosponsors were Senators George Allen (R-VA), Conrad Burns (R-MT), Saxby Chambliss (R-GA), Larry E. Craig (R-ID), Pete V. Domenici (R-NM), Lindsey O. Graham (R-SC), Kay Bailey Hutchison (R-TX), Zell Miller (D-GA), Jeff Sessions (R-AL), Ted Stevens (R-AK), Craig Thomas (R-WY), Jim Bunning (R-KY), Ben Nighthorse Campbell (R-CO), John Cornyn (R-TX), Michael D. Crapo (R-ID), Michael B. Enzi (R-WY), Charles E. Grassley (R-IA), Jim Inhofe (R-OK), Don Nickles (R-OK), Richard C. Shelby (R-AL), and John E. Sununu (R-NH).

[20]Arthur Santana, Pro-Gun Groups Split on Tactics; Cato Institute, NRA Quarrel Over Challenges to D.C. Law, Wash. Post, July 21, 2003, at B5.

and bear arms, how are courts to determine what restrictions on that right are permissible? Many gun control measures currently on the federal, state, and local books can be characterized as infringements on the right to keep and bear arms. If a gun control measure is challenged as violating an individual Second Amendment right, courts will be required to determine whether the regulation is consistent with that constitutional guarantee. An individual right interpretation of the Second Amendment thus raises a host of issues, including what the scope of the constitutionally protected activity is, whether a particular restriction on that activity is so substantial as to amount to an "infringement," and whether a given infringement is nonetheless "reasonable," given the government's justification.

This appendix attempts to identify and explore the issues that arise under an individual right interpretation of the Second Amendment, as well as to demonstrate the need for detailed empirical research on the efficacy of various gun control measures in advancing purported state interests in reducing gun-related crime and violence. Part I continues to trace the fairly recent rise of the individual right interpretation, demonstrating why such an interpretation is a distinct possibility in the future. Part II addresses some of the legal issues that arise under such an interpretation. First, this section explores efforts to define the precise scope of an individual Second Amendment right. Second, this section considers what it means to constitute an "infringement" of the right. Finally, Part II looks at the balancing involved in determining when infringements will be tolerated because they serve other important state interests. Part III briefly explains the contribution empirical research can make in the context of this balancing approach.

I. THE RISE OF AN INDIVIDUAL RIGHT INTERPRETATION OF THE SECOND AMENDMENT

The meaning of the Second Amendment's "right to keep and bear arms" has been the subject of intense scholarly debate in recent decades. The peculiar wording of the Second Amendment[21] and different readings of the history behind that amendment have offered room for differing points of view over the character of the right protected. From this debate, two general views of the extent of the Second Amendment right have emerged.

---

[21]But see Eugene Volokh, The Commonplace Second Amendment, 73 N.Y.U. L. Rev. 793 (1998) (surveying contemporary state constitutional provisions and concluding that the phrasing of the Second Amendment was not peculiar, but rather commonplace, at the time of its drafting).

First, the "states' rights" or "collective rights" view of the Second Amendment argues that the amendment guarantees only the right of the *states* to create and maintain armed militias.[22] Under this interpretation, there is no individual right of private firearm ownership, but rather a collective right of the people or the states to an armed militia. Advocates of this model focus on the amendment's prefatory clause—"A well regulated Militia, being necessary to the security of a free State"—as limiting the right granted in the operative clause—"the right of the people to keep and bear Arms, shall not be infringed." The framers intended, according to this theory, that states be free to maintain and arm the type of militias referenced in the fifteenth and sixteenth clauses of Article I, Section 8 of the Constitution,[23] which give Congress the power to organize, arm, discipline, and call forth state militias. Outside this limited context, the amendment provides no protection.

A related (yet distinct) interpretation of the Second Amendment has been called the "sophisticated collective rights" model.[24] Under this view, the right protected is an individual one, but only to the extent that the individual protected is a member of a state militia. That is, an individual has the right to keep and bear arms when the state does not itself provide the arms for its militia. Proponents of this model read the prefatory clause as qualifying the right granted by the operative clause. For many supporters of the states' rights or the sophisticated states' rights theories, the demise of the importance of and need for state militias in modern society has stripped the Second Amendment of any modern day relevance.[25]

The second general view of the Second Amendment provides that the right guaranteed by that provision is the right of an *individual* to keep and

---

[22]See, e.g., Symposium on the Second Amendment: Fresh Looks, 76 Chi.-Kent L. Rev. 1 (2000); John Dwight Ingram & Allison Ann Ray, The Right (?) to Keep and Bear Arms, 27 N.M.L. Rev. 491 (1997); Keith A. Ehrman & Dennis A. Henigan, The Second Amendment in the Twentieth Century: Have You Seen Your Militia Lately?, 15 U. Dayton L. Rev. 5 (1989).

[23]Article I, § 8, cl. 15-16 provide: "The Congress shall have Power . . . To provide for calling forth the Militia to execute the Laws of the Union, suppress Insurrections and repel Invasions; To provide for organizing, arming, and disciplining, the Militia, and for governing such Part of them as may be employed in the Service of the United States, reserving to the States respectively, the Appointment of the Officers and the Authority of training the Militia according to the discipline prescribed by Congress."

[24]See, e.g., Nelson Lund, The Ends of Second Amendment Jurisprudence: Firearms Disabilities and Domestic Violence Restraining Orders, 4 Tex. Rev. L. & Pol. 157, 184-86 (1999); Robert J. Cottrol & Raymond T. Diamond, Book Review: The Fifth Auxiliary Right, 104 Yale L. J. 995, 1003-1004 (1995).

[25]See David C. Williams, Civic Republicanism and the Citizen Militia: The Terrifying Second Amendment, 101 Yale L. J. 551, 554 (1991) ("As we today have no such universal militia and assurance that contemporary arms-bearers will be virtuous, the Second Amendment itself is—for now—outdated. . . . The militia was a precondition for the right to arms. Without a militia, the right is meaningless.").

bear arms.[26] Proponents of this model rely on several arguments in support of an individual right interpretation, including the history[27] and the text of the amendment (the operative clause grants the right, while the prefatory clause is simply "an observation, or perhaps a cautionary note"[28]). In addition, individual right supporters note that the amendment's text guarantees the right to "the people," not to the states.[29] This phrase, it is argued, has a unique meaning in the Constitution, as discussed in a recent opinion by the Supreme Court:

> "The people" seems to have been a term of art employed in select parts of the Constitution. . . . The Second Amendment protects "the right of the people to keep and bear Arms," and the Ninth and Tenth Amendments provide that certain rights and powers are retained by and reserved to "the people." . . . While this textual exegesis is by no means conclusive, it suggests that "the people" protected by the Fourth Amendment, and by the First and Second Amendments, and to whom rights and powers are reserved in the Ninth and Tenth Amendments, refers to a class of persons who are part of a national community.[30]

Giving "the people" different meanings in different contexts within the Constitution, proponents argue, would be inconsistent. These arguments lead many commentators to conclude that the Second Amendment guarantees an individual right to private ownership of firearms.

Academic Support of the Individual Right Interpretation

Support for the individual right view of the Second Amendment is relatively new to academic literature, but in recent decades this interpretation has become widely embraced in the scholarship. One commentator has suggested that the collective rights model was the uncontroversial interpretation of the Second Amendment for well over a century; then, between 1970 and 1989, the balance began to tip: 25 law review articles supporting the collective rights model were published, while 27 articles supporting the individual

---

[26]See, e.g., Volokh, The Commonplace Second Amendment, 73 N.Y.U. L. Rev. 793; Nelson Lund, The Past and Future of the Individual's Right to Arms, 31 Ga. L. Rev. 1 (1996); William Van Alstyne, The Second Amendment and the Personal Right to Arms, 43 Duke L. J. 1236, (1994); Sanford Levinson, The Embarrassing Second Amendment, 99 Yale L. J. 637 (1989).

[27]For example, the history is said to suggest that the militia envisioned by the Framers was a "militia of the whole, or at least one consisting of the entire able-bodied male population . . . equipped with their own arms." Cottrol & Diamond, The Fifth Auxiliary Right, 104 Yale L. J. at 1001.

[28]Id. at 1002.

[29]Id.

[30]*United States v. Verdugo-Urquidez*, 494 U.S. 259, 265 (1990) (citations omitted).

rights interpretation appeared in the legal journals.[31] During the 1990s, 58 law review articles were published supporting the individual rights model; only 29 favored the collective rights model.[32] In fact, some went so far as to suggest that "so great is the new 'consensus' about the Second Amendment that 'much as physicists and cosmologists speak of the Standard Model in terms of the creation and evolution of the Universe' the individual right model could now be renamed the standard model."[33] One commentator suggests that these three elements motivated the rise of the individual right interpretation: "the mass of individual right literature, the endorsement of five prominent scholars, and the use of the term standard model."[34]

Another commentator has summarized recent academic writing on the Second Amendment by noting that of the 34 law review articles substantially discussing the amendment published between 1980 and 1996, only 3 endorsed the states' rights theory.[35] He further noted that the three states' rights articles were prepared for symposia in which antigun groups were asked to provide their positions; two of these were written by "lobbyists for anti-gun groups" and one by a politician.[36] In contrast, that author observed that the individual right interpretation had attracted the support of the majority of academics, including some of the "major figures in constitutional law."[37] Another commentator pointed out, however, that a significant number of the articles supporting the individual right model published between 1970 and 1989 were written by lawyers who had either been employed by or who represented gun rights organizations, including the NRA.[38]

Of course, the dearth of collective rights scholarship may have been the result of the perceived lack of any need for a defense of this interpretation. According to one commentator, "Until recently, there was little reason for

---

[31]Carl T. Bogus, The History and Politics of Second Amendment Scholarship: A Primer, 76 Chi.-Kent L. Rev. 3, 8-10 (2000) (citing Robert J. Spitzer, Lost and Found: Researching the Second Amendment, 76 Chi.-Kent L. Rev. 349, 366 (2000)). But see David B. Kopel, The Second Amendment in the Nineteenth Century, 1998 B.Y.U.L. Rev. 1359, 1544-45 (1998) (arguing that nineteenth century commentators and courts agreed that "the core meaning of the Amendment was well-settled": that it protected an individual right to gun firearms).

[32]Id. at 14 (citing Sptizer, Lost and Found, 76 Chi.-Kent L. Rev. at 377).

[33]Id. at 22 (quoting Glenn Harlan Reynolds, A Critical Guide to the Second Amendment, 62 Tenn. L. Rev. 461, 462 (1995)).

[34]Id. at 23.

[35]See Scott Bursor, Note, Toward a Functional Framework for Interpreting the Second Amendment, 74 Tex. L. Rev. 1125, 1126 n.13 (1996).

[36]Id.

[37]Id.

[38]Bogus, The History and Politics of Second Amendment Scholarship: A Primer, 76 Chi.-Kent L. Rev. at 8-10 (noting that 16 of the 25 articles supporting the pro-individual right model published between 1970 and 1989—nearly 60 percent—were written by such lawyers).

scholars agreeing with the collective right model to address the topic."[39]
This observation came in an introduction to a Symposium on the Second
Amendment sponsored by the *Chicago-Kent Law Review* in 2000, which was
designed to "take a fresh look at the Second Amendment and, particularly, the
collective right theory. This is not, therefore, a balanced symposium."[40] The
perceived need for such a "fresh look" suggests that the supporters of the
collective rights interpretation are prepared to step up their involvement in the
debate over the interpretation of this constitutional provision.

The Federal Courts of Appeals and the Second Amendment

Those federal courts of appeals that have addressed the proper interpretation of the Second Amendment have generally taken the collective or
states' rights view.[41] Illustrative of this approach is the Seventh Circuit's
opinion in *Gillespie v. City of Indianapolis* (1999), a case in which a former
police officer challenged a federal law prohibiting persons convicted of
domestic violence from possessing a firearm as violating his Second Amendment right.[42] The court of appeals upheld the law, noting: "The link that
the amendment draws between the ability 'to keep and bear Arms' and '[a]
well regulated Militia' suggests that the right protected is limited, one that
inures not to the individual but to the people collectively, its reach extending so far as is necessary to protect their common interest in protection by
a militia."[43]

The Fifth Circuit's decision in *Emerson* is a clear break with this trend
(and the Ninth Circuit's opinion in *Nordyke* suggests further dissatisfaction
within the federal courts with the perpetuation of a collective rights interpretation). The *Emerson* decision creates an obvious split among the circuits on an important constitutional question, suggesting that the U.S. Supreme Court may wish to grant certiorari in a Second Amendment case at
some point to provide a definitive answer to this question that divides the
federal circuits. The Supreme Court's previous Second Amendment jurisprudence provides little guidance as to how the Court will rule if and when
it undertakes to answer this question.

The Supreme Court and the Second Amendment

As noted at the outset of this paper, the U.S. Supreme Court has recently declined to hear argument in two cases that squarely presented the

---

[39]Id. at 24.
[40]Id.
[41]See supra note 6.
[42]185 F.3d 693 (7th Cir. 1999).
[43]Id. at 710.

question of the proper interpretation of the Second Amendment.[44] Many scholars find this unfortunate, as the Court has addressed the proper interpretation of the Second Amendment on only a few previous occasions—and commentators sharply disagree as to what the Court actually said in those instances.

In *United States v. Miller* (1939), the Court's most recent and most extensive discussion of the amendment, the Court upheld the National Firearms Act against a challenge that it unconstitutionally infringed upon the Second Amendment right to bear arms.[45] Noting that the Constitution granted Congress the power to regulate and call forth state militias, the Court stated that "With obvious purpose to assure the continuation and render possible the effectiveness of such [Militia] forces the declaration and guarantee of the Second Amendment was made. It must be interpreted and applied with that end in view."[46] In that light, the Court found that:

> In the absence of any evidence tending to show that possession or use of "a shotgun having a barrel of less than eighteen inches in length" at this time has some reasonable relationship to the preservation or efficiency of a well regulated militia, we cannot say that the Second Amendment guarantees the right to keep and bear such an instrument. Certainly it is not within judicial notice that this weapon is any part of the ordinary military equipment or that its use could contribute to the common defense.[47]

The Court thus seemed to read the Second Amendment as inextricably intertwined with the maintenance of state militias.

Many academic commentators share the view that *Miller* supports a collective right interpretation of the Second Amendment. As one article stated, "The *Miller* Court thus clarified three things regarding the protection afforded by the Second Amendment: [including,] the right to keep and bear arms is a collective right for the benefit of the people—it is not an individual right . . . [thus] only a federal attempt to disarm organized state militias could possibly constitute a violation of the Second Amendment."[48] Another scholar has examined *Miller* in light of the Supreme Court's subsequent jurisprudence, concluding that, "These decisions suggest that, without directly facing the question, the Supreme Court has come to understand *Miller* as standing roughly for the collective right view of the Second Amendment."[49]

Other commentators have argued that the Court's opinion in *Miller* does not preclude an individual right interpretation of the Second Amend-

---

[44]See supra note 17.

[45]307 U.S. 174 (1939).

[46]Id. at 178.

[47]Id. (internal citations omitted).

[48]Ingram & Ray, The Right (?) to Keep and Bear Arms, 27 N.M.L. Rev. at 501.

[49]Michael C. Dorf, Symposium on the Second Amendment: Fresh Looks: What Does the Second Amendment Mean Today?, 76 Chi.-Kent L. Rev. 291, 298 (2000).

ment. Professor Nelson Lund has advanced three reasons for a narrow reading of *Miller*: "First, the Court's statement of its holding invites a narrow construction. Second, the logic that appears to underlie some of the Court's reasoning would lead to manifest absurdities. Third, the Court heard arguments on only one side of the case."[50] Thus, "*Miller* should be read to approve restrictions only on weapons that have the special characteristics shared by those identified in the National Firearms Act of 1934— i.e., slight value to law abiding citizens and high value to criminals."[51]

Brannon P. Denning and Glenn H. Reynolds have argued that, at the least, *Miller* does not deny that the Second Amendment protects an individual right to firearm ownership—as many federal courts have read that decision.[52] Their article first notes that the Supreme Court did not deny that the defendants in *Miller* had standing to raise the Second Amendment's guarantee as a defense to the charges against them—thus casting doubt on the argument that the Supreme Court had adopted a collective rights interpretation of the amendment (a defense that could be raised only by members of a militia).[53] The authors further argue that the Court's decision to reject the government's primary argument, an iteration of the collective rights model, undermines any conclusion that *Miller* adopted a collective rights interpretation. Rather, the Court reasoned that, assuming the Second Amendment protects an individual's right to bear arms, that right only extended to weapons suitable for use in a militia.[54] They emphasize that the government's argument was the only one before the Court; the defendants neither filed briefs nor appeared at oral argument.[55]

Recent Supreme Court opinions and other writings by the justices may provide some indication as to where certain justices stand on the question of the Second Amendment. On one hand, one commentator has noted that two current justices have suggested that the Court should reconsider the Second Amendment.[56] Justice Clarence Thomas has written that "a growing body of scholarly commentary indicates that the 'right to keep and bear arms' is, as the Amendment's text suggests, a personal right."[57] Justice Antonin Scalia has written that it would be "strange" if the Second Amend-

---

[50]Lund, The Ends of Second Amendment Jurisprudence, 4 Tex. Rev. Law & Pol. at 166.

[51]Id. at 171.

[52]Brannon P. Denning & Glenn H. Reynolds, Enduring and Empowering: The Bill of Rights in the Third Millennium: Telling Miller's Tale: A Reply to David Yassky, 65 Law & Contemp. Prob. 113, 114 (Spring 2002).

[53]Id. at 116-17.

[54]Id. at 118.

[55]Id. at 116

[56]Bogus, The History and Politics of Second Amendment Scholarship, 76 Chi.-Kent L. Rev. at 22-23.

[57]Id. at 23 n.104 (citing *Printz v. United States*, 521 U.S. 898, 939 n.2 (1997)).

ment were found not to grant an individual right.[58] On the other hand, Justice David Souter, joined in a dissenting opinion by Justices John Paul Stevens, Ruth Bader Ginsburg, and Stephen Breyer, "hinted" that the amendment might protect a collective right.[59]

At the very least, the degree of debate over the proper reading of the Supreme Court's decision in *Miller* suggests that the issue remains unsettled. Thus, it does not appear that the Supreme Court will feel bound by stare decisis to support a collective rights interpretation of the Second Amendment, if and when that issue comes before the Court again.

The Incorporation Question

A separate but important question in the interpretation of the Second Amendment is its reach. The provisions of the Bill of Rights were originally intended to limit the powers of the federal government. Beginning in the early 20th century, however, the Supreme Court began to apply some, but not all, of the Bill of Rights limitations to the states, in a process known as incorporation.[60] If the Second Amendment is found to protect an individual right to keep and bear arms, the question arises as to whether that protection extends only to federal restrictions on the right or whether it will reach state law restrictions as well.

Opponents of incorporation point to the Supreme Court's decisions in *United States v. Cruikshank*[61] (1875) and *Presser v. Illinois*[62] (1886) for the proposition that the Second Amendment has not been incorporated to apply to the states. Concededly, the *Presser* Court did say that the Second Amendment "is a limitation only upon the power of Congress and the National government, and not upon that of the States."[63] Yet it would be unfair to consider these decisions relevant today, as the doctrine of incorporation has been completely transformed since those decisions were rendered.[64] Until 1897, the Supreme Court had consistently refused to apply

---

[58]Id. (citing Antonin Scalia, A Matter of Interpretation: Federal Courts and the Law 136-37 n.13 (1997)).

[59]Id. (citing *United States v. Morrison*, 120 S. Ct. 1740, 1765 n.11 (2000) (Souter, J., dissenting)).

[60]See, e.g., *Twining v. New Jersey*, 211 U.S. 78, 99 (1908) (It "is possible that some of the personal rights safeguarded by the first eight Amendments against National action may also be safeguarded against state action, because a denial of them would be a denial of due process of law.... If this is so, it is not because those rights are enumerated in the first eight Amendments, but because they are of such a nature that they are included in the conception of due process of law").

[61]92 U.S. 542 (1875).

[62]116 U.S. 252 (1886).

[63]Id. at 265.

[64]See Don B. Kates, Jr., Handgun Prohibition and the Original Meaning of the Second Amendment, 82 Mich. L. Rev. 204, 252-57 (1983).

the Bill of Rights provisions to the states.[65] It was not until *Chicago, Burlington & Quincy Railroad v. Chicago*[66] (1897) that the Court first suggested that the Due Process Clause of the Fourteenth Amendment could be a vehicle for incorporation.

Since the early incorporation cases, the Supreme Court has followed a process of "selective incorporation"—not all provisions of the Bill of Rights are automatically made applicable to the states. Rather, individual provisions must pass the test for incorporation outlined in *Palko v. Connecticut* (1937): to qualify for incorporation, a right must be "implicit in the concept of ordered liberty."[67] In *Duncan v. Louisiana* (1968), the Court elaborated on this test: the question is "whether a right is among those 'fundamental principles of liberty and justice which lie at the base of all our civil and political institutions,' whether it is 'basic in our system of jurisprudence,' and whether it is a 'fundamental right, essential of a fair trial.'"[68]

Since outlining the modern incorporation test, the Supreme Court has not reexamined the issue of incorporating the Second Amendment's guarantee into the concept of due process.[69] Commentators have argued that a faithful application of the modern test, however, would require incorporation of the amendment.[70] These commentators suggest that the text of the Second Amendment's prefatory clause, remarking on the right being "necessary for the security of a free State," is strikingly similar to the current incorporation test: "implicit in the concept of ordered liberty."[71] If the Second Amendment is deemed to protect an individual right, resolution of the incorporation question will determine how far the guarantee reaches: which restrictions—federal only or state as well—will be affected.

II. REVIEWING RESTRICTIONS ON AN INDIVIDUAL SECOND AMENDMENT RIGHT

As previously noted, an individual right interpretation of the Second Amendment raises a number of issues: how to delineate the scope of the individual right, identify infringements of that right, and determine which

---

[65]See, e.g., *Barron v. Baltimore*, 32 U.S. (7 Pet.) 243, 247 (1833) ("The constitution was ordained and established by the people of the United States for themselves, for their own government, and not for the government of the individual states").

[66]166 U.S. 226 (1897).

[67]302 U.S. 319, 325 (1937).

[68]391 U.S. 145, 148-49 (1968) (citations omitted).

[69]See Lund, The Past and Future of the Individual's Right to Arms, 31 Ga. L. Rev. at 48 (listing three cases in which the Court has declined to address the issue).

[70]See id. at 50 ("If the Court has the slightest regard for doctrinal consistency, it will have no choice except to incorporate the Second Amendment").

[71]See id. at 53.

infringements are reasonable. Resolution of each of these issues will impact the ultimate determination of what gun control regulations will be permissible under the Second Amendment. For example, the scope of the individual right could be defined to exclude certain weapons from protection; thus, regulations touching on those weapons would not impact the constitutional guarantee at all. In addition, the definition of an infringement will determine whether a challenged regulation triggers judicial scrutiny or not, and at what level. Finally, court balancing of the extent of an infringement against the state interests offered as a justification for the infringement will be critical in determining what regulations are reasonable.

The Scope of the Second Amendment Right

Determining the scope of activity that comes within the protection of the Second Amendment is itself an undertaking that raises a number of questions. For example, what "arms" are protected? What does it mean to "keep" or "bear" a protected arm? By its very terms, the Second Amendment appears to protect the right to keep and bear arms from any restriction whatsoever: "the right of the people to keep and bear Arms, *shall not be infringed.*"[72] Yet no one seriously argues that private citizens should be allowed to possess nuclear weapons or shoulder-fired antiaircraft rockets.[73] Determining what is protected and what is not, especially given the technological and societal changes since the amendment was adopted, presents a difficult task; some have lamented that the process of outlining the scope of the Second Amendment's protections with any precision may be impossible.[74] One commentator has argued that the failure to coherently outline the scope of the right has led to an "erratic and ill-defined pattern of adjudication" that can be solved only "by developing a final and conclusive interpretation" of the amendment.[75] Determining the scope of protection is important in answering the threshold question of when the right is infringed. A narrow interpretation provides more room for the operation of gun control measures that limit an individual's ability to own a firearm

---

[72]U.S. Const. amend. II (emphasis added).

[73]See Lund, The Past and Future of the Individual's Right to Arms, 31 Ga. L. Rev. at 41-42.

[74]See, e.g., *Cases v. United States*, 131 F.2d 916, 922 (1st Cir. 1942) ("Considering the many variable factors bearing on the question it seems to us impossible to formulate any general test by which to determine the limits imposed by the Second Amendment but that each case under it, like cases under the due process clause, must be decided on its own facts and the line between what is and what is not a valid federal restriction pricked out by decided cases falling on one side or the other of the line.").

[75]Michelle Capezza, Comment: Controlling Guns: A Call for Consistency in Judicial Review of Challenges to Gun Control Legislation, 25 Seton Hall L. Rev. 1467, 1475 (1995).

without raising the difficult balancing issues discussed below. Conversely, a broad conception of the "right" will implicate a greater number of gun control regulations as potentially impinging on the right.

Commentators have proposed several means of demarcating the scope of the Second Amendment's protections. One of the most commonly advanced methods is based on looking to the history and antecedents of the amendment in an effort to construct an idea of what the Constitution's drafters had in mind when they ratified it.[76] Under this approach, individual restrictions on private firearms ownership are measured against a conception of what the framers thought the Second Amendment should protect.

For example, commentator Don Kates has suggested a tripartite test for determining what "arms" are protected, developed from his reading of the history and antecedents of the Second Amendment, as well as the limited Supreme Court jurisprudence on the subject:

> That weapon must provably be (1) "of the kind in common use" among law-abiding people today; (2) useful and appropriate not just for military purposes, but also for law enforcement and individual self-defense, and (3) lineally descended from the kinds of weaponry known to the Founders.[77]

Kates goes on to identify two further "limiting principles" on the scope of the amendment's protection.[78] First, since the amendment only protects those arms which one can "keep and bear," "weapons too heavy or bulky for the ordinary person to carry are apparently not contemplated."[79] Second, he argues that the common law right that predated the Second Amendment did not extend to "'dangerous or unusual weapons' whose mere possession or exhibition 'are apt to terrify the people.'"[80]

Another approach to defining the scope of the Second Amendment is a "functional" approach, which again relies on the history of the amendment

---

[76]For an examination of the history behind the Second Amendment, see, e.g., Paul Finkelman, Symposium on the Second Amendment: Fresh Looks: "A Well Regulated Militia": The Second Amendment in Historical Perspective, 76 Chi.-Kent L. Rev. 195 (2000); Carl T. Bogus, The Hidden History of the Second Amendment, 31 U.C. Davis L. Rev. 309 (1998); Nelson Lund, The Past and Future of the Individual's Right to Arms, 31 Ga. L. Rev. 1 (1996); David E. Vandercoy, The History of the Second Amendment, 28 Val. U. L. Rev. 1007 (1994).

[77]Kates, Handgun Prohibition and the Original Meaning of the Second Amendment, 82 Mich. L. Rev. at 259.

[78]Id. at 261.

[79]Id. But see Garry Wills, "To Keep and Bear Arms," New York Review of Books (Sept. 21, 1995) (arguing that the phrase "bear arms" was originally understood as meaning to serve in the military: "To bear arms is, in itself, a military term. One does not bear arms against a rabbit.")

[80]Id. (quoting 4 W. Blackstone, Commentaries 149; 1 W. Hawkins, Pleas of the Crown, 136 (5th ed. 1771)).

and its historical predecessors.[81] One commentator starts with the recognition that "the original understanding of the Second Amendment was based on the belief that arms should perform military, political, civil, and moral functions" and that therefore "we ought to interpret the Amendment in a way that proscribes interference with armed citizens' capacity to perform those functions. That is, the four functions should serve as benchmarks for measuring the constitutional limits of interference with the right to keep and bear arms."[82]

In attempting to draw the line between activity protected by the Second Amendment and activity that is not, a useful analogy can be made to First Amendment free speech jurisprudence.[83] That amendment provides in relevant part that "Congress shall make no law . . . abridging the freedom of speech. . . ."[84] Like the Second Amendment, this provision speaks in absolute terms, apparently barring any infringement on the right of free expression. The courts have, however, sought to define the scope of protected expression by identifying those classes of speech that do not merit protection. For example, incitements of illegal activity,[85] fighting words,[86] and obscenity[87] have been held by the Supreme Court to be outside the area of constitutionally protected speech.

In determining what is unprotected expression, the Supreme Court has on occasion looked to the history of the First Amendment.[88] But relying on the history of the amendment and the framers' intentions regarding the freedom of speech is problematic, as there is evidence that the framers did not intend the protection to reach very far; according to one constitutional scholar, "Supreme Court cases dealing with freedom of expression focus less on the framers' intent than do cases involving many other constitutional provisions. There is relatively little that can be discerned as to the drafters' views other than their desire to prohibit prior restraints . . . and their rejection of the crime of seditious libel."[89]

---

[81]Bursor, Note, Toward a Functional Framework for Interpreting the Second Amendment, 74 Tex. L. Rev. 1125 (1996).

[82]Id. at 1146.

[83]Nelson Lund has proposed using the First Amendment as a model for interpreting the Second Amendment. See Lund, The Past and Future of the Individual's Right to Arms, 31 Ga. L. Rev. at 5.

[84]U.S. Const. amend. I.

[85]See *Brandenburg v. Ohio*, 395 U.S. 444 (1969).

[86]See *Chaplinksy v. New Hampshire*, 315 U.S. 568 (1942).

[87]See *Roth v. United States*, 354 U.S. 476 (1957).

[88]See, e.g., id. at 484 ("[I]mplicit in the history of the First Amendment is the rejection of obscenity as utterly without redeeming social importance.").

[89]Erwin Chemerinsky, Constitutional Law: Principles and Policies, at 750 (1997). See also Rodney A. Smolla, Smolla and Nimmer on Freedom of Speech, at 1-18 (1994) ("One can keep going round and round on the original meaning of the First Amendment, but no clear consistent vision of what the framers meant by freedom of speech will ever emerge.").

More often, the Court has focused on a functional method of determining the scope of the First Amendment's protections. In *Chaplinsky v. New Hampshire* (1942), the Court stated that:

> [I]t is well understood that the right of free speech is not absolute at all times and under all circumstances. There are certain well-defined and narrowly limited classes of speech, the prevention and punishment of which have never been thought to raise any constitutional problem . . . . such utterances are no essential part of any exposition of ideas, and are of such slight social value as a step to truth that any benefit that may be derived from them is clearly outweighed by the social interest in order and morality.[90]

This approach focuses on the purposes behind the amendment—to foster the "exposition of ideas" and the search for "truth"—in an approach similar to the functional approach toward defining the Second Amendment discussed above.

Defining the scope of the Second Amendment's protection is one way in which the permissibility of challenged gun control measures can be evaluated. For example, if one accepts the Kates test outlined above as an accurate measure of the scope of the right, it is easy to see why handguns are clearly protected, while weapons like Saturday Night Specials or switchblade knives are not.[91] It could be argued that the amendment was never intended by the framers to protect ownership of these weapons from government regulation, because these weapons are not necessary for military, law enforcement, or self-defense purposes. Similarly, private ownership of nuclear weapons would not be protected, as such weapons are not lineal descendants of the types of weapons known to the framers. Assault rifles present a more difficult question: if one sees such weapons as direct descendants of the type of weapons used by the framers, as well as useful for modern military or law enforcement purposes, ownership of such rifles may be entitled to some level of protection. In any case, using such a test to determine the scope of protection provided by the amendment, a court could determine whether regulations that ban or otherwise restrict ownership of certain weapons implicate the Second Amendment's guarantee at all.

"Infringements" on the Second Amendment Right

Once a core of protected activity is identified, the question becomes when a particular gun control regulation impinges on that protected sphere. Answering that question is not as straightforward as it may seem: one

---

[90]Chaplinsky, 315 U.S. at 571-72.

[91]Kates, Handgun Prohibition and the Original Meaning of the Second Amendment, 82 Mich. L. Rev. at 259-60.

commentator has noted that determining whether an infringement has occurred is closely bound up with the doctrinal considerations involved in defining the scope of a right and whether an infringement is justified. "[C]losely examining the way that courts determine whether a right has been infringed may be very relevant to defining the scope of the right and to evaluating the state's justification for impairing the right."[92] This commentator goes on to observe that "often the Court does not isolate the issue of infringement, but rather implicitly subsumes it within an analysis that focuses on the scope of the right and the state's justification for any purported impairment."[93]

The Supreme Court has held that not every regulation that impacts a constitutional right rises to the level of an infringement: "As our jurisprudence relating to all liberties save perhaps abortion has recognized, not every law which makes a right more difficult to exercise is, *ipso facto*, an infringement on that right."[94] To qualify as an "infringement," a government regulation must place a significant burden on the exercise of the right; indirect or incidental burdens may not be considered to "infringe" on protected activity.[95] The Supreme Court has indicated that the key to determining whether a right has been infringed is the "directness and substantiality of the interference."[96]

Again, the Supreme Court's consideration of burdens placed on the exercise of the First Amendment right to free speech is illustrative. The critical factor in identifying whether a regulation constitutes "infringement" on speech—and the level of scrutiny the regulation will then receive—is whether the regulation is considered content-based or content-neutral. "Content-based regulations are presumptively invalid"[97] and will be permitted only if they meet the demands of strict scrutiny. Preventing all speech on a particular subject places a heavy burden on the exercise of the right (making it impossible to exercise with regard to that particular subject), clearly rising to the level of an infringement.

"In contrast, regulations that are unrelated to the content of speech are subject to an intermediate level of scrutiny."[98] Time, place, or manner

---

[92]Alan Brownstein, How Rights Are Infringed: The Role of Undue Burden Analysis in Constitutional Doctrine, 45 Hastings L.J. 867, 869 (1994) (internal citations omitted).

[93]Id. at 871 (internal citations omitted).

[94]*Planned Parenthood v. Casey*, 505 U.S. 833, 873 (1992).

[95]See Michael C. Dorf, Incidental Burdens on Fundamental Rights, 109 Harv. L. Rev. 1175, 1177-78 (1996) ("A law imposing a direct burden will be permitted to override a fundamental right only if the law is narrowly drawn to serve a compelling interest. In contrast, laws imposing incidental burdens trigger more deferential judicial scrutiny."). See also Brownstein, How Rights Are Infringed, 45 Hastings L.J. 867 (1994).

[96]*Zablocki v. Redhail*, 434 U.S. 374, 387 n.12 (1978).

[97]*R.A.V. v. City of St. Paul*, 505 U.S. 377, 382 (1992).

[98]*Turner Broad. Sys. v. Fed. Communications Comm'n*, 512 U.S. 622, 642 (1994).

restrictions are familiar examples of permissible regulations on speech. Such regulations apply to all speech regardless of its content; they simply regulate the secondary effects of the exercise of the right. Nonetheless, limiting the time, place, or manner in which one can permissibly express one's ideas does make the exercise of the right more difficult. The key difference is that the burdens created by these regulations are not so significant as to cross the threshold to become an "infringement."

Many gun control regulations burden the exercise of an individual right to private firearm ownership in one way or another, but many of these regulations may nevertheless be permissible if the burdens they impose do not rise to significant levels. At one extreme, a federal or state law that bans the possession of *any* type of firearm by an individual would clearly constitute an infringement of an individual Second Amendment right. Laws that prohibit whole classes of individuals (e.g., felons, minors, the mentally ill) from possessing firearms would similarly seem to constitute an infringement of the right as to those individuals (albeit justifiable ones).[99] Laws that prohibit the possession of whole classes of weapons would appear to make the exercise of the right more difficult.[100] Other provisions like firearm licensing or registration requirements also arguably place burdens on an individual's exercise of the right to bear arms.[101] Whether such regulations amount to "infringements" will depend on the directness and substantiality of the burden.

As the foregoing discussion illustrates, a permissible gun control regulation could be characterized in a number of ways. The regulation could be permissible because it is considered to impact activity that falls outside the Second Amendment's sphere of protection. It could be permissible because it places only an incidental or insignificant burden on the exercise of the right, and therefore does not constitute an "infringement." Finally, as the next section discusses, the regulation could be an "infringement" on protected activity, but nonetheless permissible because the infringement is justified by serving a compelling government interest.

---

[99]Felons, infants, and those of unsound mind are permissibly prohibited from possessing a firearm. See Stephen P. Halbrook, What the Framers Intended: A Linguistic Analysis of the Right to "Bear Arms," 49 Law & Contemp. Probs. 151 (1986). The permissibility of such regulations is not because the regulations do not constitute "infringements" but rather because courts have found such infringements to be "reasonable." See Part II-C.

[100]The permissibility of some of these restrictions (e.g., a ban on assault weapons) may be addressed by a definition of the scope of the Amendment's protections. See Part II-A.

[101]Don Kates has argued that licensing or registration requirements do not infringe upon the Second Amendment because "the historical background of the second amendment seems inconsistent with any notion of anonymity or privacy insofar as the mere fact of one's possessing a firearm is concerned." Handgun Prohibition and the Original Meaning of the Second Amendment, 82 Mich. L. Rev. at 266.

"Reasonable" Infringements on the Second Amendment Right

Even if a regulation is found to rise to the level of an "infringement" of the Second Amendment's sphere of protected activity, that regulation may still be permissible. The Supreme Court has made clear that constitutional rights are subject to "reasonable" restrictions. The Court has recognized that there may be legitimate and compelling reasons for a regulation that outweigh any minimal harm caused by the constitutional infringement. Determining when such infringements are "reasonable" requires courts to balance the extent of the alleged infringement against the state interest offered as a justification for that infringement.

This heightened judicial scrutiny comes in a several forms. The most demanding level of court examination is strict scrutiny, which is typically reserved for infringements on so-called fundamental rights.[102] Under the strict scrutiny regime, an infringement will be upheld only if it is narrowly drawn to serve a compelling state interest. In *Moore v. City of East Cleveland* (1977), the Supreme Court formulated the strict scrutiny test as follows: "When the government intrudes on a fundamental right, this Court must examine carefully the importance of the governmental interests advanced and the extent to which they are served by the challenged regulation."[103] In addition, the government action must be narrowly tailored: the governmental interests must not be attainable through any less restrictive means.[104]

Thus, the first question under strict scrutiny is whether the government can demonstrate a "compelling" interest that is served by the infringement of the right. Protecting the public from gun-related crime or gun-related accidents certainly seems compelling—even pro-individual right commentators have suggested that such state interests amount to "sufficiently wor-

---

[102]The Second Amendment, as an explicit provision of the Bill of Rights, may qualify as a fundamental right. The Supreme Court has indicated that the express provisions of the Bill of Rights should not be arranged in any "hierarchy." See, e.g., *Valley Forge Christian College v. Americans United for Separation of Church and State*, 454 U.S. 464, 484-85 (1982) ("[W]e know of no principled basis on which to create a hierarchy of constitutional values."); *Ullmann v. United States*, 350 U.S. 422, 428-29 (1956) ("As no constitutional guarantee enjoys preference, so none should suffer subordination or deletion. . . . To view a particular provision of the Bill of Rights with disfavor inevitably results in a constricted application of it. This is to disrespect the Constitution."). In addition, the incorporation test noted earlier provides guidance as to what rights are so "fundamental" as to require incorporation. Addressing this related question of incorporation, Professor Nelson Lund has argued, "The right protected by the Second Amendment meets the Court's test of what is 'fundamental' far more easily than other rights that have already been incorporated, some of which were never included in the fundamental documents of the English constitution." The Past and Future of the Individual's Right to Arms, 31 Ga. L. Rev. at 55.

[103]431 U.S. 494, 499 (1977).

[104]See Chemerinsky, Constitutional Law, at 643.

thy government purposes."[105] Once a compelling purpose is identified, a court must then determine whether that interest is furthered by the regulation in a narrowly tailored way. This prong of the test actually encompasses two related questions: first, whether the challenged regulation actually does further the achievement of the government interest, and second, whether the regulation furthers that interest in a manner that causes the least possible amount of infringement.

Lund has suggested that First Amendment principles are here again helpfully translated to the Second Amendment context: "In both cases, the Constitution establishes a rule that protects a human activity that its Framers regarded as a natural right. . . . In both cases, the Constitution reflects a determination that social benefits of giving legal protection to the instruments needed for the pursuit of those goals will outweigh the inconveniences arising from their misuse. In both cases, the erection of this barrier against the state governments will necessarily involve the courts in the business of balancing the public welfare against the interests of those individuals whose liberty the government wants to restrict."[106]

In the First Amendment context, different types of speech are subject to different levels of protection, based primarily on an assessment of the value or "hardiness" of the type of speech involved. For example, political speech is generally considered deserving of more protection than commercial speech. This differential treatment is implicit in the balancing process involved in reviewing restrictions on speech: "The categories of unprotected and less protected speech reflect value judgments by the Supreme Court that the justifications for regulating such speech outweigh the value of the expression."[107]

Heightened judicial scrutiny may also be applied through an "undue burden" standard. This standard was announced in *Planned Parenthood v. Casey* (1992), in which the Court held that restrictions on the right to decide whether to terminate a pregnancy were invalid if they placed an "undue burden" on the exercise of that right or, in other words, if a regulation "has the purpose or effect of placing a substantial obstacle in the path of a woman" seeking to exercise this right.[108] The "undue burden" standard, however, may be unique to the abortion context, and its applicability to the Second Amendment is unclear.

As noted above, laws that prohibit certain classes of individuals from possessing any firearms constitute an infringement of the individual Second

---

[105]Lund, The Ends of Second Amendment Jurisprudence, 4 Tex. Rev. Law & Pol. at 189.

[106]Lund, The Past and Future of the Individual's Right to Arms, 31 Ga. L. Rev. at 69.

[107]Chemerinsky, Constitutional Law, at 801 (Chemerinsky goes on to note, "For each of the categories . . . the Court's judgment can be questioned.").

[108]505 U.S. 833, 874, 877 (1992).

Amendment right. Nonetheless, courts have upheld such regulations as reasonable: the asserted state interest in protecting the public from individuals who may not have the capacity or judgment to possess and use a firearm properly clearly outweighs the extent of the infringement.

III. THE CONTRIBUTION OF EMPIRICAL RESEARCH TO JUDICIAL SCRUTINY

The balancing common to the various methods of heightened judicial scrutiny discussed above is only enhanced by empirical analysis of how well a challenged regulation actually does or does not achieve its purported state interest. The alternatives to relying on empirical data are either to trust the intuitions of judges or to completely defer to the judgments of the legislatures that enact the gun control measures. Both alternatives are unsatisfactory.

The Supreme Court has noted the importance of empirical data in resolving challenges to First Amendment restrictions. In *Nixon v. Shrink Missouri Government PAC* (2000), the Court noted that "[t]he quantum of empirical evidence needed to satisfy heightened judicial scrutiny of legislative judgments will vary up or down with the novelty and plausibility of the justification raised. . . . We have never accepted mere conjecture as adequate to carry a First Amendment burden. . . ."[109] In *Renton v. Playtime Theatres* (1986) another First Amendment case, the Supreme Court noted that, "The First Amendment does not require a city, before enacting . . . an ordinance, to conduct new studies or produce evidence independent of that already generated by other cities, *so long as whatever evidence the city relies on is reasonably believed to be relevant to the problem that the city addresses.*"[110]

Empirical data are also important in the context of the dormant Commerce Clause balancing test. The Supreme Court has stated that state-imposed burdens on the free flow of interstate commerce cannot be justified by "simply invoking the convenient apologetics of the police power."[111] On another occasion the Court warned that "the incantation of a purpose to promote the public health or safety does not insulate a state law from Commerce Clause attack. Regulations designed for that salutary purpose nevertheless may further the purpose so marginally, and interfere with commerce so substantially, as to be invalid."[112] The Court has often re-

---

[109]528 U.S. 377, 391-92 (2000).

[110]475 U.S. 41, 51-52 (1986) (emphasis added).

[111]*Southern Pacific Co. v. Arizona ex rel. Sullivan*, 325 U.S. 761, 779-80 (1945) (quoting *Kansas City S. Ry. v. Kaw Valley Dist.*, 233 U.S. 75, 79 (1914)).

[112]*Kassell v. Consol. Freightways Corp.*, 450 U.S. 662, 670 (1981).

quired states defending challenged regulations to provide extensive empirical and statistical evidence to support their proffered justifications.[113]

Resorting to the mere "incantation of a purpose to promote the public health or safety" is an intellectually empty means for a government to justify its challenged gun control regulations. As the Supreme Court has made clear in other contexts, those justifications must and should be supported by scientifically verifiable empirical evidence. If the Second Amendment is ultimately given an individual right interpretation, studies exploring the efficacy of gun control regulations in reducing gun-related crime and violence (or in promoting other compelling state interests) will be needed to accurately balance the true benefits of the regulation against the costs imposed by infringements on the right.

CONCLUSION

As demonstrated by the recent accumulation of academic support, as well as the Fifth Circuit's decision in *Emerson*, an individual right interpretation of the Second Amendment is a distinct possibility for the future. Such an interpretation would have many implications for the judicial review of challenged gun control regulations. This appendix has identified some of the issues raised by an individual right interpretation. First, courts and commentators will be required to attempt a more concrete delineation of the scope of an individual right. A comprehensive definition of the amendment's scope can be used to identify those regulations that impact constitutionally protected activity and those that do not. Second, once an area of protected activity is identified, criteria must be developed for determining when a regulation places so significant a burden on the exercise of the right as to amount to an "infringement." Finally, courts will be required to engage in fact-intensive balancing tests, weighing the cost of an infringement against the benefits to the compelling state interest in reducing gun-related crime and violence, to determine what infringements are "reasonable" and thus permissible.

With regard to the balancing of interests in making "reasonableness" determinations, courts as well as legislatures will be greatly aided by scientifically verified empirical studies that test the efficacy of various gun control measures in achieving their purported objectives. In other balancing contexts—including First Amendment and dormant Commerce Clause jurisprudence—the Supreme Court has emphasized the need for more than just appeals to the public interest. The availability of empirical data will make this balancing more accurate and reliable.

---

[113]See, e.g., Kassell, 450 U.S. at 672-75 (undertaking an extensive review of lower court findings regarding the economic impact and safety effects of state regulations restricting the length of vehicles operating on the state's roads); Southern Pacific, 325 U.S. at 770-79 (undertaking an extensive review of the lower court findings regarding the impact of train length regulations on safety and commerce).

Appendix D

Statistical Issues in the Evaluation of the Effects of Right-to-Carry Laws

Joel L. Horowitz

ifferent investigators have obtained conflicting estimates of the effects of right-to-carry laws on crime. Moreover, the estimates are sensitive to relatively minor changes in data and the specifications of models. This paper presents a statistical framework that explains the conflicts and why there is little likelihood that persuasive conclusions about the effects of right-to-carry laws can be drawn from analyses of observational (nonexperimental) data. The framework has two main parts. The first relates to the difficulty of choosing the right explanatory variables for a model. The second relates to the difficulty of estimating the relation among crime rates, the explanatory variables, and the adoption of right-to-carry laws even if the correct explanatory variables are known.

CHOOSING THE EXPLANATORY VARIABLES

The effect on crime of having a right-to-carry law in effect at a given time and place may be defined as the difference between the crime rate (or its logarithm) with the law in effect and the crime rate (or its logarithm) without the law. The fundamental problem in measuring the effect of a right-to-carry law (as well as in evaluating other public policy measures) is that at any given time and place, a right-to-carry law is either in effect or not in effect. Therefore, one can measure the crime rate with the law in effect or without it, depending on the state of affairs at the time and place of interest, but not both with and without the law. Consequently, one of the two measurements needed to implement the definition of the law's effect is always missing. To estimate the law's effect, one must have a way of "filling in" the missing observation.

The discussion of this problem can be streamlined considerably by using mathematical notation. Let i index locations (possibly counties) and t index time periods (possibly years). Let Y_{it}^+ denote the crime rate that county i would have in year t with a right-to-carry law in effect. Let Y_{it}^- denote the crime rate that county i would have in year t without such a law. Then the effect of the law on the crime rate is defined as $\Delta_{it} = Y_{it}^+ - Y_{it}^-$ under the assumption that all other factors affecting crime are the same with or without the law. The fundamental measurement problem is that one can observe either Y_{it}^+ (if the law is in effect in county i and year t) or Y_{it}^- (if the law is not in effect in county i and year t) but not both. There-fore, Δ_{it} can never be observed.

One possible solution to this problem consists of replacing the unobservable Δ_{it} by the difference between the crime rates after and before adoption of a right-to-carry law (in other words, carrying out a before-and-after study). For example, suppose that county i (or county i's state) adopts a right-to-carry law in year s. Then one can observe Y_{it}^- whenever $t < s$ and Y_{it}^+ whenever $t > s$. Thus, one might consider measuring the effect of the law by (for example) $Y_{i,s+1}^+ - Y_{i,s-1}^-$ (the crime rate a year after adoption minus the crime rate a year before adoption). However, this approach has several serious difficulties.

First, factors that affect crime other than adoption of a right-to-carry law may change between years $s - 1$ and $s + 1$. For example, economic conditions, levels of police activity, or conditions in drug markets may change. If this happens, then $Y_{i,s+1}^+ - Y_{i,s-1}^-$ measures the combined effect of all of the changes that took place, not the effect of the right-to-carry law alone. Second, $Y_{i,s+1}^+ - Y_{i,s-1}^-$ can give a misleading indication of the effect of the law's adoption even if no other relevant factors change. For example, suppose that crime increases each year before the law's adoption and de-creases at the same rate each year after adoption (Figure C-1). Then $Y_{i,s+1}^+ - Y_{i,s-1}^- = 0$, indicating no change in crime levels, even though the trend in crime reversed in the year of adoption of the right-to-carry law. Taking the difference between multiyear averages of crime levels after and before adoption of the law would give a similarly misleading indication. This has been pointed out by Lott (2000:135) in his response to Black and Nagin (1998). As a third example, right-to-carry laws might be enacted in response to crime waves that would peak and decrease even without the laws. If this happens, then $Y_{i,s+1}^+ - Y_{i,s-1}^-$ might reflect mainly the dynamics of crime waves rather than the effects of right-to-carry laws.

Finally, the states that have right-to-carry laws in effect in a given year may be systematically different from the states that do not have these laws in effect. Indeed, Lott (2000:119) found that in his data, "states adopting

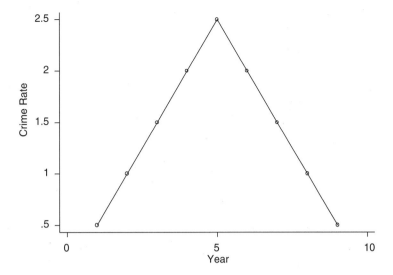

FIGURE D-1 Hypothetical crime rates by year.
NOTE: An increasing trend reverses in year 5, but the crime rate is the same in years 4 and 6. The average crime rate over years 5-9 is the same as it is over years 1-5.

[right-to-carry] laws are relatively Republican with large National Rifle Association memberships and low but rising rates of violent crime and property crime." Non-time-varying systematic differences among states are accounted for by the fixed effects, γ_i, in Models 6.1 and 6.2 in Chapter 6. However, if there are time-varying factors that differ systematically among states with and without right-to-carry laws and that influence the laws' effects on crime, then the effects of enacting these laws in states that do not have them cannot be predicted from the experience of states that do have them, even if the other problems just described are not present.

The foregoing problems would not arise if the counties that have right-to-carry laws could be selected randomly. Of course, this is not possible, but consideration of the hypothetical situation in which it is possible provides insight into the methods that are used to estimate the effects of real-world right-to-carry laws. If the counties that have right-to-carry laws in year t are selected randomly, then there can be no systematic differences between counties with and without these laws in year t. Consequently, the average value of Y_{it}^+ is the same across counties in year t regardless of whether a right-to-carry law is in effect. Similarly, the average value of Y_{it}^- is the same across counties. It follows that the *average* effect on crime of the right-to-carry law is the average value of Y_{it}^+ in counties with the law minus the average value of Y_{it}^- in counties that do not have the law. In other words, the average effect is the average value of the *observed* crime rate in counties with the law minus the average value of the *observed* crime rate in counties that do not have the law.[1]

In the real world, the counties that have right-to-carry laws cannot be selected randomly, but one might hope that the benefits of randomization can be achieved by "controlling" the variables that are responsible for "relevant" systematic differences between counties that do and do not have right-to-carry laws. Specifically, suppose that the relevant variables are denoted by X. Suppose further that the average value of Y_{it}^+ is the same across counties that have the same value of X, regardless of whether a right-to-carry law is in effect. Similarly, suppose that the average value of Y_{it}^- is the same across counties that have the same value of X. If these conditions are satisfied, then the average effect on crime of adoption of a right-to-carry law in counties with a specified value of X is the average of the observed crime rates in counties with the specified value of X that have the law in place minus the average of the observed crime rates in counties with the specified value of X that do not have the law. This is the idea on which all of the models of Lott and his critics are based.

The problem with this idea is that the variables that should be included in X are unknown, and it is not possible to carry out an empirical test of whether a proposed set of X variables is the correct one. This is because the answer to the question whether X is a proper set of control variables depends on the relation of X to the unobservable counterfactual outcomes (Y_{it}^+ in counties that do not have right-to-carry laws in year t and Y_{it}^- in counties that do have the laws in year t). Thus, it is largely a matter of opinion which set to use. A set that seems credible to one investigator may lack credibility to another. This problem is the source of the disagreement between Lott and his critics over Lott's use of the arrest rate as an explanatory variable in his models. It is also the source of other claims that Lott may not have accounted for all relevant influences on crime. See, for example, Ayers and Donohue (1999:464-465) and Lott's response (Lott, 2000:213-215).[2]

---

[1]This conclusion—but with measures of health status in place of crime rates—forms the justification for using randomized clinical trials to evaluate new drugs, medical devices, and medical procedures.

[2]Lott and his critics use panel data in which each county is observed in each of many years. Panel data provide a form of "automatic" control over unobserved factors that differ among counties but are constant within each county over time. There can, however, be no assurance that all unobserved factors that are relevant to the effectiveness of right-to-carry laws are constant over time within counties. Nor is there any assurance that the models used by Lott and his critics correctly represent the effects of such factors.

Lott is aware of this problem. In response, he argues that his study used "the most comprehensive set of control variables yet used in a study of crime, let alone any previous study on gun control" (Lott, 2000:153). There are two problems with this argument. First, although it is true that Lott uses a large set of control variables (his data contain over 100 variables, though not all are used in each of his models), he is limited by the availability of data. There is (and can be) no assurance that his data contain all relevant variables. Second, it is possible to control for *too many* variables. Specifically, suppose that there are two sets of potential explanatory variables, X and Z. Then it is possible for the average value of Y_{it}^+ to be the same among counties with the same value of X, regardless of whether a right-to-carry law is in place, whereas the average value of Y_{it}^+ among counties with the same values of X and Z depends on whether a right-to-carry law has been adopted. The same possibility applies to Y_{it}^-. In summary, it is not enough to use a very large set of control or explanatory variables. Rather, one must use a set that consists of just the right variables and, in general, no extra ones.[3]

In fact, there is evidence of uncontrolled (or, possibly, overcontrolled) systematic differences among counties with and without right-to-carry laws in effect. Donohue (2002: Tables 5-6) estimated models in which future adoption of a right-to-carry law is used as an explanatory variable of crime levels prior to the law's adoption. He found a statistically significant relation between crime levels and future adoption of a right-to-carry law, even after controlling for what he calls "an array of explanatory variables." This result implies that there are systematic differences between adopting and nonadopting states that are not accounted for by the explanatory variables In other words, there are variables that affect crime rates but are not in the model, and it is possible that the omitted variables are the causes of any apparent effects of adoption of right-to-carry laws.[4]

---

[3]Bronars and Lott (1998) and Lott (2000) have attempted to control for confounding variables by comparing changes in crime rates in neighboring counties such that some counties are in a state that adopted a right-to-carry law and others are in a state that did not adopt the law. Bronars and Lott (1998) and Lott (2000) found that crime rates tend to decrease in counties where the law was adopted and increase in neighboring counties where the law was not adopted. The issues raised by this finding (and by any conclusion that differential changes in crime levels in neighboring counties are caused by adoption or nonadoption of right-to-carry laws) are identical to the issues raised by the results of Lott's main models, Models 6.1 and 6.2 in Chapter 6.

[4]If the explanatory variables accounted for all systematic differences in crime rates, then the average crime rate conditional on the explanatory variables would be independent of the adoption variable. Thus, future adoption of a right-to-carry law would not have any explanatory power.

Lott and Mustard (1997, Table 11) and Lott (2000:118) attempted to control for omitted variables affecting crime by carrying out a procedure called "two-stage least squares" (2SLS).

There is also evidence that estimates of the effects of these laws are sensitive to the choice of explanatory variables. See, for example, the discussion of Table 6-5 in Chapter 6. Thus, the choice of explanatory variables matters. As has already been explained, there is and can be no empirical test for whether a proposed set of explanatory variables is correct. There is little prospect for achieving an empirically supportable agreement on the right set of variables. For this reason, in addition to the goodness-of-fit problems that are discussed next, it is unlikely that there can be an empirically based resolution of the question of whether Lott has reached the correct conclusions about the effects of right-to-carry laws on crime.[5]

ESTIMATING THE RELATION AMONG CRIME RATES, THE EXPLANATORY VARIABLES, AND ADOPTION OF RIGHT-TO-CARRY LAWS

This section discusses the problem of estimating the average crime rate in counties that have the same values of a set of explanatory variables X and that have (or do not have) right-to-carry laws in effect. Specifically, let $Z_{it} = 1$ if county i has a right-to-carry law in effect in year t, and let $Z'_{it} = 0$ if county i does not have such a law in year t. Let Y_{it} denote the crime rate (or its logarithm) in county i and year t, regardless of whether a right-to-carry law is in effect. The objective in this section is to estimate the average values of Y_{it} conditional on $Z_{it} = 1$ and Y_{it} conditional on $Z_{it} = 0$ for counties in which the explanatory variables X have the same values, say $X = X_0$. Denote these averages by $E(Y_{it} \mid Z_{it} = 1, X_0)$ and $E(Y_{it} \mid Z_{it} = 0, X_0)$, respectively. $E(Y_{it} \mid Z_{it} = 1, X_0)$ is the average crime rate in year t in counties that have right-to-carry laws and whose explanatory variables have the values

---

However, the 2SLS estimates of the effects of right-to-carry laws on the incidence of violent crimes differ by factors of 15 to 42, depending on the crime, from the estimates in Lott's Table 4.1 and are implausibly large. For example, according to the 2SLS estimates reported by Lott and Mustard (1997, Table 11), adoption of right-to-carry laws reduces all violent crimes by 72 percent, murders by 67 percent, and aggravated assaults by 73 percent. 2SLS works by using explanatory variables called instruments to control the effects of any missing variables. A valid instrument must be correlated with the variable indicating the presence or absence of a right-to-carry law but otherwise unrelated to fluctuations in crime that are not explained by the covariates of the model. In Lott and Mustard (1997) and Lott (2000), the instruments include levels and changes in levels of crime rates and are, by definition, correlated with the dependent variables of the models. Thus, they are unlikely to be valid instruments. It is likely, therefore, that Lott's and Mustard's 2SLS estimates are artifacts of the use of invalid instruments and other forms of specification errors.

[5]The problem of not knowing the correct set of explanatory variables is pervasive in evaluation of the effects of public policy measures. The sensitivity of estimated results to the choice of variables and the inability to resolve controversies over which variables should be used has led to the use of randomized experiments to evaluate social programs, such as job training and income maintenance.

X_0. $E(Y_{it} \mid Z_{it} = 0, X_0)$ is the average crime rate in year t in counties that do not have right-to-carry laws and whose explanatory variables have the values X_0. If the explanatory variables control for all other factors that are relevant to the crime rate, then $D_t(X_0) = E(Y_{it} \mid Z_{it} = 1, X_0) - E(Y_{it} \mid Z_{it} = 0, X_0)$ is the average change in the crime rate caused by the law in year t in counties where the values of the explanatory variables are X_0.

The models of Lott and his critics are all aimed at estimating $D_t(X_0)$ for some set of explanatory variables X. This section discusses the statistical issues that are involved in estimating $D_t(X_0)$. The discussion focuses on the problem of estimating the function D_t for a given set of explanatory variables. This issue is distinct from and independent of the problem of choosing the explanatory variables that was discussed in the previous section. Thus, the discussion in this section does not depend on whether there is agreement on a "correct" set of explanatory variables.

Estimating $D_t(X_0)$ is relatively simple if in year t there are many counties with right-to-carry laws and the same values X_0 of the explanatory variables and many counties without right-to-carry laws and identical values X_0 of the explanatory variables. $D_t(X_0)$ would then be the average of the observed crime rate in the counties that do have right-to-carry laws minus the average crime rate in counties that do not have such laws. However, there are not many counties with the same values of the explanatory variables. Indeed, in the data used by Lott and his critics, each county has unique values of the explanatory variables. Therefore, the simple averaging procedure cannot be used. Instead, $D_t(X_0)$ must be inferred from observations of crime rates among counties with a range of values of X. In other words, it is necessary to estimate the relation between average crime rates and the values of the explanatory variables.

In principle, the relations between average crime rates and the explanatory variables with and without a right-to-carry law in effect can be estimated without making any assumptions about their shapes. This is called *nonparametric estimation*. Härdle (1990) provides a detailed discussion of nonparametric estimation methods. Nonparametric estimation is highly flexible and largely eliminates the possibility that the estimated model may not fit the data, but it has the serious drawback that the size of the data set needed to obtain estimates that are sufficiently precise to be useful increases very rapidly as the number of explanatory variables increases. This is called the *curse of dimensionality*. Because of it, nonparametric estimation is a practical option only in situations in which there are few explanatory variables. It is not a practical option in situations like estimation of the effects of right-to-carry laws, where there can be 50 or more explanatory variables.

Because of the problems posed by the curse of dimensionality, the most frequently used methods for estimation with a large number of explanatory variables assume that the relation to be estimated belongs to a relatively small class of "shapes."[6] For example, Models 6.1 and 6.2 assume that the average of the logarithm of the crime rate is a linear function of the variables comprising X. Lott and his critics all restrict the shapes of the relations they estimate. Doing this greatly increases estimation precision, but it creates the possibility that the true relation of interest does not have the assumed shape. That is, the estimated model may not fit the data. This is called misspecification. Moreover, because the set of possible shapes increases as the number of variables in X increases, the opportunities for misspecification also increase. This is another form of the curse of dimensionality. Its practical consequence is that one should not be surprised if a simple class of models (or shapes) such as linear models fails to fit the data.

Lack of fit is a serious concern because it can cause estimation results to be seriously misleading. An example based on an article that was published in the *National Review* (Tucker 1987) illustrates this problem. The example consists of estimating the relation between the fraction of a city's population who are homeless, the vacancy rate in the city, an indicator of whether the city has rent control, and several other explanatory variables. Two models are estimated:

(D.1)
$$FRAC = \beta_0 + \beta_1 RENT + \beta_2 VAC + \alpha X$$
and
(D.2)
$$FRAC = \beta_0 + \beta_1 RENT + \beta_2 (1/VAC) + \alpha X,$$

where $FRAC$ denotes the number of homeless per 1,000 population in a city, $RENT$ is an indicator of whether a city has rent control ($RENT = 1$ if a city has rent control and $RENT = 0$ otherwise), VAC denotes the vacancy rate, and X denotes the other explanatory variables. The data are taken from Tucker (1987). The estimation results are summarized in Table D-1.

According to Model D.1, there is a statistically significant relation between the fraction of homeless and the indicator of rent control ($p < 0.05$) but not between homelessness and the vacancy rate ($p > 0.10$). Moreover, according to Model D.1, the fraction of homeless is higher in cities that have rent control than it is in cities that do not have rent control. This

---

[6]More precisely, the problem is to estimate a conditional mean function (e.g., the mean of the logarithm of the crime rate conditional on the explanatory variables and the indicator of whether a right-to-carry law is in effect). Nonparametric estimation places no restrictions on the specification or "shape" of this function but suffers from the curse of dimensionality. The estimation methods in common use, including those used by Lott and his critics, assume that the conditional mean function belongs to a relatively small class of functions, such as linear functions of the variables or functions that are linear in the original variables and products of pairs of the original variables.

TABLE D-1 Results of Estimating a Model of the Fraction of Homeless in a City (quantities in parentheses are standard errors)

Model	Coefficient of RENT	Coefficient of VAC or 1/VAC
(D.1)	3.17	−0.26
	(1.51)	(0.16)
(D.2)	−1.65	18.89
	(3.11)	(8.15)

result is consistent with the hypothesis that rent control is a cause of homelessness (possibly because it creates a shortage of rental units) and that the vacancy rate is unrelated to homelessness. However, Model D.2 gives the opposite conclusion. According to this model, there is a statistically significant relation between the fraction of homeless and the vacancy rate ($p < 0.05$) but not between homelessness and rent control ($p > 0.10$). Moreover, according to Model D.2, the fraction of homeless decreases as the vacancy rate increases. Thus, the results of estimation in Model D.2 are consistent with the hypothesis that a low vacancy rate contributes to homelessness but rent control does not. In other words, Model D.1 and Model D.2 yield opposite conclusions about the effects of rent control and the vacancy rate on homelessness. In addition, it is not possible for both of the models to fit the data, although it is possible for neither to fit. Therefore, misspecification or lack of fit is causing at least one of the models to give a misleading indication of the effect of rent control and the vacancy rate on homelessness.

It is possible to carry out statistical tests for lack of fit. None of the models examined by the committee passes a simple specification test called RESET (Ramsey, 1969). That is, none of the models fits the data. This raises the question whether a model that fits the data can be found. For example, by estimating and testing a large number of models, it might be possible to find one that passes the RESET test. This is called a *specification search*. However, a specification search cannot circumvent the curse of dimensionality. If the search is carried out informally (that is, without a statistically valid search procedure and stopping rule), as is usually the case in applications, then it invalidates the statistical theory on which estimation and inference are based. The results of the search may be misleading, but because the relevant statistical theory no longer applies, it is not possible to test for a misleading result. Alternatively, one can carry out a statistically valid search that is guaranteed to find the correct model in a sufficiently large sample. However, this is a form of nonparametric regression, and therefore it suffers the lack of precision that is an unavoidable consequence of the curse of dimensionality. Therefore, there is little likelihood of identifying a well-fitting model with existing data and statistical methods.[7] In summary, the problems posed by high-dimensional estimation, misspecified models, and lack of knowledge of the correct set of explanatory variables seem insurmountable with observational data.

REFERENCES

Ayers, I., and J.J. Donohue
  1999   Nondiscretionary concealed weapons law: A case study of statistics, standards of proof, and public policy. *American Law and Economics Review* 1:436.
Black, D.A., and D.S. Nagin
  1998   Do right-to-carry laws deter violent crime? *Journal of Legal Studies* 27:209-219.
Bronars, S., and J.R. Lott, Jr.
  1998   Criminal deterrence, geographic spillovers, and the right to carry concealed handguns. *American Economic Review* 88:475-479.
Donohue, J.J.
  2002   Divining the Impact of State Laws Permitting Citizens to Carry Concealed Handguns. Unpublished manuscript, Stanford Law School.
Härdle, W.
  1990   *Applied Nonparametric Regression.* Cambridge: Cambridge University Press.
Lott, J.R.
  2000   *More Guns, Less Crime: Understanding Crime and Gun-Control Laws.* Chicago: University of Chicago Press.
Lott, J.R., and D.B. Mustard
  1997   Crime, deterrence, and right-to-carry concealed handguns. *Journal of Legal Studies* 26(1):1-68.
Ramsey, J.B.
  1969   Tests for specification errors in classical linear least squares regression analysis. *Journal of the Royal Statistical Society* Series B 31(2):350-371.
Tucker, W.
  1987   Where do the homeless come from? *National Review* Sept. 25:32-43.

---

[7]Much current research in statistics and econometrics is directed at "dimension reduction." This consists of imposing shape assumptions that are much weaker than those of models like 6.1 and 6.2 but strong enough to reduce the effective number of shapes that must be considered and thereby to increase estimation precision substantially. Although these techniques show considerable promise, they have not yet been developed sufficiently to be applicable to problems like estimation of the effects of right-to-carry laws.

Appendix E

Biographical Sketches of
Committee Members and Staff

CHARLES F. WELLFORD *(Chair)* is professor and acting chair of the Department of Criminology and Criminal Justice at the University of Maryland. He also serves as director of the University of Maryland Center for Applied Policy Studies, the Maryland Justice Analysis Center, and a faculty mentor for the Gemstone Program. In Maryland he serves on the Maryland Sentencing Policy Commission, the Correctional Options Advisory Board, and the Criminal Justice Information Advisory Board. He also serves on the Advisory Commission on Sentencing for the Superior Court of the District of Columbia. He was chair of the National Research Council's (NRC) Committee on the Social and Economic Impact of Pathological Gambling and currently chairs the Committee on Law and Justice. His most recent research has focused on the determinants of sentencing, the development of comparative crime data systems, and the measurement of white-collar crime. He has a Ph.D. in sociology from the University of Pennsylvania (1969).

ROBERT F. BORUCH is university trustee chair professor of the Graduate School of Education and the Statistics Department at the Wharton School, University of Pennsylvania. He is an expert on research methods for evaluating programs and projects in the United States and other countries. In the United States, he serves on the board of trustees of the William T. Grant Foundation, the board of directors of the American Institutes for Research, the Advisory Council on Education Statistics and Evaluation Review Panel of the U.S. General Accounting Office. In his international work, he chaired the National Academy of Sciences education statistics delegation to China.

He has conducted seminars on program evaluation in Israel, Colombia, India, Cote D'Ivoire, and Kenya. He has been a consultant to the World Health Organization on AIDS prevention research and to UNESCO and the U.S. Agency for International Development on project evaluation. He has lectured in Poland, Germany, and the United Kingdom on special problems of survey research and randomized experiments for program evaluation. His work on the design of field experiments for planning and evaluating social and educational programs has received recognition form the American Educational Research Association (Research Review Award), the Policy Studies Association, and the American Evaluation Association (Gunnar and Alva Myrdal Award). He has been a fellow at the American Statistical Association, the Center for Advance Study in the Behavioral Sciences, and the Rockefeller Foundation. He is the author of about 150 articles in research journals and author or editor of over 10 books. He has a Ph.D. in psychology/statistics from Iowa State University (1968).

ANTHONY A. BRAGA (*Consultant*) is senior research associate in the Program in Criminal Justice Policy and Management of the Malcolm Wiener Center for Social Policy at Harvard University's John F. Kennedy School of Government. His research focuses on working with criminal justice agencies to develop crime prevention strategies to deal with urban problems, such as firearms violence, street-level drug markets, and violent crime hot spots. He has served as a consultant on these issues to a wide range of public agencies and private institutions, as well as numerous state and local law enforcement agencies. He was a key member of the Boston Gun Project/ Operation Ceasefire working group. He has an M.P.A. from Harvard University and a Ph.D. in criminal justice from Rutgers University.

LINDA B. COTTLER is professor of epidemiology in the Department of Psychiatry at Washington University School of Medicine in St. Louis. Her work has been in the areas of methods of psychiatric epidemiological research, with emphasis on substance abuse and dependence (drugs and alcohol) and its co-morbidity with other disorders, and prevention research. Specifically, her contributions to the field include risk factors for substance abuse, assessment of substance use and psychiatric disorders, the public health consequences of substance use, including HIV, and peer-delivered prevention models to reduce HIV and substance abuse. She is director of a postdoctoral training program in epidemiology and biostatistics of the National Institute of Mental Health (NIMH), director of a pre- and postdoctoral training program in co-morbidity and biostatistics of the National Institute on Drug Abuse (NIDA), and a consultant to the World Health Organization's Mental Health Division. She is on the advisory board of the National Center for Responsible Gaming, a member of NIDA-K

IRG, and a member of NIDA's editorial board. She served on the NRC Committee on the Social and Economic Impact of Pathological Gambling. She has an M.P.H. from the Boston University School of Public Health and a Ph.D. from Washington University, St. Louis.

ROBERT D. CRUTCHFIELD is professor of sociology and department chair at the University of Washington. He has written extensively on labor markets and crime, as well as on racial and ethnic disparities in prosecution, sentencing, and imprisonment. He is a past vice-president of the American Society of Criminology and is currently on the Council of the American Sociological Association and the American Sociological Association's Crime, Law, and Deviance Section. He served on the editorial board for the National Institute of Justice's CJ2000 project. He has been a deputy editor of *Criminology* and has served on the editorial board of the journal *Social Problems*. He is currently on the editorial boards of *Crime and Justice* and *Crime and Justice Research*. He served on the NRC's Ford Foundation minority predoctoral review panel on anthropology and sociology. He has M.A. (1976) and Ph.D. (1980) degrees in sociology fromVanderbilt University.

JOEL L. HOROWITZ is the Charles E. and Emma H. Morrison professor of economics at Northwestern University. He specializes in econometric theory, semiparametric estimation, bootstrap methods, discrete choice analysis, and inference with missing and incomplete data. He is currently working on projects involving adaptive testing, estimation of additive models with unknown links, bootstrap methods for nonsmooth models, and bandwidth selection in semiparametric estimation. He is co-editor of *Econometrica* and a member of the Econometric Society, the American Economic Association, the American Statistical Association, the American Association for the Advancement of Science, and the Transportation Research Board. He has served on several NRC ad hoc committees, including the Committee on Data and Research for Policy on Illegal Drugs, and is currently a member of the Committee on National Statistics. He has a Ph.D. from Cornell University (1967).

ROBERT L. JOHNSON is professor of pediatrics and clinical psychiatry and director of Adolescent and Young Adult Medicine at the University of Medicine and Dentistry of New Jersey, New Jersey Medical School. His research focuses on adolescent physical and mental health, adolescent HIV, adolescent violence, adolescent fatherhood and risk prevention/reduction programs with specific emphasis on substance and alcohol abuse, sexuality and sexual dysfunction, male sexual abuse, suicide, and AIDS. He currently serves on the National Institute of Mental Health's national advisory council, the board of the Violence Institute of New Jersey, and the pediatric residency review committee of the Accreditation Council for Graduate Medical Education. He has previously been a member of the advisory committee on adolescent health of the Office of Technology Assessment, chair of the Board of Advocates for Youth, and president of the New Jersey State Board of Medical Examiners. He also serves on several Institute of Medicine (IOM) committees, including the Board on Health Care Services, and was a member of the Committee on Unintended Pregnancy. He has an M.D. from the New Jersey Medical School, University of Medicine and Dentistry of New Jersey (1972).

STEVEN D. LEVITT is professor of economics at the University of Chicago. He is a research fellow at the American Bar Foundation, a faculty research fellow at the National Bureau of Economic Research, and editor of the *Journal of Political Economy*. He has studied various aspects of crime and criminality, including the impact of police and prisons on crime, the economics of gangs, the juvenile justice system, and the link between legalized abortion and crime. He has a Ph.D. in economics from the Massachusetts Institute of Technology (1994).

TERRIE E. MOFFITT is professor of psychology at the University of Wisconsin at Madison and professor of social behavior and development at the Institute of Psychiatry in the University of London. She researches the developmental interplay between nature and nurture in the genesis of antisocial behavior. She is principal investigator of the Environmental-Risk Study of the Medical Research Council and is associate director of the Dunedin Multidisciplinary Health and Development Research Unit in New Zealand. She is a fellow of the United Kingdom's Academy of Medical Sciences and a recipient of the American Psychological Association's distinguished scientific award for early career contribution to psychology in the area of psychopathology. She has a Ph.D. in clinical psychology from the University of Southern California (1984).

SUSAN A. MURPHY is an associate professor of statistics and senior associate research scientist in the Institute for Social Research at the University of Michigan. Her present research interests concern causal inference and sequential decisions, sometimes called dynamic or adaptive or tailored treatment regimes. Other interests include profile and parametric likelihood models and the development of methodology for the area of drug prevention research—in particular the use of event history analysis. In 2000, she was elected a fellow of the Institute of Mathematical Statistics. She has been a member of the NRC's Office of Scientific and Engineering Personnel. She has a Ph.D. in statistics from the University of North Carolina, Chapel Hill (1989).

KAREN E. NORBERG is assistant professor of psychiatry at Boston University and visiting research associate at the Center for Health Policy at Washington University in St. Louis. Her current research interests include economic and game theory models of parent-child interaction, social and economic factors affecting emotional and physical health of low income youth, adolescent suicide and self-injury, and social contagion. She is the principal investigator of a NIMH project to study social and economic factors in an adolescent suicide cluster. She has an M.D. from Harvard University (1978).

JOHN V. PEPPER (*Study Director*) is associate professor of economics at the University of Virginia. His current work reflects his wide range of interests in social program evaluation, applied econometrics, and public economics. He is an author of numerous published papers, conference presentations, and edited books. At the National Research Council, he has made important contributions to the work of panels of the Committee on Law and Justice, including reports on measurement problems in criminal justice research, policy on illegal drugs, and assessment of two cost-effectiveness studies on cocaine control policy. He has a Ph.D. in economics from the University of Wisconsin.

CAROL V. PETRIE is staff director of the Committee on Law and Justice at the National Research Council, a position she has held since 1997. Prior to her work there, she was the director of planning and management at the National Institute of Justice, responsible for policy development and administration. In 1994, she served as the acting director of the National Institute of Justice during the transition between the Bush and Clinton administrations. Throughout a 30-year career, she has worked in the area of criminal justice research, statistics, and public policy, serving as a project officer and in administration at the National Institute of Justice and at the Bureau of Justice Statistics. She has conducted research on violence, and managed numerous research projects on the development of criminal behavior, policy on illegal drugs, domestic violence, child abuse and neglect, transnational crime, and improving the operations of the criminal justice system. She has a B.S. in education from Kent State University.

PETER REUTER is professor in the School of Public Affairs and in the Department of Criminology at the University of Maryland. In July 1999 he became editor of the *Journal of Policy Analysis and Management.* He is currently also senior economist at RAND. He founded and directed RAND's Drug Policy Research Center from 1989 to 1993. Since 1985 most of his research has dealt with alternative approaches to controlling drug problems, both in the United States and in western Europe. He has been a member of the NRC's Committee on Law and Justice and the IOM's Committee on the Federal Regulation of Methadone and its Panel on Assessing the Scientific Base for Reducing Tobacco-Related Harm. He testifies frequently before Congress and has addressed senior policy audiences in many countries, including Australia, Chile, Colombia and Great Britain. He has served as a consultant to numerous organizations in this country and abroad. He has a Ph.D. in economics from Yale.

RICHARD ROSENFELD is professor of criminology and criminal justice at the University of Missouri, St. Louis. His research areas are violence and social organization, crime statistics, and crime control policy. He has written extensively on the social sources of criminal violence, youth homicide, and violent crime trends. His current research investigates the role of networks in sustaining violence and the impact of incarceration on homicide rates. He is executive counselor of the American Society of Criminology. In 1994, he received the Chancellor's Award for Excellence in Teaching from the University of Missouri, St. Louis. He has a Ph.D. in sociology from the University of Oregon (1984).

JOEL WALDFOGEL is a business and public policy faculty member at the Wharton School of the University of Pennsylvania and a faculty research fellow of the National Bureau of Economic Research. Prior to arriving at Wharton in 1997, he served on the faculty of the Yale University Economics Department. His research interests span law and economics and industrial organization. Within law and economics, he has conducted research on criminal sentencing, labor markets for ex-offenders, civil litigation, and the measurement of discrimination. Within industrial economics, he has conducted empirical studies of price advertising, media markets and minorities, and the operation of differentiated product markets. He has a Ph.D. in economics from Stanford University (1990).

JAMES Q. WILSON is the James A. Collins professor of management and public policy (emeritus) at the University of California, Los Angeles. He is also the Ronald Reagan professor of public policy at Pepperdine University. Previously, he was a professor of government at Harvard University. He is the author or co-author of 14 books, has edited or contributed to books on urban problems, government regulation of business, and the prevention of delinquency among children, and has published many articles. He has served on several NRC committees, including the Committee on Law and Justice, the Panel on Research on Criminal Careers, and the Committee on Data and Research for Policy on Illegal Drugs. He has a Ph.D. from the University of Chicago (1959).

CHRISTOPHER WINSHIP is professor of sociology at Harvard University. He was previously at Northwestern University as director of the Program in Mathematical Methods in the Social Sciences, and as chair of the Department of Sociology. He was a founding member of Northwestern's Department of Statistics and held a courtesy appointment in economics. He also served as director of the Economics Research Center at the National Opinion Research Center at the University of Chicago. He is currently doing research on several topics: the Ten Point Coalition, a group of black ministers who are working with the Boston police to reduce youth violence; statistical models for causal analysis; the effects of education on mental ability; causes of the racial difference in performance in elite colleges and universities; and changes in the racial differential in imprisonment rates over the past 60 years. He is currently a member of the NRC-IOM's Committee on Adolescent Health and Development. He has a Ph.D. in sociology from Harvard University (1977).

Index

A

Academic support, of the individual right interpretation, 282–284
Access, restricting, 8–9
Accidents, firearms and, 70–71
Accuracy, of research data, 43
ADAM. *See* Arrestee Drug Abuse Monitoring
AddHealth. *See* National Longitudinal Study on Adolescent Health
Administrative samples, 37–41
Aggravated assault, 64–65
    rates of aggravated assault by firearm involvement, 65
Aggregate crime, estimates of percentage change in, 145
Aggregation, of individual survey responses, 58–59
Aggregation bias, 166
AGVQ. *See* Attitudes Toward Guns and Violence Questionnaire
American Civil Liberties Union, 236
Analytic framework of illegal firearm acquisition, 82–87
    general model, 82–86
    intermediate effects of market interventions, 87
    using the framework, 86–87
Analyzing estimates for robustness, 139–150
    dummy variable model with common time pattern, 140–141

estimates of percentage change in aggregate crime, 145
estimates of percentage change in disaggregate property crimes, 148
estimates of percentage change in disaggregate violent crimes, 146–147
extending the baseline specification to 2000, 140–145
sensitivity of the results to controls, 145–150
trend model with common time pattern, 142–143
trend model with varying postlaw change durations, 150–151
Annie E. Casey Foundation, 13
ARIMA model, 228
Arrestee Drug Abuse Monitoring (ADAM), 37, 40–41, 44, 48, 87
Ashcroft, John, 278
Assault weapons, banning to reduce criminal access to firearms, 96–97
Assaults
    aggravated, 64–65
    sexual, with firearm involvement, 66
Assessment
    of individual-level studies, 183
    subjective, of self-defense with a firearm, 117
Assessment of ecological studies, 163–170
    ecological bias, 170
    proxy measures of ownership, 164–170
    substitution and confounders, 163–164

Q

R